THE TRANSFORMATION OF CITIZENSHIP IN THE EUROPEAN UNION

This book examines the electoral rights granted to those who do not have the nationality of the state in which they reside, within the European Union and its Member States. It looks at the rights of EU citizens to vote and stand in European Parliament elections and local elections wherever they live in the EU, and at cases where Member States of the Union also choose to grant electoral rights to other non-nationals from countries outside the EU. The EU's electoral rights are among the most important rights first granted to EU citizens by the EU Treaties in the 1990s. Putting these rights into their broader context, the book provides important insights into the development of the EU now that the Constitutional Treaty has been rejected in the referendums in France and the Netherlands, and into issues which are still very sensitive for national sovereignty such as immigration, nationality and naturalisation.

JO SHAW holds the Salvesen Chair of European Institutions in the School of Law at the University of Edinburgh in the UK, having previously worked at Manchester, Leeds, Keele and Exeter Universities. She has held visiting positions at Harvard Law School in the USA, and at the Institute for Higher Studies, Vienna, Austria.

CAMBRIDGE STUDIES IN EUROPEAN LAW AND POLICY

This series aims to produce original works which contain a critical analysis of the state of the law in particular areas of European Law and set out different perspectives and suggestions for its future development. It also aims to encourage a range of work on law, legal institutions and legal phenomena in Europe, including 'law in context' approaches. The titles in the series will be of interest to academics; policymakers; policy formers who are interested in European legal, commercial, and political affairs; practising lawyers including the judiciary; and advanced law students and researchers.

Joint Editors

Professor Dr Laurence Gormley,
Rijksuniversiteit Groningen, The Netherlands
Professor Jo Shaw,
University of Edinburgh

Editorial advisory board

Professor Richard Bellamy, University of Reading; Ms Catherine Barnard, University of Cambridge; Professor Marise Cremona, Queen Mary College, University of London; Professor Alan Dashwood, University of Cambridge; Professor Dr Jacqueline Dutheil de la Rochère, Université de Paris II, Director of the Centre de Droit Européen, France; Dr Andrew Drzemczewski, Council of Europe, Strasbourg, France; Sir David Edward KCMG, QC, former Judge, Court of Justice of the European Communities, Luxembourg; Professor Dr Walter Baron van Gerven, Emeritus Professor, Leuven and Maastricht and former Advocate General, Court of Justice of the European Communities; Professor Daniel Halberstam, University of Michigan, USA; Professor Dr Ingolf Pernice, Director of the Walter Hallstein Institut, Humboldt Universität, Berlin; Michel Petite, Director General of the Legal Service, Commission of the European Communities, Brussels; Professor Dr Sinisa Rodin, University of Zagreb; Professor Neil Walker, University of Aberdeen and EUI, Fiesole.

Books in the series

THE TRANSFORMATION OF CITIZENSHIP IN THE EUROPEAN UNION

Electoral Rights and the Restructuring of Political Space

JO SHAW

University of Edinburgh

CAMBRIDGE
UNIVERSITY PRESS

CAMBRIDGE UNIVERSITY PRESS

Cambridge, New York, Melbourne, Madrid, Cape Town, Singapore, São Paulo

Cambridge University Press
The Edinburgh Building, Cambridge CB2 8RU, UK

Published in the United States of America by Cambridge University Press, New York

www.cambridge.org
Information on this title: www.cambridge.org/9780521677943

First published 2007

Printed in the United Kingdom at the University Press, Cambridge

A catalogue record for this publication is available from the British Library

ISBN 978-0-521-86070-3 hardback
ISBN 978-0-521-67794-3 paperback

To the memory of Freda Shaw 1931–2004

CONTENTS

vii

FIGURES

TABLES

PREFACE AND ACKNOWLEDGMENTS

This book has been too long in the making. I owe readers, and those who have helped me over a long period of time, some explanation for its lengthy period of genesis. Its origins lie back in the mid-1990s, when Joseph Weiler invited me to present a Specialised Course on 'European Citizenship' at the 1995 Session of the Academy of European Law at the European University Institute in Florence. That presentation was eventually published in the *Collected Courses* of the Academy, and formed the basis for some other early works on citizenship which I make use of in Chapter 2. I was somewhat sceptical in the first instance about working on citizenship, but I am very grateful to Joseph Weiler for pushing me in this direction in the first place.

From an early interest in understanding how European citizenship had (or could have) what Antje Wiener has called a 'constructive potential' in the context of European integration and the project of polity-building in a non-state context, a project emerged specifically focusing on the implications of Article 19 of the EC Treaty. This provides for EU citizens resident in a Member State other than their own to be able to vote and stand in local and European Parliamentary elections, and constitutes the core of this book. Along the way, I was lucky enough to collaborate on a number of projects on citizenship topics with Antje Wiener which enabled me to sharpen my understanding of citizenship as an element of polity-building. On the subject of electoral rights specifically, I collaborated with Richard Bellamy and Dario Castiglione on an ESRC-funded research project, 'Strategies of Civic Inclusion in Pan-European Civil Society' (L213 25 2022), which supported a Research Assistantship in 1999–2000 for Stephen Day (now of Oita University, Japan), with whom I have since gone on to publish a number of papers on electoral rights,[1] and on whose early empirical work on Germany, Austria, Estonia and the UK I rely heavily in this book. I am very grateful

---

[1] Day and Shaw, 2002: 183–99; Day and Shaw, 2003: 211–36.

to the ESRC for this support. Around the same time, I also started to collaborate with Anthea Connolly, who held scholarships to undertake PhD studies in the Department of Law at the University of Leeds, and later at the University of Manchester. Anthea voluntarily chose to attach her PhD project to the broader alien suffrage project on which Stephen and I were engaged, and she duly completed her PhD in 2003 at the University of Manchester: 'The Theory and Practice of Alien Suffrage in the European Union'. She did extensive research on the historical basis of electoral rights for EU citizens in EU institutional discourses and practices and later collaborated with Stephen and me on the writing of a final project paper, drawing upon her own research;[2] her excellent work is reflected at many points in this book.

More recently, after I had written what Neil Walker kindly described as a prospectus for a larger work (i.e. a book),[3] I was grateful to receive further funding from the British Academy for a project which I now called a project on 'Moulding and Managing the Boundaries of Suffrage' (2003–5), which envisaged by that stage the preparation of a book manuscript. This, along with additional funding from the Heap Fund, School of Law, University of Manchester, permitted the part-time employment of a University of Manchester PhD student, Melanie Smith, who undertook case studies on Lithuania, Hungary and Romania, and work on the international law aspects of the protection of the political participation rights of non-nationals and of national minorities. Melanie prepared a paper for delivery at the Hart Workshop in 2004 on the Lithuania case studies, which we subsequently published jointly.[4] Melanie (now of Cardiff Law School) is one of the three people, along with Stephen and Anthea, who have literally made this project possible. Without their work it would never have happened, and I hope that they feel that what I have produced in some way does justice to their professionalism and commitment.

The same monies which funded Melanie also supported case-study work which I undertook in Slovenia (in relation to which I am grateful for the assistance and collaboration of Felicita Medved), in Malta and in Ireland. In relation to the latter case study, I am particularly grateful to Fidèle Mutwarasibo of the Immigrant Council of Ireland. He brought to my attention for the first time the work going on in Ireland in 2004 to

---

[2] Connolly, Day and Shaw, 2006.   [3] Shaw, 2003: 461–500.
[4] Smith and Shaw, 2006: 145–62.

raise the profile of the electoral rights for non-nationals in Irish local elections, work to which he himself contributed so much. He also assisted me greatly in identifying and approaching interviewees, and generously shared with me his own work on the 2004 elections and non-national civic and political activists in Ireland.

For the final writing-up stage, I am grateful to three more institutions for their support. In June 2005, the European Science Foundation supported the holding of a workshop at the University of Edinburgh on 'Citizens, Non-Citizens and Voting Rights in Europe'. I was lucky enough to be able to bring together an extraordinary group of experts on issues of citizenship, alienage and the rights of migrants for two intensive days of discussion. In this book, I refer to a number of thus far unpublished papers presented at that workshop. The School of Law of University of Edinburgh itself (and especially my colleagues in the Europa Institute) supported me by giving me time, through study leave, to work on the manuscript, and this was generously matched by an Arts and Humanities Research Council Research Leave, in the second half of the academic year 2005–6, which carried me through to completion.

Successive desk officers working on electoral rights matters within the European Commission have been exceptionally helpful over the years, notably Salla Saastamoinen and Michal Meduna. I would like to thank the many interviewees we have spoken to, and here I can speak not only for myself, but also for Anthea, Melanie and Stephen. Most have asked not to be identified other than by reference to the position where they worked. Colleagues too numerous to list have responded with patience to my persistent requests for information or for help in locating a document or unravelling some conundrum which was puzzling me. Without their willingness to help, this book would be immeasurably poorer (although, perhaps, somewhat thinner!). Inevitably, there has been material which I have collected over the years which I have so far been unable to use. I do not see the present volume as the closure of my attempts to understand the theory and practice of EU electoral rights, in their wider political context; on the contrary, I hope to be in a position to publish a number of further, smaller works, which draw upon some of the unused case-study material and delve into areas which have been omitted from this volume, as well as to develop a broader perspective on the transnational political practices of EU citizens and residents more generally.

As I have brought the manuscript to completion, I have built upon the discussions on citizenship issues I have had over the years with Dario Castiglione, Richard Bellamy, Alex Warleigh, Chris Hilson and other participants in the ESRC 'Civic' project, as well as with Miriam Aziz, Daniel Halberstam, Miguel Poiares Maduro, Damian Chalmers and Sybilla Fries. I have given papers or presentations which have shaped my thoughts in locations as diverse as New York (Fordham Law School), Michigan Law School, Lisbon (on several occasions and at several locations), Oslo (Arena), Florence (EUI), Turin (ECPR), Toronto (ECSA Canada), Vienna (EURCIT), Budapest (IMISCOE), Stirling (SLSA), Cambridge (CRASSH and the Law Faculty), Oxford (Law Faculty), Durham (DELI), Zagreb (Faculty of Law), Dubrovnik (Advanced Course on EU Law) and Ljubljana (Peace Institute). I have benefited greatly from comments and criticisms encountered on these occasions. In writing the book, I have relied heavily upon a number of colleagues to read sections of the manuscript and to save me from a whole variety of possible infelicities. In no particular order, I would like to thank John O'Dowd, University College Dublin, for his compendious knowledge of Irish constitutional law; Rainer Bauböck of the Austrian Academy of Sciences and the European University Institute, who commented on the very first draft paper which Stephen Day and I delivered in Vienna in 2000; Neil Walker of the European University Institute and the University of Edinburgh, for his comments on 'Sovereignty at the Boundaries of the Polity'; Antje Wiener of Queen's University Belfast, for her reading and comments which helped to put the whole manuscript in its broader context; Erika Harris of the University of Liverpool and Istvan Pogany of the University of Warwick for guidance on citizenship in Central and Eastern Europe; and Zenon Bańkowski of the University of Edinburgh, for some helpful comments on citizenship issues more generally. However, I wish to pay particular tribute to two busy colleagues at the University of Edinburgh who found time to read the entire manuscript and make comments upon it: Christina Boswell and Neil MacCormick. Without such colleagues able and willing to give their time in that manner, the academic profession would indeed be a much poorer one. I alone, of course, remain responsible for any (undoubted) remaining infelicities or misinterpretations. This is perhaps inevitable considering the wide-ranging (and often rapidly changing) legal and political ground which the book covers, and I would be happy to hear from any readers who are unhappy about how I have presented some issue or question, or who wish to point out some egregious error or omission. The law is stated as I understood it on 1 November 2006, although the book fully anticipates the accession of Bulgaria and Romania to the EU on 1 January 2007.

Finally, I would like to thank my family for bearing with me. Leo Shaw has been with me throughout, but during the time it has taken me to complete the project has mutated from primary school child into university student. As mother and son, it is hard to say whether we give each other more stress or more support. Sometimes it seems to be both simultaneously. But, along the way, we have certainly had some fun, and learnt quite a lot together. More recently, Alfred Thomas has been close by, and he has helped me to relax and put the work in its place, when necessary, by providing distraction and tender care. Most importantly, however, I would like to dedicate this book to the memory of my mother, Freda Shaw, née Baxter (1931–2004). My mother studied Modern Languages in the late 1940s and early 1950s at the University of Reading and went on to spend a 'year abroad', in the days before SOCRATES, in Clermont-Ferrand in central France. But, even before going to university, she was a pioneering participant in the early exchanges which developed in the post-war years between the West Riding of Yorkshire, where she was born and brought up, and Lille in northern France. She maintained an enduring attachment to the people of northern France whom she met and became friends with, attachments which extend across our family and their families, and which have lasted beyond her death. While I perhaps owe my interest in the law to my father, I certainly owe my interest in the languages and cultures of other European states primarily to my mother. I am very sad that she is not here, today, to see what I tried to build, with the help of others, on the basis of these ideals of transnational exchange and cooperation.

Small parts of many of the chapters of this book, particularly Chapters 1, 2, 3, 5, 7, 8 and 9, reproduce and substantially develop material first published in J. Shaw, 'Sovereignty at the Boundaries of the Polity', in N. Walker (ed.), *Sovereignty in Transformation*, Oxford: Hart Publishing, 2003, pp. 461–500, and are reproduced with the permission of Hart Publishing Limited.

Parts of Chapters 2 and 3 reproduce and substantially develop material first published in S. Day and J. Shaw, 'EU Electoral Rights and the Political Participation of Migrants in Host Polities' (2002) 8 *International Journal of Population Geography* 183–99, which is copyright of, and is reproduced with the permission of, John Wiley & Sons Limited.

Parts of Chapters 4 and 5 reproduce and develop material first published in A. Connolly, S. Day and J. Shaw, 'Alien Suffrage in the European Union: Contested and Incomplete?', in R. Bellamy, D. Castiglione and J. Shaw (eds.),

Making European Citizens, Basingstoke: Palgrave, 2006, and are reproduced with the permission of Palgrave Macmillan.

Parts of Chapter 6 reproduce material originally published in J. Shaw, 'EU Citizenship and Political Rights in an Evolving European Union' (2007) 71 *Fordham Law Review* 101–30, and are reproduced with the permission of the editors of the *Fordham Law Review*.

Parts of Chapter 10 reproduce and develop material originally published in M. Smith and J. Shaw, 'Changing Polities and Electoral Rights: Lithuania's Accession to the EU', in P. Shah and W. Menski (eds.), *Migration, Diasporas and Legal Systems in Europe*, London: Routledge-Cavendish, 2006, pp. 145–63, and are reproduced with the permission of Thomson/Taylor and Francis Books (UK).

Other parts of Chapter 10 reproduce and develop material first published in S. Day and J. Shaw, 'The Boundaries of Suffrage and External Conditionality: Estonia as an Applicant Member State of the EU' (2003) 9 *European Public Law* 211–36, and are reproduced with the permission of the editor of *European Public Law*.

PART I

Electoral rights in legal and political context

Introduction: electoral rights and the boundaries of the suffrage

This book explores some of the relationships between the contested concepts and practices of citizenship and membership, of nation and nationality, and of states and 'state-like' polities, such as the European Union.[1] Its frame of reference is the EU and its Member States, and its primary prism of analysis is the concept of citizenship. To illuminate these relationships, the book uses the case of electoral rights for non-nationals,[2] or 'aliens' as they are still sometimes anachronistically called. That is, it looks at the cases where non-nationals, i.e. those who, without the formal nationality of the state where they reside, are permitted to vote (and indeed to stand) in elections in the host state. These are most often local elections, or, in the special case of the EU, European Parliament elections; occasionally, non-nationals are permitted to vote or stand in national or 'regional' elections (that is, elections to the devolved or 'state'-level authorities in Member States which have federal or devolved systems of government). In addition, the book also looks at

---

[1] Or 'EU', or 'Union'.

[2] A note on terminology: this book refers throughout to the voting rights of 'non-nationals' rather than 'non-citizens', in recognition of the fact that the term 'citizenship' implies contested and textured concepts of membership of different types of communities (and not just states) which stretch beyond 'national citizenship'. The term 'non-nationals' is used to refer, legally speaking, to those without formal legal nationality or national citizenship of a state, in the sense in which the term 'nationality' is recognised and used under international law, and is used without reference to ethnic or even civic implications of terms such as 'nationalism', 'national identity' or 'nation state'. Thus, so far as possible, I use the terms 'nationality' or 'national citizenship' to denote legal membership of a state and 'citizenship' (without the attachment of national) to denote a broader socio-political concept of membership, while recognising that these usages are not shared by other authors, and thus in some quotations citizenship is used in a different sense. Moreover, all these terms need to be used with especial care when applied to the cases of the states of Central and Eastern Europe, where nationality has historically meant something quite different to the concept as developed in international law; it often refers in that context to membership of a national community defined ethnically, culturally and/or religiously.

many cases where non-nationals are denied those same rights, on the premise that the denial of rights is often as illuminating as the granting of them.

The extension of electoral rights beyond the boundaries of national citizenship is almost always a highly contested political and legal move, although a recent opinion poll highlights that, despite generally negative attitudes towards foreigners and immigrants within the Member States, there are often positive attitudes amongst citizens to the proposition that non-nationals who pay taxes should also enjoy the right to vote in local elections.[3] Indeed, the suggestion that EU citizens should have the right to vote in all elections organised in the Member State in which they live, regardless of national citizenship, came in third place when respondents in a Eurobarometer survey were asked to nominate (from a list) which two measures they thought offered the best ways of strengthening European citizenship.[4] This seems to indicate quite widespread support for the general liberal and cosmopolitan principle of alien suffrage, which holds that states ought to ensure that long-term-resident non-nationals have rights of political participation in any host polity to the greatest extent possible, in accordance with respect for democracy and fundamental rights, especially the principles of equality and non-domination of minorities by majorities. On that view, residence is a sufficiently strong factor of affinity and belonging to ground a claim for political equality on the part of someone lacking the formal badge of national citizenship. On the other hand, opposition to extending electoral rights finds expression in a more state-focused communitarian principle which holds that it would be wrong to reduce the incentives for the formal acquisition of national citizenship, because to do so might undermine the quality and character of that citizenship, by watering it down by reference to an ever wider range of foreigners' rights.

---

[3] *Migration and Citizenship Rights in Europe: European Citizens' Attitudes*, Quaderni FNE, Collana Osservatori, No. 21, November 2005. The results show the following percentages in favour of electoral rights at the local level: France: 82%; Italy: 74%; Germany: 62%; Poland: 56%; Czech Republic: 45%; Hungary: 32%. Of these Member States, only Hungary actually confers local electoral rights on third country nationals and it produces, ironically, the lowest results!

[4] Eurobarometer Special 251, *The Future of Europe*, May 2006, at 45–6. The adoption of a European welfare system and the adoption of a European Constitution were cited most commonly by the respondents as the measures most likely to strengthen European citizenship. However, 8 per cent of respondents, and 25 per cent of respondents questioned in the UK, spontaneously stated that they did not wish to be European citizens.

As the basis for looking at the contestability of electoral rights for non-nationals, this chapter introduces the basic building blocks of the argument, by setting out the legal framework for electoral rights, especially in the European Union but also – in brief – in the Member States. It outlines the research questions which the book seeks to address, although these will be elaborated more fully later, towards the end of Chapter 3, after we have looked in detail at the concept of citizenship and at the theories and practices of alien suffrage.

We should begin, however, with the right to vote. The right to vote is one of the most important formal legal indiciae or 'hallmarks' of citizenship (Gardner, 1997: 39):

> as one of the political rights, the right to vote enables citizens to partici-
> pate, through the medium of elected representatives, in the exercise of
> political power. The right is thus relevant to all other hallmarks, since the
> content of the rights and duties of citizens at any one time can indirectly
> be influenced or determined by its exercise.

Thus elections can be seen as moments which are central to the production and reproduction of democracy and democratic institutions, moments at which communities are formed and form themselves. Consequently, the capacity to participate in an election must be seen as central to the complex notion of citizenship. But is the converse always true? Is it right to assume that nationality, as a primary legal indicator of national citizenship, is or should always be crucial to the franchise? Are there circumstances in which those without formal citizenship in that legal sense should be able to vote in elections? Indeed, should they be given any political participation rights at all in the host polity? Given their status as non-citizens, it is arguable that both their interest in and loyalty to the host polity could be regarded as suspect. In other words, is it legitimate to restrain the political speech and freedom of association of resident non-nationals, as well as denying them the normal participation rights given to nationals and/or special participation rights, such as the right to elect foreigners' councils or similar bodies?

A paradox faces all polities: so long as the criterion for allocating political rights of participation, especially electoral rights, has been overwhelmingly the formal one of nationality and so long as the gateways to nationality have been limited by states operating restrictive nationality laws, many who live and indeed are born within the boundaries of any given polity have been unable to participate politically, fully or even partially. Whether this is regarded as an anomaly of the present system of Westphalian states, a natural or desirable consequence of that same system, or indeed evidence of its decline and increasing irrelevance, it is clearly a fact as only a minority of states grant electoral rights to non-nationals. We can observe that the mixing of 'national' populations results from a number of factors: globalisation and the interpenetration of economies in the modern world, coupled with the uneven distribution of economic well-being and labour-market opportunities, are clearly key factors promoting mobility and migration, but so too are repressive state regimes which deny political and personal freedoms and give rise to refugee populations, and also the fact that state boundaries sometimes change whether by consent or force and thus generate 'minority' populations separated from their 'homelands' (e.g. the break-up of previously multinational states or empires). There are also positive causes of mixity, such as the existence of entities like the European Union which positively encourage mobility, at least within and amongst its own Member States and at least for market or near-market reasons. All of these factors in different ways generate mobility and create groups of residents within states who lack the formal legal badge of citizenship: nationality. In turn, those who lack nationality are quite commonly denied the right to vote. This results in the selection of political representatives at the national, regional and local level by a limited group of residents, even though the results of those elections affect all residents, and not just nationals as a limited group. For the elected representatives will exercise political power throughout the jurisdiction of the state and *vis-à-vis* all residents, without regard to whether individuals hold nationality or not.

Particular attention is paid in this book to the limited passive and active electoral rights conferred by Article 19 of the Treaty establishing the European Community[5] on citizens of the Union. They are treated as a test case to show how changes in certain legal rules within the context of the EU are linked to a broader process of transformation of citizenship in the context of migration, globalisation and associated challenges to the viability and future of the nation state.

Introduced initially by the Treaty of Maastricht (or Treaty on European Union[6]) as part of the wider 'citizenship package', Article 19(1) provides that a citizen of the Union residing in a Member State other than the one of which she is a national shall have the right to vote

---

[5] Hereinafter referred to as the 'EC Treaty'.   [6] Hereinafter referred to as the 'EU Treaty'.

and stand as a candidate in municipal elections 'under the same conditions as nationals of that State'. That is, a citizen of the Union has a non-discrimination or equal treatment right. In very similar terms, in relation to elections to the European Parliament, Article 19(2) lays down the right to vote and stand as a candidate for a citizen of the Union residing in a Member State other than the one of which she is a national. Electoral rights at the Union level are limited in two crucial respects: first, they cover only a limited range of elections, namely, municipal or local elections[7] and European Parliament elections, the latter being unique to the European Union as a form of supranational electoral competition; secondly, they extend only to those privileged non-nationals covered by the definition of citizenship of the Union as provided for in Article 17(1) EC, namely, the nationals of the twenty-seven Member States (twelve Member States at the time of entry into force). Article 19 is very limited. It does not cover access on the part of EU citizens to the most important elections taking place within the Member States, namely, general or national elections (or indeed to 'state' or regional elections such as those which take place in federal states or states with devolved authorities[8]). It also excludes from consideration the much larger group of non-nationals resident in the Member States, namely, the citizens of third countries (or 'third country nationals').

The Article 19 electoral rights comprise one part of the limited package of explicit rights conferred by Part Two of the EC Treaty on citizens of the Union. Article 17(1) EC declares that 'Citizenship of the Union is hereby established'. This might seem rather impressive at first sight, but, in a phrase added by the Treaty of Amsterdam, citizenship of the Union is declared in Article 17(1) to be *complementary* to national citizenship, which it shall not *replace*. In many respects, the inclusion of the citizenship provisions in the EC Treaty in 1993 marked a

---

[7] The term 'municipal elections' is used in the EC Treaty specifically in order to link the Treaty's coverage to 'municipalities', which are commonly recognised as the smallest administrative subdivision with democratically elected self-government. In practice, common usage in English generally refers to 'local elections', and on the whole this term is used throughout this book, except where reference is made to the specific texts of the EC Treaty and the implementing Directive, where the term 'municipal elections' is generally adopted. However, the two should be treated for the purposes of this book as synonymous.

[8] The UK is an important exception to this, in that EU citizens can vote in elections held in Northern Ireland, Scotland and Wales to the assemblies/parliaments exercising devolved powers in those regions/countries. This is laid down in the relevant UK statutes. The implications of this are explored further in Chapter 8, Section VI.

codification of existing legal and especially judicial approaches to the status and rights of persons under EC law which some already described as a form of 'Community citizenship' based largely upon the concept of the free movement of persons and the principle of equal treatment.[9] It would therefore hardly be appropriate to characterise the Maastricht citizenship 'package' as a major constitutional innovation for the European Union, although the electoral rights are amongst the small number of genuine novelties which it did introduce, along with the right to diplomatic and consular protection from the authorities of any Member State for a citizen of the Union when in a third country (Article 20 EC).[10] Also covered in the package is a more generalised right to move and reside freely within the territory of the Member States than previously existed under EC law (Article 18 EC), the right to write to the institutions or bodies of the Union in any of the official languages of the Union, and to receive a reply in the same language, the right to petition the European Parliament, and the right to apply to the Ombudsman for redress in relation to maladministration by the Union institutions (all set out in the three paragraphs of Article 21 EC). However, as Articles 194 and 195 EC make clear in texts which articulate in a little more detail the provisions of Article 21, the latter two rights are not confined to Union citizens, but also extend to all resident natural and legal persons, and ought more properly to be seen as part of the constitutional arrangements underpinning transparency and democracy at the Union level, rather than as 'rights' attaching to those designated as the 'members' of the Union understood as a polity, namely, Union citizens (Article 17(1) EC).

In that respect, Union 'citizenship rights' share much in common with national 'citizenship rights', in the sense that in both cases the boundary between insiders and outsiders is commonly blurred. In practice, at national level, it is often hard to distinguish between the formal rights of citizens (i.e. those with formal national membership) and non-nationals, in

---

[9] For an analysis of the case law, see, for example, O'Leary, 1996 and Wilkinson, 1995, and, for an early example of the scholarly use of the notion of citizenship in relation to free movement of persons, see Plender, 1976.

[10] A Presidency working document in preparation for a meeting of the Ministers of Foreign Affairs engaged in the negotiations towards the Treaty of Maastricht commented à propos the first Gulf War that 'Drawing from the experience of the Gulf crisis, it was considered that Community citizens, irrespective of their Member States, should have the right, when outside the Community and when necessary, to avail themselves of the protection of the diplomatic missions of any Member State': Council Document 8724/1/90, 2 October 1990, 16.

the sense that the latter often enjoy most of the formal rights of the former, with the exception of certain political rights, and access to employment in many parts of the public service.[11] This seems to be the case, also, with many Union citizenship rights, but not the electoral rights as framed in Article 19 (i.e. the right of EU citizens to vote when resident in other Member States), which are exclusive to EU citizens.

Where Union citizenship differs sharply from national citizenship is in its top-down constructed character. This is emphasised not only by the rather false solemnity whereby Union citizenship is 'established' by Article 17, but also by Article 22 which allows Member States to adopt amendments to the citizenship provisions, developing the list of rights, through a truncated treaty amendment procedure which avoids the need for a full intergovernmental conference. The Commission is mandated to report periodically to the Council on progress relating to the issues covered by the citizenship provisions. Bearing in mind the contents of these reports, the Council can act unanimously on a proposal from the Commission, after consulting the European Parliament, to adopt amendments to the citizenship provisions. However, such amendments will not enter into force until they have been ratified by all the Member States in accordance with their respective constitutional requirements, just like a full amending Treaty. The Article 22 procedure has never so far been invoked. Its existence reinforces the fact that the developmental potential of the citizenship provisions lies clearly in the hands of the Member States and not the EU institutions (Preuss *et al.*, 2003: 5), even though it is for the Commission to make the initial proposal for a change. There is little scope under the normal legislative procedure for the concept of citizenship to be developed other than within the frame provided by the legal basis in Article 18 to develop measures on freedom of movement, given the limitations on EU competences in the other fields covered by citizenship. As we shall see in later chapters, there is, however, a limited developmental potential within the citizenship provisions themselves, not least because they have already been given a broader, more teleological reading by the Court of Justice in recent cases.

In addition to the short explicit list of citizenship rights in Part Two of the EC Treaty, however, EU citizens also enjoy other important rights

---

[11] That does not mean that in practice they enjoy 'equal' citizenship with nationals, because in many states those of immigrant origin, whether with or without formal nationality, are often amongst the most socially excluded groups, especially those with racial or ethnic origins or religious affiliations which differ from majority populations.

under the EC Treaty which are 'attached' to citizenship of the Union by virtue of Article 17(2) EC, in particular other rights associated with free movement such as access to employment, many welfare benefits and public services, including health care and education on the same basis as nationals, and the right to non-discrimination on grounds of nationality more generally (Article 12 EC). The centrality of these equal treatment rights as the core of Union citizenship at the present time has led Paul Magnette (2005: 177) to use the term 'isopolity', drawn from the Greek traditions of city states, to describe the basis of EU citizenship:

> The fact that the authors of the treaty have developed this horizontal dimension of citizenship, rather than the vertical bonds between the citizens and the Union, confirms that they intended to build a 'federation of states' rather than a 'European state'. In the EU, as in the ancient leagues of Greek cities, the *isopoliteia* is more developed than the *sympoliteia*.

However, the vertical relationship may be starting, in a tentative way, to develop. It was suggested by Advocate General Tizzano, in the Opinion which he gave on two cases brought before the Court of Justice on the scope of the franchise for European Parliament elections, that the right of Union citizens to vote for the European Parliament in European elections is implicit in the system of EU law and is thus one of the rights guaranteed under Article 17(2) EC.[12] Indeed, he argued that it was 'perhaps the most important' of the rights inhering in the status of Union citizenship.[13] If the right to vote is an EU citizenship right, then it would clearly be a very significant right, given the weakness of the vertical dimension of citizenship in the EU context has long been noticeable by its absence. This (vertical) right – which is separate from the (horizontal) right granted by the Treaty to resident non-national EU citizens to vote under the same conditions as nationals (Article 19(2) EC) – is derived, Advocate General Tizzano argued, from the 'principles of democracy on which the Union is based', in particular the principle of universal suffrage. However, that right can be subjected to limitations, such as qualifications based on age or residence; in other words, it does not require the Member States to vest a right to vote for the European Parliament on all nationals including those who are resident in third countries. It remains up to the Member States to decide

---

[12] See Opinion of Advocate General Tizzano in Case C-145/04 *Spain* v. *United Kingdom (Gibraltar)* and Case C-300/04 *Eman and Sevinger* v. *College van burgemeester en wethouders van Den Haag (Aruba)*, 6 April 2006, paras. 67–8.
[13] Para. 82 of the Opinion.

whether or not to confer expatriate voting rights on their nationals who are EU citizens when resident either elsewhere in the Union or in a third country (e.g. in order to preserve their connection with the home state) provided any differences in treatment can be objectively justified.

In the event, the Court of Justice, in deciding the cases,[14] declined to make any general statements about whether voting for the European Parliament should be seen as an EU citizenship right, although this may be regarded as implicit in its approach. It certainly confirmed that the right to vote for the European Parliament is not an *exclusive* EU citizenship right, even if it is such a right, as Member States may grant the right to third country nationals under certain conditions. We shall look in more detail at these cases in Chapter 6.

It is thus worth emphasising that the right to non-discrimination on grounds of nationality, like the limited electoral rights under Article 19 which amount to specific applications of that general principle of equal treatment, is truly an exclusive 'citizenship right' of citizens of the Union at the present time. The only circumstances in which a third country national will derive certain equal treatment rights, such as the right of residence in a Member State on the same basis as nationals or the right to certain educational benefits, is indirectly from a citizen of the Union if the third country national is a member of the family of that Union citizen, who is in turn herself exercising free movement rights. Accordingly, such equal treatment rights as are enjoyed by those who are members of the families of mobile Union citizens are largely derived from secondary legislation, such as the detailed Directive of 2004 which governs the right of residence and the other entitlements of citizens of the Union, and their families, who have exercised the right of free movement.[15] There are also groups of privileged third country nationals holding the nationality of a state which has an Association Agreement with the Union. For example, while Turkish citizens do not derive any rights of entry and residence in the Member States under the Association Agreement between Turkey and the EU, once lawfully resident they are protected by an equal treatment principle adopted in Decisions of the Association Council, and interpreted by the Court of Justice as

---

[14] Case C-145/04 *Spain* v. *United Kingdom (Gibraltar)*, 12 September 2006; Case C-300/04 *Eman and Sevinger* v. *College van burgemeester en wethouders van Den Haag (Aruba)*, 12 September 2006.

[15] Directive 2004/38/EC of the European Parliament and Council of 29 April 2004 on the right of citizens of the Union and their family members to move and reside freely within the territory of the Member States, OJ 2004 L158/77.

conferring rights on Turkish citizens which they can rely upon directly before courts in the Member States.[16] The principle whereby there is no general right to equal treatment on grounds of nationality for third country nationals, but only certain limited (and usually derived) rights under secondary legislation, has never been explicitly stated by the Court of Justice, but is widely asserted by commentators (e.g. O'Leary, 1996: 35).[17] It can be derived from the Court's clear approach to the provisions on the free movement of workers (e.g. Article 39 EC). In numerous cases it has held that these provisions only apply to nationals of the Member States.[18] It follows from this that there is at present no imperative in EU law to extend the electoral rights such as they exist in Article 19 EC for EU citizens to third country nationals.

Notwithstanding the weaknesses of EU law, in the majority of the twenty-seven Member States of the Union[19] the EU electoral rights do operate in tandem with other *national* laws allowing some or all non-nationals outwith the category of Union citizens (i.e. third country nationals) to vote in some or all elections, although, most commonly, these provisions are limited to conferring electoral rights in relation to local elections. The Member States can still broadly be grouped into the three categories identified by Síofra O'Leary in the mid-1990s, although the balance in terms of numbers between the categories has shifted somewhat in the ensuing period. She distinguishes between those states which extend local electoral rights to all non-nationals, those which do certain rights on the basis of an historical connection between the Member State and certain other countries, and those which reserve all electoral rights to nationals (O'Leary, 1996: 191). The first category includes Ireland, the

---

[16] Case C-192/89 *Sevince* v. *Staatssecretaris Van Justitie* [1990] ECR 3461.

[17] For a critical discussion of the possible scope of Article 12 EC, see Nic Shuibhne, 2003. This point will be discussed further in Chapter 7.

[18] E.g. Case 12/86 *Demirel* [1987] ECR 1573.

[19] The twenty-seven Member States of the European Union are the following (with dates of joining the Union): Belgium, France, Germany, Italy, Luxembourg, the Netherlands (founding states: 1952); Denmark, Ireland, the United Kingdom (1973); Greece (1980); Portugal, Spain (1986); Austria, Finland, Sweden (1995); the Czech Republic, Estonia, Hungary, Latvia, Lithuania, Poland, Slovenia, Slovakia (the so-called A8 (or, after accession, the EU8) states, from Central and Eastern Europe, 2004); Cyprus, Malta (also 2004); Bulgaria, Romania (2007) (whose accession was not able to be completed in the first tranche of Central and Eastern European states). Croatia and Turkey opened accession negotiations with the EU in October 2005. Macedonia was recognised as a candidate state in December 2005, with a view to opening negotiations for membership. Norway has flirted on several occasions with membership, but this has been rejected twice in national referendums in 1972 and 1994.

Netherlands, Belgium, Luxembourg, the Scandinavian countries and quite a number of the new Member States. In the second category, the unusual examples of the UK and Ireland should be mentioned, as the UK gives electoral rights in national elections (and European Parliament elections) to Commonwealth[20] and Irish citizens, on the basis of historic connections, and Ireland has since the 1980s given electoral rights to UK citizens to vote in Dáil (i.e. lower house of parliament) elections, reciprocating the rights of Irish citizens in the UK. France, Germany, Austria, Greece, Italy and Poland are amongst the Member States in the last category, although there have been political campaigns in most Member States in recent years to institute electoral rights.

Timing can also be significant. In some cases, such as the Scandinavian countries, the Netherlands, Spain, Portugal, the United Kingdom and Ireland, the provisions allowing non-nationals to vote predate the institution of the EU electoral rights and/or the date of accession to the Union. In other cases, such as Belgium and Luxembourg, they have been instituted since the Treaty of Maastricht. Timing is also important, often in quite complex ways, in relation to the new post-2004 Member States which have granted electoral rights to non-nationals. In all cases, this has occurred since the transitions of the early 1990s to democracy, and in most cases the electoral rights have been instituted in circumstances which are broadly associated with accession to the Union, and the taking on of the obligations associated with membership.

In sum, a majority of the twenty-seven Member States, namely fifteen, confer some electoral rights on at least some third country nationals, under national law, and some of the Member States confer additional electoral rights on EU citizens, above and beyond the requirements of EU law. It should be noted, however, that these electoral rights are clustered for the most part in the smaller and medium-sized Member States, and thus do not benefit the majority of third country nationals resident in the Member States.

There are no Union-level measures requiring Member States to institute voting rights for third country nationals in any elections, and indeed it is a widely held view that there is no competence on the part of the Union in this domain to enact legally binding measures, and so there have not been any proposed legislative measures to this effect forthcoming from the European Commission. The whole field of policy relating to the integration of immigrants presents challenges to the European Commission, as there is no clear competence to create or

---

[20] Two EU Member States are members of the Commonwealth: Cyprus and Malta.

even encourage integration policies in the Member States in the current Treaties. Article 63(4) EC only refers to 'the rights and conditions under which nationals of third countries who are legally resident in a Member State may reside in other Member States', suggesting a focus on a level playing field rather than an attempt to raise the standards of protection for third country nationals.[21] Thus electoral rights were not included in the range of rights that Member States are required to extend to third country nationals under the Directive on the right of residence of long-term-resident third country nationals adopted on the basis of Article 63.[22] However, electoral rights are covered in the context of the looser and merely persuasive 'common basic principles' on the integration of immigrants, adopted by the Council in 2004 and aimed at securing improvements in the status and treatment of third country nationals within the Member States.[23] Fleshing out these basic principles, the Commission's 2005 Communication on the integration of immigrants refers to the benefits of electoral participation:

> The participation of immigrants in the democratic process, particularly at the local level, enhances their role as residents and as participants in society. Providing for their participation and for the exercise of active citizenship is needed, most importantly at the political level and especially at the local level.[24]

This suggests a strong political awareness of the issues raised by political rights within the EU institutions and the Member States.

A consistent theme of this book concerns the interactions between the limited electoral rights provided for *citizens of the Union* under the EC Treaty, the *national* rules on electoral rights which cover both citizens of the Union *and* third country nationals, as well as the *national and*

---

[21] Article III-267(4) of the Treaty establishing a Constitution for Europe ('Constitutional Treaty') would – if ratified – provide for the adoption of European laws or framework laws establishing 'measures to provide incentives and support for the action of Member States with a view to promoting the integration of third country nationals residing legally in their territories, excluding any harmonization of the laws and regulations of the Member States'. However, even this complementary competence is currently in doubt, as ratification of the Constitutional Treaty stalled in mid-2005 after the no votes in the French and Dutch referendums.

[22] Council Directive 2003/109/EC of 25 November 2003 concerning the status of third country nationals who are long-term residents, OJ 2004 L16/44.

[23] Council Document 14615/04 of 19 November 2004.

[24] Commission Communication, *A Common Agenda for Integration: Framework for the Integration of Third Country Nationals in the European Union*, 1 September 2005, COM(2005) 389, at 20.

international contexts in which all of these sets of rules operate. It is important to note that Article 19 EC is not the only 'international' legal provision which engages in some way with the transnational question of the electoral participation rights of non-nationals resident in a host polity. There are also a number of international instruments which address the question of extending electoral rights as a dimension of democratic consolidation more generally, or as one means to improve the rights of immigrants. However, these do not have the binding character of the rights under EU law.

A number of Member States have signed and ratified the Council of Europe's Convention on the Political Participation of Foreigners in Local Life (1992),[25] which focuses not only on formal electoral rights, but also on other forms of political participation such as the guaranteeing of basic freedoms of association and expression to non-nationals and the development of specialised representational outlets for non-nationals such as 'foreigners' councils', as can be found in a number of Member States such as Denmark, Italy, France and Germany. The provisions of the Convention are intended to operate for the benefit of all non-nationals, regardless of whether they are nationals of the Member States or third country nationals. The Parliamentary Assembly of the Council of Europe adopted a Recommendation in January 2001, urging contracting states to introduce further rights for migrants, including the right to vote and stand in local elections for those resident and settled for a minimum of three years.[26] The Organization for Security and Cooperation in Europe (OSCE) and the Council of Europe have also engaged with issues such as the treatment of resident minorities and migrants, in ways which have impinged directly or indirectly upon the sovereign rights of states under international law to determine who may vote in elections within the territory. While there is limited protection of the right to vote and other political freedoms under the European Convention on Human Rights and Fundamental Freedoms (ECHR), the European Court of Human Rights in the *Matthews* case intervened directly in relation to the scope of EU law, by requiring the UK to institute voting rights in European Parliament elections for citizens of Gibraltar.[27]

---

[25] ETS No. 144; opened for signature on 5 February 1992; entered into force 1 May 1997; www.conventions.coe.int.

[26] Recommendation 1500 (2001), 26 January 2001.

[27] *Matthews* v. *United Kingdom* (App. No. 24833/94), judgment of 18 February 1999, (1999) 28 EHRR 361. This is discussed in more detail in Chapter 6.

These, and many other aspects of the laws and politics of electoral rights for non-nationals in the EU and the Member States, will be investigated in more detail in the chapters which follow. For, while the starting point of this discussion has been the issues raised by the granting, or non-granting, of electoral rights to non-nationals on the basis of residence and in particular the specific case of EU electoral rights, the objectives of this book are rather wider in character. This book uses the case of electoral rights for non-nationals as the basis for a broader enquiry into the transformation of the nature of citizenship in contemporary Europe. In that context, law is recognised as both a reactive and a proactive 'force', structuring certain aspects of institutional change, but also one which itself is in turn susceptible to change as a result of political pressures. In practice, this book is most concerned with 'constitutional questions', so far as these deal with the structural and ideological foundations of polities, including the question of membership. In terms of approach, it shares much in common with the methodological approach of 'constitutional ethnography', most associated with the work of Kim Lane Scheppele.[28] Scheppele (2004: 395) describes constitutional ethnography as:

> the study of the central legal elements of polities using methods that are capable of recovering the lived detail of the politico-legal landscape.

Its goal is not prediction, in the social-scientific sense, but comprehension; 'not explained variation but *thematization*' (Scheppele, 2004: 391; emphasis in the original). It allows constitutionalism, as a result, to emerge

> as a set of practices in which the transnational ambitions of legal globalization flow over and modify the lived experience of specific local sites, and as a set of practices in which local sites inescapably alter what can be seen as general meanings.
>
> (Scheppele, 2004: 394)

In this case, the 'nestedness' of national polities within the broader legal framework of European integration, and the opportunities and constraints that this offers, is one of the primary focuses of attention.

---

[28] Compare the more 'scientific' approach to defining a methodology for comparative constitutional law as deployed in Hirschl, 2005, drawing explicitly on the case-selection traditions of comparative politics.

The empirical core of the book is to be found in Chapters 4 to 10. While the empirical focus starts with the Union electoral rights sketched here, including the pressure points associated with these rights such as the nature of the European Parliamentary electorate and the question whether Union citizens will ever be granted rights to vote in *national* elections across the territory of the Member States, it then widens out to consider the electoral rights which the Union does not lay down (for third country nationals), but which it leaves at present to national law. Finally, the book considers the role of Union laws and policies, amongst other legal and political factors such as the wider contexts of national immigration laws and policies, and policies on citizenship and nationality, in relation to those electoral rights which are made available (or in some cases denied) under national law within the Member States. However, the concerns of the book will be wider than this empirical focus, in the sense that the work contributes to debates about the 'condition' of citizenship (van Steenbergen, 1994) and how it is operating to delineate insiders and outsiders in the multiple polities (supranational, national, subnational) which comprise the European Union and its Member States. It is consequently with the problematic concept of citizenship that we must begin, a task which, in turn, will assist us in reflecting upon what citizenship might mean for the European Union, building upon the brief presentation earlier in this chapter. In Chapter 3, we will then return to look more closely at the boundaries of the suffrage, and the arguments which are made to include or exclude outsiders.

2

Political membership in and beyond the state

I Introduction

In this chapter, I analyse the multivalent and controversial concept of citizenship, in both its political and its legal guises. The particular focus is upon teasing out the extent to which citizenship has a resonance outwith and across the borders of individual states, and in the context of international developments such as human rights law. What meanings of a post-national, transnational, supranational or international character can citizenship have? To what extent can citizenship and nationhood be mapped according to the same criteria? The analysis leads to a set of interim conclusions about the normative attractiveness, but generally empirically underspecified nature, of claims about the possibilities of citizenship beyond the state. These reflections in turn lead on to a more detailed consideration of the limited concept of 'citizenship of the Union' which was identified in Chapter 1 as providing the legal framework within which electoral rights are granted to citizens of the Member States across the European Union.

II Citizenship as membership

There are as many definitions of citizenship as there are texts about this essentially contested concept.[1] Some variant of the notion of 'full membership' of the relevant community or polity, an approach which builds directly upon the work of sociologist T. H. Marshall (1950: 28–9), seems a favoured starting point. It stresses, above all, the relational aspects of citizenship. For example, David Held (1991: 20) offers the following definition:

---

[1] I use 'essential contestability' in the W. B. Gallie sense, namely, the possibility that two persons 'could disagree substantively about a certain concept and yet agree that some example could be a paradigm for the concept': Gallie, 1955–6; see also Connolly, 1993: 10 *et seq.*

Citizenship has meant a reciprocity of rights against, and duties towards, the community. Citizenship has entailed membership, membership of the community in which one lives one's life. And membership has invariably involved degrees of participation in the community.

But what is *full* membership of any given community or polity? Many different ways of 'cutting the cake' of membership have been suggested. Yasemin Soysal (1994: 159), for example, highlights the two elements of rights and identity which she says make up 'modern citizenship'. Antje Wiener (1999: 200–1; 1998) isolates the vital constitutive role of 'citizenship practice' as a historical element of state formation, and focuses on the three elements of rights, access and belonging as making up citizenship practice. 'Rights' can be broken down into the traditional 'Marshallian' triad of civil, political and social rights. 'Access' expresses the participation element in relation to both the political sphere and the welfare state, and operates 'as a means of testing the meaningfulness and hence the integrative power of formal rights' (Wiener, 1994). 'Belonging' likewise has two elements, namely, an identity element expressed both through a common we-feeling and responsibilities and duties (such as a duty to pay taxes), and a legal in/out marker, which has come to mean, in a world of Westphalian states, the notion of nationality. Linda Bosniak (2003: 185–6) breaks the distinctions down still further by identifying five separate, but interrelated, dimensions of membership, namely, status, rights, political engagement, responsibilities and identity/solidarity/belonging. Clearly, some of these elements have a stronger legal dimension than others, and some are related more closely to the Greek and Roman roots of citizenship, while others are related to modernist and indeed postmodernist conceptions of identity.

Another way of thinking about the demands of *full* membership is to draw the distinction between formal membership and practical access to the benefits of membership (Shaw, 2000). In principle, citizenship – and especially its ascription to given groups on the basis of certain boundaries – appears to be about the distribution of life opportunities. In practice, given unequal wealth distribution, as well as prejudice or hostility towards certain groups marked out by factors such as gender, skin colour, ethnic origin, religious affiliation, disability or sexual preferences, even within a group formally defined as the 'citizens' of a given polity, many will enjoy more of the actual benefits of membership than others. Conversely, many of the practical benefits of membership of a polity are in some circumstances extended also to those who lack formal citizenship, such as civil rights, other human rights, and access to public services. Does that make such persons, in some practical if not formal sense, 'citizens'?

III Citizens and aliens

The final element of the definition of citizenship as membership is the one most central to this book, namely, the question: 'membership of what'? Coy references to polities and communities fail to hide the fact that, under the modern states system, there has been a tendency to prioritise the linkage between state and citizen above all else. For example, liberal nationalists such as David Miller continue to argue that the nation state is the only 'real' basis for identification and for fostering the glue which holds communities together, and allows democracy to operate effectively (Miller, 1995). Back in 1974, French sociologist Raymond Aron categorically denied the possibility of *European* citizenship, or any form of multinational citizenship (Aron, 1974). Yet historically the original Greek and Roman references to citizenship as a political concept were not necessarily linked to any given form of political organisation, and certainly not the state or even the nation state as we know it today (Magnette, 2005). Thus many other scholars concentrate on the blurring of the boundaries of membership resulting from migration and other elements of globalisation, and see challenges to the primacy of the nation state in the lexicon of citizenship from supranational and international developments such as the European Union and international human rights law. Consequently, such scholars suggest that supranational citizenships such as citizenship of the European Union can offer a real added value beyond national citizenship.

The definition of the scope of membership in relation to the scope of the polity is important for the argument in this book because of this tension between the universal and the particular. On the one hand, citizenship appears to be a universal status, a badge of personhood, based upon an irreducible and enforceable commitment to equality; yet, at the same time, it is also commonly used as a means of defining the particular and of delineating the inside from the outside. In other words, by its very essence, the ascription of citizenship could be seen to be a recognition of inequality or at least difference. This seems to follow from Hannah Arendt's (1973: 296) famous comment that the core citizenship right is the 'right to have rights', namely, the right to be recognised as belonging to a community. By way of contrast, the universalistic reading of citizenship would seem to lead necessarily towards a global and cosmopolitan concept of citizenship, without reference to the particularisms of individual polities or states. This is an aspirational idea which founders at the present time upon the rock provided by the reality of modern life, namely, that the most basic badge of membership, *national* membership, continues to be ascribed on the basis of the (legal) nationality of Westphalian states recognised under international law.[2]

It has commonly been the case that strands of thinking about national citizenship which derive moral force precisely from concepts of universal personhood (e.g. the Republican citizenship tradition in France) have found it hard to accept these arguments being extended beyond the border of the state, especially when faced by challenges such as unprecedented demands being placed upon the asylum system as happened in the 1990s (Boswell, 2000). States thus remain the archetypal bounded communities, albeit that the boundaries between them are becoming, as we shall see, increasingly blurred. As Arendt commented in this regard, 'Theoretically, sovereignty is nowhere more absolute than in matters of emigration, naturalization, nationality and expulsion' (1973: 278). In similar terms, other scholars have noted that migration law – the right on the part of states to control the movement of peoples and to categorise some movement as 'legal' and some as 'illegal'[3] – is 'the new last bastion of sovereignty' (Dauvergne, 2004: 588). States are the key to the issue: 'If there were no such things as state borders, then we would not be studying international migration. It is states and their borders that make migration visible' (Geddes, 2005: 802). The same could be said about the boundaries of citizenship. The boundedness of communities immediately reveals the problem of 'aliens' or 'foreigners', constructed as the obvious and direct counterpoint to citizens. Are they the same as, or different from, citizens defined in the national sense? Is the future of citizenship to remain intertwined with concepts of nationalism (Shaw, 1998a)? Is the only effective justification for retaining citizenship

[2] Like Nancy Fraser (2005: 70), I view the notion of 'Westphalia' not as a strict legal rendition of the conditions articulated in the Treaty of Westphalia 1648 but as 'a political imaginary that mapped the world as a system of mutually recognizing sovereign territorial states'.

[3] In this book, I use most often the term 'irregular' to cover the category of persons 'who are liable to be deported for issues related to immigration status'. The term is preferable to 'illegal' because it does not have the same connotations of criminality: see IPPR Factfile, *Irregular Migration in the UK*, April 2006, at 5.

internally within the state, as Stephen Legomsky (1995) has argued, the fact that it operates in the international sphere to delineate political space? The answers to these questions have evolved over the years, as political formations themselves, and the legal frameworks which reflect these formations, have evolved.

In an era of sovereign non-overlapping polities (i.e. under conditions in which the political imaginary of Westphalia is dominant[4]), the differentiation of nationals and non-nationals was rather easy to determine. Membership is ascribed in large measure internally by nationality law ('the juridical link between a person and a State'[5]), by reference to a range of factors such as place of birth, affiliation, marriage or long-term residence. States, as sovereign entities, have the power to make determinations of nationality.[6] They are largely free to choose whether to allow dual nationality and to determine the conditions under which naturalisation or registration as a citizen for migrants and their descendants is permitted. Rainer Bauböck (1994a: 207) terms this order of formal membership a case of territorial sovereignty; its distinctive feature is that it claims to be complete and discrete:

> Completeness means that everybody is at any point in time subject to the territorial sovereignty of a state; discreteness implies that nobody is subject to more than one state simultaneously.

Unsurprisingly, formal membership is a necessary precursor, in this system, to the acquisition of voting rights and thus to this formal dimension of political membership. The power of the distinction between nationals and others is clear: 'Although citizenship is internally inclusive, it is externally exclusive. There is a conceptually clear, legally consequential, and ideologically charged distinction between citizens and foreigners' (Brubaker, 1992: 21).

In addition to recognising nationality as an ascription of membership (Hailbronner, 2006a), public international law, especially – in the modern era – international human rights law, can step in to deal with failures in the system of discrete states and separate systems of nationality such as the withdrawal of nationality, expulsion from the national territory

---

[4] See above n. 2.

[5] Article 2 of the European Convention on Nationality, European Treaty Series (ETS) No. 166; opened for signature 6 November 1997; entered into force on 1 March 2000; www.conventions.coe.int.

[6] *Nottebohm Case* (*Liechtenstein* v. *Guatemala*) [1995] ICJ Reports 4 (judgment of 6 April 1955).

and any other denial of rights, to regulate or prevent conditions such as statelessness, and to protect groups such as refugees and those in need of temporary protection. It has also been challenged, at various times, to address the issues raised by national minorities, that is, minority ethnic groups with the internal badge of national citizenship, who experience issues of social exclusion or prejudice, and who are therefore not 'full' citizens in practice. Private international law, meanwhile, deals with certain types of conflicts of law (or, perhaps better, dissonances) which can occur between different national legal orders in relation to the differing conditions of recognition of, for example, the acquisition of nationality on marriage or affiliation conditions relating to children or grandchildren.

Historically, international law tended to set its face against dual nationality as an unnecessary source of confusion, and so states could feel justified in disallowing it or seeking to reduce instances of its occurrence. In some quarters, dual nationality has also been seen as a contradiction in terms, on the grounds that no one – at least theoretically – can be a servant of two masters. More recent developments, such as the 1997 European Convention on Nationality, acknowledge its utility, in particular as a means of allowing women to pass on their citizenship more easily and as a means of facilitating the integration of immigrants without forcing them arbitrarily to renounce their former citizenship. Some authors contend that there is an increasing convergence towards a European 'norm' in nationality law (Hansen and Weil, 2001), with greater tolerance of dual nationality (Hansen and Weil, 2002; Spiro, 1997). Whether nationality laws in different states are converging around a norm of simpler acquisition is a moot point (Howard, 2005), although evidence in some states such as Germany, which previously had extremely restrictive citizenship policies, seems to point in this direction (Green, 2004: Ch. 4). Some have contended that European Union citizenship has also had an impact on national citizenship laws, encouraging convergence in soft 'reflexive' ways (Rostek and Davies, 2006). However, the better view, which is based on the most comprehensive recent research in this field, is that there is a 'bewildering complexity of rules and regulations for the acquisition and loss of nationality' and 'no overall "European model" of citizenship legislation' (Bauböck *et al.*, 2006c: 20).

Be that as it may, what such approaches to the question of membership have in common is that they deal with the problem of 'aliens' by eliminating the category, through citizenship acquisition, if not by first generation immigrants, then certainly by the successor generations of the children and grandchildren of immigrants. Yet, while in any system there will always be some who choose to remain aliens, in practice there will be many others for whom there is effectively no choice. Into this category would fall the large numbers of undocumented migrants who experience increasingly repressive border control mechanisms and widespread comprehensive denial of rights. Are they to be left wholly out of account, as quasi-non-persons in any reckoning of the evolution of the rights of migrants and of citizenship? As Liza Schuster and John Solomos comment: 'For everyone who can claim to enjoy global citizenship, there are many more who are shut out of every aspect of citizenship' (2002: 52).

For whatever reason it exists, whether through choice or effective lack of choice, 'alienage' presents a continuing challenge to the state, to nationality and to citizenship, raising issues in particular for democracy and democratic practices[7] if large numbers of aliens are excluded from electoral participation. It has been suggested that we use the term 'alien citizenship' (Bosniak, 1994, 2000a, 2000b, 2002, 2003, 2006) precisely to highlight how difficult it sometimes is, *pace* Brubaker, to see clear distinctions between citizens and aliens, but also to highlight that:

> citizenship at the border and citizenship within the community are not always jurisdictionally separate projects but are, instead, sometimes deeply imbricated with one another.
>
> (Bosniak, 2003: 199)

Indeed, as Ciara Smyth (2005: 21) comments:

> On an intuitive level, the concepts of citizen, denizen, legal alien and illegal alien with corresponding rights may make sense. But these concepts mask the prior processes that determine the acquisition of citizenship, whether an immigrant is legal or illegal, and who qualifies for long-term residence. As far as immigrants are concerned, the process is often portrayed as a choice exercised by the individual. But much larger forces are at play, not least the dynamics of forced displacement (including economic hardship), the politics of immigrant selection and the economic interest in allowing the presence of undocumented workers in the State.

---

[7] On the relationship between foreignness and democracy, see Honig, 2001.

In international law, there have been some limited moves towards a blurring of a distinction between aliens and citizens. Smyth, for example, points to the development of commentary by the UN Human Rights Committee on Article 12 of the International Covenant on Civil and Political Rights, which governs the 'right to return' to one's 'own country'. General Comment 27 by the Committee notes that the 'scope of "his own country" is broader than the concept "country of his nationality" ... [and] ... is not limited to nationality in a formal sense', and could include various categories of long-term residents with close connections to a particular country.[8] Such texts lead Smyth to agree with Oscar Schachter who has commented that 'the Covenant on Political Rights does not grant aliens rights to political participation. On the other hand, that does not mean that they should be denied such rights. It simply has not gone that far' (Helton *et al.*, 2000: 284). Smyth (2005: 3) adds: 'yet'.

However, the problem with alien citizenship and indeed any form of semi-citizenship for aliens is the problem of duties and the lack of reciprocity. If, as Held commented, citizenship is about a reciprocity of rights and duties, how should the state – or any political entity conferring membership – react to the fact that the primary polity to which an alien owes her duties is another one? This problem is sharply brought into focus by the fact that states are increasingly following a trend amongst European countries to set tests, requiring minimum levels of knowledge about the host state, its language, history and culture, as prerequisites for citizenship acquisition through naturalisation.

IV Evolving polities: tensions and pressures

Even if this were indeed once the case, and that itself is already doubtful, it is certainly clear today that states can no longer be regarded as hermetically sealed units, from the perspective of the allocation of citizenship rights and obligations. There can be little doubt that the state has transformed in fundamental ways, with consequential impacts upon citizenship, especially since the Second World War (Zürn and Leibfried, 2005: 1). Processes of globalisation, Europeanisation and indeed subnational change have all contributed to this. Bauböck (1994a)

---

[8] Human Rights Committee General Comment 27, Freedom of Movement (Art. 12), 2 November 1999, CCPR/C/21/Rev.1/Add.9.

usefully suggests two additional scenarios of 'orders of membership' involving increasing areas of overlap between states and memberships, namely, 'nominal citizenship' and 'societal membership'. The former scenario complements rather than undermines the pattern of territorial sovereignty, bringing in a more complex political and legal map in which the possibilities of changes of nationality through naturalisation for mobile populations are regarded as crucial to the preservation of democracy and stability via a principle of formal inclusiveness; the latter scenario, however, begins to separate out the civic, civil and social dimensions of citizenship, by focusing upon the areas of participation and entitlement ascribed to non-national migrants *without* the necessity for formal membership, such as participation in welfare state institutions, and access to public goods such as education and health care. Many have used the term 'denizen' to describe this form of 'semi-citizen' condition, in which territoriality and residence replace nationality and legal citizenship as the badge of membership.[9] To complicate matters even further, as Kees Groenendijk points out, there are certain groups of 'almost-citizens' in some states, who are often historically connected to the host state, who enjoy 'a status of enhanced denizenship that entails almost the same rights as those enjoyed by resident nationals, including voting rights at some level (local or national) or access to public office and full protection from expulsion' (2006: 411). Although they do not enjoy protection from expulsion, the situation of Commonwealth or Irish citizens in the UK would fall under this broad category.

It is interesting that only in this final subcategory within the broader category of denizenship does the right to participate in elections finally start to become clearly detached from the acquisition of formal membership, although there are other groups of the more general category of denizens who do enjoy local electoral rights at least. In practice, many modern states still proceed in relation to non-nationals on the basis of inclusion with respect to civil and socio-economic rights, and exclusion in respect of most political rights. Yet debates over alien suffrage can be, as Christian Joppke puts it, 'foundational debate[s] over the meaning of citizenship in the nation-state' (Joppke, 1999: 195).

---

[9] Its usage in the modern migration literature is ascribed to Thomas Hammar, although the term was used much earlier by John Locke: Hammar, 1990; Layton-Henry, 1990; for background see also Bauböck, 1994b.

The scenarios painted here together highlight how states are able to deliver the paradox of internal inclusiveness founded on external exclusiveness (Joppke, 1999: 6). They do not fully address the complexities of the challenge to patterns of belonging which emerge in a multi-level polity such as the EU, viewed in conjunction with both its Member States (some federal, some unitary in nature) and an emerging trans-European legal domain constructed by the Council of Europe and the Organization for Security and Cooperation in Europe (OSCE). In this context, there are many different pressures operating at different levels which the snapshot of sovereign or even semi-sovereign overlapping states offered thus far fails adequately to capture. Each of these is in turn pertinent to the task of defining the boundaries of the suffrage.

First of all, it must be observed that the supranational and international *legal* context has developed within a wider frame of globalisation, and especially global economic forces. The European Union and all of its Member States are by no means immune to the pressures of globalisation. The limited concept of citizenship of the Union, briefly discussed in Chapter 1, represents one possible supranational response to the breaking down of the linkages between state, nation and citizenship in relation to intra-EU mobility, but this is only one small part of a bigger story involving global population movements and a much wider frame for migration policies and politics. Global population movements are often precipitated by the search for greater economic prosperity, by the volatility of capital investment and commodity markets, as well as by attempts to escape repressive or ineffective government regimes. All of these trends often give rise to clandestine and irregular immigration, which states view as 'illegal'. There are larger populations of third country nationals in many of the Member States (and almost all of the pre-2004 group of Member States) than there are of nationals of other Member States (second-country nationals), and it is such population movements, combined with growing prosperity within a neo-liberal frame of economic management, which have transformed, for example, a Western European country such as Ireland which was traditionally a state of emigration into a state of immigration within a few short years (Ruhs, 2004).

Writers from North America and Western Europe are fond of stating that migration is at the centre of any reconceptualisation of the lenses which citizenship provides us with in order to view the human condition (e.g. Heisler, 2005). It is important not to reject, but rather to review, the importance of this insight, in the light of the fact that the EU8 Member

States of Central and Eastern Europe, along with a number of other accession and candidate states such as Bulgaria, Romania and Croatia, are themselves increasingly states of immigration as well as states of emigration. It is certainly true that large numbers of Poles and Lithuanians, for example, took advantage of the free movement possibilities made available in just a few EU Member States, notably Ireland and the United Kingdom, in the immediate post-enlargement phase.[10] In addition, however, states such as Poland and Lithuania are also now experiencing immigration in larger numbers, notably from countries of south-eastern Europe, the former Soviet Union and the Middle East,[11] and may become in due course not only transit countries in a continued East–West migration flow, as they are at present, but also net immigration countries. In the future, therefore, what are seen as the challenges of managing diverse communities and many different cultures and languages within Western European states at the present time can be expected to emerge in many of the Central and Eastern European countries as new migrants enter those countries.

In the short term, the 'free movement' of workers from those states often appears to have more in common with large-scale migratory movements from low-income to high-income states than it does with the rather more restrained and restricted population mobility which has taken place under the aegis of the EU free movement rules in recent years. At least, this is certainly true for mobility from some states such as Poland and the Baltic countries, especially to Ireland and the UK, which were the only two countries, along with Sweden, to accept labour mobility (under certain conditions) from the date of accession in 2004. For example, income disparities and unemployment have been significant push factors, leading to (often highly qualified) workers from Central and Eastern Europe filling many low-income and low-skill jobs in countries such as Ireland and the UK, which are otherwise 'hard-to-fill' jobs. In contrast, EU mobility is predominantly that of persons with high levels of skills and/or qualifications into similar jobs/activities in

---

[10] A. Travis, 'Poles Top List for Work Applications in Britain after EU Expansion', *Guardian*, 23 November 2005, http://www.guardian.co.uk/guardianpolitics/story/0,,1648512,00.html; for a full analysis of the situation in the UK, see *Accession Monitoring Report May 2004–June 2006*, a joint online report by the Home Office, the Department for Work and Pensions, HM Revenue & Customs and the Department for Communities and Local Government, available at http://www.ind.homeoffice.gov.uk/aboutus/reports/accession_monitoring_report/.

[11] See Country Profile No. 3, Poland, July 2005, available from http://www.focus-migration.de; and Iglicka, 2005.

the host state, and is often based on life-style choices, such as student or retirement migration, or migration in order to follow a partner.[12] In the longer term, it might be expected that migration from (and to) the Central and Eastern European Member States may conform to these characteristics.[13] Indeed, it already does share some of those characteristics, as right across the twenty-seven Member States the major factor determining levels of migration remains educational level: highly educated citizens are twice as likely to take advantage of cross-border mobility opportunities than those with low or average levels of education (Krieger and Fernandez, 2006: 7). Furthermore, persons with equivalent levels of education in the identified 'low mobility' EU8 countries (Czech Republic, Hungary, Slovakia and Slovenia) are much less likely to exercise their right of free movement than those in the 'high mobility' states of the 'old' fifteen, that is Denmark, Finland, Ireland and Sweden, and in particular show much lower intentions to exercise mobility, whether these are firm intentions or so-called 'basic intentions'[14] (Krieger and Fernandez, 2006: 10).

Even so, there are other reasons to take more specific account of the effects of EU enlargement for questions of 'citizenship' in its broadest sense, especially in the short term (Reich, 2005; Krūma, 2004). In the early 1990s, Jürgen Habermas noted that the geographical arena of the continent of Europe was seeing two historical movements which touched upon the relation between citizenship and national identity. The first stemmed from the break-up of the Soviet Union, the decline of communism and state socialism in Europe, the reunification of Germany, the reinvention of many of the countries of Central and Eastern Europe as liberal democracies, and finally the re-emergence of some age-old ethnic conflicts in certain eastern and south-eastern European countries and those carved out of the former Soviet Union. The second historical movement was the process of economic and political integration amongst and within the Member States of the European Union (Habermas, 1994: 20). With enlargement, these movements have, to some extent, been married together.

---

[12] *Europeans Move for Love and a Better Quality of Life*, IP/06/389, 28 March 2006.
[13] There is, for example, already retirement migration to Croatia, even before it becomes a Member State.
[14] That is, the contemplation of mobility in the short or medium term, but without firm plans.

Thus enlargement has greatly increased the diversity of the domestic legal and political regimes of citizenship, nationality and membership which are nested within the wider frame of 'citizenship of the Union', but in addition the dramatic processes of post-Cold War modernisation have thrown questions of membership into sharp relief in many of these states. One of the most influential theories conceptualising differences in approaches to nationalism in Western and Eastern Europe in the post-Cold War period, which saw an upsurge of violent ethnic conflict and of nationalist sentiments, was based on the distinction between a concept of civic nationalism based around institutions and the rule of law, increasingly applicable in Western Europe, and an ethnic nationalism apparently continuing to dominate in Eastern Europe. This distinction was originally developed by Hans Kohn (1944) in the Second World War, and then largely forgotten about until the post-1989 period demanded new explanations for some unpalatable political developments (Brubaker, 1996). Although widely criticised as overly schematic and offering at the most ideal types by reference to which certain forms of political movement can be analysed (Janmaat, 2006), the concepts of civic and ethnic nationalism have been used to underpin thinking about concepts of citizenship and nationality as they have evolved in contrasting ways in different states (Péteri, 2000). For example, there are a number of states with a strongly ethnic descent-based or *ius sanguinis* conception of nationality in Central and Eastern Europe. This is true of Poland at least in the post-Second World War period, but has also been substantially the case in Germany, at least until the nationality law was recently amended to permit citizenship acquisition on a residence basis and as a birthright for the children of non-nationals who have been settled for a minimum of eight years (Hailbronner, 2006b).

On the other hand, there is also a strong historical tradition in Central and Eastern Europe of the multi-nation state (or empire), in which nationality as a form of affinity needed to be distinguished from citizenship as a legal badge of membership conferring, for example, voting rights. This involves different terminological distinctions to those common in the Western European and North American literatures, which have commonly focused on nationality as the externally recognised badge of membership, and citizenship as the more open-textured social and political concept of societal membership; a term to describe ethnic belonging in the way that the term 'nationality' and 'nation' was used in the multi-nation states of Central and Eastern Europe, such as the Austro-Hungarian empire, was lacking. 'Nationality' involves the drawing of conceptual distinctions based on national affiliation (based on descent) and in some cases religion, which are separate from the ascriptions of political membership within the state or the empire. Such distinctions have simply had no place in the literatures focusing on post-Second World War Western European or North American states in the context of discussions of citizenship or migration.

1919 and 1945 were not the only periods or moments of intense state formation and re-formation in Europe in the twentieth century. Many new states also emerged in the aftermath of the Cold War after 1989, with the break-up of the multi-national states of the Soviet Union, Czechoslovakia and Yugoslavia (SFRY).[15] In each case, successor states such as the Baltic states of Estonia and Lithuania, and Slovakia and Slovenia, which are all examples of EU8 Member States which have chosen to adopt rules conferring local electoral rights on third country nationals, were faced with the task of defining, *de novo*, the concept of citizenship, and thus the concept and status of aliens. Such countries have had to define citizenship status either from scratch, or by reference to historic boundaries and concepts of peoplehood, many of which are inevitably quite controversial. Some states such as Lithuania adopted a 'zero-option', according nationality at the point of state re-foundation to all legal residents, but placing subsequent restrictions upon citizenship acquisition. In addition, there have been both newly created 'national minorities' (e.g. Russians in the Baltic states; and citizens of other former SFRY countries in Slovenia), as well as so-called autochthonous minorities, whose status as minorities often dates back to the break-up of the Austro-Hungarian Empire after the First World War, and subsequent boundary alignments under measures such as the Treaty of Trianon (1920). These were part of boundary changes which saw Hungary lose one-third of its pre-war territory and a similar percentage of its Magyar population. Thus there are very significant Hungarian minorities in Slovakia and Romania, and smaller groups in countries such as the Ukraine, Slovenia, Serbia and Austria. As a result, the citizenship debate in both the political and legal senses has become linked into the difficult policy challenges to be resolved by such states of institutionalising relationships between national homelands and minorities abroad (Iordachi, 2004a). Some of the minority groups have

---

[15] Or, more correctly, the Socialist Federal Republic of Yugoslavia, or SFRY, as it is referred to in Chapter 10, where the consequences of the break-up for issues of citizenship and belonging are dealt with in more detail.

typically acquired the citizenship of the host state (such as most Russians in Lithuania, or Hungarians in Romania), but equally some have chosen not to acquire this citizenship, or have been unable to do so (e.g. many Russians in Latvia). It is interesting that the strains of post-communist transformation have been felt not only in ethnically mixed states such as the Baltic states, but also in ethnically homogeneous states such as Hungary, because of the increased awareness of diasporic communities outside the boundaries of the state. The raised awareness after 1989 was the result of the fact that such matters could only now begin to be publicly discussed (Fowler, 2004a).

All of these factors have exercised an influence, as we shall see in later chapters, on how and where the boundaries of the suffrage are fixed and, more broadly, they have challenged some of the conventional literatures on the interaction between domestic traditions of statehood and nationality and the gradual accretion of migrants' rights. For all these reasons, the countries of Central and Eastern Europe provide important contrasts with the citizenship and nationality narratives of the states of Western Europe, narratives which have often dominated debates about the integration of immigrants and minorities in scholarship hitherto.

When looking at the pressures upon the state in terms of notions of membership, the impact of pressures from the regions and localities 'below' the state should not be ignored (Painter, 2003). The dilemmas of citizenship within multi-national and multi-level democracies are especially difficult to conceptualise using the vocabulary of linkages between citizenship and the (unitary) 'nation state' (Tully, 2000), and thus there is a need for other conceptual frameworks to make sense of the trends towards regionalisation and the recognition of sub-state nations which has occurred in a number of Member States. As Guy Kirsch put it: 'at a time when Western Europe strives to impose its new-found supranational identity on future history, it is rediscovering its own plurality, as infranational identities from past history are reborn' (Kirsch, 1995: 59). The narratives and practices of intra-state federalism within the European Union have undergone significant development in the last twenty years, both in terms of the creation and the disintegration of states which may broadly be described as federal. One existing federation, Austria, has acceded to the EU in the last fifteen years, joining Germany which was an original member of the European Communities. Belgium, Italy, Spain and – latterly – the United Kingdom have each gone down *sui generis* routes towards devolution and regional autonomy involving the decentralisation of 'national' power, in response to internal pressures for species of federalisation or even full-blown independence. New sites of electoral power and distinctively 'regional' politics have been created, often precisely in order to diffuse claims to national autonomy. Interestingly, however, many of the states of Central and Eastern Europe which acceded to the Union in 2004 emerged out of the ashes of failed federations, notably the Baltic states, the Czech and Slovak Republics, and Slovenia, and their post-federal claims to national autonomy have marked in significant ways their transitions to statehood and thence to membership of the European Union as independent European states. Many writers also highlight the city as the locus within which many citizenship practices are realised in the modern world (Uitermark *et al.*, 2005; Isin, 2000), with the 'global city' seen more as a transnational rather than a national actor in the context of multiculturalism and globalisation, one which disrupts internal hierarchies and systems of power ordering, often with policies 'at odds with the nation state of which they are a part' (Ford, 2001: 209). The point is particularly pertinent in the migration context, as most immigrants tend to live within cities in their host polities (Penninx *et al.*, 2004).

In sum, overlapping polities, complex constellations of power and authority linked with a variety of international, supranational, state-level and sub-state institutions, along with substantial populations of non-national residents, are the features which characterise the EU and its Member States at present. These are features which seem likely to persist and intensify with future enlargements over the next few years to include yet more states with historically rather fuzzy notions of statehood and citizenship joining those states in transition which acceded already in 2004.

V Towards post-national citizenship?

The consequences of these developments in citizenship theory have been investigated by many scholars. Some envisage various forms of 'post-national' membership emerging. Noel Pickus (1997: 3) puts the dilemma neatly:

> Are we, as some contend, on the verge of developing new notions of citizenship and community, ones that successfully weave together our multiple allegiances from the local to the universal? Should the notion of individual membership in a single nation state be replaced by an

emphasis on group representation, cultural rights, and membership in multiple countries? Or would such new notions of transnational and multicultural citizenship threaten basic principles of [national] democracy? Will the shared civic identity that makes both self governance and the protection of rights possible suffer if these changes come to pass?

Thus some argue that citizenship has acquired 'postnational' features (Tambini, 2001), and others that it now has 'transnational' ones (Fox, 2005). In both cases, this is because in substantial measure there has been a de-linking of questions of rights (especially), and (to a more limited extent) access and belonging, from the exclusive purview of a single nation state. Certainly, various forms of multiple and even flexible (Ong, 1999) citizenships now seem empirically real even if they are not (yet) the norm, since the majority of people still remain throughout their lives in one (national) polity. They are also theoretically and normatively justifiable by reference to the complex polities in which they occur and the need to create institutions for those polities especially where legislative competences have been conferred, as in the case of the European Union. It is harder to say, however, precisely why and how these changes have occurred, and what patterns have replaced the national paradigm. For example, can we say that the de-linking of rights from states is the consequence of changes at the state level or of the influence of international (human rights) norms? Are the forms of affiliation, if no longer to one state, now attached to multiple polities at the state level each of which makes a claim to nation statehood, or to putative supranational entities such as the European Union which cannot make a plausible claim to statehood? Or is dual (national) citizenship to be the archetypal postnational way forward in a complex world (Spiro, 2005)?

The problems of many of these visions are illustrated starkly by Rogers Smith (2001: 74):

> normatively, I too would like to see a complexly federated world of 'weak' political peoples in which individuals could freely choose to belong to many roughly equal and only 'semi-sovereign' communities at once. [But] . . . the political dynamics of people-building make the achievement of such arrangements on an enduring basis precarious. Those of us with normative reservations about absolutist senses of allegiance thus face major challenges in considering how we can forge stable forms of political membership that eschew them.

Thus, normatively, postnational or transnational forms of membership do seem to offer attractive alternatives to bounded versions of citizenship which are simply empirically closer to the reality of life within complex polities, particularly those which are diverse or are deeply divided (Soysal, 2004). Certainly, it is quite tempting to attach the label of 'postnational' to the emergent concept of European citizenship under the EC and EU Treaties (Shaw, 1998a), and the label 'transnational' to the complex citizenship practices of mobile populations of immigrants, within diasporic groups and faith communities in particular (Kastoryano, 2005). Up to a certain point, these labels have a symbolic and rhetorical power, in particular as an aspiration to combat hierarchical and unequal relationships between states (Castles, 2005). However, empirically it still remains important to specify the precise changes and evolving institutional practices which constitute or construct forms of membership which are not attached solely to traditional state-level forms of polity organisation. It is also important to specify the circumstances in which the boundaries of citizenship seem less permeable to exogenous influences, such as the case of acquisition and loss of formal national citizenship (Bauböck *et al.*, 2006a, 2006b).

Insisting on a high degree of empirical specification, whether of post/ trans-national or of revived national forms of citizenship practice at least gets over some of the difficulties associated with the fact that, if the term is used too generally, the risk arises that 'citizenship' becomes 'simply too multivalent to play the kind of central analytical and aspirational role that it has come to play in the work of many contemporary scholars' (Bosniak, 2003: 200). In this way, we can avoid the pitfalls identified by Christian Joppke in relation to what he terms 'hyphenated citizenships', that is, concepts such as sexual citizenship or ecological citizenship. He argues that 'such "citizenship" is less a distinct and clearly demarcated object of study than a conceptual metaphor for a bewildering variety of rights-based claims in contemporary societies, particularly if raised by marginal groups' (Joppke, 2003: 429). On the contrary, if the analysis is carefully restricted to specific new institutional forms of participation, which cross or transgress state boundaries and which are based, wholly or in part, on supranational and/or international legal structures and/or on the interactions between multiple national legal structures, then these problems should be satisfactorily avoided, especially if the analysis is predominantly empirical, rather than normative, in its approach. It is therefore to the excavation of the institutional dimensions of citizenship as applied in the EU context that we shall now turn, building upon the brief presentation in Chapter 1.

VI Citizenship and the European Union: market or polis?

Much has been made, over the years, of the weakness of the citizenship concept applied in the EU context. Perhaps the harshest commentary on the text of the Treaty comes from an author who nonetheless sees merit and utility in the project of European citizenship, Joseph Weiler. He states that 'the Citizenship clause in the TEU [Treaty on European Union] is little more than a cynical exercise in public relations' (Weiler, 1998: 10). The underlying doubt is whether citizenship in the EU context can have any 'normative or empirical significance', as Joseph Carens has bluntly put it (Carens, 2000: 165). Rhetorically, Jonathan Fox asks the sceptics' question for them: 'what rights do "EU citizens" get – really – beyond what their states already provide?' (Fox, 2005: 195). He answers his own question by evoking precisely the paradigm right relating to migration: 'One answer is the right to move and work freely across national borders, a right that most migrants can only dream of.' Here, then, is where the value-added of citizenship of the Union for nationals of the Member States must clearly lie, but the difficulty for students of EU law is that this question immediately leads to another which implicates the complex genealogy and history of the Union citizenship concept: given that the EU, or more precisely the European Community as it then was pre-Maastricht, already guaranteed free movement rights not only for workers and their families, but also for most other categories (self-employed, students, retired persons, those of independent means), why should the Union choose to adopt the language of citizenship in the context of the Treaty reforms of the early 1990s? Was this merely to acknowledge, in more political terms, what was already a legal development driven by the imperatives of the economic integration framework of the EC Treaty? Furthermore, what value-added lies in the adoption of language at the Union level consciously aping the narratives of citizenship at the state level? Why did the Union move onto the terrain of citizenship, given that the European integration project – and thus the European Community – was originally conceived as a process of economic integration between sovereign states, each of which has its own separate citizenship?

Clearly, that move must be related to the emergent, but nonetheless controversial, political identity of the Union, as it has evolved through successive enlargements, treaty reforms, and processes of institutional and policy intensification from the 1980s onwards. This process of political development accelerated with the formal creation of the

European Union in the 1990s, through the Treaty of Maastricht. That was the same treaty which instituted the citizenship concept, as we have noted, albeit as an amendment to the EC Treaty, rather than as part of the EU Treaty.[16] In terms of 'political union', the free-standing EU Treaty institutes what is now known as the 'pillar structure' of the European Union. This is based around the long-standing EC Treaty, with its single market framework and more recent rules on the establishing and functioning of a single currency (the euro), plus flanking policies such as those on the environment or social and regional policy, now designated in political parlance as the 'first pillar'. The Common Foreign and Security Policy (Title V of the EU Treaty) is often known as the second pillar, and what is now termed Cooperation in Police and Criminal Justice Matters (Title VI of the EU Treaty) as the third pillar.[17] However, the EU Treaty does not treat the situation of the individual under EU law in any substantial way, leaving this largely to the domain of the EC Treaty, although it contains important provisions on fundamental rights which bind the Union, its institutions and the Member States, and thus protect the position of individuals (Articles 6 and 7 EU).

It is interesting to note that the emergence of the formal concept of citizenship of the Union in the 1990s coincided with a general resurgence of scholarly and political interest in citizenship as a concept, and as a prism of analysis for the human condition, and the ascription of multiple functions to that concept (e.g. van Steenbergen, 1994). Analytically and normatively, citizenship has been used by scholars and by political actors to express notions of identity, both in terms of commonality (citizenship as one of the ties that bind within communities) and in terms of difference (citizenship as expressing multivalent identities). Such re-articulations of the case for using citizenship to describe certain collective attributes have often been bottom-up in nature, resulting from pressures of globalisation and migration, as well as from the politics of identity and recognition (Kymlicka and Norman,

---

[16] Logically, the Treaty of Maastricht should probably have termed the legal structure established under Part Two of the EC Treaty 'Community citizenship', rather than 'citizenship of the Union'.

[17] As will be apparent when we discuss the position of third country nationals under EU law in Chapter 7, the legal and constitutional framework associated with the third pillar has changed since the original Treaty of Maastricht. The third pillar still exists, but is reduced in scope compared to the original position in 1993 when it first came into force, as a result of the Treaty of Amsterdam which came into force in 1999.

1994). It has not only been commentators who have articulated arguments about identity or political recognition in citizenship terms, but also NGOs and other social movements at all levels – local, state level and international (Ong, 2005). But the specific motivation for the institution of a concept of citizenship via the Treaty of Maastricht was a top-down concern with facilitating the creation of European identity, and even a European *demos* which could be the basis for a European democracy. It is hard, of course, not to observe such developments, one might even say such manipulations, without a degree of cynicism, since there hardly seemed any grassroots movement for European citizenship. That is not to say that there have not been proponents of a concept of European citizenship which goes beyond the economic roots of European integration and into the political realm, but such proponents have been primarily scholarly rather than societal in nature, or if societal have been limited to a small number of predominantly Brussels-based NGOs.

What could this citizenship mean? Mouffe (1992: 8) has argued that:

> If Europe is not to be defined exclusively in terms of economic agreements and reduced to a common market, the definition of a common political identity must be at the head of the agenda and this requires addressing the question of citizenship. European citizenship cannot be understood solely in terms of a legal status and set of rights, important as these are. It must mean identifying with a set of political values and principles which are constitutive of modern democracy.

In similar terms, discussing European citizenship, Richard Bellamy refers to citizenship as more than 'mere membership', but also entailing 'the leverage such membership gives for changing its terms and conditions' (i.e. of a given system, of which an individual may be a member) (Bellamy, 2001: 65). These concerns about the political condition of European citizenship have played an important role in recent debates in the European Union about the possible finality of the European integration process, and more specifically what role a constitutional text might play in relation to any such finality. That led to the debate, after the Treaty of Nice, about the 'future of the Union', the Laeken Declaration of December 2001 which convened the Constitutional Convention of 2002–3, and finally to the Treaty establishing a Constitution for Europe, which was signed by the then twenty-five Member States in Rome in October 2004.[18] That text, part innovation and part recapitulation of

---

[18] Hereafter referred to as the 'Constitutional Treaty'.

well-established provisions and principles, would have made little formal difference to the Union's existing legal and constitutional provisions regarding citizenship. Moreover, more generally, even if it were ratified, the Constitutional Treaty would not institute a brand new constitutional framework where one does not exist at the moment. Rather, it would inaugurate the perhaps uneasy co-existence of a formal text with the underlying incremental and dynamic constitution on the basis of which the Union presently operates under its existing treaties, in what might prove to be an uneasy relationship (Shaw, 2005). However, what was of course important about the overall debate on the drafting of the Constitutional Treaty, and indeed what was one of the themes in its rejection in two referendums held in France and the Netherlands in May and June 2005 which brought the ratification process to a sudden halt, was the nature and purpose of European integration (and the related question of enlargement, especially the possibility of Turkey entering the Union), the question of democracy for European citizens, and, as a subsidiary question, but nonetheless one of considerable importance, the treatment of outsiders and immigrants in the Union context. It is of considerable significance to the study of citizenship of the Union that the Member States have often tended to veer towards so-called 'Fortress Europe', namely, the collective embrace of repressive measures towards outsiders.

Notwithstanding the absence of suggested formal changes to the existing provisions, the treatment of the citizenship issue in the context of the debate about the 'future of the Union' and about the drafting of the Constitutional Treaty forms part of a long-standing tendency within EU studies to link the question of citizenship to the issue of polity formation (Keane, 2005). Perhaps inevitably, most arguments within this intellectual current have tended to offer rather 'thin', vague and unsubstantiated formulations of the constitutional or political 'glue' which citizenship could represent for the European Union if its potential is tapped. Nonetheless, it is possible to see in the legal developments which have occurred since the institution of the formal concept of citizenship of the Union in 1993 some evidence that citizenship is becoming a more cohesive and a less fragmented concept in the EU context. In turn, these developments can be related to the case for studying the electoral rights of non-nationals as one aspect of the wider transformation of citizenship in the European political space. Hence we must now examine these developments in citizenship of the Union in more detail.

VII Interpreting citizenship of the Union

Throughout the period of development of citizenship in the EU context, it has remained very difficult to define or to capture the concept (Lyons, 1997; Douglas-Scott, 1998). In an early commentary on the European citizenship concept, Ulrich Preuss (1995: 267) urged that it should be treated as an opportunity rather than an entity:

> European citizenship does not mean membership in a European nation, nor does it convey any kind of national identity of 'Europeanness'. Much less, of course, does it signify the legal status of nationality in a European state. Rather, by creating the opportunity for the citizens of the Member States of the European Union to engage in manifold economic, social, cultural, scholarly, and even political activities irrespective of the traditional territorial boundaries of the European nation-states, European citizenship helps to abolish the hierarchy between the different loyalties ... and to allow the individuals a multiplicity of associative relations without binding them to a specific nationality. In this sense, European citizenship is more an amplified bundle of options within a physically broadened and functionally more differentiated space than a definitive legal status.

In similar terms, Dora Kostakopoulou (2000: 490) comments that European citizenship is 'neither a neat nor a consistent entity. Rather, it is a continuum of possibilities and therefore also an almost infinite source of potential disagreement.' But, again, the point must be made that these potentialities are shaped by the fact that the European Union is an entity based on limited powers conferred by the Member States. That is why Article 17(2) EC refers to the fact that citizens of the Union enjoy the rights, and are subject to the duties, contained in the EC Treaty.

In earlier work on the issue of citizenship of the Union, which had a primarily theoretical and legal doctrinal focus, rather than a focus on wider legal and political developments within and across the Union and its Member States, I concentrated on identifying the space within which citizenship of the Union makes sense as more than just a formal legal concept (Shaw, 1998a, 1998b). I argued that citizenship of the Union, as it developed, would be structured by a variety of endogenous and exogenous influences. Those endogenous influences coming from within the logic of EU law itself include processes of spillover into the domain of claims-making for legal rights. These are the inevitable products of the closer interactions fostered by the multitude of political, economic, legal, social and cultural contacts between the Member States, based on the framework of Treaties which link them together. Another way of putting this point is that cases based on the denial of EU rights would be raised at the state level, resulting in references to the Court of Justice under Article 234 EC, and the case law of the Court of Justice on the exercise of freedoms and rights under the Treaty would contribute constructively to the interpretation of citizenship of the Union.[19] This prediction has turned out to be correct, with a steady flow of significant cases shaping EU rights especially since 1998 (Kostakopoulou, 2005; Mather, 2005). To that extent, citizenship has conformed to the expectations of, for example, neo-functionalist theories of integration, as deployed in some of the early works on European citizenship (Meehan, 1993). However, it is also clear that the evolution of citizenship in the EU context can be understood in terms of theories of institutionalism and/or social constructivism, which also provide powerful explanations for the development of some, if not all, facets of European integration (Wiener, 2003; Wiener, 2006: 50–1; Kostakopoulou, 2005). On all these accounts, the development of citizenship is related in different ways to other changes of both an institutional and an ideational nature which can be seen within the scope of European integration processes, and also to developing understandings of the role of norms.

In addition, the obvious point about the scope of European Union law requires reiteration: any rights arising under EU law are confined by the scope of the EU treaties, and in particular by the scope of the EC Treaty, which contains all of the competences conferred upon the Union institutions to adopt measures which can regulate directly the status and rights of individuals within the Member States. The scope and nature of EU competence thus remains a powerful endogenous force.

But, of course, EU citizenship is also nested within the wider forces of globalisation and Europeanisation, including changes at the state and sub-state levels, as noted in earlier sections of this chapter. Formally speaking, citizenship of the Union is shaped by the nationality laws of

---

[19] This point was made in an early case raising the citizenship question by Advocate General Léger, albeit that the Court in that case chose not to resolve the issue which arose using the citizenship provisions: 'it is for the Court to ensure that its full scope be attained'. Case C-214/94 *Boukhalfa* v. *Federal Republic of Germany* [1996] ECR I-2253, at para. 63 of the Advocate General's Opinion.

the Member States as a powerful exogenous force. Member States are free to determine who are their nationals, subject to the requirement that, where a person possesses dual nationality, the Member State may not arbitrarily fix upon the nationality of a Member State as being the decisive nationality for some matter relating to the allocation of rights under EU law (de Groot, 2004).[20] More generally, national traditions of citizenship are an important set of structures influencing the trajectory of citizenship (Preuss *et al.*, 2003). Equally, the pressures are not one way: there is increasing evidence of aspects of EU citizenship, in particular the boundary between EU citizens and third country nationals, exercising reciprocal influences upon patterns of national citizenship, especially nationality laws (Rostek and Davies, 2006).

Having articulated the proposition that Union citizenship is developing within a dense environment of mutual pressures and influences, the next logical step, when trying to shed light upon this environment or to unravel the complex network of pressures and influences, is, as I have argued in the previous section, to concentrate on the specific institutional forms which citizenship practices have taken. In this case, it is important to concentrate on the impact of EU citizenship upon the development of a portfolio of rights for migrants, not least because the EU has specifically encouraged mobility, at least amongst 'its' citizens. This is a necessary precursor to understanding the EU electoral rights in Article 19 as an incident of those mobility rights.

The focus on migrants' rights as citizenship rights in the EU context is particularly visible in the case law on rights associated with free movement of EU citizens in the post-Maastricht era. In a rhetorical flourish, in the *Grzelczyk* case,[21] the Court stated that citizenship of the Union is 'destined to be the fundamental status' of nationals of the Member States, but that in itself is a rather empty statement. More significantly, since the mid-1990s and its first positive invocation of the symbolic power of Article 17 EC in the *Martínez Sala* case,[22] the Court has created significant constraints upon the sovereignty of the Member States as exercised in relation to welfare provision, the provision of public services, and even nationality law, by applying the non-discrimination provision to protect the interests of citizens of the Member States

---

[20] Case 369/90 *Micheletti* [1992] ECR I-4258.

[21] Case C-184/99 *Rudy Grzelczyk* v. *Centre Public d'Aide Sociale d'Ottignes-Louvain-la-Neuve (CPAS)* [2001] ECR I-6193.

[22] Case C-85/96 *Martínez Sala* v. *Freistaat Bayern* [1998] ECR I-2691.

lawfully resident in a Member State other than the one of which they have the nationality (Fries and Shaw, 1998). In *Martínez Sala*, that conclusion resulted in the Court requiring the German authorities to grant non-discriminatory access on the part of a Spanish national to childraising benefits in Germany; similarly, in *Bidar*, the Court applied the non-discrimination principle to the provision of subsidised loans to students in higher education in the United Kingdom for the benefit of certain students from other Member States residing in the UK for the purposes of studying.[23] In both cases, the claimant had a prior lawful residence in the host Member State. Bidar was not a student who moved in order to study in a different state, but a French national who was residing with his grandmother and who completed his secondary education in the United Kingdom. He could therefore be regarded as substantially integrated in the United Kingdom. However, he nonetheless did not satisfy the ordinary residence test in order to qualify for access to subsidised loans as a student of higher education. As the Court pointed out in *Bidar*, a certain degree of financial solidarity between the Member States can be expected under the citizenship provisions, combined with the non-discrimination provision:[24]

> a citizen of the Union who is not economically active may rely on Article 12 EC where he has been lawfully resident in the host Member State for a certain period of time or possesses a residence permit.

Such a conclusion can be justified by reference to the text of the relevant secondary legislation covering the free movement rights of students; it is stated in the Preamble to the Directive on students' rights of residence that beneficiaries of the right of free movement must not become an *unreasonable* burden upon the Member States.[25]

However, the rights acquired by EU citizens are by no means unconditional in relation to economically inactive persons. For example, in *De Cuyper* the Court held that Belgium was justified in imposing a residence condition precluding a national from exporting an unemployment benefit to another Member State, although this would be possible under the relevant EU legislation regarding the coordination of social

---

[23] Case C-209/03 *R* v. *London Borough of Ealing, ex parte Bidar* [2005] ECR I-2119.
[24] *Ibid.*, para. 56.
[25] Council Directive 93/96/EC on the right of residence for students, OJ 1993 L317/59; see also recital 10 of the Preamble to Council Directive 2004/28/EC on citizens' free movement rights which replaced Directive 93/96/EC and other secondary instruments as of April 2006; this also refers to citizens not becoming an 'unreasonable' burden upon the host state (OJ 2004 L158/77).

security schemes – with a view to encouraging mobility – in the event that a person wanted to move to live in another Member State in order to seek work.[26]

Perhaps more startling has been the interference in the immigration sovereignty of a Member State which results from the *Chen* case.[27] This case arose as a consequence of the effects of the Irish rules on *ius soli* or birthright citizenship, which was granted to all babies born on the island of Ireland at the time when the facts arose regardless of the status of the mother. A baby girl born to a Chinese mother in Northern Ireland thus automatically became an EU citizen, by virtue of the Irish provisions, and furthermore as an EU citizen resident in a Member State other than the one of which she was a national, young Catherine Chen was fully protected by the non-discrimination provisions of EU law. The issue which arose before the Court of Justice concerned the implications of this for the child's mother, as primary carer. She wished to reside in the United Kingdom with the child but otherwise had no right of abode. The effects of this rather unusual situation on the UK's immigration sovereignty in the sense of its capacity to decide which third country nationals may lawfully take up residence within its borders is quite significant. As a member of the family of an EU citizen, Mrs Chen was held by the Court of Justice to have the right to reside with, and care for, her child, as this was necessary for her child in practice to enjoy the benefit of her EU citizenship; this meant that Mrs Chen could not be denied the right to reside in the United Kingdom. As we shall see in Chapter 8, which presents a more detailed study of electoral rights and associated developments in Ireland, such developments in free movement rights, which represent the outer limits of the Court's case law so far as they have resonance for third country nationals, can also interact in interesting ways with developments in the field of electoral rights.

It is worth recalling, finally, that the Member States have been reluctant in some cases to give up their immigration sovereignty even in the case of the free movement rights of EU citizens, and this has often gone unchecked in the context of EU law. It was only in March 2006 that the Court of Justice finally confirmed, in a case brought by the Commission against Belgium, that it was impermissible for a Member State to issue *automatic deportation orders* to a national of a Member State resident on its territory who had failed, at the end of an allowable period of residence

---

[26] Case C-406/04 *De Cuyper* v. *Office national de l'emploi* [2006] ECR 6947.
[27] Case C-200/02 *Chen* v. *Secretary of State for the Home Department* [2004] ECR I-9925.

of three months, to produce necessary documentation to prove that, in the absence of employment, he or she had support from another source or independent means.[28]

In some of its case law on the consequences of the non-discrimination principle protecting citizens of the Member States when they take advantage of their free movement rights, the Court of Justice has sought to emphasise a view of citizenship as a status rather than merely a bundle of rights ascribed to a socio-economic actor. This can be found in its repetitive invocation in all recent cases of citizenship of the Union as the 'fundamental status' for nationals of the Member States, drawn from the *Grzelczyk* case. The point can also be related back to much earlier developments. The impetus of the free movement rights (goods, services, labour, capital, enterprise) was the construction of the market citizen or *Marktbürger* as the first figure of EC law (and the primary actor in the new European market) – those 'acting as participants in or as beneficiaries of the common market'.[29] Arguably, however, legislative[30] and judicial[31] developments which have generalised the right of free movement (of persons) and given it a broader 'citizen-focused' character have moved at least that element of the range of free movement rights into the sphere of civil rights for citizenship purposes. This version of free movement rights as civil rights was stated most eloquently by Advocate General Jacobs in *Konstantinidis*.[32] He stated that:

> a Community national who goes to another Member State as a worker or self-employed person under Articles [39, 43 and 49] of the [European Community] Treaty is entitled not just to pursue his trade or profession

---

[28] Case C-408/03 *Commission* v. *Belgium* [2006] ECR I-2647.

[29] H. Ipsen, *Europäisches Gemeinschaftsrecht*, Tübingen: J. C. B. Mohr, 1972, quoted in Everson, 1995: 73.

[30] See the directives introduced by the institutions of the European Community even in the pre-Maastricht citizenship era to create a more generalised free movement right: Council Directive 90/365/EEC on the right of residence for employees and self-employed persons who have ceased their occupational activity, OJ 1990 L180/28; Council Directive 93/96/EC on the right of residence for students, OJ 1993 L317/59; Council Directive 90/364/EEC on the right of residence, OJ 1990 L180/26.

[31] Case 186/87 *Cowan* v. *Le Trésor public* [1989] ECR 195 (right of a UK tourist attacked on the Paris underground to French criminal injuries compensation payments by virtue of his status as a recipient of services and entitlement to freedom of movement, coupled with the right to non-discrimination on grounds of nationality) and Case 293/83 *Gravier* v. *City of Liège* [1985] ECR 593 (right of a French student to non-discriminatory treatment by a Belgian university, as migrant students come within the scope of protection of the EC Treaty).

[32] Case C-168/91 *Konstantinidis* v. *Stadt Altensteig* [1993] ECR I-1191 at 1211.

> and to enjoy the same living and working conditions as nationals of the host State; he is in addition entitled to assume that, wherever he goes to earn his living in the European Community, he will be treated in accordance with a common code of fundamental values, in particular those laid down in the European Convention on Human Rights. In other words, he is entitled to say 'civis europeus sum' and to invoke that status in order to oppose any violation of his fundamental rights.

This status-driven vision of the mobile Euro-citizen invoking his or her legal right to European citizenship should not, however, be regarded as an authoritative statement of the law, at least not in terms of the time at which it was written (early 1990s). The Court of Justice did not follow the suggestion of the Advocate General in the *Konstantinidis* case and instead adopted a narrower economic rationale to underpin its conclusions regarding the 'Community rights' of a self-employed masseur of Greek nationality living in Germany who complained that the German authorities were infringing his EU rights in their official translation (or better transliteration) of his name (from Greek letters into Roman ones). The transliteration lost the essence of the original Greek name. The Court of Justice concluded that in such circumstances the German authorities were not entitled to insist on a spelling of the applicant's name in such a way as to misrepresent its pronunciation since 'such distortion exposes him to a risk of confusion of identity on the part of his potential clients'. What is notable about this case is that the Court focused specifically on the economic considerations, highlighting the role of Konstantinidis as economic actor within the EU system as a 'market' citizen. These economic rights created the necessary nexus for the application of the non-discrimination principle.

Since then, the constitutional and political situation has evolved, as has judicial argument, at least in some cases. In *Garcia Avello*,[33] the Court applied the non-discrimination rule when examining the treatment of the surnames, under Belgian law, of those with Belgian nationality and those with dual Belgian and Spanish nationality. The result of treating two different situations in the same way was that the latter would have different surnames under different national legal systems, and this was a form of discrimination on grounds of nationality. The Court had no difficulty concluding that the case fell within the scope of EU law, because, like the applicant at the centre of the *Martínez Sala*

---

[33] Case C-148/02 *Garcia Avello* v. *Belgium* [2003] ECR I-11613.

case, the applicants were simply nationals of one Member State lawfully resident in another. In *Standesamt Stadt Niebüll*,[34] the Court was faced with a situation where a child of German nationality, who was born in Denmark and was domiciled there, found that the surname which is registered for him in his Member State of nationality is different to that which he bears in his Member State of birth and normal residence. It is interesting to note that Advocate General Jacobs, in his Opinion, did not pursue the provocative line of argument that he deployed in *Konstantinidis* regarding citizenship as a status under EU law when faced with another case on surnames under national law. On the contrary, arguing that there was indeed a case for applying EU law to this situation and for finding that there has been discrimination on grounds of nationality, Jacobs referred to the significance of the post-Maastricht citizenship provisions for a case which is not dissimilar in nature to *Konstantinidis*, concluding that 'the combined effects of Articles 17 and 18(1) EC mean that it is now unnecessary to establish any economic link in order to demonstrate an infringement of the right to free movement'.[35] The Court of Justice did not express a view on this point, as it disposed of the case on the narrow and technical basis that it had no jurisdiction to hear the questions referred by the national court, because the latter was acting in the context of the case in an administrative and not a judicial capacity. Consequently, there was no case for applying the preliminary reference procedure under Article 234 EC.

Notwithstanding the absence of a full judgment on the issue of surnames in the *Standesamt Stadt Niebüll* case, can we now say with confidence that citizenship under EU law is finally throwing off the shackles of the 'legacy of the market citizen' (Everson, 1995)? The consequence may be a clearer vision of Union citizenship in the future as a civil status of nationals of the Member States, a vision which could have significant spillover into other domains of Union citizenship rights, such as the electoral rights which are the primary focus of this book. However, it should be emphasised that the basis for that civil status still remains a reference point of equal treatment between nationals of the Member States, rather than some additional and exclusive relationship between the Union and 'its' citizens (O'Leary, 1996). To put it another way, the horizontal 'isopolity' concept continues to

---

[34] Case C-96/04 *Standesamt Stadt Niebüll* [2006] ECR I-3561.
[35] *Ibid.*, Opinion of 30 June 2005, para. 54.

dominate the political possibilities of EU citizenship, and the horizontal element remains under-developed (Magnette, 2005).

VIII Union citizenship and electoral rights for non-nationals

The EU electoral rights are somewhat different in legal and constitutional nature to the free movement and non-discrimination rights which have evolved incrementally through a combination of treaty provision and judicial intervention over thirty years. The electoral rights emerged as a comprehensive package in a single set of constitutional changes, followed by implementing measures. The package comprises Article 19 EC, and two directives adopted by the Council.[36] In contrast to the other citizenship provisions, Article 19 and its associated directives clearly innovate both in the field of EU competence and in relation to law and policy-making. In turn, these EU provisions are dependent upon detailed constitutional, legislative and administrative application (and, inevitably, interpretation) at the state, sub-state and local level as the Member States have been tasked with giving effect to the requirement to confer local and European Parliamentary election rights of both an active and a passive nature upon nationals of the Member States.

I would argue that with the electoral rights, and the consequential construction of the citizen of the Union as an active political citizen (albeit within limits), EU law has stepped into a domain which is driven as much by a political imperative of 'citizenship-as-political-participation' as it is by either the notion of 'citizenship-as-rights' or indeed 'citizenship-as-status'. The electoral rights thus carry EU law into a new domain by providing a distinctive political nexus between the individual and another polity. This is one reason why in several Member States constitutional amendments were needed to give effect to Article 19 EC. In the case of European Parliamentary elections, this polity is the European Union itself, and it could easily be said that the electoral rights are concerned with the question of developing a distinctive European identity, which is often – so far as it goes – the symbolic underpinning

---

[36] Council Directive 93/109/EC laying down detailed arrangements for the exercise of the right to vote and stand as a candidate in elections to the European Parliament for citizens of the Union residing in a Member State of which they are not nationals, OJ 1993 L329/34; Council Directive 94/80/EC laying down detailed arrangements for the exercise of the right to vote and stand as a candidate in municipal elections by citizens of the Union residing in a Member State of which they are not nationals, OJ 1994 L368/38.

given for EU citizenship itself. This involves the enhancing of the 'sympolity' element of EU citizenship (Magnette, 2005). However, in the case of electoral rights in local elections, the reality is that these are concerned with the integration of non-national EU citizens within the *host* polity, and thus arguably have the effect not of making the beneficiaries necessarily more European, but rather perhaps more French or more German or indeed perhaps more Parisian or more Bavarian, if city or state is more important than nation state. But like the other instances involving the application of the non-discrimination principle discussed in this chapter – such as the cases of *Martínez Sala* and *Bidar*, as well as the 'right to a name' cases – all these rights are parasitic upon the exercise of free movement rights by citizens of the Union. That is, the rights are precisely there to equalise the situation of Union citizens resident in a Member State other than the one of which they possess the nationality, with nationals of that state. The EC Treaty simply would not apply if there were no cross-border element. The same is true of the electoral rights which protect the interests of the mobile European citizen. But applying the argumentation developed by Advocate General Jacobs in *Standesamt Stadt Niebüll* by analogy, the crucial nexus is not the economic one, but lawful residence in another Member State, that is, a civil status rather than an economic one. However, in the case of the European Parliamentary electoral rights, the rights additionally ensure that, if the migrant EU citizen is unable or unwilling to vote in his or her home polity in periodic European Parliament elections,[37] he or she does not lose out on the opportunities for democratic self-expression created by the institution of direct elections for the European Parliament. Finally, it was argued by Advocate General Tizzano in the *Gibraltar* and *Aruba* cases[38] that Union citizens have a general citizenship right to vote for the European Parliament which is unrelated to the exercise of free movement rights. If so, this right could be regarded as the first non-situation-specific European citizenship right. In the event, the Court of Justice declined to offer a

---

[37] The situation on expatriate voting in European Parliament elections differs from Member State to Member State, although it is allowed in principle in almost all Member States, and the typical preferences of EU citizens also differ. Some prefer to use expatriate voting rights, and others prefer to vote in the host state. Under Directive 93/109/EC, to prevent double voting, voters resident in another Member State must choose whether to vote in the home or the host state (Article 4, OJ 1993 L329/34).

[38] See Opinion of Attorney-General Tizzano in Case C-145/04 *Spain* v. *United Kingdom (Gibraltar)* and Case C-300/04 *Eman and Sevinger* v. *College van burgemeester en wethouders van Den Haag (Aruba)*, 6 April 2006, paras. 67–8.

similarly dramatic statement about the scope of Union citizenship, but its judgment in particular in *Aruba* supports the argument that it sees the right to vote for the European Parliament as a Union citizenship right, albeit not an unconditional or an exclusive one.[39] These cases are discussed in detail in Chapter 6.

Making an argument about the constitutional significance of the EU electoral rights does not carry with it any *a priori* claims about the effectiveness or significance of the EU electoral rights which currently exist. As Strudel (2002, 2003, 2004) has argued, the EU electoral rights are wholly dependent upon national action if they are to be effective. It is also the case that the provisions of the EC Treaty on citizenship guarantee limited electoral rights without any accompanying broader political freedoms, such as the right of association or the right to join or to found a political party, although these are guaranteed elsewhere under EU law as fundamental rights. Without such freedoms, how can the electoral rights truly empower citizens of the Union as democratic actors within the Union and the Member States? The profound limitations of the rights as they have emerged and applied will be rehearsed in much more detail in Chapters 4 and 5, while the arguments around possible extensions and developments will be canvassed in Chapters 6 and 7.

However, a more general case can be made that electoral rights for non-nationals can offer an interesting case study, where the study of 'citizenship-as-status', and the questions of formal membership, nationality and immigration cut across the study of 'citizenship-as-political-engagement', and thus the question of democracy, whilst at the same time drawing down on the distinctively liberal discourse of 'citizenship-as-rights'. In other words, it engages all three dimensions of citizenship rights and practices. But, unlike the market and socio-economic rights attaching to free movement, where some if not all of the rights provided by EU law concern the regulation of economic relationships between private citizens as well as the regulation of relationships between citizens and public institutions in relation to welfare or public service entitlements or benefits, electoral rights operate fully in the domain of the public sphere and change the premise upon which the electorate for a particular election is based, into a premise based on citizenship of the Union, that is, a supranational legal status.

---

[39] Case C-145/04 *Spain* v. *United Kingdom (Gibraltar)*, 12 September 2006; Case C-300/04 *Eman and Sevinger* v. *College van burgemeester en wethouders van Den Haag (Aruba)*, 12 September 2006.

EU electoral rights are nested within a set of contestations about the scope of citizenship of the Union, most notably its institution of a sharp delineation between citizens of the Union and citizens of third countries. It is worth recalling that a number of Member States already had electoral rights in local elections for the benefit of *all* non-nationals (e.g. Denmark, Ireland and the Netherlands at the time of the Treaty of Maastricht), rights which they were at perfect liberty to maintain in respect of third country nationals even after the institution of the EU electoral rights. However, so far as pertains to citizens of the other Member States, such rights have had to be adjusted to the requirements of Article 19 EC. Moreover, access to citizenship of the Member States, and thus via Article 17 EC to citizenship of the Union, remains essentially a matter for national law. Consequently, two immigrants to two different Member States originating in the same third country, with equal periods of residence and similar degrees of employment, community and family connection to their host state, can be in very different positions with regard to political participation as a consequence of different rules on access to nationality of the host state (as well as perhaps other personal choices about whether to seek the nationality of the host state if this will mean relinquishing their statehood of birth because of differing rules on dual nationality). That citizenship of the Union should indeed be contested terrain is not necessarily a negative statement about its effects or importance. There can be equally sharp disagreements about the nature and qualities of *national* citizenship, and perhaps it is a statement about the normality of Union citizenship to observe that it constitutes a terrain of contestation.

In the next chapter, I look in more detail at electoral rights for non-nationals both as a practice adopted by certain polities and as a contested principle regarding the treatment of those lacking that badge of citizenship to which we have made reference so much in this chapter, nationality. This discussion leads, at the end of the chapter, into a fuller presentation of the argument which this book will seek to make about the role of electoral rights for non-nationals in the broader narrative of the transformation of citizenship in the European political space, and to an outline presentation of the empirical issues to be covered in the following chapters.

3

Electoral rights for non-nationals: theoretical, legal and political accounts

I Introduction

This book is not a general normative or empirical enquiry into the topic of electoral rights for non-nationals, or the theme of alien suffrage. As I shall show in more detail at the end of this chapter, this book is not concerned with arguing the case for increasing, or restricting, the voting rights of non-nationals in the context of particular polities, including the European Union. On the contrary, it uses electoral rights for non-nationals, in the first place those granted (or denied) at the EU level and in the second place those granted (or denied) at the national level, as one possible framework within which to examine the multiple and varying meanings of citizenship in the contemporary European political space. It is particularly concerned with both the 'nestedness' and the contest-edness of those rights, as these can provide powerful messages about what type of normative principles underpin any given polity (Jachtenfuchs, Diez and Jung, 1998).

Citizenship is, of course, only one possible paradigm which can be used to analyse evolving political spaces, institutions and relationships such as those which exist within the complex constitutional polity of the EU and its Member States. It would, perhaps, make just as much sense to use the ideal of democracy as the basis for a normative enquiry, or the networks of accountability which exist between institutional actors at different levels of government as the basis for an empirical enquiry. Instrumental reasons might suggest using citizenship just because the Article 19 EC electoral rights are treated in the EU as *citizenship rights*, but that hardly seems a convincing rationale on its own. However, as the previous chapter has hinted, despite the difficulties in grasping and applying a concept of citizenship, in particular beyond and sometimes even within the confines of the traditional nation state, citizenship retains a certain hegemonic character as a reference point for measuring matters of rights, access and belonging within systems of law and governance. But it follows from the adoption of the premise of citizenship as a framework of analysis that this focus must equally pervade what follows in this chapter by way of a more detailed account in theoretical, political and legal terms of ideas and practices of alien suffrage, or electoral rights for non-nationals. Following a presentation of what types of normative political arguments can be and are used in relation to the question of electoral rights for non-nationals, I turn in the middle of the chapter to a review of the extent of, patterns of and platforms for non-national voting rights at the present time, concluding the chapter with a presentation of the core argument of the book along with an outline of the contents of later chapters.

II The nature of the principle of alien suffrage

As I have noted already, as a normative political principle, the principle that non-nationals ought to be able to participate in elections is frequently discussed in terms of 'alien suffrage'.[1] One could formulate this principle as holding that, in a liberal democratic, constitutionally based polity which adheres to fundamental rights precepts, lawfully resident non-nationals ought, in principle, to be included amongst the group of persons entitled to participate politically within the host polity, *inter alia* through rights to vote and stand in some, if perhaps not all, elections. Joseph Carens (2002: 101) asserts that:

> liberal democratic justice, properly understood, greatly constrains the distinctions that can be made between citizens and non-citizen residents. The longer people stay in a society, the stronger their moral claims become, and, after a while they pass a threshold that entitles them to virtually the same legal status as citizens.[2]

In other words, length of residence appears to be the only valid criterion for distinguishing between privileged and non-privileged groups of non-nationals. Carens suggests that it remains permissible to restrict

[1] I would like to acknowledge the contribution to the development of the ideas in this chapter of my ongoing discussions with Anthea Connolly about the principle of alien suffrage during her doctoral studies at the Universities of Leeds and Manchester between 1999 and 2003. See A. Connolly, 'The Theory and Practice of Alien Suffrage in the European Union', unpublished PhD dissertation, University of Manchester, 2003.

[2] The argument of the parallelism of rights of nationals and non-nationals is made from a contextualist philosophical position: see most recently Carens, 2005, and for a fuller statement of the underlying philosophical position, based on grounds of justice, Carens, 2000: Ch. 7.

voting in national elections to citizens alone, but only provided that residents have proper access to naturalisation procedures. The reason is that this activity (voting in national elections) is intimately connected to the exercise of *democratic* autonomy, and so, one assumes, can be restricted to members of the *demos*, defined by national citizenship. Thus even those who argue strongly for the assimilation of the rights of nationals and non-nationals in all spheres (political, civil, socio-economic) frequently admit that the right to vote in national elections and the right to stand for high elected office can legitimately be reserved in democracies as a privilege of national citizenship.[3]

The allocation of electoral rights on the basis of residence rather than nationality can be contrasted with the strongly 'statist' principle associated with what is often called the 'Westphalian' period of (nation) state development whereby 'only nationals could be citizens, only people of the same national origin could enjoy the full protection of legal institutions, [and] persons of different nationality needed some law of exception until or unless they were completely assimilated and divorced from their origin' (i.e. by naturalisation) (Arendt, 1973: 275). This principle was, according to Aristide Zolberg (2000: 513), adopted to 'sharpen the institutional delineation of national boundaries', in the 'hypernationalist' phase in citizenship's development. In contrast, the principle of inclusion is associated with a status of 'cosmopolitan denizenship' (Zolberg, 2000), emphasising the half-way house status of resident non-nationals.

The strength – in practice – of the case against extending voting rights to non-nationals is well evidenced by the fact that, although a majority of EU Member States do now grant at least some electoral rights to non-nationals above and beyond the requirements of EU law, the majority of the six large Member States grant no rights to third country nationals (France, Germany, Italy, Poland) and the other two grant only rather restricted rights (Spain, United Kingdom). Since on the whole the larger states have also the largest populations of third country nationals (although not necessarily the highest ratio of non-nationals to nationals),[4] despite the availability of electoral rights for all third country nationals in local elections in quite a number of smaller and medium-sized Member States (Belgium, Denmark, Estonia, Finland,

---

[3] For a challenge to this, see López-Guerra, 2005: 218–31.
[4] See Chapter 7 for more detailed coverage of the numbers of third country nationals resident in the Member States.

Hungary, Ireland, Lithuania, Luxembourg, the Netherlands, Slovakia, Slovenia and Sweden), and for some in others (Portugal), it remains the case that access by the majority of non-nationals resident in the Member States of the European Union to the local franchise is excluded at the present time.

On the other hand, Heather Lardy (1997: 98–9) perhaps pessimistically overstates the current situation when she suggests that the fact

> that such proposals have rarely been discussed seriously in modern times is, however, more likely a reflection of the preoccupation with territorial sovereignty which characterizes the modern State than an objection to the franchise extension based on principles rooted in political theory ... In many States the issue appears never to have arisen; the restriction of voting rights to legal citizens is regarded as a reasonable and administratively convenient device for delimiting the electorate, and one which requires no justification.

In fact, there has been over the last twenty years a substantial amount of political mobilisation around the question of electoral rights for non-nationals, even in states where access to the franchise by non-nationals is effectively blocked by constitutional *fiat*, such as Austria and Germany, although it is true that much of the debate has been instrumental at a political level rather than concerned with the niceties of political theory. But debates about electoral rights should not simply be seen in terms of 'successes' – i.e. successful attempts by mobilising groups to bring about a change in the law. Sometimes failure can be as expressive of the fundamental questions which arise as can success. This point is illustrated in Chapter 8 with a contrast between the debates in the Netherlands and in Belgium.

In practice, the continuing case *against* alien suffrage in modern polities is generally premised upon versions of communitarianism combined with more formalist notions of sovereignty, boundaries and membership. Assumptions are sometimes made about the capacity of the non-national to play the role of the active citizen in a 'thick' republican conception of citizenship, because of doubts about shared commitments or loyalties (Honig, 2001). These are the types of fears that lie behind the leniency shown towards state restrictions on the political activities of aliens in the European Convention on Human Rights,[5] an instrument which dates from just after the Second World War. It is

---

[5] Hereinafter referred to as the ECHR.

worth noting that during this war there was large-scale and routine recourse by Allied governments, especially the US, Canada and the UK, to internment as a method of dealing with groups which were seen as threats on the inside, such as the Japanese, Italians and Germans. Internment was applied in some cases, such as the Japanese in North America, not only to more recent migrants, but also to those with settled residencies and US or Canadian citizenship. The same treatment was meted out to Italians and Germans in the UK. Such persons were characterised as enemy aliens, even if they possessed the formal badge of citizenship. This was notwithstanding a willingness to rely – at the same time – upon foreigners who were prepared to serve as soldiers (Vagts, 1946).

Proponents of alien suffrage must address the conundrum of how to combine a sense of cosmopolitanism as a defence against tribalism with a sense of bounded communities as a defence against rootlessness. In fact, Heather Lardy (1997) has argued that it is difficult to reconcile the complete exclusion of those who lack formal national citizenship from the franchise with accounts of political participation based on either liberal or communitarian theories. It is an oft-cited communitarian justification for denying electoral rights for non-nationals that the idea of the suffrage of aliens offends against a thick principle of citizens as active members of a (national) community. It is paradoxical, she argued, that non-nationals are denied the right to vote on the grounds that they are insufficiently part of the *demos*, and yet if they can pass a 'thin', and often highly discretionary, citizenship test permitting them access to nationality they will automatically be sufficiently well-qualified members of the polity to exercise the vote. Yet, since Lardy wrote those words in the 1990s, in fact, the Member States of the European Union have become increasingly concerned about tests of integration not only as conditions for access to national citizenship but also, although still more rarely, as conditions of access to the national territory altogether.[6]

The case *for* alien suffrage is typically supported by versions of liberalism/liberal democracy premised on equality and autonomy, with a splash of cosmopolitanism (e.g. a putative international 'right to democracy'), and a desire to bring voting rights into a continuum of inclusion rather than confining them to the dichotomy of membership (i.e. yes/no and in/out). Consequently, it downplays the significance of

---

[6] See Chapter 8, Section II.

(formal legal) national citizenship, and concentrates upon concepts of 'societal membership', such as that articulated by Rainer Bauböck, which was discussed in Chapter 2.[7] In addition, the principle of 'affected interests' is often emphasised to justify inclusion in the franchise (Lardy, 1997: 92; Bauböck, 2005: 766; Hilson, 2006): this holds that all those who are resident in a polity are affected by measures taken by the legislature.[8] This argument is easier to make in respect of local democratic representative institutions than it is in respect of national legislatures, in particular because it is hard to argue that national and non-national residents of a particular locality are not affected in the very same way by measures of a local character which in practice they pay for through taxation, e.g. on the funding of schools or the organisation of waste collection and disposal.

In sum, the questions that theorists and observers typically ask are the following. Do non-national residents have a moral, a human rights-based or a democratic claim to political inclusion in the host polity even if they retain a formal political and legal connection (citizenship) to another polity, one perhaps where they were not born and have never lived and of which they may not even speak the language, but which remains their state of 'heritage'? What difference do the obstacles to naturalisation placed by the host polity make? Has the host polity a duty to include the resident non-national through forms of automatic citizenship registration, thus avoiding the need for 'alien' suffrage as such, by removing most people from the category of aliens? Is it correct to say that consistent exclusion will enhance the sense of isolation and exclusion experienced by resident alien communities, and hence weaken the fabric and legitimacy claims of the society in which they are living (Lardy, 1997: 98)? Does denial of political inclusion diminish the human rights of the migrant? Or the democratic credentials of either the host state or the state of origin? If a case is successfully made for inclusion, what form should the political participation of migrants take? Are electoral rights the only solution, and, in which case, should they include the right to vote *and* stand, or just the former; and to which elections should the electoral rights extend – local, regional and/or national (or, indeed, supranational)? Is the guarantee of freedom of

---

[7] See the fuller discussion of the arguments of Rainer Bauböck in Chapter 2, Sections III and IV.

[8] The argument is originally drawn from Robert Dahl's work on democracy: for a more detailed discussion, see López-Guerra, 2005.

political expression and association for migrants, including effective access to political representatives such as parties and officials a sufficient degree of protection? Alternatively, should political inclusion recognise the specific interests of migrants as minorities, and include support for group-based collective representation and consultation within mainstream decision-making processes? Might the strength of the case for political inclusion depend upon the surrounding legal framework such as access on the part of migrants and their descendants to naturalisation or registration as a citizen of the host state, or the availability of cross-cutting legal statuses such as dual citizenship/nationality? Finally, can arguments for the extension of electoral rights support the selective extension of such rights to privileged categories of migrants only, as in the case of citizenship of the European Union and EU electoral rights?

III Voting and elections

Alien suffrage requires us to consider in a little more detail the role of elections in democracies. If, as we suggested at the beginning of Chapter 1, voting is a hallmark of citizenship and elections are 'the defining institutions of modern democracy' (Katz, 1997: 3), then we need to look more closely at elections and the definition of electorates.

Democracy has a dual quality. Philip Pettit contrasts the contestatory with the electoral aspect of democracy (Pettit, 2005). At one level, elections can be seen as vital moments of discursive democracy, moments at which communities are formed and form themselves. But, equally, democracy 'is not just a formula for aggregating votes, but is also a system of collective deliberation and legitimation' (Kymlicka, 1999: 119). Democratic self-government is a much larger project or process than the simple act of voting, vital though that is – and the concentration on the boundaries of the suffrage offers only a narrow perspective upon the wider question of democracy within any given polity. The idea of a right to political participation, above and beyond the right to vote, must also include elements providing the conditions of freedom, knowledge and security within which the notion of exercising individual choice in an election is meaningless. These are collective rather than individual conditions of life. Thus elections too (and the act of voting) have a collective as well as an individual dimension. Moreover, legal forms, such as voting rights or indeed the formal openness of the political regime at the national level, tell us relatively little about the overall political culture of the host polity, and indeed elections themselves should not be conflated with a concept or practice of democracy. There may be other obstacles to participation, such as the lack of recognition at the national level of cultural rights or cultural difference (Koopmans and Statham, 2000a). Hence, in this context we must proceed with considerable caution.

Moreover, electoral law is 'not merely a technical set of rules for administering elections, but a collection of coded pronouncements about who counts as a full member of the political community and why' (Lardy, 1997: 100). No polity ascribes voting rights universally even to all citizens. There are age bars, capacity/competence bars and often bars related to criminality or deviance (i.e. virtue bars). Historically, there have been gender bars, race/colour bars and bars based on property and wealth. In practice, the suffrage is always a multi-textured framework of rules, involving a patchwork of restrictions based on community membership, competence and autonomy, which may sometimes overlap (Blais, Massicotte and Yoshinaka, 2001). These issues are frequently contested in modern polities, as witness the October 2005 judgment of the European Court of Human Rights concluding that a comprehensive ban in the United Kingdom on voting by all convicted prisoners whilst in prison was contrary to Article 3 of Protocol No. 1 to the ECHR, bearing in mind that all restrictions on the right to vote needed both to pursue a legitimate aim, and to be proportionate in character (Duff, 2005; Easton, 2006).[9]

Since voting is not just an individual act, but a collective process, it is clear that it is in the definition of the collectivity – the *demos*, the citizenry – that so many of the paradoxes must lie, just as we saw in Chapter 2 that it is in the definition of some of the collective elements of citizenship, particularly citizenship's *edges*, that the most acute challenges in respect of that concept necessarily arise. The *New Oxford Dictionary of English* gives the following as the definition of the 'electorate': 'all the people in a country or area who are entitled to vote in any election'.[10] This is an example of the circular nature of so many arguments about the boundaries of the suffrage and hence the boundaries of the polity. *Who* are those 'entitled to vote'? In a democracy aspiring to apply the principle of popular sovereignty and to translate this into a

---

[9] *Hirst v. United Kingdom (No. 2)*, App. No. 74025/01, judgment of 6 October 2005.
[10] *The New Oxford Dictionary of English*, Oxford: Clarendon Press, 1998.

practice of more or less universal suffrage,[11] this should surely be the 'people' in the sense of the *demos*. Who, then, are the 'people'? The 'members' of the given country or area, that is, those who *belong*, would seem to be the obvious answer. It remains, then, to determine who decides who belongs, on what authority and how. The act of determining the group of people entitled to vote (the electorate) certainly seems logically prior to the holding of an election, but the fact of determination seems equally to presuppose some pre-political authority which claims to determine the boundaries of the polity and thus to distribute political power. The conclusion must be, however, that the definition itself has taken us no closer to understanding who the 'electorate' actually is. On the contrary, we need a pre-existing theory of the polity and in particular of the boundaries of the polity to lend meaning to the concept of the 'electorate' (López-Guerra, 2005).

Even if it is accepted that, in principle, polities are, and will be for the foreseeable future, bounded in a number of ways, not least by the norms of nationality laws and by structures controlling immigration and border crossings but also by other more symbolic structures (Bańkowski and Christodoulidis, 1999), it is still the case that any normative claim to moral purchase made on behalf of a particular version of citizenship as the membership badge for a bounded community needs to be evaluated by reference to the standards according to which the boundaries have themselves been set. Justice is not, *contra* the common interpretation given to Walzer's approach, essentially an internal matter only or at least a matter involving principles which distinguish sharply between the internal and external spheres (Walzer, 1993). On the contrary, a polity's claim to be a liberal constitutionalist democracy (a claim made on behalf of all of the Member States of the European Union by Article 6 EU), and to offer 'universal citizenship', must be tested not only by reference to what happens within the polity (majoritarian practices, rule of law, protection of minorities, fundamental rights, etc.), but also by reference to the boundaries that it sets with the rest of the world and the extent to which those boundaries are treated as permeable, fuzzy or negotiable.

---

[11] Wider struggles over the extension of the suffrage (e.g. to women, to prisoners and/or those previously convicted of criminal offences, to those suffering mental disabilities, and to those aged between 16 and 18) fall outwith the scope of this research. The symbolic and practical importance of the scope of the suffrage is reflected in measures as diverse as Article 21(1) of the Universal Declaration of Human Rights, the Declaration of Independence (1776) or the Declaration of the Rights of Man and Citizen (1789), especially insofar as the latter focus upon popular sovereignty.

Certainly, the alien suffrage debate in both its empirical and normative guises poses severe tests to political theories which proceed blindly on the basis of the fiction of a 'closed society' with non-porous borders. Thus Rawls' assumption 'that a democratic society, like any political society, is to be viewed as a complete and closed social system' (Rawls, 1993: 41) has encountered considerable criticism (e.g. Benhabib, 2004: Ch. 3), not least from Nancy Fraser, who warns that 'globalization is changing the way we argue about justice' (Fraser, 2005: 65). And yet, despite these criticisms, it remains relatively common amongst theorists of democracy to continue largely to assume that the boundaries of the polity are comfortably set at the point where legal citizenship begins and ends, even if at the same time arguments are being made for multiple overlapping concepts of citizenship and belonging (Goodin, 2003).

IV Voting rights and human rights

Moves towards conferring the local franchise on resident alien communities, visible not only in a number of European countries but also in some parts of the United States, are often linked to the increased mobility not only of persons and labour, but also of capital, goods and culture. They also posit the significance of the boundaries of the suffrage for democratic practice. Jaime Raskin's case for non-citizens voting in local elections in the US is based on a combination of 'classical American democratic principles and an emerging global ideology of local democracy' (Raskin, 1993: 1441). From democratic theory he draws three classic principles to sustain his argument: government by consent; no taxation without representation; and 'good-enough-to-fight-good-enough-to-vote', which refers to the long-standing willingness of some polities, particular empires of various types, to include foreigners in the military. Perhaps somewhat idealistically, he goes on to argue that:

> as the world grows closer in terms of population mobility, capital, investment, labour markets, cultural production, and high technology, it is imperative that we create political norms to make the most of these processes of integration consistent with democratic values. The possibilities for exploiting displaced persons are too great if we make capital and labour mobile but political rights immobile. We cannot read the world as a global economic village but define it as a collection of remote islands for the purposes of political participation. Eventually we may define a human right to democratic participation.
>
> (Raskin, 1993: 1460)

The case for a human-rights-based claim can be founded, if one follows Saskia Sassen's arguments, upon very significant changes which have occurred in the political status of human rights in recent years, especially their capacity to generate claims for *universal* equal treatment. In a powerful passage, she argues that:

> Human rights are not dependent upon nationality, unlike political, social, and civil rights, which are predicated on the distinction between national and alien. Human rights override such distinctions. Even where rooted in the founding documents of nation-states, as is the case with the United States and France, we need to understand the specific developments of these rights over the last few years. Human rights today are a force that can undermine the exclusive authority of the state over its nationals and thereby contribute to transform the interstate system and international legal order.
>
> (Sassen, 1998: 70)

Human rights have an impact, she contends, upon nation state citizenship, the boundaries of the nation and the very legitimacy of the state. In similar terms, Yasemin Soysal (1994: 164) asserts that:

> today ... individual rights, expansively redefined as human rights on a universalistic basis and legitimized at the transnational level, undercut the import of national citizenship by disrupting the territorial closure of nations. The same human rights that came to be secured over the centuries in national constitutions as the rights and privileges of a proper citizenry have now attained a new meaning and have become globally sanctioned norms and components of a supranational discourse.

It may be that these statements suggest overly optimistic characterisations of the supposedly universally integrative effects of human rights discourse and claims-making, and indeed of the current effectiveness of international human rights norms. No matter that the experience in numerous divided societies has hardly been one in which human rights discourse has invariably operated as an integrative mechanism, or that the existence of international human rights norms has not prevented substantial human rights infringements (especially of non-nationals) even in states which claim to be compliant.[12] Certainly, at the level of

---

[12] The types of cases which the critics of the 'human rights' case (e.g. Koopmans and Statham, 2000a) draw attention to involve the expulsion to the home state of the children of migrant workers (e.g. Turks) who have committed even quite minor crimes by states such as Germany.

rhetoric, though, it should follow that states now have a very weak capacity to resist claims made for better or fairer treatment by resident migrants, even where these claims may encounter resistance from counterclaims brought by other disenfranchised groups, including resident intercultural minorities such as indigenous peoples (Dobson, 2006). The argument finds support in cases such as the House of Lords decision declaring that a United Kingdom statute and executive order making provision for the indefinite detention without trial of non-nationals certified as 'suspected international terrorists' was contrary to the European Convention on Human Rights, as enshrined in UK law by the Human Rights Act 1998, specifically Article 5 ECHR guaranteeing the right to liberty.[13] In this case, the court found no justification for treating UK and non-UK persons differently.[14]

In a similar vein, William Barbieri (1998) provides a theory of the ethics of political membership which uses a human-rights-based theory of non-domination to justify the view that political membership in a society should be open to all who reside there. Barbieri argues for a matching of the ethics of the inclusive polity and the provision of equal representation to all resident within its boundaries. All must have a share. Citizenship (membership of the polity) is, for Barbieri, an examination of the nature and basis of equality and it is also entwined with questions regarding the relations between moral and legal rights and the foundations of law. Democracy, moreover, 'is grounded in the human rights of individuals to self-determination and only this right forms the basis of the state's claim to sovereignty' (Barbieri, 1998: 59). In other words, the idea is that only democracy provides the legitimating force for state sovereignty but democracy is only attained when the polity is ethical, that is, when there is equality. This is, of course, a fundamentally liberal idea and ideal.

V The role of international law in relation to electoral rights

A different line of argument treats electoral rights for non-nationals as part of a wider portfolio of migrants' rights. This focuses on the responsibilities of states in relation to this group of people, and any measures

---

[13] *A (FC) and Others* v. *Secretary of State for the Home Department* [2004] UKHL 56, [2005] 2 AC 68.

[14] On the general possibility of using (international) human rights law to ground claims for equal treatment of nationals and non-nationals, see Cole, 2006.

which states have agreed to within international law, or indeed at the national level, are more specialised than the general body of international and national human rights law which is universally applicable. That does not mean to say that such arguments do not have recourse, as a foundation stone, to the discourse of human rights as well, but the primary vehicle for the argument is an instrumental reason, namely, the disenfranchisement that occurs (in a world of supposedly universal suffrage of citizens) as a consequence of population mobility.

The language of the various international instruments that directly or indirectly address the rights of migrants is somewhat mixed on the question of electoral rights for non-nationals.[15] For example, Article 42(3) of the most important general international instrument on migration and migrants, the UN Convention on the Protection of the Rights of All Migrant Workers and Members of Their Families,[16] merely states that 'migrant workers *may* enjoy political rights in the State of employment if that State, *in the exercise of its sovereignty*, grants them such rights' (emphasis added).[17] This text therefore conceives of a limited curtailment of national sovereignty in the political arena in the name of international responsibility.[18] Likewise, Ciara Smyth (2005) finds little support in international human rights instruments, including those on racial discrimination, for the argument that there is an evolving norm in international human rights law in favour of political inclusion of non-nationals. She describes the picture as 'rather discouraging' (Smyth, 2005: 9). At the regional level, there is more encouragement, although not in the form of the ECHR, which still contains in Article 16 a derogation specifically permitting the High Contracting Parties to impose restrictions on the political activity of aliens although it is interpreted relatively restrictively by the European Court of Human Rights (Kokott and Rudolf, 1996). Furthermore, the full potential of

---

[15] See also the brief discussion of international human rights law distinctions between aliens and citizens in Chapter 2, Section III.

[16] Adopted by General Assembly Resolution 45/158 of 18 December 1990; entered into force in 2003.

[17] A recent House of Lords report urged the UK Government to reconsider its decision not to ratify the Convention, and in that context it noted that both the European Parliament and the European Economic and Social Committee have urged the Member States to ratify the Convention: House of Lords Select Committee on the European Union, *Economic Migration to the EU*, Session 2005–6, Fourteenth Report, 16 November 2005, at 39.

[18] It is worth recalling – as a substratum for this argument – that the very existence of a right to democratic governance in international law is contested: Fox and Roth, 2001.

Article 1 of Protocol No. 3 to the ECHR, which requires the High Contracting Parties 'to hold free elections at reasonable intervals by secret ballot, under conditions which will ensure the free expression of the opinion of the people in the choice of the legislature' has yet to be fully explored. Meanwhile, the Council of Europe Framework Convention for the Protection of National Minorities[19] refers in a rather vague manner likewise in Article 15 to the 'effective participation' of persons belonging to national minorities 'in cultural, social and economic life and in public affairs, in particular those affecting them'. Clearly, however, there is no necessary overlap between groups of migrants and members of national minorities.[20]

A number of Member States have joined other European states in signing up to the Council of Europe's Convention on the Political Participation of Foreigners in Local Life.[21] Concluded in 1992, the Convention entered into force in 1997. Of the Member States, Denmark, Finland (most recently), Italy, the Netherlands and Sweden have ratified. The United Kingdom, Cyprus and the Czech Republic have signed, but not ratified. It offers a template of incremental steps towards enhancing the political participation rights of non-nationals, up to and including the right to vote in local elections; signatories commit themselves to implementing these, but there are – as with most international instruments – no sanctions for non-compliance. The case made for the Convention is strongly 'liberal democratic', as is made clear by the direct references in the Explanatory Report to the values of the Council of Europe including 'individual freedom, political liberty and the rule of law, which form the basis of all genuine democracy, and its attachment to the universal and indivisible nature of human rights and fundamental freedoms'. These inspirations are reflected in the Preamble. The Convention envisages a staged introduction of three levels of political participation rights by signatory states, although the states may 'opt out' of the second and third stages. The first stage, which in essence just complements the ECHR, protects the basic civil liberties of foreigners by according them freedom of expression and freedom of assembly and association, on the same basis as nationals. The second level involves

---

[19] ETS No. 157; opened for signature 1 February 1995; entered into force 1 February 1998; www.conventions.coe.int.

[20] See also the more extended discussion of the relationship between migrants and minorities in Chapter 10, Section II.

[21] ETS No. 144; opened for signature on 5 February 1992; entered into force 1 May 1997; www.conventions.coe.int.

consultative bodies to represent foreign residents at local level; and the third and final level involves the right to vote in local authority elections.

Smyth (2005, 13–14) draws attention to some positive and negative aspects of the Convention. On the one hand, the Convention contains the first unambiguous statement in international law upholding the rights of non-national residents to vote in local elections. She notes that the Convention does not draw any distinction between second-country nationals (i.e. nationals of other Council of Europe states) and third country nationals (i.e. nationals of other non-Council of Europe states), quoting from the Explanatory Report as follows:

> The considerations adduced in the preamble concerning the participation of foreign residents in the life of the local community and the fact that they generally have the same duties as citizens at the local level apply to foreign residents of all nationalities. To create a distinction between those foreign nationals who enjoy voting rights and those who do not, would be politically problematical.[22]

As Smyth comments, 'this reasoning is interesting in view of the distinction introduced at the EU level between EU citizens and third country nationals for the purpose of voting in member state local elections' (Smyth, 2005: 14). We shall examine this distinction in more detail in Chapter 7, which looks at the case for extending electoral rights under EU law to third country nationals. On the other hand, the Convention has a number of weak aspects, notably the absence of effective enforcement mechanisms, and indeed mechanisms for implementation and monitoring. Furthermore the fact that less than one-quarter of the Council of Europe's (nearly fifty) Member States have actually signed and ratified the Convention also undermines any claim that it lays the foundations for 'an emerging norm against traditional preferences for nationals in the enjoyment of political rights' (Smyth, 2005: 14).

The political institutions of the Council of Europe have returned to the theme of political participation of foreigners in local elections in more recent times, with the Parliamentary Assembly adopting a Recommendation in January 2001 urging contracting states to introduce further rights for migrants, including the right to vote and stand in local elections to those established for a minimum of three years.[23] It

---

[22] Para. 36(iii) of the Explanatory Report, available at http://conventions.coe.int/Treaty/en/Reports/Html/144.htm.
[23] Recommendation 1500 (2001), 26 January 2001.

repeated this call in a more wide-ranging Resolution in 2005 on the abolition of all possible restrictions on the right to vote more generally.[24] Also in 2005, the Parliamentary Assembly extended the scope of its recommendations in this respect by supporting the right to vote in local referendums for non-nationals with five years of residence in line with the principles of the Convention on the Participation of Foreigners in Public Life at the Local Level, as part of its recommendations on good practices in relation to referendums more generally.[25] Within the Council of Europe's other institutions, the European Commission for Democracy through Law, or Venice Commission as it is better known, includes a recommendation on extending the right to vote to non-nationals in local elections after a certain period of residence, as part of its Code on Good Practice in Electoral Matters.[26] The Congress of Local and Regional Authorities has worked on the details of the participation of people of immigrant origin in Europe's towns, cities and regions, with a Recommendation and a Resolution on a pact for integration and participation adopted in 2004, calling *inter alia* upon the governments of the Member States of the Council of Europe to sign and ratify measures such as the Convention on the Participation of Foreigners in Public Life at the Local Level.[27] These latter texts convey the important message that the political participation and successful integration of non-nationals comprises necessary measures beyond the scope of local electoral rights.

D'Oliveira has questioned whether the Convention, which refers of course to 'every foreign resident', is not part of a framework of international law (he is not specific about the other instruments upon which he relies for his argument) which casts doubt on whether it is permissible for a distinction to be drawn between nationals of the Member States and others when granting voting rights (d'Oliveira, 1994: 142–3). There are few other clear sources of international law which could be said to

---

[24] Resolution 1459 (2005), 24 June 2005.
[25] Recommendation 1704 (2005), 'Referendums: Towards Good Practices in Europe', 29 April 2005.
[26] CDL-AD (2002) 23, 23 May 2002, point 1.1.b.ii.
[27] Congress of Local and Regional Authorities, Recommendation 153 (2004) on a pact for the integration and participation of people of immigrant origin in Europe's towns, cities and regions, 27 May 2004 (addressed to the Committee of Ministers of the Council of Europe and the governments of the Member States); and Resolution 181 (2004) on a pact for integration and participation of people of immigrant origin in Europe's towns, cities and regions, 27 May 2004 (addressed to the local and regional authorities of the Member States).

buttress the approach taken in the Convention, although one important document comprises the Lund Recommendations on national minorities adopted within the context of the work of the OSCE. These are aimed at 'national' minorities who can be expected to have national citizenship, but who find themselves otherwise excluded, and so they have limited relevance to the immigration scenario.[28] The efforts of the European Parliament to link the references to voting rights in the Charter of Fundamental Rights of the European Union (adopted in 2000 as a declaratory instrument[29]) to a wider set of international law guarantees of the right to vote are somewhat undermined by the fact that Articles 39 and 40 of the Charter essentially replicate the provisions of Article 19 EC on electoral rights for EU citizens, and cannot be interpreted as going any further than the scope of those provisions as they stand.[30]

Some writers have therefore argued that, while the relevant provisions are not entirely consistent, the right to vote is one of the few rights in international law which may validly be limited to citizens (Gardner, 1997: 42). In the fullest review yet of international practice in this area, Ciara Smyth concludes:

> A conclusive answer to the question . . . regarding whether the right to vote is a citizen's right or a human right has proved elusive. At the universal level, the right appears to be exclusively a citizen's right. At the European level, the law is progressively developing towards recognition of a right of long-term residents to participate in local politics. But the right has not yet fully emerged and State practice in the coming years will be determinative.
>
> (Smyth, 2005: 21)

---

[28] OSCE High Commissioner on National Minorities, 'Lund Recommendations: Effective Participation of National Minorities in Public Life' (September 1999). These provide: 'Effective participation of national minorities in public life is an essential component of a peaceful and democratic society . . . (1) These Recommendations aim to facilitate the inclusion of minorities within the State and enable minorities to maintain their own identity and characteristics, thereby promoting the good governance and integrity of the State. (2) These Recommendations build upon fundamental principles and rules of international law, such as respect for human dignity, equal rights, and non-discrimination, as they affect the rights of national minorities to participate in public life and to enjoy other political rights. (3) States shall guarantee the right of persons belonging to national minorities to take part in the conduct of public affairs, including the rights to vote and stand for office without discrimination.'

[29] OJ 2000 C364/1.

[30] See the references to the international law on the right to free and fair elections collected on the Parliament's website: http://www.europarl.eu.int/comparl/libe/elsj/charter/art39/default_en.htm.

In later chapters, we will look at that 'State practice' to which Smyth refers, taking account of the international obligations to which states have signed up, or which they find are imposed upon them by virtue of emerging international or European norms especially in the context of EU enlargement. First, however, it is important to look in more detail at the characterisation and conceptualisation of electoral rights as migrants' rights, before surveying the extent to which states have in fact thus far adopted electoral rights for non-nationals.

VI Conceptualising electoral rights as migrants' rights

It is now well accepted that, when voting rights were in fact given to groups of non-nationals in the nineteenth-century United States, at least in some states and some territories, this was with the specific aim of encouraging immigration and settlement (Tienda, 2002: 605; Raskin, 1993; Harper Ho, 2000; Hayduk, 2004, 2006; Varsanyi, 2005; Evia, 2003). Equally, they were removed at a later stage as a consequence of revised instrumental views about migration and participation, particularly hostility to certain national groups as migrants. Moreover, other types of instrumental goals can clearly be seen in play in the twenty-first century, revolving around the question of the integration of immigrants, when non-national voting rights are granted, along with other social, economic and political rights, as part of an integration package. There are purely pragmatic arguments at play as well, such as those which point out the links between access to the electoral register and access to the credit society for migrants in many credit-based economies. It may be difficult to secure a bank account and doubly difficult to obtain a credit card for a migrant who is not on the electoral register, thus effecting a double form of political and financial exclusion.

Overall, the question of the integration of immigrants often seems to be given just as much salience in arguments about non-national voting as claims that non-national voting raises the democratic quality of a community by allowing all those who are affected to have a say. By 1997, the European Commission was claiming that the benefits of the electoral rights granted under the EC Treaty to resident non-national EU citizens would be precisely in terms of 'a greater integration of Union citizens in their host Member State'.[31] Some claim that there is empirical evidence

---

[31] European Commission, 'Second Report on Citizenship of the Union', COM(1997) 230, 25 July 1997, at 11.

that giving political participation rights to incomers has positive effects on integration processes (Penninx et al., 2004). In this respect, they are often backed up by politicians, with a British Minister remarking to a House of Commons Committee in 2002 that increased registration of non-national EU citizens could give rise to increased participation of EU citizens which in turn gives rise 'to benefits such as further integration between citizens of different backgrounds within the United Kingdom and increased interest and involvement in local democracy generally'. In other words, paradoxically the effect of such provisions should be seen to be making non-nationals benefiting from Article 19 more *British*, not more *European*.[32] It is a challenge to nation-state citizenship, for sure, but one which is of a *transnational* rather than a *postnational* or *supranational* character.

Political decisions in relation to non-national voting are affected by a whole host of closely related issues relating to migration and mobility, the rules of citizenship, and the political system more generally. These include the political salience of the question of political participation of migrants, their descendants and indeed other minorities (national or otherwise defined) in the host polity (Odmalm, 2005; Martiniello and Staham, 1999; Ireland, 2000). Voting rights must also be seen in relation to other forms of political participation and political freedoms in the polity such as guarantees of freedom of expression and association, membership of (and right to found) political parties, creation of and voting for special representative councils, and the activism of social movements and voluntary associations. In addition, increasing attention is now paid to the mirror image of non-nationals voting in host polities, namely, the political participation in the polity of origin of emigrants, and the impact of this both upon the individual emigrant and upon the quality of democracy in the polity of emigration (in particular if this is a polity which is losing population as a consequence of emigration, or at least suffering the flight of significant well-qualified sectors of the population) (Bauböck, 2005; Barry, 2006; Rubio-Márin, 2006; Spiro, 2006; López-Guerra, 2005).

The ascription of limited voting rights as part of a package of integration measures in advance of formal national citizenship acquisition can

---

[32] Select Committee on European Scrutiny of the House of Commons, Thirty-Eighth Report, Session 2001–2, HC 152, 16 October 2002, Document 35: The Right to Vote and Stand as a Candidate in Municipal Elections, 93; comments by Nick Raynsford MP, then Minister for Local Government and the Regions, in the context of discussion in the Select Committee on European Scrutiny of the Commission Report on the application of Directive 94/80/EC (COM(2000) 843 of 18 December 2000).

be seen as a part of the overall integration process. The alternative view, which prefers the reservation of all voting rights to national citizens alone, suggests that these rights should be reserved as a type of 'prize' for those who pass the relevant tests of membership, such as residence requirements, affinity rules, and other conditions such as linguistic or other socio-cultural tests. This is the approach applied to the majority of third country nationals in the Member States of the European Union, notwithstanding that quite a number of the (typically smaller) Member States have instituted local electoral rights for some or all third country nationals.

Migration, like citizenship, is a contested and complex practice and concept (Seglow, 2005).[33] As Allan Williams (2001: 103–4) comments, it is wrong to assume that all migration is temporary, legal and for work purposes. In fact, more diffuse patterns are in play, a point reinforced by the fact that, as he notes, 'across Europe, the pattern of national provision has produced a bricolage of territories with differentiated rights for different migrant groups'; the EU remains 'a highly fragmented migration space', borders have 'varying degrees of permeability and closure', and overall the EU can be described as a 'mosaic of migration spaces'. The complexity of Europe as a migration space continues to grow, following the enlargement of the European Union in 2004 to include eight new countries from Central and Eastern Europe, and two Mediterranean states (Salt, 2005). Certainly, at least until enlargement, the migration movements involving the states of Central and Eastern Europe and the then Member States of the European Union appeared to be primarily circular in character, and substantially smaller in scale, than was often feared (Wallace, 2002). As noted in Chapter 2, there have been some more dramatic movements since enlargement – the most notable being the number of movements (in both directions, it should be noted, since many migrants also later return home) between Poland, on the one hand, and the UK and Ireland, and the quite severe population and skills drains also being experienced in Latvia and Lithuania, although the total numbers in those states are lower. However, overall the trends have not seen as large an increase in either actual mobility, or the demand for mobility, across the EU8 as was thought likely by some commentators.[34]

---

[33] Report of the Global Commission on International Migration, 'Migration in an Interconnected World: New Directions for Action', October 2005.

[34] 'Report on the Functioning of the Transitional Arrangements Set Out in the 2003 Accession Treaty', Communication from the Commission, COM(2006) 48, 8 February 2006.

Perhaps the most sustained case in recent writings for the generalised inclusion of resident aliens within the suffrage has come from Ruth Rubio-Marín, whose approach is based upon positing immigration as a democratic challenge to the polity (Rubio-Marín, 1998, 2000). She recognises and attempts to deal with the paradoxes which can arise between a liberal principle of equal inclusion ascribing full membership rights to all those resident on a permanent basis within a polity (regardless of whether they are natural born citizens or immigrants) and the understandable wish in a world of states to preserve some relevance to a concept of nationality and national citizenship. Empirically, many Western states face this paradox with large populations of non-national immigrants. A balance can be achieved, she argues, with a reworked and perhaps 'thinner' conception of national citizenship, which is not marked by 'outdated notions' such as exclusive loyalty:

> The concept of national citizenship should thus become more open and inclusive, and adequately take into account the social reality posed by the new forms of residential communities [i.e. resident immigrants] ... [T]his requires first that the concept of nationality be redefined and 'democratized' to accommodate the recognition of the new members and their cultural and political specificities.
>
> (Rubio-Marín, 2000: 245)

So far as the implementation of these principles is concerned, she acknowledges that different polities will respond in very different ways to the challenges of matching constitutional reality with moral aspiration to liberal democracy. However, Rubio-Marín's default position on the incorporation of non-nationals is that this, thinner, reworked conception of national citizenship would be conferred automatically upon long-term-resident non-nationals, although without prejudice to other memberships they wished to retain.[35] Thus what she calls 'ascriptive nationality' should not be seen as a

> freedom-restricting imposition on resident aliens especially when multiple citizenship becomes the rule ... [A]scriptive nationality serves a protective function by ensuring inclusive communities of citizens and avoiding the vulnerability generated by either statelessness or the holding of merely nominal citizenship. Moreover, automatic nationality does not have to be seen as imposing a certain identity on resident aliens as long as

---

[35] For a related argument on alien incorporation, see Kostakopoulou, 2003 and 2006.

nationality is previously redefined to deal with the existing plurality of identities, attachments and loyalties.

(Rubio-Marín, 2000: 243)

Following a not dissimilar line of argument, Rainer Bauböck's position on the issue of political rights for resident aliens stems from his search for answers to some of political theory's most enduring questions, regarding the legitimacy of political rule and the group of persons on whom that legitimacy must be focused (Bauböck, 1994a). As he points out, resident aliens have a peculiar status in modern democracies, as they are affected by political decisions but unable to participate in them. What steps do democratic states have to take in order to satisfy liberal norms of inclusion, especially in terms of voting rights? The answer is derived from the need for all political ideologies claiming to offer a coherent basis for political order to set some standard for inclusion. Crucially, therefore, it is the choice of political ideology made in any given polity that appears to be decisive for the extent to which political rights should follow the *de facto* situation of 'societal membership' achieved by permanent resident aliens, living, working, paying taxes and participating in the welfare state institutions of the host state. Normatively, Bauböck's preference is for establishing a liberal democratic norm of inclusion, balanced with norms of equality and consent. In policy terms, he derives from this the universality of basic political liberties such as freedom of thought, expression, association and assembly, as against the particularity of core political rights such as participation in national elections and the right to hold high political office. However, this condition can only apply in circumstances where there is reasonably open admission to nationality in the host state through naturalisation and automatic acquisition of citizenship rights. On the other hand, as residence is the relevant criterion of access even for citizens in relation to local political communities, it should – likewise – be the criterion for resident aliens. On that basis, a minimum period of residence should be the only criterion for admission to the local political community, and no distinction should be drawn by reference to formal or nominal citizenship.

In a more recent work addressing both the voting rights of non-resident citizens and those of resident non-citizens, Bauböck points to a principle of 'stakeholder citizenship' combining elements of both the republican and liberal perspectives on citizenship, and links back to two principles: 'affected interests' and 'inclusion':

From the former it retains the idea that citizenship is a status of full membership in a self-governing polity and that voting rights should generally be attached to such status. From the latter it derives a principle of inclusion that would give stakeholders a subjective claim to membership and electoral rights. Stakeholdership should, however, be less vague and overinclusive than affected interests. It is best described as expressing an interest in membership that makes an individual's fundamental rights dependent on protection by a particular polity and that ties an individual's well-being to the common good of a particular polity.

(Bauböck, 2005: 766)

Although stakeholder citizenship is a term more commonly associated with corporate governance and the rather controversial idea of 'corporate citizenship' (Wheeler, 1997), Bauböck seeks to make the term do useful work in the context of political communities more generally. One important proposition he derives from his argument is that, unlike Rubio-Marín, he would normally expect aliens to apply for naturalisation rather than to enjoy automatic conferment of citizenship status, and he would moreover expect the common condition of non-citizens' political involvement in the polity precisely to be that they become national citizens, and seek naturalisation. Long-term alienage seems, therefore, to be excluded by definition.

Writers such as Carens and Bauböck see the long-term trend as being towards the acquisition of citizenship in the host state by migrant non-nationals, and consequently argue that citizenship acquisition by immigrants should not be too burdensome. Naturalisation should be fairly straightforward, and largely based on a length-of-residence qualification with few if any competence or connection tests, and citizenship of the host state should also be easily obtainable by the children of migrant non-nationals, even where the latter choose not or are unable to naturalise. Dual and even multiple nationality should be permitted, and even encouraged, and there should not be differential treatment as regards dual nationality as between those who naturalise and those who are citizens by birth or descent (Aleinikoff and Klusmeyer, 2001b; Hansen and Weil, 2002). Conversely, some opponents of voting rights for non-nationals ground their opposition precisely on a normative preference for naturalisation not least in order to maintain the distinction between citizens and non-citizens, to sustain the incentives to naturalise and to maintain the privileges associated with citizenship (Schuck, 2004). That assumes, of course, that there are not too many legal and bureaucratic obstacles to citizenship acquisition, an issue which was alluded to also in Chapter 2.

Bauböck does not expect – *contra* many republican perspectives on citizenship – an exclusivity on the part of the attachment of the migrants. Stakeholder citizenship would be able to recognise multiple polities, multiple citizenships and multiple systems of identity and loyalty on the part of the migrant. These would include both overlapping horizontal systems of polities, and also polities nested within polities – as is the case both with federal states and with the European Union itself. Since stakeholder citizenship does not require rules to be identical at different levels, he argues that this can explain the electoral rights arrangements under EU law, covering European Parliament elections and local elections, but missing out national elections.

Bauböck concludes by offering two pathways to making sense of the phenomenon of voting by resident non-nationals and non-resident citizens, namely:

> 1) retain the mental framework of a Westphalian state system with clear cut boundaries between polities and revise our conception of citizenship by disconnecting status from rights and regarding the latter as a global commodity offered by states to mobile populations, or: 2) adapt the republican concept of citizenship as equal membership in a self-governing polity to a world in which political boundaries are increasingly overlapping or nested within each other.
>
> (Bauböck, 2005: 766)

He expresses a preference for the latter route as more promising both to explain actually existing patterns and policies, and to enable the development of democratic principles for how such rights ought to be allocated.

Even if naturalisation is one possible route to inclusion, it does not hide the challenge of alienage itself to the bounded polity. Seyla Benhabib (2004) develops an interesting argument which eschews the call for open borders, but embraces a tradition of cosmopolitan federalism drawn from Kant. In that context, bounded communities – traditionally states – continue to be important sites where practices, such as democratic political inclusion of 'others' (i.e. aliens) are contested and 'democratically iterated' in conjunction with the evolution of domestic institutional forms such as nationality laws and access to the suffrage. She points to the example of the extension of electoral rights to third country nationals in a number of EU Member States as important examples of the disaggregation of citizenship as status and citizenship as rights.

In common with a number of writers, Benhabib looks in detail at the case of Germany, where there have been both debates over electoral rights for non-nationals (ultimately blocked by the Constitutional Court) and also reforms of citizenship laws in recent years. For Benhabib, the interpretation given by the German Federal constitutional court to the concept of the people, which blocked the inclusion of third country nationals into the local franchise following a legislative proposal at the level of the *Land* in Hamburg and Schleswig-Holstein,[36] appeared in retrospect to be a 'swan song to a vanishing ideology of nationhood' (Benhabib, 2004: 207).[37] However, at the same time the constitutional court issued a challenge to the legislature, to open up alternative pathways to inclusion by reform of Germany's notoriously restrictive citizenship laws, which had blocked citizenship acquisition not only by immigrants themselves, but also by their descendants of the second and third generations. This affected in particular so-called 'guestworkers' from Turkey. The case brought out into the open hitherto difficult concepts such as the reconceptualisation by Germans of their state as a country of immigration, in particular through the arguments posed by the two *Länder* which sought to make the legislative changes to widen the franchise. These ideas have in turn been more widely disseminated into political discourse, through democratic iterations. Part of Germany's process of reconstructing the idea of the 'German' polity has been the reform of the restrictive citizenship laws both to allow the children born of non-national parents in Germany to acquire citizenship by birth in certain circumstances and to reduce the qualifying residence period for naturalisation (Hailbronner, 2006b). Of course, though, what neither these arguments nor these reforms have brought about – notwithstanding the constitutional amendment introduced in Germany for the purposes of giving effect to the Treaty of Maastricht's electoral rights conferred on nationals of Germany's fellow Member States of the European Union – is any widening of the political participation rights of third country nationals in Germany.

VII How widespread are electoral rights for non-nationals at the present time?

It is clear that neither normative arguments in favour of extending the boundaries of the suffrage, nor indeed the international law instruments

---

[36] BVerfGE 63, 37 (Schleswig-Holstein); BVerfGE 63, 60 (Hamburg), 31 October 1990.
[37] These cases will be placed in a wider context in Chapter 9, Section II.

which have been drawn up such as the Council of Europe's Convention on the Political Participation of Foreigners in Local Life, have received anything like universal approval either amongst the Member States of the European Union, or more widely across Europe and the rest of the world. In this context, it is a serious question whether the Article 19 EC electoral rights which were presented in Chapter 1 should be regarded as part of a (still relatively small, but growing) corpus of electoral rights for non-nationals, or as a special case linked to the dynamics of European economic and political integration. This question goes to the heart of this book's objectives, as articulated in more detail at the end of this chapter.

Table 3.1 shows the current position in the fifteen Member States which were members of the Union before May 2004, and Table 3.2 complements this with the position as it now stands in the post-2004 Member States.

There are around forty-five democracies worldwide which provide for electoral rights for at least some non-nationals, in at least some elections (Bauböck, 2005). To enable comparisons, Table 3.3 gives a summary of the main cases of electoral rights for non-nationals outside the EU. Thus the EU, with twenty-seven Member States giving rights under Article 19 EC, dominates this list. It is also useful to note that, insofar as there are fifteen Member States which provide for additional rights in some respect (additional rights for EU citizens and/or rights for third country nationals), this too represents a cluster which is unmatched anywhere else, inside or outside Europe. There are a number of other European countries with electoral rights provisions in place, in particular other Nordic states (Iceland, Norway) which have universal alien suffrage for local elections developed originally in partnership with Nordic states now in the EU. Switzerland has much more restricted rights limited to certain cantons only. Beyond Europe, it is important to note the case of New Zealand which has the most generous alien suffrage rights of all, including access to national as well as local elections, for all non-nationals on the basis of one year's residence, plus permanent residency (i.e. a formal right to remain indefinitely).[38] A number of other Commonwealth countries (especially in the Caribbean) provide for electoral rights, including the right to vote in national elections, for other Commonwealth citizens (Blais et al., 2001; Bauböck, 2005).

---

[38] Uruguay also allows non-nationals to vote in general elections, but only after fifteen years' residence.

Table 3.1 *Summary of the position on non-nationals voting in the 'old' Member States[a]*

	Local elections		National elections including regional/state elections		COE?[b]
	EU citizens	TCNs	EU citizens	TCNs	
Austria[c]	Yes	No	No	No	No
Belgium[d]	Yes	Yes	No	No	No
Denmark[e]	Yes	Yes	No	No	R
Finland[f]	Yes	Yes	No	No	R
France	Yes	No	No	No	No
Germany[g]	Yes	No	No	No	No
Greece	Yes	No	No	No	No
Ireland[h]	Yes	Yes	UK citizens	No	No
Italy[i]	Yes	No	No	No	R
Luxembourg[j]	Yes	Yes	No	No	No
Netherlands[k]	Yes	Yes	No	No	R
Portugal[l]	Yes	Some	No	Some	No
Spain[m]	Yes	Some	No	No	No
Sweden[n]	Yes	Yes	No	No	R
United Kingdom	Yes	Common-wealth citizens	Some[o]	Common wealth citizens for all elections	S

^a As of October 2006. Sources include: Groenendijk *et al.*, 2000; Blais *et al.*, 2001; Waldrauch, 2005; and the Council of Europe website, http://conventions.coe.int.

^b Signed (S) or ratified (R) the Council of Europe's Convention on the Participation of Foreigners in Public Life at Local Level.

^c Third country nationals voting at local level proposed in city level legislation in Vienna and Graz; the Viennese local law was declared unconstitutional by the constitutional court in a judgment of 30 June 2004.

^d Constitutional amendment in place to allow third country national voting in local elections after 2001. Change instituted in 2003.

^e Third country nationals' rights in local elections include county elections (regarded as part of local self-government); country is part of the Nordic Council which recognises reciprocal rights.

^f Country is part of the Nordic Council which recognises reciprocal rights.

^g Third country nationals excluded from franchise by interpretation of concept of *Staatsvolk* by Federal Constitutional Court.

^h UK citizens may only vote in elections for the lower house, the *Dáil*. However, in the event of reciprocity by another Member State, Ireland could extend electoral rights in these elections to nationals of that state, under the existing legislation.

ⁱ Italy has not yet adopted a constitutional amendment to permit third country nationals to vote in local elections.

^j Third country nationals only have the right to vote, and not to stand. Legislative change in 2003.

^k Third country nationals may not vote in provincial elections.

^l Local and national election voting rights for third country nationals on the basis of reciprocity; thus far includes Brazil, Cape Verde, Argentina, Israel, Norway, Peru, Uruguay and Venezuela at local level, Brazil at national level.

^m Reciprocity basis in principle, but thus far only Norway; hence the provisions could be regarded at present as largely symbolic.

ⁿ Third country national rights in local elections include county elections (regarded as part of local self-government); the country is part of the Nordic Council which recognises reciprocal rights.

^o Irish, Maltese and Cypriot citizens for all elections (the latter two are part of the Commonwealth); all EU for 'regional' elections to the devolved assemblies/parliament.

Table 3.2 *Summary of the position on non-nationals voting in the post-2004 Member States*

	Local elections		National elections including regional/ state elections		
	EU citizens	TCNs	EU citizens	TCNs	COE?[a]
Bulgaria[b]	Yes	No	No	No	No
Cyprus	Yes	No	No	No	S
Czech Republic[c]	Yes	No	No	No	S
Estonia[d]	Yes	Yes	No	No	No
Hungary	Yes	Yes	No	No	No
Latvia	Yes	No	No	No	No
Lithuania	Yes	Yes	No	No	No
Malta[e]	Yes	No	No	No	No
Poland	Yes	No	No	No	No
Romania[f]	Yes	No	No	No	No
Slovenia[g]	Yes	Yes	No	No	No
Slovakia	Yes	Yes	No	No	No

[a] Signed (S) or ratified (R) the Council of Europe's Convention on the Participation of Foreigners in Public Life at Local Level.
[b] Joined the EU only as of 1 January 2007.
[c] In relation to the possibility of third-country nationals voting, the reciprocity principle has been enacted but not yet applied.
[d] Third country nationals cannot stand as candidates.
[e] Reciprocity principle is used in principle but only applies to the UK in local elections.
[f] Joined the EU only as of 1 January 2007.
[g] Third country nationals cannot stand as candidates.

The provision of electoral rights on a reciprocal basis is one of the important aspects of the 'glue' which holds this loose alliance of states together, although, unlike the case of the EU, the reciprocity is essentially voluntary and not driven by compliance rules such as those contained in the EC Treaty, notably Article 10 EC. Likewise, a number of other South American countries with histories of colonial domination are also linked by reciprocal rights to former imperial powers in Europe (e.g. the relations between Brazil and Portugal).

Table 3.3 *Summary of the position on non-nationals voting in selected third countries*

	Local elections	National elections including regional/state elections	COE (where relevant)?[a]
Iceland	Yes	No	R
Norway	Yes	No	R
Switzerland	Some cantons	Some cantons[b]	No
Australia	Some[c]	Some regional elections/UK only in national elections[d]	
Canada	No	No	
New Zealand	Yes	Yes[e]	
US	Some[f]	No	

[a] Signed (S) or ratified (R) the Council of Europe Convention on the participation of foreigners in public life at local level.
[b] Non-nationals do not have the right to stand for election.
[c] UK citizens may vote in local elections throughout Australia. In South Australia, Tasmania and Victoria, all non-nationals may vote in local elections, provided they fulfil certain conditions such as being owners and occupiers of property. Non-nationals do have the right to stand for election.
[d] Non-nationals do not have the right to stand for election.
[e] Non-nationals do not have the right to stand for election.
[f] Restricted to a very small number of localities, in particular to elections to school boards.

Interestingly enough, voting rights extensions have not invariably been associated with the policies of liberal or social-democratically oriented states. One of the few recent examples of the extension of the right to vote to non-nationals involved the case of foreign workers, or *VertragsarbeiterInnen*, in the German Democratic Republic. Right at the death of the GDR, in 1990, a new law was promulgated that enabled this group of 100–200,000 persons to vote at all levels after six months of residency. Ironically, few of them remained much longer in the united Germany. Many foreigners were sent home with one-way tickets just before German reunification in 1990.[39]

---

[39] On the reality of life for foreigners in the GDR, see S. Geyer, 'Ausländer in der DDR. Frischfleisch für den Sozialismus', *Der Spiegel*, 5 May 2001.

It is worth noting at this stage, however, that theory and practice may not always converge. Despite the *existence* of electoral rights for non-nationals in a not insignificant number of states, these may not always be simple to *exercise* in practice, if there are barriers to entry such as complex electoral registration arrangements, linguistic barriers, and rules restricting membership of political parties or associations or indeed just simple ignorance on the part of officials responsible for implementing statutory rights.

VIII Electoral rights and the transformation of citizenship: the approach of this book

The tables included in the previous section, along with the accompanying comments on the spread of alien suffrage, are not intended to provide the basis for a detailed review of state practice on electoral rights, as this lies beyond the scope of this book. Nor is it intended here either to argue the case for the extension of existing state practices or even to buttress calls from certain quarters, such as NGOs, for more electoral rights to be granted under EU law, whether to EU citizens themselves (e.g. rights to vote in national elections in the Member State of residence) or to third country nationals (e.g. rights to vote in local elections). As a normative endeavour, such calls need to be based on a coherent political theory of the European Union as a multilevel constitutional project. This book does not seek to provide such a theory or to use the existing theories in this way. A similar point needs to be made about arguments for the European Union to be based on a citizenship of residence (allowing the entry of third country nationals into citizenship of the Union), rather than a citizenship combining the separate nationalities of the Member States. To defend this point of view would likewise be a normative endeavour which would need to be grounded in political theory (Føllesdal, 1999).

It may be, of course, that the consequences of the predominantly empirical analysis of electoral rights policies (including the limits of those policies) at the Union and national level in this book might be to demonstrate the existence of certain anomalies in the current EU policies on electoral rights. The analysis of these anomalies might in turn seem to point in the direction of extending electoral rights both for EU citizens and for third country nationals, either as a consequence of extensions to Union competences, or as a result of steps taken autonomously by the Member States as part of a gradual process of

Europeanisation. Instrumental conclusions about the potential integrative contribution of measures on electoral rights, or indeed other mechanisms to foster political participation, might also easily be drawn from the analysis, especially in relation to the argument that for local elections there need to be strong rebuttal arguments to deny the positive inclusionary effects which would result from having universal residence-based access to the franchise.

However, this is not a book about the ethics of inclusion and exclusion, or about the stories of political peoplehood, which animate writers such as Rogers Smith (2003). Thus it does not contain any attempt to tease out whether the allocation of electoral rights to non-nationals is a desirable or undesirable element of national democratic systems, or policies and measures on immigration, nationality and citizenship (Beckmann, 2006). Nor am I trying to 'explain' the existence of cases of non-national voting as political practices, and to show definitively that this results from 'national' or 'postnational'/international factors. Given the diversity of practices amongst states, inside and outside the European Union, and given the failure of earlier researchers fully to do just that, this does not seem a satisfactory avenue for research (Earnest, 2003, 2004, 2006). Within the wider frame of migration policy and migration politics, there are similar levels of controversy amongst researchers as to the determinants and explanations for policy developments, particularly those which are 'liberal' towards immigrants such as measures fostering political participation, against a background of increasingly restrictive state policies on entry and residence (Boswell, 2007). In this matter likewise the book does not claim to make a decisive contribution to knowledge and understanding.

What this book seeks to do, instead, is to use the case of non-nationals voting in elections in order better to illuminate the processes of development and transformation of concepts of citizenship in modern Europe, particularly in the context of the development of the European Union as an increasingly political integration project, but also in the context of wider economic forces of globalisation and other relevant processes such as Europeanisation and regionalisation. As I noted at the end of Chapter 1, this is a form of 'constitutional ethnography' (Scheppele, 2004). Here the key constitutional building blocks are citizenship, and citizenship practices, and, in that context, I privilege the institutional forms of Union citizenship, especially the Article 19 electoral rights. However, the empirical focus is not exclusively upon Union citizenship and consequently later chapters focus directly upon national cases of electoral rights in the wider policy context which has framed such debates. My argument is that the development and transformation of 'new' forms of citizenship (i.e. broader changes in the 'quality' or nature of polity membership) are best revealed by studying two sets of (interrelated) changes:

1. the diffuse, gradual and incremental changes in the formal arrangements which govern various forms of citizenship, which are examined with a particular eye to seeing how the international and/or supranational level is supplementing or interacting with the national level; and
2. the contestations, conflicts and debates about definitions of, and rights and obligations of, polity membership, which occur whenever the *leitmotiv* of citizenship is invoked.

These are the 'lived details' of the polities under study, in Scheppele's ethnographical schema (Scheppele, 2004: 395). The study of changes in formal governing arrangements will focus initially on developments in the European Union, in terms of Treaty change, legislation and its implementation at the national level, and the case law of the Court of Justice, with an eye to both change which *has* occurred (i.e. the institution of limited electoral rights for EU citizens) and that which has *not* occurred (i.e. the absence of equivalent provisions regarding third country nationals and the extension of EU citizens' rights to include national elections). This is the material covered in Chapters 4 to 7. The presentation does not seek to suggest that there is a definitive withering away of national citizenship and an associated growth in importance of European citizenship, or indeed to deny that such a development could be taking place, whether in the short term or the long term. One of the difficulties of any such argument would inevitably be the misfit between assessing the trajectory of 'citizenship policies' in the Union, and the trajectory of citizenship policies at the national level. The former policies are *largely* although *no longer exclusively* concerned with the status and legal regulation of the situation of nationals of the Member States when they are resident in a Member State other than the one of which they hold the nationality. They are concerned in only much more limited ways with the legal status and treatment of third country nationals, and with the status of EU citizens when they are resident in their home state. The latter group of national policies remain, at least at the theoretical level, universally applicable as the means for distinguishing between national citizens and *all aliens*. In practice, such citizenship policies are now substantially limited and mediated both by virtue of the effects of EU law and also by virtue of the often diffuse effects of Europeanisation in relation to national political debates and institutions. These limiting and mediating factors operate not only in relation to EU citizens, but also in certain respects in relation to third country nationals. Not all studies of the so-called limits of European citizenship, especially if they involve the study of matters relating primarily to the regulation of the status of third country nationals such as immigration policy at the national and EU level, appear fully to appreciate these complex interactions (Vink, 2005).

In terms of broader contestations over definitions of polity membership, including the use of electoral rights for non-nationals as one means of expressing the boundaries of polity membership at national level,[40] these are teased out through the analysis in Chapters 8, 9 and 10. Amongst other matters, emphasis will be placed in these chapters upon the diffuse and often indirect role which the EU plays in relation to (national) citizenship in the wider European arena (Rostek and Davies, 2006). Here the specific modes of national polity building which are characteristic of the different Member States are crucial to the mediating role which EU laws and policies can take in practice. Understanding this role, along with the role of the laws and policies which emanate from other international or transnational bodies, such as the Council of Europe or the OSCE, is central to the task of assessing the rate and nature of policy change and thus of changes in the broader constitutional environment. While debates about electoral rights will be central to the presentation, reflections on the wider 'nestedness' of controversies inevitably requires detailed consideration of issues which are not ostensibly directly connected to this question, such as debates about the emergence of a putative European Union policy on immigration and asylum since the mid-1990s, debates about citizenship acquisition (e.g. the referendum in Ireland in June 2004 on birthright citizenship for the children of non-nationals) and debates about the treatment of national minorities such as the Russians in the Baltic states. The complex relationships between these analyses and debates about electoral rights will be made clearer as the argument is developed through the separate chapters, but again as with the study of electoral rights themselves, it should be emphasised that treatment of such questions is neither

---

[40] For an example in the US context of the role of contestations around alien suffrage in the definition of the polity at both the state and the federal level, see Varsanyi, 2005.

comprehensive nor systematic in relation to the EU or its Member States, but merely illustrative of particular types and sites of contestation.

Whenever laws – for whatever reason – confer electoral rights on residents who are not part of the national *demos* defined by nationality, this inevitably gives rise to *contestation* if there is any element of discrimination between different groups. That is not the same as saying that the rights are necessarily *controversial*. For example, in the UK, the full range of electoral rights in all elections (local, national, European) is conferred on certain groups of non-nationals: Irish citizens and Commonwealth citizens. These represent the relics of an earlier 'imperial' citizenship enjoyed by all former 'subjects' of the British Crown. These electoral rights are not generally regarded as controversial within current political discourse. Claims that they should be rescinded are rarely, if ever, heard, although it is sometimes said that, if the rights were being instituted today, it is likely that different principles would be applied. However, like any discriminatory electoral rights, they can give rise to contestation, in the sense that other groups of non-nationals may also lay claim to be part of the suffrage, and there are anomalies between different groups of non-nationals, some of whom have full electoral rights, some of whom have none, and some of whom have the limited range of rights conferred by EU law.

Contestations also arise around the interactions between electoral rights and laws and policies on (legal and illegal) immigration and the status and integration of immigrants, on the status of emigrants, on the acquisition of nationality by birth or by other means, on asylum-seekers and refugees, on the protection of individuals and groups against xenophobia and discrimination based on race and ethnic origin, and on political participation more generally, including the rules governing the conduct of elections, political parties and political freedoms. More generally, the contestations are influenced by wider legal, political and economic conditions, such as the state of the labour market and the manner in which it is regulated, patterns of associational life, including the role of political parties, and the national constitutional framework for each polity. Contestations are not simply a matter of either public opinion or elite political discourse, but also involve formal legal phenomena such as case law and court judgments. Referring to the role of law in regulating the status of non-citizens within a territorial jurisdiction (as well as the status of emigrants), Peter Spiro has commented that 'law will be both an inscription and an accelerant of these new meanings and practices, both a lagging and a leading indicator' (Spiro: 2006: 208). To put it another way, in all twenty-seven national polities which constitute the EU, both the EU electoral rights and those which are granted by national law alone are nested within a complex framework of legal and political structures, with long and complex histories of their own which are hardly susceptible to generalisation. But one point is clear: the role of law in the transformation of citizenship is linked not only to formal institutional change, but also to the patterns of political and ideological contestation which provide the more informal framework within which formal institutions are nested. Moreover, the influence is not a one-way track: the diversity of those citizenship regimes also reflects back onto the construction and development of Union citizenship. Although Union citizenship is often criticised as being top-down in nature, it is never completely impervious to the influence of the diverse citizenship regimes of the Member States.

Following on from this main research question concerning the identification and analysis of sites of contestation, a number of subsidiary research questions will be pursued. First, I will try to figure out precisely how the interrelatedness of national policies on electoral rights for non-nationals, on the one hand, and wider European debates about polity membership, on the other, actually works. What (political and legal) principles govern the interactions between the different spheres of competence, such as competence definition and delimitation, subsidiarity, federal 'drift', or indeed the retrenchment of national sovereignty? At what points, and in what ways, do the national and 'European' debates about polity membership questions intersect, with particular reference to debates about electoral rights? Where, precisely, are the tensions and misfits between the levels to be found and what consequences should be drawn from these tensions? And, finally, how can one judge 'changes' in the quality or nature of polity membership? At what point does the holding of rights and obligations *vis-à-vis* polities other than the *nation* state become significant? When exactly has a 'transformation' in the nature and quality of polity membership taken place?

IX An outline of the issues to be discussed

The second part of the book focuses on the past, present and future of EU electoral rights. Chapters 4 and 5 look at EU electoral rights in detail, tracing their origins and the process whereby Article 19 EC came to be enacted and implemented in EU law. Chapter 4 takes the story from the inception of what was then the European Economic Community (1958) and the creation of the supranational institutions, in particular the Assembly which proved central to debates about electoral rights, up to the point of agreement amongst the Member States on the Treaty of Maastricht in 1991, which enshrined the Article 19 electoral rights in the EC Treaty. Chapter 5 highlights developments since 1993 when the Treaty of Maastricht came into force, analysing the competing interpretations which have been given to these provisions and some of the most salient aspects of their implementation through EU legislation and national measures since that time. In both chapters, the wider issue of a 'citizenship for Europe' (which remains a question rather than a statement) provides the context in which electoral rights must be examined.

Chapters 6 and 7 turn to the future of electoral rights in the EU, and consider three dimensions of change. The first concerns the status of the European Parliamentary *demos*: how 'European' is it? What rights, other than the equal treatment right in Article 19(1) EC, do EU citizens have in relation to voting and standing in European Parliament elections? The second considers the argument that the local and European Parliamentary electoral rights given to non-national EU citizens resident in the Member States should logically be extended to cover regional and national elections, to improve the democratic engagement of EU citizens in their state of residence. This latter section of Chapter 6 evaluates some mechanisms which could be pursued to make this objective a reality. The final dimension considered in Chapter 7 concerns the status of third country nationals under EU law. There is no competence under EU law as it stands for the EU to adopt measures requiring Member States to adopt electoral rights at the local level for resident third country nationals. However, in practice the story of the development of EU competences in relation to third country nationals is a more complex one, and this is reflected especially in the gradually increasing impact that EU laws and policies have upon national immigration and integration policies.

The third part of the book turns to national contestations over policies on electoral rights. Chapters 8 and 9 focus upon these policies from the national perspective, reflecting back upon issues of EU law where necessary. Chapter 8 focuses on practices of inclusion and Chapter 9 upon practices of exclusion. A variety of perspectives are adopted, including looking at electoral rights through a constitutional prism, from the perspective of the rules on citizenship acquisition, and from the perspective of the roles of political parties in democratic processes.

Taking a slightly different perspective, Chapter 10 looks at the special problems of new states with new citizenships and new minorities, and at the interaction between electoral rights and policies on minorities, in the context of EU enlargement. Its particular geographical and geopolitical focus is upon the post-2004 Member States in Central and Eastern Europe.

Chapter 11 brings the book to a conclusion, with an essay which seeks to re-examine the research questions articulated in the previous section.

PART II

The past, present and future of EU electoral rights

4

The emerging constitutional framework for electoral rights in the era of European citizenship

I Introduction

This chapter investigates the historical origins of the electoral rights guaranteed under European Union law and the development of a constitutional framework for these rights, in the wider context of the evolution of European citizenship in legal and political terms.[1] It is the first of four chapters on the past, present and possible future of electoral rights in the European Union. In essence, the story of electoral rights in the EU can be seen as a microcosm of some of the key variables at play within the story of EU integration more generally: the shift from a concern with economic questions to a concern with political and social questions; the role of legal rights in structuring key political developments; the gradual hardening of 'soft' institutions into hard legal and constitutional form, with all the attendant questions raised about legitimacy and effectiveness of such institutions; and finally the question of national implementation and the interaction between EU developments and the national constitutions and constitutional traditions of the Member States.

In setting the scene for the study of electoral rights for non-nationals, the basic principles of citizenship of the Union were presented and discussed in Chapter 1. In Chapter 2, I took the argument further by presenting the tension existing within citizenship of the Union between the market and the polity. Is Union citizenship at root an economic concept, or a political one? The post-Maastricht case law of the Court of Justice on citizenship of the Union was highlighted as arguably moving the concept away from a primary focus on the economic nexus between the free-moving EU citizen and the host Member State, and I will return

---

[1] This chapter draws upon Connolly, Day and Shaw, 2006. That paper was the result of the collective endeavours of its authors for which they are equally responsible; its early sections, on which this chapter relies, likewise owed a great deal to the work of Anthea Connolly. See Connolly, 2003.

to that specific question when referring to the post-Maastricht developments in citizenship as one context in which to draw conclusions about the current state of EU electoral rights in Chapter 5. In addition, I have stressed the difficulty of the task of discerning precisely 'what is' EU citizenship, and what is its 'value-added' in comparison to an underlying Treaty system which from the beginning sought to enshrine free movement rights for economic purposes and to guarantee equality of treatment regardless of nationality. One dimension concerns the question whether the texts and rights which were announced in the Treaty of Maastricht were merely declaratory of the *status quo* under which a limited citizenship concept was already recognised for nationals of the Member States under European Community law, or whether they offered a significant constitutional step towards creating a constitutionally defined political citizenship for the Union. Is it possible to discern, post-Maastricht, a concept of a European polity albeit with a thinly defined 'European *demos*'? Do the electoral rights included in the Maastricht package contribute to understanding the EU in this context as an emergent polity with a thinly defined European *demos*?

When the Treaty of Maastricht instituted a limited range of EU electoral rights in 1993 as part of the citizenship package, this represented for the EU institutions, especially the Commission and the European Parliament, the culmination of a long-standing debate, and not a surprising innovation. Debates about the scope of the EU suffrage dated back to the early 1960s when they were first raised in the European Parliament in the context of discussions on direct elections. Tracing the debates through the years, it is possible to discern that there are a number of historical roots to the discussions which led towards, and have led on from, the institutionalisation of citizenship of the Union in the Treaty of Maastricht. For example, Hans Ulrich Jessurun d'Oliveira highlighted the twin roots of the current electoral rights: 'the emergence of a Community or Union collectivity' and the 'principles of democracy' (d'Oliveira, 1994: 142). Thus, on the one hand, the debates about electoral rights grew out of the development of free movement rights under the Treaty and through the case law of the Court of Justice, so that in legal literatures dating back to the 1970s there were calls for such 'free movers' to be conceived as 'Community citizens'.[2] Electoral rights on

---

[2] See Böhning, 1972, cited in Wilkinson, 1995: 418; Plender, 1976; Evans, 1984. Ress, 1981: 302, contains a section entitled 'Are we on the way towards creating European citizenship?'.

this view are rights ancillary to the practice of migration by EU citizens, rights to be established by the EU acting as a protective polity in order to foster a deeper sense of involvement on the part of the EU migrant with the host state and with certain aspects of its political culture, and to limit the prejudice in terms of the loss of political rights which the migrant may suffer as a result of moving away from her home state.

This in turn connects to the second root of EU electoral rights, namely, the impulse towards greater formal internal democratisation of the institutions of European integration through popular participation, especially moves coming from within the European Parliament. Members of the original 'Assembly' discussed the issue of allocating certain voting rights on the basis of residence rather than nationality, when debating the introduction of direct elections, from 1960 onwards. It seemed illogical to many participants in the debate to suggest direct elections to the European Parliament *without* safeguarding the completeness of the democratic principle by extending voting rights in those elections also to those who had taken advantage of the free movement rights guaranteed by the Treaty. However, that step alone was not enough. In addition, a link to a putative 'citizenship' for the emergent 'Euro-polity' was again then swiftly made, especially by the European Commission, which later made concrete suggestions for local election voting rights, only finally adopted in the Treaty of Maastricht.[3]

This chapter returns first to the earlier stages of the development of a discourse of citizenship within EC law, linking that in particular to the first root of EU electoral rights, before focusing in more detail on the second root of EU electoral rights, the emergence of a discourse of polity-building and in particular democratisation in European Parliament debates from the 1960s onwards. From this discussion we move to a more general discussion of the debates about citizenship-related measures leading up to the conclusion of the Treaty of Maastricht, on which political agreement was reached in late 1991. The chapter concludes with a reflection upon what the developments up to 1993 meant for the idea of creating a concept of European citizenship under what we can now term EU law, and specifically what the

---

[3] See Commission Report to the European Parliament on 'Voting Rights in Local Elections for Community Nationals', COM(86) 487, also published as Bull. EC Supp. 7/86; Commission Proposal for a Council Directive on Voting Rights for Community Nationals in Local Elections in Their Member State of Resident, COM(88) 371; Amended Proposal, COM (89) 524.

prospects for electoral rights might be, which were conceived from the very beginning as having a central role to play in the development of European citizenship.

II The emergence of a (distinctively legal) discourse of citizenship in European Community law

The earliest examples of the use of the term 'citizenship' to describe the connection under EC law between those enjoying the benefits of free movement rights under what was then the Treaty establishing the European Economic Community (EEC Treaty) and the Community itself are to be found in various statements of members of the Community institutions, especially the European Commission (O'Leary, 1996: 17). Examples of references to citizenship date right back to the early 1960s, although probably the most significant early statement came from the Commission Vice-President, Lionello Levi Sandri, who referred in 1968 to the development of a body of rules relating to free movement of workers as 'an incipient form – still embryonic and imperfect – of European citizenship'.[4] Scholarly discourse (Böhning, 1972; Plender, 1976; Evans, 1984; Ress, 1981) followed on, therefore, from an emergent institutional discourse. Furthermore, in the early literatures it was legal scholarship and legal analysis which made most use of the discourse of citizenship in the European integration context, and less frequently political science.

There is no single interpretation of what it means or meant to invoke citizenship in this context. Much of the legal literature made reference to the distinction between treating those who are beneficiaries of the free movement rules as factors of production under a system of economic integration and treating them as humans, with social and cultural needs, with families, and with rights going beyond the economic sphere, including fundamental rights. This ideology is certainly present in the preamble to the first basic Regulation adopted by the Council in 1968 on freedom of movement for workers within the Community,[5] which refers to freedom of movement as a fundamental right for workers and their families. Furthermore, substantial parts of the Regulation are concerned with the rights of workers' families, in relation to initial family

---

[4] See Bull. EC 11/68, at 5–6.
[5] Council Regulation (EEC) No. 1612/68 on freedom of movement of workers within the Community, OJ Spec. Ed. 1968, L257/2, at 475.

reunification, and access to educational and other types of social benefits. Provisions such as Article 7(2) of the Regulation guaranteeing the
worker's right to the same 'social and tax advantages as national workers' have been interpreted by the Court of Justice very broadly as
including rights for the workers' children, and thus as benefits for the
worker herself.[6] On the other hand, there is equally ample evidence from
the time period when the rules on free movement were under development that, while the Member States, in the form of legislation adopted in
the Council, had conceded the need to pursue a broad equal treatment
programme in respect of the entitlement of workers and their families
post-admission, in other respects they regarded their immigration sovereignty as undisturbed. For example, the Member States negotiated for
themselves the inclusion in the original Treaty of derogations allowing
the exclusion or deportation of nationals of other Member States on
grounds of public policy, public security and public health (now Article
39(3) EC; formerly Article 48(3) EEC). Moreover, the Council's 1964
measure concerning the implementation of these derogations was essentially concerned with procedural matters, rather than any questions
about whether it was legitimate for the Member States, in the face of
increased integration, to continue to require such exceptions.[7]
Interestingly, the very first reference from a UK court to the Court of
Justice after accession concerned the discretion of the state to deport a
national of another Member State for activities deemed undesirable on
public policy grounds (membership of the Church of Scientology)
which were lawful when carried out by a national.[8] These activities
could be regarded in very broad terms as 'political' in character. It was
not until the case of *Rutili* that the Court of Justice significantly miti-
gated the effects of the public policy exception, requiring Member States
to interpret it strictly and narrowly.[9]

It should be noted, however, that the Member States imposed restrictions not only in relation to the allegedly problematic effects of political
activities on the part of aliens, who, by definition, do not owe allegiance
to the host, but also in relation to the boundaries of the welfare state. The
situation of workseekers, as opposed to workers, remained very unclear,

---

[6] Case 32/75 *Fiorini (née Christini)* v. *SNCF* [1975] ECR 1085; see generally Ellis, 2003.
[7] Council Directive 64/221/EEC on the co-ordination of special measures concerning the
movement and residence of foreign nationals which are justified on grounds of public
policy, public security or public health, OJ Spec. Ed. 1964, No. 850/64, at 117.
[8] Case 41/74 *Van Duyn* v. *Home Office* [1974] ECR 1337.
[9] Case 36/75 *Rutili* v. *Ministère de l'Interieur* [1975] ECR 1219.

both in relation to their right of access to the territory of the host Member State to seek work (and for how long), and especially in relation to their right to draw unemployment benefit to cover the period of workseeking (which in principle they should draw upon from the Member State in which they previously worked, rather than from the one in which they are seeking work) (Wilkinson, 1995: 419–22).

Article 39(4) EC (formerly Article 48(4) EEC) furthermore contains a 'public service' exception, under which the provisions on the free movement of workers are not to apply to employment in the public service within the Member States. The Court of Justice has given a narrow interpretation of the discretion of the Member States to exclude non-nationals from the public service, limiting the derogation merely to cases where there is participation in the exercise of powers conferred by public law, duties designed to safeguard the general interests of the state and other public authorities, and posts assuming the existence of a special relationship of allegiance to the state and reciprocity of rights and duties which form the foundation of a bond of nationality. Thus the Court prevented, for example, Belgium from excluding from the free movement and equal treatment guarantees a whole raft of lower grade public service posts including jobs as train drivers, railway signallers, nurses, plumbers and electricians.[10] However, the inclusion of such a clause in the Treaty in the first place (not to mention its continued presence in the Treaties right up to the present day[11]) casts doubt on whether a citizenship-focused interpretation of the provisions is truly plausible, when the provisions are looked at in the round. It is difficult in the longer term to marry a limitation on employment in the public service with policies promoting the political representation of migrants, including the right to vote and stand in local elections.

While the frame of reference provided by the free movement provisions constituted the dominant means for conceptualising the putative emergence of the citizenship concept, alternative means of viewing the development of a legal concept of European citizenship draw upon various concepts of rights within EC law.[12] Scholars have, for example, frequently pointed to the development of a conception of fundamental

---

[10] Case 149/79 *Commission* v. *Belgium* [1981] ECR 3881.

[11] See Article III-133(4) of the Constitutional Treaty, which reproduces Article 39 EC: 'This Article shall not apply to employment in the public service.'

[12] For an attempt to distinguish between different 'classes' of rights under EU law, namely, 'Community rights' (which would include free movement rights), fundamental rights, and citizenship rights, see Hilson, 2004.

rights for the European Community, based on the notion of general principles of law, enshrined in Article 220 EC as a source of law within the European Union as the most constructive basis for future development of a special bond between the EU and 'its' citizens (O'Leary, 1995). Alternatively, one can focus on the enforceability of EC law by individuals, such as the limited recourse of individuals to bring direct actions before the Court of Justice itself (more recently, the Court of First Instance) and the development of concepts such as direct effect by the Court of Justice which allowed individuals to rely upon enforceable Community rights as against Member States before national courts.[13] Thus, in 1979, Commissioner Etienne Davignon declared that 'it could be said that the status of "Community citizen" had been officially recognized from the moment when the Treaties granted rights to individuals and the opportunity of enforcing them by recourse to a national or Community court'.[14] These alternative conceptualisations, like those based on the free movement rights, owe a great deal in terms of their evolution to the creative role of the Court of Justice as a motor of integration, especially during the 1960s and 1970s when political impetus for European integration was relatively weak.

III From a legal to a political discourse of citizenship

Although it is possible to argue that the legal position in relation to free movement, as a putative basis for European citizenship, remained somewhat contingent and conditional, it is also important to note a series of political developments which occurred from the date of the first enlargement (1973) onwards, which could be said to buttress claims of an emergent citizenship concept. Although commitments such as that made at the Paris Summit in October 1972 to convert the (economic) Community into a (political) European Union proved largely empty, as the Member States were incapable of translating words into actions in particular within the unrealistic timetable of eight years they set themselves, some of these early attempts at constructing citizenship policies were picked up again in the late 1980s and 1990s, as ideas about political union constructed around a notion of membership were revitalised.

---

[13] Case 26/62 *Van Gend en Loos* [1963] ECR 1.

[14] Statement reproduced in *Proceedings of the Round Table on 'Special Rights and a Charter of the Rights of the Citizens of the European Community' and Related Documents*, Luxembourg: European Parliament, 1979, 25.

One section of the Tindemans Report of 1975 on 'European Union', drawn up at the instance of the European Council, was concerned with the construction of 'a Citizens' Europe',[15] and it addresses the policy measures in relation to rights and entitlements which could be instigated (e.g. in fields such as consumer protection and environmental protection) to bring Europe 'closer to its citizens'. This is an appeal which has had resonance through the years, and is referred to on the very first page of the Laeken Declaration which mandated the establishment of the Convention on the Future of Europe, which in turn drew up the first draft of the Constitutional Treaty.[16]

The change in focus in political rhetoric from economic integration to political integration in the early 1970s is termed a 'paradigm shift' by Antje Wiener (1998: 66). This formed the basis for the introduction of debates about citizenship, initially on an informal basis, and later on a more formal basis as the Member States gradually agreed a number of initiatives such as the measures on the uniform passport and – outside the immediate European Community framework – the Schengen Convention eliminating borders between the Member States and removing the need for passports or identity cards to be shown at the internal borders of participating states. In addition, from the early 1970s onwards the European Council was agreed upon the need to work towards instituting certain 'special rights' for nationals of the Member States to distinguish them as 'citizens', and the types of measures which were contemplated under this heading included local election voting rights. The Communiqué from the Meeting of the Heads of Government of the Community in Paris, 1974,[17] was of critical importance in the development of European citizenship in so far as it led to a working party to study the conditions and timing for the process under which the citizens of the nine Member States could be given special rights as members of the Community. The Commission's technical reports on the topic of special rights identified 'special rights' as rights which were at that time

---

[15] Bull. EC Supp. 1/76, at 26–7.

[16] *Annexes to the Presidency Conclusions – Laeken, 14 and 15 December 2001*, SN 300/01 Add.1, Annex 1, Laeken Declaration on the Future of the European Union, http:// european-convention.eu.int/pdf/LKNEN.pdf.

[17] Passport Union and 'special rights' were dealt with in points 10 and 11 of the final communiqué issued at the European Summit held in Paris on 9 and 10 December 1974 (what we would now recognise as the European Council meeting which brings to a conclusion each six-monthly rotating Council Presidency). The Commission was mandated to work on various proposals relating to these matters, and produced a report and proposals, which are published in Bull. EC Supp. 7/75.

reserved for nationals living in their own Member States. Accordingly, it stated that,

> since civil rights and liberties are at least in principle generally granted to all foreigners and since economic and social rights as well as the right to become an official of the European Communities and the right to vote and to stand for election to the [European Parliament] are real or potential rights, acquired on the basis of the Community Treaties, it follows that the special rights referred to in Point 11 ... are first and foremost other rights which exist in the Member States ... [T]he most important would seem to be the rights to vote, to stand for election and to become a public official at local, regional, or national levels.[18]

Although the political approach of the Commission at the time was cautious, noting that it believed there to be no legal powers under the EEC Treaty at the time (including what is now Article 308 EC (formerly Article 235 EEC)) to grant political rights to the nationals of the Member States and thus that an *ad hoc* legal instrument would be required, it did comment in passing that the 'complete assimilation with nationals as regards political rights is desirable in the long term from the point of view of *a European Union*' (emphasis added).[19]

On the basis of this type of rhetoric, it is unsurprising that Wiener should draw a parallel between citizenship in the European Community and citizenship within states, arguing that (1998: 8):

> citizenship when it first appeared on the EC's policy agenda in the early 1970s, had been strategized precisely on the conceptual and normative grounds of modern citizenship ... [P]olicy makers drew on the idea of citizenship as an identity generating concept in the 1970s ... [E]arly interest in the creation of a 'European citizenship' was embedded first and foremost in the notion of citizenship as a state-building component.

IV Linking the suffrage in European and local elections

The roots of the debate on citizenship and electoral rights go even deeper than these institutional discussions in the 1970s immediately reveal.[20] Developments in the European Parliament specifically around the question of 'universal suffrage' as the basis for direct elections to the European Parliament were also central to the emergence of a notion of

---

[18] Bull. EC Supp. 7/75, point 2.2.2.   [19] *Ibid.*, point 3.1.
[20] See more generally on the evolution of parliamentary democracy, Pinder, 2000.

citizenship as a polity-building instrument,[21] so far as they contributed to creating out of the Assembly established by the 1951 Treaty establishing the European Coal and Steel Community the directly elected proto-legislature for the European Communities from 1979 onwards. At that point, the Assembly took on the features of what we now recognise as the European Parliament.

In its early days, the Assembly[22] was composed of parliamentarians delegated by their national parliaments, who thus held dual mandates. More than a few of these were elderly statesmen and women who had been rewarded for a lifetime of service at home with what was understood to be a rather comfortable and undemanding position abroad, but amongst them were parliamentarians who were also keen 'Europeans' and who believed that the European Parliament could hold a key position in leading European integration. Two factors can be identified as impelling the Parliament first to consider the right to vote and to stand in European elections, and secondly to consider the right to vote and to stand in European and local elections in the place of residence. One of these concerned the seriousness with which the designation of 'parliament' was taken. Many parliamentarians carried with them conceptions about parliamentarianism and democracy that were embedded in their own national orders. The other related to the fact that post-war parliamentarians were beginning to witness the basic consequences of Western European collaboration to provide freedom of movement, namely, that, by moving from one country to another, 'factors of production' (that is, people conceived as economic migrants) were disenfranchising themselves. Hence, democracy considerations plus the growing awareness of a new category of market 'citizens' were two crucial reasons why a debate on voting rights took place in the European Parliament.

According to Article 21(1) of the 1951 Treaty of the European Coal and Steel Community (ECSC):

> The Assembly shall consist of delegates whom the Parliaments of each of the member states shall be called upon to appoint once a year from

---

[21] I use the term 'polity-building' rather than 'state-building' to emphasise the limited and ambiguous notion of the EU as a polity: Shaw and Wiener, 2000.

[22] The conventional title was changed from 'Assembly' to 'Parliament' by Resolution of the Assembly of 30 March 1962. JO 1962, 1045, and this became the term used by most commentators and politicians, although Margaret Thatcher famously insisted on continuing to call it the Assembly right through the 1980s. The official title was changed by the first substantial amendments to the founding European Treaties since the 1950s, the Single European Act of 1986.

among their own membership, or who shall be elected by direct universal suffrage, according to the procedure determined by each respective High Contracting Party.

This reference to 'direct universal suffrage' marked the start of the Parliament's debate on voting rights, especially voting rights for non-national citizens in European elections. From 1960 onwards, the idea of direct elections to the Parliament animated the Parliament as it focused on and used arguments about 'building Europe'[23] and establishing democracy to support this aim.[24] In 1960, the Parliament adopted a proposal for a uniform electoral procedure for direct elections to the European Parliament, including the proposal that elections by direct universal suffrage would include the right of nationals of the Member States to vote in Member States other than their own.[25] But it dropped this controversial suggestion in the next version of its proposal on the uniform electoral procedure, which was a more minimal text adopted in 1975 with a view to facilitating the initiation of direct elections which were eventually held in 1979 (Evans, 1984: 705), only for it to reappear again in the 1982 proposal, which was once again not adopted.[26] The basis for the Parliament's work in this area lay in what was then Article 138(3) EEC, which mandated the Parliament to propose, for unanimous adoption by the Council of Ministers, proposals for the election of the Parliament by direct universal suffrage.

Although the Parliament received support from certain quarters for direct elections,[27] it encountered opposition in other places. A principal reason for this was the belief that, under the founding Treaties, the Parliament did not have sufficient powers to justify being directly elected. By contrast, parliamentarians themselves tended to think it

---

[23] Ninth General Report on the Activities of the Community, 1 February 1960 to 31 January 1961.

[24] 'The European Parliament demands that the application of the principles of a constitutional theory based on democracy and the primacy of the law should be reinforced in order to ensure the future development of the Community.' 4 *Bulletin de la Communauté Européene du Charbon et de l'Acier*, Chronologie Années 1950–60, Luxembourg 1967, 68.

[25] The proposal is to be found in a Resolution dated 17 May 1960, JO 1960, 834, Article 7.

[26] OJ 1982 C87/61.

[27] The Italian Government had introduced measures concerning the direct election of Italian members of the European Parliament, and in 1968 Christian Democrat MEPs asked the Italian Government to invite other European governments to begin the direct election of their members; see *Cahiers de documentation européenne*, Octobre–Décembre 1968, Parlement Européen, 69.

would be undemocratic for the powers of the Parliament to be augmented without its first being directly elected. This conflict reached a pinnacle with the Commission's 1972 report on 'The Enlargement of the Powers of the European Parliament'.[28] Whilst the Parliament inclined towards the view that it should be directly elected and that subsequently as the most democratic body in the Community it should have stronger powers, the report concluded that the powers of the Parliament should be increased first. It found that '[t]he new powers would, of their very nature, constitute means of influencing events in such a way as to promote the application of Article 138 of the EEC Treaty' and also that 'the present mode of recruiting the Parliament involves a certain degree of democratic legitimacy justifying the exercise of true parliamentary powers'.[29]

When the Summit Meeting of the Heads of State and Government took place in Paris in 1974, the Heads of Government of Belgium and Italy had suggested, for the first time, that the right to vote and to stand should be granted at the local level to all Community nationals.[30] These governments had been the first also to consider the direct election of their own members of the European Parliament,[31] and bills to extend the right to vote in local elections in their territory had also come before their own parliaments. When the proposed law for direct elections reached the Belgian Parliament, Article 4 provided that 'nationals of the Member States of the European Communities who have their residence in Belgium may take part in the elections to the European Parliament under the same conditions as Belgian citizens'.[32] First, this implied that there was no question mark over direct elections to the European Parliament, and secondly it helped to launch the idea of extending the boundaries of the suffrage in both European and local elections. Given the problems that Belgium faced much later in transposing European legislation on the right to vote in local elections of European citizens,[33] this may be viewed as somewhat incongruous. Nonetheless,

---

[28] Vedel Report, Bull. EC Supp. 4/72.   [29] *Ibid.*, 60.
[30] This point is reported in the Commission's subsequent report in Bull. EC Supp. 7/75, point 2.2.3.
[31] It is also notable that the Luxembourg Socialist Party had made it a standing stipulation that there should be direct elections to the European Parliament, and, in 1969, it called on the government to table a bill to this effect. European Documentation – A Survey, April–June 1969, European Parliament, 67.
[32] Patijn Report, EP Working Doc. 368/74, 13 January 1975, 43.
[33] See the discussion in Chapter 5.

the Parliament took up Belgium's position with regard to the universal right to vote in European elections and was sympathetic to the right to vote in local elections in the place of residence;[34] by reflecting upon these issues, the Belgian Government had assisted their introduction onto the Community's agenda. The Commission did not refer to the right to vote and stand in European elections as one of the 'special' rights connected with citizenship and this was undoubtedly because the question of direct elections to the Parliament remained at that time contested and the project incomplete.

When the first direct elections to the Parliament did eventually take place in 1979, after the adoption of the Council Act on Direct Elections,[35] nationals of the Member States resident in another Member State were not able to vote, unless this had been provided for at national level (O'Leary, 1996: 207). The only provision at European level on this matter was a prohibition on double voting,[36] which was largely aimed at those with dual nationality as they are the group historically most likely to double vote. This was just one of the several respects in which the vocation of Article 138(3) EEC to see the adoption of a uniform electoral procedure as the basis for the elections based on direct universal suffrage was sacrificed on the altar of political expediency in order to secure agreement amongst the nine Member States, some of whom feared interferences in the national sovereignty as one of the consequences of direct elections (van den Berghe, 1979). For example, the United Kingdom feared that it might be forced to introduce elections by proportional representation.[37]

However, soon after the first direct elections, the Parliament settled down once again to examine the criteria for extending the right to vote as an entitlement under EU law, not least because Article 7(2) of the Council Act provided for the European Parliament to draw up a further more detailed proposal on the uniform procedure. The Seitlinger Report[38] suggested that Member States ought to give the right to vote

---

[34] Article 7 of the Parliament's draft Convention on direct universal elections to the Parliament called for voting rights for all Community citizens irrespective of their place of residence.

[35] OJ 1976 C278/5.   [36] Article 8.

[37] Except in Northern Ireland, where it introduced proportional representation based on a single transferable vote from the very beginning, the UK maintained a first-past-the-post constituency system until the 1999 European Parliamentary elections, when it introduced the d'Hondt system for multi-member constituencies under the European Parliament Elections Act 1999: Farrell and Scully, 2005.

[38] Seitlinger Report, draft text on the electoral procedure, A1-988/81, 26 February 1982.

in European elections to those who had been resident in their country for five years or more, and persons who had not resided in another Member State for five years must be given the right to vote by their country of origin in their country of origin. The right to stand for election was to be guaranteed in the Member State of nationality alone. The report justified the right to vote in the Member State of residence by the principle of long-term residence. However, the Parliament in plenary took a different approach. It maintained that the right to vote should be a right conferred by the Member State of nationality alone.[39] On the other hand, however, the Parliament did propose that the right to stand for election should be given by the country of residence after five years; this would have meant that an individual could stand for election in a country where they could not vote in the same elections.[40] The issue of proportional representation rather than voting rights continued to dominate, including in the debate in the Parliament's plenary session.[41] The Council did consider the Seitlinger Report and the Draft Act several times within the Committee of Permanent Representatives (COREPER) but no further action was taken.[42] Overall, the voting rights debate fell victim to an advanced level of stagnation in the European Community, and conflicting positions on the Common Agricultural Policy and the crisis over the UK's budget rebate were not conducive to consensus. Meanwhile, the debate about 'special rights' had also run aground, not least because of the lack of 'formal resources' (Wiener, 1998: 100), *inter alia* in the sense of clear competences under the Treaties to push any proposals forward.

Following a second set of European elections in 1984, and with the aim of reviving the debate within the Council, the Parliament put forward a new proposal on the electoral procedure.[43] In an opinion, the Committee on Legal Affairs stated that it wished the electoral procedure to be genuinely uniform, and pointed out that, from the legal point of view, the

---

[39] See Article 5 of the Parliament's Draft Act on a uniform electoral procedure, adopted by resolution on 10 March 1982, OJ 1982 C87/61. If the national has left the territory of the Member State, this, of course, raises the question of expatriate voting, and the degree of connection which expatriates should have before voting. Clearly, to institute such an electoral rule by means of the uniform electoral procedure would have been as substantial an interference in national sovereignty as the institution of electoral rights for non-nationals.

[40] Article 6 of the Draft Act.   [41] *The Week*, European Parliament, 8–12 March 1982.

[42] See the further Resolution of the European Parliament of 9 March 1983, deploring the lack of action on the part of the Council of Ministers before the 1984 elections, OJ 1983 C96/28.

[43] Bocklet Report, EP Working Doc. A2-1/85.

existence of a 'uniform procedure' meant that the actual procedures used to achieve the principles, objectives and results of the electoral system should all be uniform.[44] Although the Parliament as a whole did not vote on the draft report which had been adopted by the Political Affairs Committee on 28 February 1985, not least because of the absence of a consensus across the political groups in the Parliament on the question of how uniform the direct election procedure should be, the Political Affairs Committee had made a clear proposal on the residence criteria, stating that:

> Nationals of a Member State shall be entitled to vote in the country of which they are nationals. The Member States shall take all the necessary measures to enable their nationals whose place of residence is outside their country of origin to exercise their electoral rights without hindrance in the Member State of which they are nationals.[45]

Changing the focus away from the issue of electoral procedure to the question of the rights of nationals of Member States in the context of their migration from one Member State to another, a clear approach to the question of electoral rights emerged from 1983 onwards.[46] A resolution in June 1985 on the guidelines for a Community policy on migration stipulated that the right to vote in European elections in the country of residence would be given to Community citizens who had spent five years or more in a Community country other than their country of origin.[47] This resolution also stated that the right to vote and to stand for

---

[44] See the commentary on this report in Report on a proposal for an electoral procedure incorporating common principles for the election of Members of the European Parliament, Committee on Institutional Affairs, Rapporteur Mr Anastassopoulos, A4-212/98, 2 June 1998.

[45] Above n. 44, Art. 2(i). Although 1983 was the last time that the Parliament voted on a Draft Uniform Electoral Procedure as a whole before the adoption of the Treaty of Maastricht which introduced one element – the right to vote in the Member State of residence – and changed the rules contained in what was then Article 138(3) EC on the adoption of the uniform electoral procedure, it did adopt other isolated resolutions on the right to vote as such: e.g. Resolution on the exercise of voting rights in the European Parliament elections of 14 to 17 June 1994 by citizens of the Community who are not nationals of the Member State in which they have their permanent residence, OJ 1984 C10/73.

[46] European Parliament Resolution on the right of citizens of a Member State residing in a Member State other than their own to stand for and vote in local elections, OJ 1983 C184/28.

[47] Resolution on guidelines for a Community policy on migration, OJ 1985 C141/462; see also Resolution on the problem of migrant workers, OJ 1983 C342/140.

election at local level should be given to migrant workers from Member States 'living for a certain period – to be specified – in a Member State other than their country of origin'.

A further obstacle to voting rights in the mid-1980s appeared to be erected by the Adonnino Committee, set up in 1984 after the Fontainebleau European Council, and comprising personal representatives of the Heads of State and Government and their foreign ministers. Its mission was to come up with concrete suggestions to implement a People's Europe and thereby to enhance 'European identity'. The Committee submitted its first report to the Milan European Council, but it was ambiguous as to the basis of voting rights. The report argued that:

> It is *desirable* to increase the citizen's involvement in and understanding of the political process in the Community institutions [and that] the electoral procedure . . . shall ensure either that a citizen should be entitled to vote for candidates from his own country . . . or that a citizen residing in another Member State should be allowed to vote for candidates from that Member State.[48]

Thus the report recommended that discussion of the matter should continue, but at the same time made it categorically clear that the subject remained within the competence of the Member States to decide. This view was endorsed by the Council in its response to a written question from an MEP in which it confirmed that it was of the view that the reciprocity, non-reciprocity and grant of voting rights was a matter for individual Member States and also that, therefore, the intergovernmental approach was the preferred one (O'Leary, 1996: 236).

V From stagnation to action via market-making

When Jacques Delors took over from Gaston Thorn as President of the Commission in January 1985, he rapidly introduced a timetable for the completion of the internal market before the end of 1992.[49] That proved to be an initiative which galvanised the Member States into political action to reform the Treaties and to foster the political conditions under which the necessary measures could be adopted within the Council of Ministers and the European Parliament. The Commission that he led

---

[48] Bull. EC Supp. 7/85, 'A People's Europe' (emphasis added); see also the Commission's response in Bull. EC Supp. 2/88.

[49] Commission White Paper on completing the Internal Market (COM(85) 310).

was not so immediately supportive of the right to vote in local and European elections, however, and progress on the subject of the right to vote was not achieved at the same pace or in the same relatively smooth fashion. The Commission's report on 'Voting Rights in Local Elections for Community Nationals'[50] (for which the Parliament had waited three years since its resolution on migrant workers in 1983) was positive in its initial paragraphs saying that the cornerstone of democracy is the right of voters to elect the decision-making bodies. It acknowledged that:

> There is no doubt that Community legislation has had the effect of breaking the link between national territory and the legal implications of nationality. (The gradual achievement of a People's Europe will consolidate this trend) ... However ... the disassociation between national territory and the legal implications of nationality does not extend to political rights.[51]

The report revealed that, as in the Parliament, negotiations in Council on the right to vote had centred on whether or not eligibility for such rights should come down to residence or nationality, observing that: 'The gulf between countries in favour of the nationality qualification and countries in favour of the residence qualification proved so wide that no solution could be found.'[52] The report additionally pointed out the problem of constitutional amendment which would be needed in many of the Member States to enable changes to the electorate in local and European elections, and, from the Parliament's point of view, concluded on a discouraging note. The report asked whether it would be politically consistent to propose giving local elections a European character which was not enjoyed by the European elections themselves, and claimed that logic and political consistency demanded that the first step should be to give a European character to the elections which were intrinsically European. Thus, '[o]nce a European electoral procedure is adopted, local electoral law could develop on a reciprocal basis'.[53] In other words, the view taken was that there should be no consideration of local election rights without reconsidering the uniform procedure, which was still swamped in controversy.

The Parliament was highly critical of the report and produced a report and a resolution stating that the European Parliament,

---

[50] COM(86) 487, Voting rights in local election for Community nationals – Report from the Commission to the European Parliament transmitted for information to the Council; also published as Bull. EC Supp. 7/86.
[51] Above n. 50 at 8. Brackets added. [52] Ibid., 43. [53] Ibid., 44.

4. Rejects, in particular the Commission's attempt to tie the right to vote and stand in local elections to the uniform procedure for elections to the European Parliament;

5. Considers that the attitude which the Commission has adopted on this matter so far has severely strained the relationship between the Commission and the Parliament, which is founded on co-operation.[54]

It insisted that, while the Commission might see an indisputable link between a uniform electoral procedure and the right to vote and stand in local elections, the Commission could not set aside progress on local elections and

> absolve itself of responsibility by pointing to the work on the uniform electoral procedure for the European Parliament. The two types of election have virtually nothing in common other than the fact that they are both elections. Still less can the uniform electoral procedure for the European Parliament be regarded in any way or at any stage as a precondition for the submission of a legislative proposal on the right to vote and stand in local elections.[55]

Lastly, the report frankly asserted that, 'in the face of Parliament's unambiguous wish, it [the Commission] has sought to mask its indecision with stalling tactics'.

Endeavouring to rectify the impasse towards the end of 1987, Commissioner Ripa di Meana undertook before the Legal Affairs Committee of the European Parliament to present a proposal for a directive on voting rights in the first half of 1988. During 1987, a qualitative change in the thinking of the Commission appeared to have taken place and in the 1988 proposal for a directive the Commission announced that it had been working steadily to move from 'theoretical discussion to legislative action'.[56] Furthermore, it recognised and acknowledged that the right to vote in local elections is the political complement to economic and social integration, stating that this imperative is 'underlined by the goal of

---

[54] 'Vetter Report, Drawn up on Behalf of the Committee on Legal Affairs and Citizens' Rights on Voting Rights in Local Elections for Community Nationals Residing in a Member State Other Than Their Own', A2-197/87, 6 November 1987, confirmed by a European Parliament Resolution on voting rights in local elections for Community nationals residing in a Member State other than their own, 15 December 1987, OJ 1988 C13/33.

[55] See above n. 54, point 12.

[56] Proposal for a Council Directive on voting rights for Community nationals in local elections in their Member State of residence, COM(88) 371, OJ 1988 C246/20, Bull. EC Supp. 2/88, at 27.

creating a European area' and a 'commitment to a People's Europe'. Moreover, echoing debates about electoral rights as migrants' rights rehearsed in the previous chapter, the Commission stated that:

> As far as local elections in the Community are concerned, residence appears to be a more appropriate criterion for determining the place of voting than nationality. Actually living in a municipality means that various aspects of daily life are influenced by decisions taken by the elected body which runs the municipality.

Even the fact that implementing such a measure would require constitutional amendment in some Member States was for the Commission no longer an obstacle to making a concrete proposal. For the Commission, the difficult part of the proposal was the task of demonstrating why it could now find a legal basis for a directive in a – in this respect unchanged – EEC Treaty, having previously denied that it could. In its broader justification of the proposal, in the explanatory memorandum, the Commission referred to the 'declared objective of the Single European Act of promoting democracy'.[57] This is true only in the more general sense, as Síofra O'Leary points out, given that it is the Preamble to the Single European Act which refers to the promotion of democracy, not its provisions addressing objectives as such (O'Leary, 1996: 240–1). It can certainly be claimed, with conviction, that the SEA marked a qualitative turning point in the evolution of what we now term the European Union, but this is largely a view which has been formulated with the benefit of hindsight and at the time its provisions were generally assessed by commentators as rather too pragmatic and limited in character (Pescatore, 1987), especially in relation to the institutional conditions needed to enable the so-called 1992 programme to be driven through by the political leaders in the Commission and the Council of Ministers.

The draft directive proposed that nationals of the Member States resident in another Member State should be granted the right to vote, on application, in the municipality of their residence, after a period of residence not less than the term of office of the relevant municipal council, whatever that might be. Potential voters would have to be informed of their right to vote, and to be entered in the register, and have to fulfil certain conditions such as demonstrating that they had not been deprived of their civic rights in their state of nationality and that they could no longer exercise the right to vote in their Member State of

---

[57] Bull. EC Supp. 2/88, at 29.

origin (either because expatriate voting was not allowed, or because they had voluntarily renounced the right to vote in their state of origin), as well as proving residence for the necessary period of time.[58] To stand for election, a period of residence equal to two terms of office of a municipal council would be needed.[59] Member States could exclude non-nationals from holding offices such as Mayor, or Deputy Mayor.[60] Otherwise, in respect of conditions on voting and standing, the Member States were obliged to accord equality of treatment between nationals and non-nationals seeking to vote and stand.[61]

The Parliament continued to press actively for progress on voting rights following the Commission's 1988 draft directive, and in March 1989 it approved the Commission proposal subject to minor amendments.[62] However, notwithstanding the Parliament's enthusiasm, and the Commission's willingness to present a revised proposal,[63] the measure was never adopted, which is unsurprising since its legal basis in Article 235 EEC – already contestable given the Commission's willingness in previous years to follow the general Member State line that political rights were a matter for intergovernmental action, not legislation under the Treaties – would have required a unanimous vote amongst the Member States. This would have been impossible to achieve in the circumstances.

Síofra O'Leary (1996: 241) describes the 1988 proposal as 'premature' in the absence of any new legal basis in the Treaties, in particular in view of the controversy which surrounded the adoption of the Maastricht citizenship provisions, not least those on local electoral rights. On the other hand, it is possible to argue that, notwithstanding the eventual non-adoption of the proposal, its very existence and the discussion between Community institutions which it prompted had a wider resonance. In other words, reflecting perhaps a wider set of pressures brought to bear upon the Commission and the Member States, pressures which culminated *inter alia* in the adoption in December 1989 by eleven of the twelve Member States of the declaratory Community Charter of Fundamental Social Rights of Workers[64] (the UK alone dissenting), the Commission as initiator of legislation recognised the imperative of linking the social

---

[58] See Articles 2–4 of the draft directive.   [59] Article 8 of the draft directive.
[60] Article 10 of the draft directive.   [61] Articles 5, 6 and 9 of the draft directive.
[62] OJ 1989 C96/106.   [63] COM(98) 524.
[64] Curiously, the Charter was never published in any official series of EU documentation such as the *Official Journal* or the *Bulletin of the European Communities*, but it was published rather informally as European File 6/90. The text is available in the University of Pittsburgh Archive of European Integration at http://aei.pitt.edu/archive/00004629/01/003998_1.pdf.

and political dimensions of migration between the Member States (including political rights) to the economic process of building a single market. According to the Commission, a 'socio-economic approach' to a People's Europe was not enough.[65] This was in contrast to its earlier view which was more protective of the role of the Member States. This could be described as the beginnings of a process of classical 'spillover' from the sphere of economic integration into fields which historically the Member States have jealously guarded, such as political rights and citizenship more generally. That process continued after 1989 as the political discussions began increasingly to concentrate on the subject of hastening economic and monetary integration, and, at the insistence primarily of the German Government, the European Council meeting in Dublin in June 1990 affirmed that an intergovernmental conference on constitutional reform and political union should also take place alongside that on economic and monetary union. This negotiation reached its conclusion in agreement on the Treaty of Maastricht in November 1991, incorporating the provisions on citizenship of the Union introduced already in previous chapters of this book.

VI The negotiations leading to the Treaty on European Union

Most explorations of how European citizenship emerged as a topic at the 1990–1 intergovernmental conference on political union refer to the Spanish memorandum, 'The Road to European Citizenship', of September 1990, which followed an earlier letter by the Spanish Prime Minister Felipe Gonzalez addressed to the European Council (O'Leary, 1996: 23–30; Wiener, 1998: Ch. 11). Until this point, European citizenship had been constructed in the context of an inter-institutional discourse about the assumed progress towards 'Europe', as can be demonstrated in a narrower sense by the debates about electoral rights charted in the previous sections. 'The Road to European Citizenship' was keenly supranational and it consequently exposed the conflict that would inevitably arise between the intergovernmental and the supranational perspectives. Its intention and its effect was to re-situate the citizen at the heart of the European process. The document pointed out that the Community had had little effect on the daily life of citizens and that, although there had been initiatives to heighten the profile of the Community citizen, 'the practical context has not made it possible to

[65] Bull. EC Supp. 2/88, at 29.

advance resolutely along the road to making the whole body of Community citizens the fundamental point of reference for Community successes and achievements'.[66] The importance that the document accorded to citizenship is illustrated by the fact that citizenship was defined as one of the three pillars of European political union. Citizenship was defined in the Spanish memorandum as:

> The personal and indivisible status of nationals of the Member States, whose membership of the Union means that they have special rights and duties that are specific to the nature of the Union and are exercised and safeguarded specifically within its boundaries, without dismissing the possibility that such a status of European citizen may also extend beyond those boundaries. Acquisition and loss of the citizenship would be coincidental with citizenship of one of the Member States.

With regard to the right to political participation in the place of residence, the memorandum said that political participation would begin with the freedoms of expression, association and assembly and would be gradually extended to participation in electoral processes; participation in European elections would occur in two stages – the adoption of a uniform electoral procedure followed by the recognition of the right to vote at the place of residence.

Even before the two intergovernmental conferences formally opened in December 1990 at the European Council meeting in Rome, the minutes of the General Affairs Council of 4 December 1990 were able to record, in relation to what might be expected to appear in the new Treaty, that 'the great majority of delegations agree that [the concept of European citizenship] should form part of the new Treaty'.[67] This was on the basis of preparatory work undertaken in a group comprising the personal representatives of the Ministers of Foreign Affairs and of the Commission President during the course of the latter part of 1990. The notion that was being worked on was dubbed 'Citizenship of the Union' in Council Secretariat documents of late 1990, long before the specific texts of what was to become the Treaty of Maastricht or Treaty on European Union had been drawn up.[68] The Commission's October 1990 Opinion on the

---

[66] 'Towards a European Citizenship', *Europe Documents*, No. 1653, 2 October 1990. Reprinted in Laursen and Vanhoonacker, 1992: 328.

[67] Council Document 10545/90, Draft Minutes of the General Affairs Council held on 4 December 1990, 6 February 1991.

[68] Council Document 10356/90, Add.2, 30 November 1990, Annex 3 dated 19 November 1990.

convening of the intergovernmental conference, a formal requirement under the Treaty for amendment processes to occur, also approved the inclusion of provisions on European citizenship, including voting rights in local elections and European elections.[69] In February 1991, the Spanish Government proposed a specific Title of the new Treaty to be dedicated to citizenship. The Preamble to the proposed Title (drafted in grand style) claimed that the Community was:

> Resolved to lay the foundation for an integrated area serving the citizen, which will be the very source of democratic legitimacy and a fundamental pillar of the Union, through the progressive constitution of a common citizenship, the rights and obligations of which derive from the Union.[70]

The novelty of such a proposal lies in its explicit invocation of a link between citizens and the Union, and in its statement that rights and obligations derive 'from the Union'. In fact, as the final version of the citizenship provisions (which did not include this clause) makes clear, Union citizenship is derived from national citizenship, since the criterion of membership is nationality of a Member State. In addition, as the European Community and the European Union have remained entities grounded in international law on a voluntary sharing of sovereignty between the Member States on the basis of treaties, it remains tricky to develop an interpretation of a concept such as Union citizenship which derives its formal legitimacy from the Union rather than the Member States.[71]

The first full formal draft of the citizenship provisions appeared very much in the form that they were finally adopted in late 1991. On 18 June 1991, the Luxembourg Presidency produced its Draft Treaty on the Union, in time for it to be discussed at the European Council meeting concluding the Luxembourg Presidency.[72] It contained, in a proposed new Part Two of the EC Treaty, a set of draft Articles A–F, the same six

---

[69] Bull. EC Supp. 2/91.

[70] CONF-UP 1731/91, 20 February 1991; reprinted in Laursen and Vanhoonacker, 1992: 325.

[71] A similar controversy arose over a draft of Article 1 of the Treaty establishing a Constitution for Europe drawn up by the Praesidium to the Convention on the Future of Europe which stated that 'this Constitution establishes the Union' (CONV 528/03, 16 February 2003 (Articles 1–16 of the draft Treaty establishing a Constitution for Europe)). The clear derivation from the international law nature of the Union is that the Member States *establish* *the Union* and that the powers of the Union *flow from* the Member States, so that the Constitutional Treaty has only a derived and not an original status.

[72] *Europe Documents*, No. 1722/1723, 5 July 1991; reprinted in Laursen and Vanhoonacker, 1992: 358.

provisions as are now to be found in the EC Treaty. There were no amendments of substance after that time by the Member States. Article C contained essentially the same two clauses on local and European Parliamentary electoral rights as exist today. Thus, whatever controversy attended the issue of including a concept of citizenship in the Treaty on European Union during the course of the pre-IGC preparatory period or the early negotiations chaired by Luxembourg, this had been resolved into a consensus on a rather minimalist set of provisions by the end of the Luxembourg Presidency. As a result of that, the Dutch Presidency was able to concentrate on other aspects of political union which caused controversy, such as the reference in the very first provision of the Treaty to the Union's federal vocation. This reference did not survive the Dutch Presidency, as it was vetoed categorically by the United Kingdom.

The various drafts proved rather unsatisfactory to the Parliament which was adamant that the Union should provide a constitutional guarantee of the fundamental rights that were additional to those contingent upon membership of a Member State.[73] The proposal to create an independent basis for fundamental rights for the Union, shared with the Commission, was not adopted at that time.[74] Notwithstanding the Parliament's agitation, the Maastricht intergovernmental conference did take a more or less intergovernmental approach to Union citizenship and consequently the Parliament claimed that the new treaty contained major shortcomings and 'fails to develop the concept of citizenship and protection for fundamental rights and freedoms'.[75]

---

[73] 'Citizens and others must be given a framework of equality and solidarity. Unless it is seriously distorted, this concept can no longer tolerate a legal and political framework which denies the full enjoyment of fundamental freedoms. In essence it is no longer possible today to dissociate the concepts of citizenship and democratic freedom': EP Interim Report of the Committee on Institutional Affairs on Union Citizenship, Bindi I, A3-139/91, at 6; see also EP Report of the Committee on Institutional Affairs on Union Citizenship, Bindi II, A3-300/91.

[74] Only from 1999 onwards did the EU return to the topic of a Charter of Fundamental Rights, when the first so-called Convention was established by the European Council after its meeting in Cologne in June 1999, to work on the elaboration of a Charter of Fundamental Rights for the Union. This was elaborated during the course of 2000, accepted in declaratory form at the European Council meeting in Nice in December 2000 which approved the Treaty of Nice, but later incorporated into the Treaty establishing a Constitution for Europe which was agreed by the subsequent Convention on the Future of Europe and the IGC of 2003–4.

[75] Report of the Committee on Institutional Affairs on the results of the intergovernmental conferences, EP Doc. A3-123/92, 26 March 1992, at 4.

It is worth noting that, as an alternative to the approach taken to local electoral rights via the institutionalisation of citizenship, the Member States were offered a clause which would have introduced local electoral voting rights via an amendment to the provisions on the free movement of workers. This proposal, put forward by the Danish delegation to the intergovernmental conference, would have matched the personal scope of these provisions by covering citizens of the Member States who were migrant workers as *primary* beneficiaries, and members of their families – including third country nationals – as *secondary* beneficiaries with derived rights:

> Citizens in the Member States and members of their families who are legally resident in one of the Member States of the European Community shall have the right to vote and be eligible for election to local Councils in their State of residence provided they have been resident in that State for three years prior to the election.[76]

To the extent that third country nationals who were members of the families of migrant EU citizens would have been included, it would have been notably broader than the eventual provision adopted. Such a proposition anticipates the extended discussion about the personal scope of EU citizenship and its exclusion of all third country nationals which appears in Chapter 7.

The text approved in November 1991 at the Maastricht intergovernmental conference, and incorporated into a Treaty which was signed in February 1992 and finally entered into force in November 1993 after national ratification, contained a clause conferring local and European Parliamentary electoral rights on citizens of the Union in the following terms:

> 1. Every citizen of the Union residing in a Member State of which he is not a national shall have the right to vote and to stand as a candidate at municipal elections in the Member State in which he resides, under the same conditions as nationals of that State. This right shall be exercised subject to detailed arrangements adopted by the Council, acting unanimously on a proposal from the Commission and after consulting

---

[76] Conference of the Representatives of the Governments of the Member States, Political Union, CONF-UP 1777/91, 21 February 1991, copy of a letter from Ambassador Riberhold, Danish Delegation to the IGC on Political Union to Mr Ersbøll, Secretary General of the European Council of Ministers.

the European Parliament; these arrangements may provide for derogations where warranted by problems specific to a Member State.

2. Without prejudice to Article 190(4) and to the provisions adopted for its implementation,[77] every citizen of the Union residing in a Member State of which he is not a national shall have the right to vote and to stand as a candidate in elections to the European Parliament in the Member State in which he resides, under the same conditions as nationals of that State. This right shall be exercised subject to detailed arrangements adopted by the Council, acting unanimously on a proposal from the Commission and after consulting the European Parliament; these arrangements may provide for derogations where warranted by problems specific to a Member State.

This clause can now be found in Article 19 EC.[78] It is one of six provisions on the topic of citizenship, Article 17 establishing the basic principle, Article 18 dealing with the question of free movement, Article 20 addressing diplomatic and consular protection, Article 21 covering the right to petition the European Parliament and the right to apply to the Ombudsman, and Article 22 expressing the developmental capacity of the citizenship provisions. Article 22 requires the Commission to report every three years to the other institutions on the application of the citizenship provisions, taking into account the development of the Union. The second paragraph of Article 22 contains an important shortcut to other Treaty amendment processes, since the Council may unanimously adopt, on a proposal from the Commission and after consulting the European Parliament, measures to strengthen or add to the rights laid down in Part Two. Thus the full convening of an intergovernmental conference effectively to amend the citizenship provisions is not required. However, such a measure would have to be ratified by the Member States in accordance with their respective national constitutional requirements, like any other amending treaty, before it could enter into force. It also reinforces that effective development of citizenship in the EU context does not fall within the ordinary legislative process of the Union.

---

[77] This refers to the establishment of a uniform electoral procedure for the European Parliament.

[78] Article 19 EC is the numbering used since the renumbering of the EC Treaty brought about by the Treaty of Amsterdam from 1999 onwards. Previously, it was Article 8b EC. Under the Constitutional Treaty, if ratified, the text of Article 19 EC will be carried forward essentially unchanged as Articles I-10(2)(b) (basic principle) and III-126 of the Constitutional Treaty (implementation rules) if the Constitutional Treaty is ratified.

VII Conclusions

Detailed discussion and interpretation of the Maastricht electoral rights clauses and their subsequent implementation is reserved to the following chapter. However, a brief conclusion is appropriate here in relation to the question as to whether, with the inclusion of citizenship of the Union in the EC Treaty from Maastricht onwards, it could be said that citizenship was now 'achieved' for the Union. Can one view the provisions adopted as the final and successful culmination of the debate on 'special rights' for nationals of the Member States dating back to the early 1970s? What of the process of institutional democratisation which preoccupied members of the European Parliament from the 1960s onwards: what contribution has the institution of citizenship made to this, in the absence of other necessary elements of the process of democratisation, including the uniform electoral procedure and the full inclusion of the Parliament in the legislative process without exceptions and reservations, which was achieved neither by the Treaty of Maastricht, nor by subsequent amending treaties?

At one level, the Maastricht provisions can be judged a success in the sense that they marked a move away from an unhappy phase of rhetorical posturing which began in the 1970s, with the Member States declaring grand ideals such as the completion of European Union within less than ten years, but then matching this with almost no concrete action. If, however, one clause is to be judged a definite triumph for the incremental approach in which the informal resources of citizenship have gradually coalesced into a formal framework for special rights, it is the electoral rights clause. Electoral rights were given a firm constitutional basis in the EC Treaty in 1993, with the unanimous agreement of the Member States – an expression of collective will on a question of political and constitutional significance both for the EU itself and also for the Member States. This outcome contrasts with the signal failure of those same states just a few years before either to proceed with the Commission's proposal on local electoral rights or to follow up the suggestions of the European Parliament on European Parliamentary electoral rights on the basis of the uniform electoral procedure.[79] This is an area where clear new supranational competences to adopt the necessary implementing legislation were adopted in the

---

[79] The question of the uniform electoral procedure remained, of course, outstanding in 1993, and developments in that area will be discussed further in Chapter 5.

Treaty of Maastricht, overcoming previous barriers to progress which had been erected based on an ostensible desire only to proceed in this area on the basis of intergovernmental agreements. Equally, there is no particular evidence that this was an initiative driven by specific national factors such as the existence of a trend at the national level. At the time when the measures were instituted in the EU Treaties, only Denmark, the Netherlands and Ireland had local electoral rights for all third country nationals, and there is no particular evidence – aside from the Danish delegation's clause discussed in the previous section – that their specific considerations either drove or constrained the institution of electoral rights for a limited range of *privileged* foreigners. In fact, as we shall see in Chapter 8, at the time of the Treaty of Maastricht, the local electoral rights for non-nationals applicable in Ireland had exceptionally low political salience.

On the other hand, if citizenship is viewed as an important figure on the EU constitutional landscape, the retention of the right to define entry and exit from European citizenship in the hands of the several Member States is clearly a significant rebuff to the notion of an independent supranational 'European' citizenship. Writing soon after the entry into force of the Treaty of Maastricht, Síofra O'Leary (1996: 308) concluded that: 'Perhaps most importantly of all, the survival of Member State nationality as the basis for the enjoyment of Union citizenship suggests that Member State sovereignty, rather than individual rights are central to the determination of the scope and content of Union citizenship.'

Furthermore, it was certainly too early in 1993 when the Treaty of Maastricht entered into force, and may well still be too early even now to conclude that there is a 'minimum consensus about what Community citizenship does and should entail and thus consensus about the Community's integration project as a whole' (O'Leary, 1996: 303). In any event, the difficulty with applying this as the test of whether citizenship has truly taken root in the Union or not is that it makes citizenship in the European Union context entirely vulnerable to a reversal in a forward logic of European integration, since as a legal and constitutional concept it would then be premised on a sense of shared common goals and values on the part of the Member States and their citizens in relation to the political project of integration.

The very first threat to this thin consensus could be said to have occurred during the course of the Maastricht ratification process, with Danish citizens voting in an initial referendum on the Treaty of

Maastricht in June 1992 to reject its ratification, albeit by quite a narrow margin. Steps were taken within the European Council to mollify Danish public opinion, which had revealed, *inter alia*, some concerns about the inclusion of European citizenship in the EC Treaty. A Decision adopted at a European Council meeting in Edinburgh in December 1992 under the UK Presidency reiterated that citizenship of the Union was intended to be additional to national citizenship and not to take its place.[80] While this measure did not amend the Treaties as such, although it was adopted in a form which intended to express its binding nature for the Member States, it found its reflection in the amendment to the citizenship provisions made by the Treaty of Amsterdam, agreed in 1997. This added a clause to Article 17(1) EC, providing that: 'Citizenship of the Union shall complement and not replace national citizenship.'

However, the reaction to the doubts engendered by the Maastricht ratification experience did not in fact push successive treaty reforms – which in turn often reflected an elite desire for closer political integration – decisively off the agenda. On the contrary, that logic and trajectory of treaty change continued throughout the 1990s with the Treaty of Amsterdam and the Treaty of Nice, and, with renewed vigour, into the 2000s with the post-Nice Laeken Declaration and the Convention on the Future of Europe. The role of these events in framing the subsequent development of citizenship in the European Union is considered at the end of the following chapter. However, in each case, the formal outcome has not been as grand as the rhetoric which has framed the debate, and, under the surface veneer of that often grandiose rhetoric, the process of incremental change has continued. It is to the post-Maastricht period of the incremental development of electoral rights that we now turn.

---

[80] Denmark and the European Union, OJ 1992 C348/1, Section A.

5

EU electoral rights since 1993

I Introduction

This chapter presents the story of EU electoral rights from the date of the coming into force of the Treaty of Maastricht in 1993 onwards. Thus it covers a period in which these electoral rights have become crystallised in EU law and practice in the form of the two EU implementing directives,[1] and in national law and practice. However, the chapter will concentrate on presenting the story from the perspective of EU law and policy. So far as national developments and the process of national adjustment are concerned, these are considered primarily from the perspective of the requirements of EU law, bearing in mind the supremacy of EU law, and the obligation on the Member States under Article 10 EC to 'take all appropriate measures, whether general or particular, to ensure the fulfilment of the obligations arising under this Treaty'. The perspective from within the Member States, especially so far as concerns the relationship between EU electoral rights and other electoral rights under national law, as well as the interdependence between electoral rights and the wider framework of immigration law and policy, nationality law, and policies on minorities, will reappear in those specific national contexts in Chapters 8, 9 and 10. Possible extensions of the scope of EU electoral rights, derived from some of the controversies which they raise within the framework of EU law, are discussed in Chapters 6 and 7.

---

[1] Council Directive 93/109/EC laying down detailed arrangements for the exercise of the right to vote and stand as a candidate in elections to the European Parliament for citizens of the Union residing in a Member State of which they are not nationals, OJ 1993 L329/34; Council Directive 94/80/EC laying down detailed arrangements for the exercise of the right to vote and stand as a candidate in municipal elections by citizens of the Union residing in a Member State of which they are not nationals, OJ 1994 L368/38.

II The impact and significance of EU electoral rights

Tracing the story of EU electoral rights through from 1993 to the present day, this chapter inevitably raises the question of the impact and significance of EU electoral rights, particularly as viewed from the perspective of the evolution of EU citizenship. In its Second Report on Citizenship of the Union in 1997, the Commission commented that:[2]

> Voting rights for non-national Union citizens are indeed the most important of the new rights conferred by the Treaty. But the benefits that may ensue from its application . . . are most likely to be felt only in the long term.

The evidence about how the EU electoral rights are measuring up to this challenge remains so far rather scanty. Initial commentary concentrated on the potential of these rights, both in terms of the more general vocation of citizenship of the Union to foster a closer relationship between the Union and 'its' citizens and thus to offer a potential legitimacy benefit, and in terms of the specific benefits which would be experienced by migrant EU citizens as regards a closer relationship with the host polity in which they would be allowed limited voting rights. Early legal studies of the electoral rights charted the process of legal development in the early and mid-1990s, before the rights started to have a practical impact (Oliver, 1996; O'Leary, 1996). Since that time, there have been very few detailed scholarly studies of the application of the electoral rights, either by lawyers or political scientists, and in large measure those which have been made have been either national or broadly 'European' rather than comparative in character (Besch, 2004; Strudel, 2003, 2004; Bidegaray and Strudel, 2002; Hedrich, 2001; Méndez Lago, 2005; Jacobs, Martiniello and Rea, 2002). Sylvie Strudel, basing her assessment primarily on the room for manoeuvre given to, and eagerly used by, the Member States in the implementation of the details of the electoral rights in local elections, gives a rather negative assessment of the whole project of Article 19, at least from the point of view of ensuring equality between citizens (Strudel, 2003). However, as she notes, it is not only the resistance of the Member States to interferences with their sovereignty which has resulted in Article 19 having a lower impact than might be

---

[2] European Commission, 'Second Report on Citizenship of the Union', COM (1997) 230, 25 July 1997, at 11.

desirable, but also the apparent reluctance of EU citizens themselves to engage with the rights which they have been granted, for example, by registering to vote in their state of residence (Strudel, 2002).

As to official evidence, there have been since 1993 a number of reports from the European Commission on both types of EU electoral rights,[3] as well as more general periodic reports on citizenship which touch upon the issue of electoral rights alongside the other citizenship rights conferred by Part Two of the EC Treaty. Four of these have so far been issued under Article 22 EC which gives the Commission the task of reviewing the citizenship provisions.[4] The reports on electoral rights are partially based upon questionnaires completed by the Member States, which offer some interesting insights into how the electoral rights are perceived by the Member States, but they also provide evidence of how the European Commission has used the process of monitoring compliance with the directives and threatening enforcement actions which can be brought under Article 226 EC to ensure that national legislation *and practice* satisfactorily implement the formal requirements of the directives. However, as we shall see, so far only one Article 226 action has been brought before the Court of Justice; this concerned the implementation of the local elections Directive by Belgium.[5] However, threats of infringement proceedings on the part of the Commission have on several occasions prompted amendments to national legislation, and encouraged compliance during the course of the initial segment of the proceedings, which is administrative rather than judicial in nature.

Another source of primarily legal information has come from the EU Network of Independent Experts on Fundamental Rights, established after the EU institutions solemnly proclaimed the EU's Charter of

---

[3] 'Commission Report on the Application of Directive 93/109/EC to the June 1994 European Parliament Elections', COM(1997) 731; Commission 'Report on the Application of Directive 93/109/EC to the June 1999 Elections to the European Parliament', COM(2000) 843, 18 December 2000; 'Commission Report on the Participation of European Union Citizens in the Member States of Residence (Directive 93/109/EC) and on the Electorate Arrangements (Decision 76/787/EEC, as amended by Decision 2002/772/EC, Euratom)', COM(2006) 790; 'Commission Report on the Application of Directive 94/80/EC on the Right to Vote and Stand as a Candidate in Municipal Elections', COM(2002) 260, 30 May 2002.

[4] Apart from the 1997 report (above n. 2), reports were issued in 1993 (First Report, COM(93) 702, 21 December 1993), in 2001 (Third Report, COM (2001) 506, 7 September 2001) and in 2004 (Fourth Report, COM(2004) 695, 26 October 2004).

[5] Case C-323/97 *Commission* v. *Belgium (Right to Vote and to Stand as a Candidate in Municipal Elections)* [1998] ECR 4281.

Fundamental Rights[6] in December 2000 at the Nice Intergovernmental Conference. The task of the Network is to monitor the fundamental rights situation in the Member States and in the Union, and to draw up reports. Each year, annual reports are written by experts in each of the Member States and published,[7] and an annual report summarising national reports, and a synthesis report containing recommendations, are drawn up and published by the Commission.[8] The national reports 'shadow' the provisions of the Charter of Fundamental Rights with national experts being asked to comment each year on significant developments under each heading.[9] As Articles 39 and 40 of the Charter in turn echo the provisions of Article 19 EC on European Parliamentary and local electoral rights, this effectively invites the experts to review progress on Article 19 each year. However, the results are fairly patchy.

However, what evidence there is, aside from being scanty and of a largely national rather than comparative nature, is also distinctly equivocal about the value-added of EU electoral rights. The rate of participation in elections by those benefiting from the rights (voting and standing) is low in respect of both types of elections covered. There are high levels of ignorance about EU electoral rights on the part of their intended beneficiaries, and even where citizens have knowledge about their rights they often encounter a certain degree of mainly passive resistance on the part of public authorities which tends to impede effective exercise of these rights. The involvement of EU migrants (as voters and as candidates) in the electoral life of the host polities also remains marginal in almost all regions of almost all EU Member States, with little evidence of political parties or other political groups engaging with this relatively small electoral group in order to foster mobilisation or to gain electoral advantage. Even so, the symbolic importance of the Article 19 electoral rights should not be underestimated. This is particularly evident when they are examined in the light of other contested issues regarding citizenship and participation, such as the treatment of third country nationals under EU law and the 'nestedness' of electoral rights debates within the wider frame of reference provided by national debates about immigration, citizenship and nationality.

---

[6] OJ 2000 C364/1.
[7] See the website of the Interdisciplinary Research Cell in Human Rights (CRIDHO) at the Catholic University of Leuven in Belgium, http://cridho.cpdr.ucl.ac.be, where the reports are made available each year.
[8] http://europa.eu.int/comm/justice_home/cfr_cdf/index_en.htm.
[9] See below Section IX.

The perception that the electoral rights are akin to lame ducks – with low levels of participation by those to whom the entitlements are granted in all Member States and low levels of visibility in terms of their impact upon electoral politics – contrasts somewhat with some positive early comments especially from legal commentators. David O'Keeffe predicted that, although it was too early to expect Member States to grant electoral rights in *national* elections to nationals of other Member States, 'as it is, the effects of the change in local elections could be substantial' (O'Keeffe, 1994: 96). But he did not see the Maastricht rights as substantially *new* rights since they already existed in a disparate way prior to their adoption in the Treaty in the laws of at least some of the Member States. Some states already gave local electoral rights to all non-nationals and others had given electoral rights to nationals of other Member States to allow them to participate in European Parliamentary elections. In contrast, Síofra O'Leary (1996: 265) argued that 'Article [19] represents a significant departure from the traditional exclusion or limitation of the rights of non-nationals in the field of political participation'. The early controversy attached to Article 19 was linked in particular to the fact that constitutional amendments were needed in several Member States to ensure implementation of the electoral rights provisions (unlike most of the rest of the 'citizenship package' which did not require specific national constitutional adjustments).[10] O'Leary cautioned that 'the importance of these amendments of national conceptions of sovereignty, what it entails and who can exercise it, should not be underestimated' (O'Leary, 1996: 265).

Hans Ulrich Jessurun d'Oliveira pointed explicitly to the radical power of the new provisions, highlighting the absence of a clear link between *local* electoral rights and *citizenship* at the *Union* level. He suggested:

---

[10] Constitutional amendments to accommodate electoral rights, especially in local elections, were required in France, Germany and Spain, where the issue was also discussed in cases brought before the respective constitutional courts, and in Portugal. For a discussion of the case of Germany, with references to the other states, see Kadelbach, 2003: 21; Oliver, 1996: 476–8; and O'Leary, 1996: 219–33. There has also been subsequent constitutional court discussion of Article 19 in relation to both local elections and European Parliamentary elections in France and in Poland, with both the French *Conseil Constitutionnel* and the Polish Constitutional Tribunal ruling that the Article 19 rights did not contravene the national constitutional provisions in either case: *Conseil Constitutionnel*, 98-400 DC, 20 May 1998; Polish Constitutional Tribunal, judgment of 31 May 2004 K15/04.

that granting rights at local elections [has] more to do with unexpressed
endeavours to dissolve the identities of the Member States, and indeed
their statehood, than with democracy on a European level.

(d'Oliveira, 1994: 139)

His concern focused on the apparent incompatibility of Article 19 with
what is now Article 6(3) of the EU Treaty requiring the Union to 'respect
the national identities of its Member States'. He foresaw:

> the breaking up of those direct links, which until recently existed between
> the definition of the legitimation of the State in terms of the sovereignty
> of the people belonging to that State on the basis of nationality, and the
> exercise of political powers in the State concerned. To my mind, the two
> provisions are mutually exclusive. Insofar as [Article 19(1)] entails revi-
> sions of constitutions of certain Member States . . . one may conclude that
> the Union does not respect the national identity of the Member States;
> assuming that a constitution could qualify as a repository of the national
> identity.

(d'Oliveira, 1994: 139)

This suggests that, by stepping into the territory traditionally associated
with the principle of alien suffrage, the EU was now engaging with a
contentious political issue closely tied to issues of national sovereignty
and identity. This is true even though the EU's engagement was partial
(local and European parliamentary elections only) and modified (not *all*
non-nationals but only EU citizens). Indeed, it could also be said that
the EU electoral rights introduced additional elements of dissonance
into the national legal orders because they required those Member States
which already had local electoral rights for *all* non-nationals
(i.e. Denmark, Finland, Ireland, the Netherlands and Sweden) either
to change the existing rules in order to make sure they complied with the
conditions laid down in the implementing Council Directive 94/80/EC,[11]
or to introduce an element of legal discrimination between third
country nationals and EU citizens which did not exist previously (e.g.
in relation to prior qualifying residence periods where the EU rules
stipulate a specific regime which may differ to that hitherto in place
for non-nationals generally). Potentially, therefore, the electoral rights
could be seen as a threatening Trojan Horse on the territory of national
sovereignty.

---

[11] Above n. 1.

In some quarters, the exclusion of national elections did provoke critical comment. Heather Lardy was particularly harsh in her criticism of the partial nature of the electoral rights. Viewed from the perspective of the theory of citizenship, 'the absence of a right to vote in national elections as an incident of Union citizenship creates imbalances in the distribution of rights between Union citizens which undermines the very idea of citizenship ... [O]ne may question whether a status which carries with it such limited political rights is really a form of citizenship at all' (Lardy, 1996: 613). For Elizabeth Meehan, 'these rights confer a second-class order of citizenship because they do not include the right to vote and to stand for office in general elections throughout the Member States' (Meehan, 1993: 149), and David O'Keeffe tempered his welcome for the local electoral rights by commenting that:

> local voting rights are a pale substitute for participation in national parliamentary elections, in direct presidential elections ... and in referenda. These are the votes which most affect the political life of a Member State, and its participation in the process of European integration.
>
> (O'Keeffe, 1994: 95)

Similar sentiments come from d'Oliveira (1994: 139):

> Exercise of voting rights in national elections would be a much more relevant aspect of European citizenship, given the involvement of (some) national bodies of representation in the framing and implementation of the European legal and political order.

Somewhat more pragmatically, Malcolm Anderson et al. commented that:

> some expected the Treaty to be more ambitious, and proposals from the Spanish and others did call for the right to vote and stand for election in national elections ... The Maastricht ratification process showed, however, that this area is a political minefield, for the fact that the Treaty gave voting rights to 'foreigners' was one of the most potent weapons its opponents could mobilise against it.
>
> (Anderson et al., 1994: 111)

This latter comment highlights the perpetual enigma of the citizenship provisions of the EC Treaty, and of the topic of citizenship in the EU context more generally, namely, the capacity of citizenship discourse simultaneously both to excite and to disappoint. Early commentators almost universally saw EU citizenship as a dynamic concept, 'capable of being added to or strengthened, but not diminished' (O'Keeffe, 1996: 373; O'Keeffe, 1994: 107). Furthermore, as Anderson *et al.* note (1994: 121), 'although the description "federal" was rejected by the IGC, the inclusion of citizenship may ultimately prove to be more radical, and it gives federalists something positive on which they might build in future'. To these commentators, the inclusion of political rights in the Maastricht package is 'encouraging'. At the same time, the rights which were actually introduced – however they were viewed – were clearly very limited, and often contingent. They were also, crucially, dependent upon implementation first by the EU institutions and then subsequently by the national and in some cases regional and local authorities.

III The implementation of Article 19 EC

Both paragraphs of Article 19 EC refer to 'detailed arrangements [to be] adopted by the Council, acting unanimously on a proposal from the Commission and after consulting the European Parliament' in order to implement the electoral rights in relation to municipal/local and European Parliamentary elections respectively. The legislative procedure chosen by the Member States at the Maastricht intergovernmental conference for the measures implementing Article 19 was highly intergovernmental in character. Although the Commission has the right of legislative initiative (which also means that it can withdraw a proposal if it feels that it is in danger of being adopted by the Council in a form which it regards as unsatisfactory), the European Parliament is only to be 'consulted' once during the procedure, has no right of co-decision, and can only propose amendments. Finally, when taking the decision, the Council of Ministers must act unanimously. This gives each individual Member State a veto over implementing legislation.

It is conceivable with such a legislative procedure that, after the entry into force of the Treaty of Maastricht, the Member States could have found themselves unable to agree unanimously upon implementing measures. This would have raised the difficult question as to what the effects of Article 19 EC might have been if it had not been implemented, and whether individuals might have been able to rely upon the rights granted to them under Article 19 especially *vis-à-vis* the national authorities, and whether such rights would have been upheld by national courts and by the Court of Justice. The issue has so far proved hypothetical, although it is conceivable that the effects and scope of Article 19 could still be invoked in a case before national courts, concerning the exercise of rights to vote and stand at the national level under the two implementing directives, and consequently come before the Court of Justice via a reference under Article 234 EC from the national courts (Zuleeg, 2001). However, there have been only a very small number of cases so far at the national level invoking the EU electoral rights, and none of these has given rise to a reference to the Court of Justice.

In any event, the Member States proved themselves capable of swift action, removing any immediate need to speculate upon the effects of Article 19. The chosen form of legal instrument was the directive, an EU measure which requires national implementing measures. Directives are EU instruments which lend themselves to the minimal harmonisation of national laws around agreed basic principles, without necessarily requiring national laws to be identical in every respect.[12] Within a matter of weeks of the Treaty of Maastricht coming into force in November 1993, the Council had adopted Directive 93/109/EC on 6 December 1993, which was necessary to implement Article 19(2) EC on European Parliamentary elections. This allowed only six months for the Member States to get their arrangements in place in advance of the next elections in June 1994, but all twelve were successful in ensuring the formal arrangements were put in place.[13] One year later, in December 1994, the Council adopted Directive 94/80/EC implementing Article 19(1). The Member States were supposed to put in place the necessary implementing laws for local elections by 1 January 1996, although in fact only four of the then twelve Member States fully complied with that deadline.[14] The process of gradually bringing Directive 94/80/EC into practical effect was not completed until March 2001 when the rules were first applied in local elections in France, although Belgium was the last Member State formally to bring its legislation into compliance. This was achieved in 1999, but only after an enforcement action under Article 226 EC had been brought before the Court of Justice by the Commission against Belgium, resulting in a judgment formally declaring Belgium's

---

[12] This follows from the definition of the directive in Article 249 EC as a measure which is binding, as to the result to be achieved, upon the Member States to which it is addressed, but which leaves them the choice of form and methods in relation to implementation.

[13] For details of the relevant laws, see O'Leary, 1996: 218. Obviously, as further states have acceded to the EU, they too have implemented the terms of Directive 93/109/EC in national law, while the 'old' Member States have adjusted their national laws to the arrival of new Member States.

[14] Denmark, Ireland, Luxembourg and the United Kingdom. See Commission Report on Directive 94/80/EC, above n. 3, at 5.

non-compliance.[15] There are some significant differences in relation to implementation issues between Article 19(1) and 19(2) EC and the respective directives, and these questions are dealt with in the following sections.

IV Directive 93/109/EC and electoral rights in European Parliament elections

In October 1993, the Commission presented a proposal for a directive laying down detailed arrangements for the exercise of the rights to vote and to stand in elections to the European Parliament.[16] Amongst the controversial aspects of the proposal was the inclusion of a residence qualification allowing the Member States to prevent EU nationals from voting until they had been resident for five years in that state. After objections by the European Parliament,[17] this was replaced by an equivalence provision in Article 5, according to which residence in another Member State counts towards any minimum period of residence in the electoral territory of the host state imposed on nationals. However, Member States are still allowed to impose minimum residence periods in respect of residence in a particular constituency or locality.

The Parliament also objected to the inclusion of derogations making special arrangements for particular states, such as those allowing Member States with large proportions of non-national EU citizens amongst their voting-age population to impose minimum residence periods for EU citizens wishing to vote or stand as a candidate. Despite its objections, such a derogation was included in the Directive for the benefit of a Member State 'where the proportion of citizens of the Union of voting age who reside in it but are not nationals of it exceeds 20% of the total number of citizens of the Union residing there who are of voting age' (Article 14(1)). In practice, that clause can only be used by Luxembourg, and that state has indeed acted to restrict the right to vote to non-national citizens of the Union who have resided in its territory for five of the last six years, and the right to stand as a candidate to non-national citizens of the Union who have their legal domicile in Luxembourg and who have resided there for ten of the last twelve years. In 2003, when the Commission reported on the operation of the

---

[15] *Commission* v. *Belgium*, above n. 5.
[16] COM(93) 534, 27 October 1993, OJ 1993 C329.
[17] Froment-Meurice Report, EP Doc. A3-357/97, 15 November 1993.

Luxembourg derogation to the other institutions, it noted that the number of non-national citizens of the Union of voting age residing in Luxembourg represented 32.93% of the total number of citizens of the Union of voting age resident in Luxembourg, at the time of the 2001 population census.[18] There is a risk that such a rule may deprive EU citizens of their right to vote completely if they lose their vote in their 'home' state under tight expatriate voting rules before acquiring it in Luxembourg through lengthy residence under the qualifying provisions. Article 1(2) specifically excludes any effect of the Directive upon national provisions affecting the right to vote or to stand as a candidate on the part of nationals who reside outside its electoral territory.

For the most part, however, the negotiation of Directive 93/109/EC did not engender great controversy between the Member States, or amongst the various institutions involved in the legislative process. This was important given the short timescale for its adoption caused by the imminence of European Parliament elections in June 1994.

The Directive is structured around the concept of the 'Community voter', that is, the national of one Member State (thus a person enjoying citizenship of the Union) who is resident in another Member State and who has the right to vote in European Parliament elections by virtue of the Directive. The Directive is based on a number of key principles which allow considerable scope for national variation in implementing measures. Community voters have freedom of choice between voting in the host state or in the home state (where available), but may only vote in one state (Article 4(1)). They may also only stand as a candidate in one state (although this may be a different state to the one where they vote) (Article 4(2)). To protect that freedom of choice, Community voters are not entered automatically on the electoral register in the first instance (e.g. simply by virtue of their residence in a particular locality), and the first entry on the electoral register in the Member State of residence can occur by application only. However, after first registration, Community voters must not be removed from the electoral roll until such time as they request to be removed, or they are removed automatically because they no longer satisfy the conditions applicable under the Directive. The basic principle of non-discrimination between Community voters and the nationals of the host Member State is applied, as required by Article 19(2) EC itself. Member States are not allowed to apply any rules on compulsory voting until an individual

---

[18] COM(2003) 31, 27 January 2003.

Community voter has expressed the wish to vote in that state (Article 8(2)). However, the non-discrimination principle cannot be used to avoid the application of national rules in the home state so that, for example, rules on the removal of the right to vote or the disqualification of candidates are given extraterritorial effect (Article 6(1)). Where a Community voter seeks to stand as a candidate for the European Parliament elections in the state of residence, he or she must provide an attestation demonstrating that he or she has not been disqualified from standing as a candidate (Article 6(2)). The Member State of residence may furthermore check with the home state whether Community voters seeking to exercise their rights to vote have been disqualified from voting (Article 7(1)). In practice, the requirements in Article 7 on the exchange of information between Member States about voters and candidates has necessitated the construction of quite a complex bureaucratic system for information exchange, which could endanger in practice the right to vote.

V The application of Directive 93/109/EC

Directive 93/109/EC has already been applied three times, in 1994, 1999 and 2004, on a cross-EU basis (as well as in separate elections held in Austria, Finland and Sweden after the fourth enlargement in 1996). Special arrangements were made to ensure the effective application of Article 19(2) EC in the June 2004 elections which took place just over one month after the accession of ten new Member States on 1 May 2004. The Commission has now reported three times, on the 1994, 1999 and 2004 elections.[19]

From the very beginning, the Parliament was concerned that EU citizens would not be aware of their new rights and that the Member States would not take proper action to increase their awareness. Article 12 of the Directive states that Member States 'shall inform Community voters and Community nationals entitled to stand as candidates in good time and in an appropriate manner of the conditions and detailed arrangements for the exercise of the right to vote and stand as a candidate'. A resolution on the June 1994 elections drew to the attention of the Commission and the Member States the need for an awareness and information campaign on European elections and expressed concern,

> at the confusion that may arise from: (a) the lack of a clear understanding
> between the countries of origin and the countries of residence with regard

---

[19] See COM(1997) 731, COM(2000) 843 and COM(2006) 790, above n. 3.

to dual entry on the electoral role, (b) lack of knowledge of the new electoral systems.[20]

This resolution was followed, two months later, by a second resolution on the European elections which said that the Parliament was,

> disturbed that in some Member States citizens of other EU countries entitled to vote, unlike the Member State's own nationals, must themselves take steps to ascertain the election date, [and] ... convinced that it is unacceptable, and clearly contravenes the preamble to Council Directive 93/109/EC ... that many citizens have to apply in person – sometimes twice – to the relevant office in order to register as voters.[21]

The Parliament's fears about ignorance of and access to the new rights seem to have been confirmed by the turnout to the 1994 elections. Although it is possible to know only who registered to vote and not who actually voted, because of the low rate of registration it is generally agreed that these elections saw a small percentage of eligible voters taking advantage of their right to vote, and just one non-national candidate (out of fifty-three who stood) was successfully elected in her Member State of residence.[22] Conversely, it is also generally assumed that most of those who bothered to register, given the effort this sometimes involved, did in fact vote. Lack of information was attributed as a significant reason for this and the Commission's Second Report on Citizenship declared that an improvement in the participation of Union citizens in European elections required effort on the part of the institutions and the Member States to improve the information available to citizens.[23] Moreover, varying levels of participation between the Member States provided a strong indication that some of the Member States were being much more receptive than others about the whole question of facilitating the participation of Community voters, and this led to a feeling in 1999 in the Commission that 'much of the problem lay at the feet of the Member States'.[24]

---

[20] Resolution on voting rights for citizens of the Union in the European elections, OJ 1994 C44/159, 20 January 1994.

[21] Resolution on obstacles to, and discrimination against, EU citizens participating in the European elections, OJ 1994 C128/317, 21 April 1994.

[22] Wilmya Zimmermann, a Dutch national who was elected for the SPD (social democrats) in Germany; see COM(1997) 731, above n. 3, at 14.

[23] Above n. 2, at 2.

[24] Interview with an official from Directorate General of Justice and Home Affairs, Brussels, November 1999.

When the Commission reported again in 2000 on the 1999 elections, it did so against a background of falling turnouts generally across the Member States in European Parliament elections.[25] Again, the proportion of Union citizens entered on the electoral roll of their Member State of residence was generally low although it had improved from the previous election. Whilst turnout for the 1999 elections fluctuated considerably between the Member States, in all of the Member States the number of non-nationals registering to vote was consistently lower than the corresponding number for nationals. A European Parliament report expressed concern at the low registration and falling turnout figures, particularly since it felt that this phenomenon could delegitimise the process whereby its members were elected especially in the context of a significant increase in Parliamentary powers.[26] The Commission's figures are backed up by research undertaken under the aegis of a European Commission Framework Five funded project entitled 'Pioneers of European Integration "From Below"', which examines mobility and the emergence of European identity by looking specifically at those who move within the EU and those who do not. The research results noted a lower level of participation in European elections by mobile Union citizens than by those who do not exercise their right to mobility.[27]

Some Member States (Denmark, Finland, the Netherlands, Spain, Sweden, Ireland and the UK) send letters about electoral rights directly to potential electors whenever they have contact with the local or national authorities, making forms available in various languages. Others have limited their information campaigns to ministerial press conferences, notices in newspapers, provision of information leaflets in public libraries and similar locations, provision of information to consulates and embassies, and radio and TV advertising.[28] Greece has had

---

[25] Turnout has fallen steadily since the first direct elections in 1979, although there were some upward trends in the old 'EU15' in the 2004 elections: http://www.elections2004.eu.int/ep-election/sites/en/results1306/turnout_ep/turnout_table.html. The most widely adhered-to thesis about turnout in European Parliament elections concerns their so-called 'second order' nature, namely, that in comparison to national elections they do not truly decide who is in power: Schmitt, 2005.

[26] European Parliament Report on the Third Commission Report on Citizenship of the Union, Committee of Citizens' Freedoms and Rights, Coelho, A5-0241/2002, 20 June 2002.

[27] See Executive Summary of PIONEUR, available at http://www.obets.ua.es/pioneur/difusion/PioneurExecutiveSummary.pdf, at 7–8.

[28] See the summary for the 1994 European Parliament elections in O'Leary, 1996: 217; and COM(2000) 843, above n. 3, at 15–17.

the weakest information campaign, consisting only of media and advertising leaflets, and a registration rate in 1999 of 1.8 per cent. As the Commission commented in its 2000 report, there is a difference between knowing about the rights themselves and knowing about the procedures for exercising those rights.[29] The Parliament has also expressed unhappiness with the absence of specific deadlines in the Directive regarding the submission of applications to be entered on the electoral register, since some of the Member States apply what are, in its view, unreasonably early deadlines. In Greece, France and Luxembourg, registration for the European elections meant submitting an application between six and fifteen months in advance, and in Italy the process for registration has been criticised for being highly complex:

> First you have to go to the police for a resident's card ('*carta di soggiorno*'), then to the city council to become a resident and then back to the city electoral office twice to put your name on the two supplementary electoral rolls (one for the local elections and the other for the European Parliament).[30]

With regard to improving voter registration, a motion for a Parliamentary resolution on e-democracy and e-European citizenship encouraged the Member States to promote electronic voting and to put in place e-voting for the 2004 European elections,[31] but this has yet to happen anywhere in the EU for European Parliament elections.

In the 1999 elections, sixty-two non-national candidates stood for election in their Member State of residence and four were elected. This represented an improvement from 1994 but illustrates the problems that parties have faced in putting forward non-nationals on their party lists. The Federation of Greens heralded the highest-profile successes with Daniel Cohn-Bendit (a German national elected in France)[32] and

---

[29] COM(2000) 843, above n. 3, at 8.

[30] Dr James Watson, Chair of the British Labour Party in Rome, private correspondence, August 2000.

[31] Motion for an EP resolution on e-democracy and e-European citizenship, tabled by Marco Cappato and others pursuant to rule 48 of the Rules of Procedure, B5-0115/2002, incorporated in A5-2002/241.

[32] Cohn-Bendit is a unique and high-profile individual, not least because of the ban on his residence in France imposed by the government because of his activities in student protests in 1968, although he had been born in France to German parents, and, although stateless at birth, was entitled to French and German citizenship at the age of eighteen. It was revoked in 1978. He has been a German MEP from 1994 to 1999, a French MEP from 1999 to 2004, and a German MEP once again from 2004 onwards.

Monica Frassoni (an Italian national elected in Belgium). The Parliament's Resolution on the Second Commission Report on Citizenship of the Union called on political parties to accept more Union citizens who were not nationals of the country concerned as party members and candidates on electoral lists, and to encourage them to take part in the political life of their country of residence.[33] Subsequently, the Parliament's proposed introduction of transnational lists for the 2009 European elections has been seen as one way of providing the necessary stimulus for legitimising the adoption of non-nationals.[34] This would enable 10 per cent of seats to be elected via a transnational list through transnational political parties (Day and Shaw, 2006).

In 2000, the Commission reported that the Directive had been 'satisfactorily transposed' in all Member States, some of which have made minor amendments to their legislation at the Commission's request.[35] Difficulties arose in relation to Germany, which traditionally destroys its electoral register after each election. However, when drawing up the new register for the next election, use is made of the population register for nationals, but not for non-nationals who had to repeat their request for registration. This is contrary to Article 9(4) of the Directive, since re-registration should be automatic after the first request. The incorrect transposition by Germany had 'significant repercussions' for the participation of EU citizens in the 1999 European Parliament elections, where the proportion of EU citizens registered to vote declined from 6.7 per cent in 1994 to 2.1 per cent in 1999.[36]

Before the 2004 enlargement, the Commission became concerned about the tight timescale between the accession of the new Member States on 1 May 2004 and the European Parliament elections of June 2004. This necessitated extensive prior planning on the part of both the existing 'old' Member States and the accession states, including what amounted to the provisional bringing into force of EU law in advance of accession, and the making of the necessary practical arrangements to

---

[33] EP Resolution on the Second Commission Report on Citizenship of the Union, OJ 1998 C226/61. The 2004 elections saw a drop in the number of candidates to fifty-seven, with only three elected (COM(2006) 790, at 7–8).

[34] See Recommendation on the draft Council decision amending the Act concerning the election of representatives of the European Parliament by direct universal suffrage, annexed to Council Decision 76/787/ECSC, EEC, Euratom of 20 September 1976. Committee on Constitutional Affairs, A5-212/2002.

[35] COM(2000) 843, above n. 3, at 4–5.   [36] *Ibid.*, 5.

Table 5.1 *Selected figures from the 1994 and 1999 European Parliamentary elections*

Member State	Electoral turnout (%)		Number of eligible EU nationals		Number of registered EU nationals		Percentage of registered electors who were subsequently believed to have voted	
	1994	1999	1994	1999	1994	1999	1994	1999
Austria	67.73	49.4	91,385	97,359	7,261	14,659	7.94	15.06
Belgium[a]	90.7	90.8	471,277	496,056	24,000	38,236	5.1	7.71
Germany	60	45.19	1,200,000	1,573,316	80,000	33,643	6.6	2.14
Denmark	52.9	50.5	27,042	46,400	6,719	12,356	24.85	26.6
Spain	59.1	64.38	192,074	290,085	24,227	64,904	12.61	22.37
Finland	60.3	30.14	11,296	13,898	2,515	3,911	22	28.14
France[a]	52.7	46.76	1,427,315	1,427,315	47,508	70,056	3.38	4.91
UK	36.4	24	400,000	400,000	7,845	92,378	1.96	23.1
Greece[a]	71.2	75.30	40,000	40,000	622	736	1.55	1.84
Ireland[a]	44	50.21	13,600	67,900	6,000	29,804	44.11	43.89
Italy	73.7	70.81	152,139	109,800	2,809	10,136	1.8	9.23
Luxembourg[a]	88.5	88.5	105,000	111,500	6,907	9,811	6.58	8.8
Netherlands	36	29.89	160,000	167,332	–	28,284	–	16.90
Portugal[a]	35.5	40.03	30,519	30,519	715	4,149	2.34	13.59
Sweden	41.64	38.8	150,000	148,470	36,191	40,433	24	27.2

Source: Information from Commission official, November 1999. See also COM(2000) 843.

[a] Belgium, Greece and Luxembourg have compulsory voting; in France and Portugal, no new information for the number of potential voters in 1999; the figures for Ireland do not include British citizens.

allow voter registration so that in practice voters could vote.[37] The figures on the impact of enlargement on electoral rights which were supplied by the Commission (see Table 5.2), indicated that enlargement of the European Union would increase the number of Community voters entitled to vote in European Parliament elections and local elections on the basis of residence from approximately 5.5 million to around 6.5 million. However, these figures were compiled before enlargement and do not take into account population movements which have occurred since, whether to or from the new Member States. The new Community voters comprised citizens of the accession states resident in the 'old' Member States and citizens of the other accession states and the 'old' Member States resident in the accession states. Emphasising its general view about information campaigns, the Commission reinforced this message by stating that:

> The Commission considers that States must *specifically* inform new Community voters of the detailed arrangements and conditions for exercising their electoral rights. This means that a State cannot fulfil its obligation under Article 12 merely by providing the information it normally provides for its own nationals. The information must be tailored to meet the specific information requirements of Community voters. The Commission encourages all member states and acceding States which have not yet done so to use a system of direct personal letters mailed to Community electors residing on their territory. States can also provide them with appropriate information whenever they have contact with local or national authorities. As far as possible, States should enable citizens to enter their names on the electoral roll simply by filling in a form and returning it by post.[38]

In a press release issued in early 2004, the Commission maintained a relentlessly upbeat tone, declaring that 'participation of a further one million EU citizens living outside their home country [was] successfully guaranteed'.[39]

The Commission's report on the 2004 elections was published in December 2006, and it observed that 11.9 per cent of potential Community voters registered to vote in their Member State of residence, so it was too early to make a judgment on how this claim translated into

---

[37] COM(2003) 174, 8 April 2003, Commission Communication on measures to be taken by Member States to ensure participation of all citizens of the Union to the 2004 elections to the European Parliament in an enlarged Union.

[38] COM(2003) 174, at 5 (emphasis in the original).   [39] IP/04/126, 29 January 2004.

Table 5.2 *Non-national citizens of the Union residing in the Member States*

Country	Nationals	Non-national citizens of EU15	Non-national citizens of new Member States	Community voters in total
Germany	61,432,000	1,621,000	418,000	2,039,000
France	41,970,000	1,004,000	53,000	1,057,000
UK	42,870,000	790,000	62,500	852,500
Spain	34,350,000	611,500	38,500	650,500
Belgium	7,576,000	516,500	12,000	528,500
Austria	5,796,000	95,000	150,000	245,000
Netherlands	11,612,000	194,000	9,000	203,000
Italy	46,552,000	150,000	35,500	185,500
Sweden	6,566,000	147,000	23,000	170,000
Ireland	2,659,000	140,000	1,000	141,000
Luxembourg	219,000	107,000	8,000	115,000
Portugal	7,751,000	52,000	500	52,500
Denmark	4,064,000	32,000	8,000	40,000
Finland	3,960,000	17,000	13,000	30,000
Greece	8,244,000	16,000	7,500	23,500
Sub-total	**285,621,000**	**5,493,000**	**839,500**	**6,333,000**
Czech Republic	8,228,000	17,000	63,000	80,000
Estonia	868,000	(2,500)	(2,500)	5,000
Cyprus	576,000	13,000	2,000	15,000
Latvia	1,300,000	(1,500)	(2,000)	3,500
Lithuania	2,600,000	500	500	1,000
Malta	312,000	6,500	(Not known – 0)	6,500
Hungary	8,070,000	11,500	5,000	16,500
Poland	29,865,000	12,500	2,500	15,000
Slovenia	1,588,000	1,000	500	1,500
Slovakia	4,316,000	1,500	2,000	3,500
Grand total	**343,344,000**	**5,560,500**	**919,500**	**6,480,500**

Shaded boxes = new Community voters at 2004 elections, in total 987,800.
Source: Working Paper, EP Elections in 2004, Number of Community Voters under Directive 93/109/EC in the 2004 Elections, JAI.C.3/SAS/2001-1, 23 March 2004, which incidentally reports quite different figures to those presented in an earlier press release by the Commission, 'Towards the First European Parliament "Enlarged Elections": Participation of a Further One Million EU Citizens Living Outside Their Home Country Successfully Guaranteed', IP/04/126, Brussels, 29 January 2004.

Notes for table 5.2 (cont.)
Note: The numbers are relatively rough estimates that serve to give an overall picture of new Community voters. They were based on population statistics of Eurostat, but come from different years, from different collections of population data (e.g. estimations drawn from total population/active population etc.), and information supplied from the population registers of some of the Member States. They were compiled *before* enlargement actually occurred, and therefore did not take account of any changes caused by enlargement.

concrete participation in the 2004 elections.[40] In the new Member States in particular, overall turnout was exceptionally low, not least because voters in the new Member States were probably experiencing 'Euro-fatigue' after the national accession referendums held during the course of 2003 and 2004, and the accession celebrations coinciding with enlargement in May 2004.[41] It is interesting (but probably not at all coincidental in view of the enlargement of the EU in May 2004 to include the former communist countries of Central and Eastern Europe which had experienced OSCE scrutiny of their elections after 1989) to note that for the first time the Office for Democratic Institutions and Human Rights of the OSCE was invited to observe the European Parliament elections in 2004.[42] On this occasion, the OSCE merely issued a pre-election review which is largely descriptive of the process at the Union level, and it did not follow the process at the national level. Comments were made in the report about the fact that information may not always be readily available to Community voters in their language of choice, and that there are some difficulties in relation to the application of the prohibition on double-voting and the system for information exchange between Member States, bearing in mind the differences in electoral registration schemes across the EU and the lack of a genuinely 'European' solution to this problem. The report also commented upon some 'anomalies' in

---

[40] COM(2006) 790, at 7. A copy of the questionnaire sent by the European Commission to Member States regarding feedback on the June 2004 elections, with a deadline for return of October 2004, was made available on the Europa website: http://europa.eu.int/comm/justice_home/doc_centre/citizenship/political/doc/eu_questionnaire_ep2004_en.pdf.

[41] See details of turnout, above n. 25. For discussion, see Chan, 2004.

[42] Elections to the European Parliament 10–13 June 2004, OSCE/ODIHR Pre-Election Review, Warsaw, 3 June 2004, ODIHR/GAL/40/04, available at www.osce.org/odihr/. The Commission in 2006 proposed amendments to Directive 93/109/EC to abolish the information-exchange system: COM(2006) 791.

relation to the franchise, such as the fact that the UK allows Commonwealth citizens to vote in European Parliament elections, the fact that France extends voting rights to inhabitants of the French overseas territories and three of its seventy-eight seats are elected in these territories, and the fact that in Latvia and Estonia around 20 per cent and 12 per cent of the residents in these states are not permitted to vote because they are not citizens. The specific case of Cyprus, where elections were not organised in the northern part of the island where the government of the Republic of Cyprus does not exercise effective control, was also commented upon. We return to the question of the scope and nature of the European Parliamentary *demos* in the light of the evolution of direct elections and the development of European citizenship in Chapter 6.

VI Directive 94/80/EC and electoral rights in local elections

In relation to the local elections Directive, it proved more difficult to reach agreement amongst the institutions (Commission, Parliament, Council) than it had been in relation to Directive 93/109/EC. Establishing a consensus between the Parliament and the Commission would prove to be particularly problematic. The Parliament repeated a similar objection to residence qualifications which it made in relation to Directive 93/109/EC, rejected recitals in the Commission proposal for a directive which allowed non-national Union citizens to be required to produce pieces of information over and above those required of national voters and placed much weight on automatic entry onto the electoral register.[43] It added a recital stating that Member States must provide that sufficient time be allowed to inform people of their right to stand and vote (and, where applicable, to be entered onto the electoral register) and categorically opposed a derogation which was proposed for Belgium, where there are very large numbers of Community voters in certain municipalities of Brussels. Consequently, the final version of the Directive attracted considerable criticism from the Parliament, as a watered-down

---

[43] Proposal for a Council Directive laying down detailed arrangements for the exercise of the right to vote and to stand as a candidate in municipal elections by citizens of the Union residing in a Member State of which they are not nationals: COM(94) 38, OJ 1994 C105/8. For the European Parliament's reply, see Report of the Committee on Legal Affairs and Citizens' Rights and the opinions of the Committee on Institutional Affairs and the Committee on Regional Policy, A4-11/94 and its Opinion published at OJ 1994 C323/75.

version of what was originally on the agenda for electoral rights,[44] and both the Parliament and the Economic and Social Committee felt that they had been disenfranchised in this sensitive matter by the legislative process adopted for Article 19 EC.[45] But this was necessary because, as Jeffrey Lewis has shown, in relation to agreement amongst the Member States, the local elections Directive proved to be most problematic.

Lewis' presentation of the negotiation of the terms of the local elections Directive was developed as a case study of the work of the Committee of Permanent Representatives (COREPER) as a crucial cog in the EU's decision-making structures (Lewis, 1998). COREPER, which brings together the diplomatic representatives of the Member States to the European Union at ambassador and lesser levels, prepares the work of the Council of Ministers, and in many cases presents fully prepared texts to the ministers for formal agreement (Bostock, 2002). This was indeed the case with the local elections Directive, which went through all of its crucial negotiating phases within this supposedly technocratic body, rather than at the political level of the Council of Ministers.

It is interesting that Lewis' interview data reveals that the key actors in this context – i.e. the Member States – were of the view that the Treaty of Maastricht was decisive in giving the European Community the necessary competence to adopt the local elections Directive. In other words, without Article 19 EC there could have been no progress on the basis of, for example, Article 308 EC. Although the issue had had plenty of political salience when it was a proposal from the Commission in the late 1980s, and not inconsiderable support from some quarters – including, ironically given its later eagerness to seek exemptions and tardiness in complying, from Belgium – Lewis' interviewees at COREPER doubted whether the EC Treaty conferred on the European Community the necessary competence to act in advance of the amendments introduced by the Treaty of Maastricht. This, in a sense, is a political rather than a purely legal decision. For – where they have considered it appropriate – the Member States have previously been willing in policy domains as sensitive as sex equality law, environmental policy and consumer protection

---

[44] European Parliament Resolution on Council Directive 94/80/EC, OJ 1995 C109/40; 'EP/ Citizens' Europe', *Agence Europe*, No. 6345, 27 October 1994, at 9.

[45] Own-initiative opinion of the Economic and Social Committee on the proposal for a Council Directive laying down detailed arrangements for the exercise of the right to vote and to stand as a candidate in municipal elections for citizens of the Union residing in a Member State of which they are not nationals, OJ 1994 C393/186.

to use the residual legal basis of what was then Article 235 EEC (now, post-Amsterdam, Article 308 EC) to adopt legislation by means of a unanimous vote in order to further the Community's objectives when there was no other specific legal basis in the Treaty. The 'lack of competence' argument was more likely to have been a technique for reinforcing that it was simply too early for the then European Community – until citizenship had been constitutionalised by the Treaty of Maastricht – to intrude so deeply into the local electoral sovereignty of the Member States. In particular, only with the 'constitutionalisation' of citizenship, could those Member States which needed national constitutional amendments in order to implement the electoral rights be expected to act.[46] Lewis acknowledges this point by referring to the effects of the 'grand bargain' and package deal of Maastricht.

The Commission's draft Directive was presented to Council in April 1994, but was referred back to COREPER soon thereafter. It only came back to the General Affairs Council in December 1994, where it was effectively rubber stamped by the ministers on the basis of the political compromise reached in COREPER (Lewis, 1998: 493). COREPER was given the file to deal with not because it was a narrow technical issue – the traditional image of what COREPER is there to deal with in the EU institutional system – but precisely because it was too political. Had the debate been politicised, through Council discussions, a decision might never have been reached – and certainly not so quickly as it was. Lewis argues that the socialisation processes of COREPER have created an ideal decision-making environment for this and other challenging dossiers, creating, in the case of the local elections Directive, the frame for cross-national understanding of crucial domestic political difficulties of some Member States, whilst also achieving what might be regarded as a surprisingly high level of 'equal treatment' for resident non-national EU voters. Hence generalised residency requirements were removed from the original Commission draft, but the capacity to reserve leadership roles such as the position of mayor for nationals marked the recognition of internal sensitivities over national sovereignty. The right to vote of *Community* voters must also be regulated through specific measures at national level, so that states such as Denmark were not allowed to deem

---

[46] This can also be discerned from a Council Press release of 1990 cited by Lewis, 1998: 494: when the foreign ministers discussed this dossier in June 1990, they noted 'political, constitutional and legal problems in connection with this proposal which prevent certain Member States from taking up a final position'.

compliance with the Treaty and the Directive simply by applying their existing arrangements for local elections which subjected all non-nationals to a three-year residency requirement. This reinforced the process of distinguishing between second- and third country nationals. Likewise, French attempts to institute a partial quota system for EU representatives in municipalities with over 20 per cent non-national EU citizens in the electorate were received sympathetically, but ultimately the quota system proposed fell victim to political pressure to enact a measure within the spirit of the Maastricht citizenship provisions. Even so, a special derogation was effectively enacted for Luxembourg, so far as it covered the case of whole Member States where the proportion of EU voters on 1 January 1996 was more than 20 per cent of the electorate; such Member States are entitled to restrict the right to vote to those satisfying a qualifying residence period of no more than the term of office of the municipal council, and the right to stand to those satisfying a qualifying residence period of no more than twice the term of office of the municipal council (Article 12(1)). Only Luxembourg falls into this category.[47]

Particular attention was paid in COREPER to the case of Belgium, where it was evident that the application of the Directive could alter delicately balanced linguistic majorities/minorities within municipalities (involving French speakers, Flemish speakers and German speakers). This is recognised by Article 12(2) which allowed Belgium to apply the same derogation as in Article 12(1) to 'a limited number of local government units'. Since its original 'communautaire' enthusiasm for local electoral rights as a nation state 'at the heart of Europe', Belgium has had to face up to a very different political problem in the context of its own very delicately balanced federal arrangements for the various linguistic communities. The essence of the problem concerned representation for the Flemish-speaking community in Brussels, which could be endangered in specific municipalities within 'greater' Brussels if a substantial group of Community voters showed itself more sympathetic to voting in tandem with the French-speaking community. It became evident that it would be impossible for the Belgian government to achieve the necessary constitutional change which required the consent of all communities if it were not given some form of derogation. Lewis maintains that the members of COREPER were able to be sympathetic to and react to the Belgian Ambassador's need for a derogation,

---

[47] On this, and the role of the Commission in policing this derogation, see above n. 18.

based on specific and well-articulated domestic political constraints. These constraints were better understood by the Ambassadors, socialised in the world of COREPER and living in Brussels themselves, than they would have been by the Ministers, who might have been tempted to make political capital out of the difficulties faced by one partner.[48] Unlike some of the other arguments put forward by national delegations, the Belgian argument was seen to be a 'good' argument, one which could be accepted in the national capitals provided it was carefully presented by the Ambassadors to their political superiors. Overall, COREPER operated as a functional decision-making forum in which national arguments for special treatment could be heard, evaluated and either accepted or rejected, without posturing or threats of vetoes, or *quid pro quo* concessions which would have led to a 'race to the bottom' in terms of the content of decisions adopted. This proved to be more important than the impotent rage of the European Parliament, which refused to 'endorse' the terms of the Directive in a *post hoc* resolution, on the grounds that it had specifically not been consulted during the legislative process on the terms of Article 12(2). It concluded that the 'Council's action can scarcely be considered compatible with the founding principles of European integration, in particular the principle of transparency and the objective of closer contact with the citizens'.[49]

Ultimately, the principles upon which Directive 94/80/EC are based are very similar to those that underpin Directive 93/109/EC, including, wherever possible, the preservation of the diversity of national electoral laws, the application of the principle of non-discrimination and equal access to electoral rights, preservation of freedom of choice on the part of the voter (to avoid in particular the imposition of compulsory voting by the host state, rather than the problem of double voting which arose in relation to European Parliament elections), and imposition of an information-giving obligation on the host state to alert resident non-national EU citizens of the possibility of voting. As with the European Parliament elections Directive, residence in another Member State is deemed to satisfy residence qualifications related to residence in the host state, but Member States are entitled to apply the same qualifications as

---

[48] I have corroborated this finding, at least so far as it pertains to this particular Directive, through discussions with the UK Permanent Representative of the time.

[49] European Parliament Resolution on Council Directive 94/80/EC, above n. 44, point 5.

they might apply to nationals, such as requiring a person to have their principal residence in the territory of the basic unit of local government where they wish to vote or stand, or subjecting the right to vote or stand to a minimum period of residence in that territory (Article 4). However, unlike Directive 93/109/EC, the local elections Directive does not use a concept of the 'Community voter' as a shorthand term, but rather defines entitlements under the Directive according to a combination of citizenship of the Union within the meaning of Article 8 EC plus the fact of *not* having the nationality of the Member State of residence, but otherwise satisfying *all* of the conditions to be able to vote in that state apart from nationality (Article 3).

VII The application of Directive 94/80/EC

It was noted above that the Member States were somewhat tardy in implementing Directive 94/80/EC into national law, and that only four of the then twelve Member States managed this task by the due date of 1 January 1996.[50] Inevitably, the implementation exercise was bound to be a complex matter. Even though the Member States determined in an Annex to the Directive what constituted the 'basic unit of local government' for the purposes of application of the Article 19 rights,[51] the proliferation of statements in the minutes from the various national delegations reproduced in the *Official Journal* alongside the Directive about how they understood various terms used in the Directive, plus the inclusion of the two contested derogations in Article 12, offer ample evidence of the sensitivity of the whole issue. In many respects, compliance at national level has been a field of contestation between the Member States and the Commission. At the very least, the high level of variation in arrangements for local government organisation and local government elections at the national level combined with the absence of a provision in the Directive requiring Member States to report comprehensively on implementation have made this a difficult dossier for the

---

[50] Details of the implementing measures for the EU15 of pre-2004 Member States are set out in Annex I to the 2002 Commission Report on the Application of Directive 94/80/ EC, above n. 4.

[51] The basic units of local government in Austria, Finland and Sweden were included in an amending directive: Directive 96/30/EC, OJ 1996 L122/14; for the 2004 enlargement, the adaptation provisions were included in the Act of Accession, Annex II.2.D to the Act of Accession, OJ 2003 L236/334.

Commission to pursue.[52] Furthermore, in terms of ascertaining what the impact of the electoral rights has been, this has proved to be much more difficult than in the case of the European Parliament rights, for a number of reasons. These include the fact that obviously there is no one single Europe-wide event which can be studied and evaluated by way of assessing the impact of the electoral rights. On the contrary, local elections occur at different times, under different electoral rhythms and subject to very different conditions across what are now twenty-seven Member States. There is a variety of clauses under the Directive which Member States *may* make use of, but are not obliged to, thus creating even greater levels of variation, such as the possibility of reserving for their own nationals the offices of 'elected head, deputy or member of the governing college of the executive of a basic local government unit' (Article 5(3)) and the power to designate or elect the delegates from a representative council to a parliamentary assembly (Article 5(4)) (Waldrauch, 2005: 8–9). Not all Member States systematically collect participation data relating to local elections or records of successful non-national candidatures, and few of them seem to make much useful data available to the European Commission when requested. Finally, in a number of states, the interaction of the EU rights with wider alien suffrage rights for all non-nationals makes it difficult for both public officials and scholars to disaggregate the precise nature of the impact of EU electoral rights.

The most obvious case of non-compliance with the local elections Directive was that of Belgium; despite its special derogations, Belgium still failed to implement the Directive, until after it had been the subject of an enforcement action in the Court of Justice brought by the Commission.[53] On 26 June 1997, the Commission decided to bring an action against Belgium, which had so far failed to notify the Commission of the national measures which it was taking to implement the Directive. According to Mario Monti, the then Single Market Commissioner:

> We cannot expect people to take seriously efforts made by the Union to make citizens' concerns a priority if Member States fail to implement

---

[52] For some background regarding the Commission's understandings about the differences and commonalities between the various local government arrangements which it made use of when devising the proposed legislation, see the Explanatory Memorandum to the Commission's Proposal for a Council Directive, COM(94) 38, 23 February 1994, reprinted in Marias, 1994: 205.

[53] Case C-323/97 *Commission* v. *Belgium* [1998] ECR I-4281, above n. 5.

their rights in practice ... In the case of Belgium the Directive incorporates special rules to take account of the large number of people from
other Member States. In particular, there is a specific derogation allowing
the Belgian authorities to request a minimum residence period before
granting the right to vote in a limited number of municipalities where
people from other Member States exceed 20% of eligible voters. Despite
this, Belgium has failed to fulfil its obligations to implement this Directive
on time.[54]

Belgium had previously claimed that difficulties amending the
Constitution had caused the delay and representatives of the Belgian
Government subsequently told the Court that the Directive would be
implemented in the second quarter of 1998. In essence, the Court's
finding of an infringement by Belgium was a mere formality. The law
transposing Directive 94/80/EC in Belgium was finally adopted on 27
January 1999 and published in *Moniteur belge* on 30 January 1999. By the
deadline for registration, some 17.3 per cent of the eligible 496,000 EU
nationals had registered to vote in the October 2000 local elections in
Belgium, which were the first set of municipal elections in which they
could vote, and this despite the compulsory nature of voting in Belgium.
This was, however, a considerable increase on the 7.71% of eligible EU
citizens who registered to vote in the 1999 European Parliament elections. Belgium did not seek to apply the derogation it had negotiated
under Article 12, despite the political controversy that this had elicited
during the negotiation phase.[55]

By the end of January 1999, although all of the Member States had
transposed the Directive, the Commission faced ongoing problems in
ensuring that they had all transposed it properly.[56] In Germany, for
example, electoral rights at the local level are implemented through
measures adopted at the level of the *Land* and thus there is a wide variety
of different regimes relating to registration (Dill, 1999: Ch. 3). In Saxony
and Bavaria, the non-national voter was required to make a sworn
statement that he or she had been resident in the municipality for at
least three months without interruption. Non-national voters were

---

[54] See 'Municipal Voting: European Commission Decides to Refer Belgium to the Court of
Justice', http://europa.eu.int/comm/internal_market/en/people/voting/573.htm.
[55] 'Report from the Commission on Granting a Derogation Pursuant to Article 19(1) of the EC
Treaty, Presented under Article 12(4) of Directive 94/80/EC on the Right to Vote and Stand
as a Candidate in Municipal Elections', COM(2005) 382, 22 August 2005, at 4.
[56] 'EU Citizenship: Commission Decides to Send Reasoned Opinions to Germany and
Greece Concerning Voting Rights', IP/99/602, 30 July 1999.

additionally required to apply for inclusion on the electoral list before each election. At the Commission's behest, the legislation was amended to remove these 'excessive' requirements.[57] In August 1999, the Commission issued a reasoned opinion to Greece for failing correctly to transpose the Directive on a number of points. According to the Greek legislation, persons were only entitled to vote if they had knowledge of the Greek language and had been resident in Greece for at least two years. No such requirements were in place for Greek nationals. Furthermore, provisions in Greek legislation prohibited citizens of other Member States voting or standing in Greek elections from taking part in elections in their Member State of origin. Since neither Article 19 EC nor Directive 94/80/EC implied that EU nationals have to choose between exercising their right to vote and stand as a candidate in municipal elections in their country of origin or their country of residence, this constituted a breach of both. Although the Commission came closest in the Greek case to bringing a case of incorrect implementation before the Court of Justice under Article 226 EC, in practice again informal pressure has proved successful in ensuring the necessary changes at the national level. In 2002, when reporting on the application of the Directive, the Commission declared itself satisfied that the Member States have actually implemented the Directive, and declared the quality of the national transposition measures to be 'satisfactory'.[58] The 2002 report also carries an annex detailing the transposition measures in all of the then fifteen Member States of the European Union.

At the national level, despite generalised apathy which has led the Commission to comment that it has received few complaints about the operation of the electoral rights,[59] some EU citizens have found themselves dissatisfied with the scope of the provisions. For example, an Italian citizen resident in Vienna began an action in the Austrian courts, contesting his exclusion from the electoral roll in relation to the Vienna city elections. Vienna is both a city and a *Land*, and elections to the latter are not included in the EU provisions; for the purposes of the local elections Directive, it is the *Bezirke*, not the city itself, which represent the relevant local governmental authorities where EU citizens can vote. It was held by the Austrian Constitutional Court that, because the city

---

[57] See COM(2002) 260, above n. 3, at 7. [58] See *ibid.*, 5.
[59] *Ibid.*, 7. For one such complaint, see European Parliament Committee on Petitions, Petition 964/2003, Notice to Members, 23 July 2004, PE 346.797, CM/536446EN.doc.

council has the power to make laws, it is quite proper that both the local elections Directive and also the implementing Austrian legislation should provide that an EU citizen does not have the right to vote in the city council elections, but only in elections at the level of *Bezirke*. Consequently, the exclusion of EU nationals was in conformity with Austrian law and EU law.[60] The Court also refused to refer the case to the Court of Justice under Article 234 EC, and sidestepped an attempted challenge by the complainant to the legality of the local elections Directive itself, on the grounds that it infringed the principle of non-discrimination between EU nationals.

In 2003, Belgium became a concern once again for the Commission in relation to the implementation of Article 19(1). In the Belgian municipal elections of 2000, 133 non-Belgian EU citizens residing in the municipality of Honnelles applied to be included in the electoral register within the prescribed time. However, the municipal council took the decision concerning the electoral rolls too late, after the deadline set in the Belgian legislation. Inconclusive litigation at the national level resulted from these events, and the EU citizens were unable to vote. The Commission decided to send a reasoned opinion to Belgium in July 2003, in accordance with the procedures under Article 226 EC,[61] but, after Belgium wrote to the aggrieved EU citizens informing them that they would definitely be registered for the next municipal elections on the basis of their initial application, the Commission closed the proceedings in 2004.[62]

The Directive does not oblige Member States to report on implementation; as a result, in spring 2001 the Commission sent all the Member States a questionnaire to gather the necessary information. Only France and Denmark did not reply to requests for information, but even so the information provided to the Commission provided at best a rather patchy picture of the application of Directive 94/80/EC. Only one Member State, Luxembourg, has so far been able to avail itself of the derogation, and the Commission judged this to be justified, since in 1999 32–4 per cent of the total number of voters were non-national EU citizens, having risen from 28.7 per cent at the time of transposition of

---

[60] Judgment of the Austrian Constitutional Court of 12 December 1997, B3113/96, B3760/96.

[61] 'Right to Vote at Municipal Elections: Commission Pursues Infringement Proceedings against Belgium', IP/03/1090, 23 July 2003.

[62] '22nd Annual Report from the Commission on Monitoring the Application of Community Law (2004)', COM(2005) 570, 5 November 2005, at 7.

the Directive.[63] Figures cited in a 2005 report on the application of the derogation seemed to emphasise this trend, with Luxembourg reporting that 37.6 per cent of the voting population of EU citizens in Luxembourg by that time were non-national EU citizens.[64]

In some Member States, there have been, locally speaking, some quite significant increases in the electorate in the municipalities with high percentages of non-national EU citizens. The Commission asked the Member States to report upon these specifically, but none of the Member States reported that any particular difficulties had arisen as a result of this. However, there is evidence in some Member States where retirement migration is quite prevalent of active organisation of non-national EU citizens (Méndez-Lago, 2005), and a constant trickle of anecdotal evidence in the press about the difficulties which are faced.[65] There is no comprehensive information available concerning the *general* turnout in all the Member States; one of the reasons for this is that, whilst some Member States can provide accurate registration figures, other Member States cannot provide any figures at all as a result of the fact that central government has virtually no involvement in municipal elections.[66] However, the Commission was particularly concerned by the low voter registration in Greece and Portugal (both 9 per cent). The number of non-national candidates elected in the Member States was: Finland, 5; Sweden, 408; Spain, 30; Portugal, 3; and the Netherlands, 2. Once again, some Member States sent letters informing potential electors of their right to vote, although Michael Schlikker of the Office of the federal government's Commissioner for Foreigners' Issues in Germany has asserted that, 'even where towns and cities took the decision to inform EU-nationals with a letter the turnout wasn't any higher than where they didn't'.[67]

In the past few years, there have been numerous initiatives at EU-wide level seeking to enable EU citizens to make use of their Article 19(2) EC rights with information on how to register, vote and be a candidate in

---

[63] See COM(2002) 260, above n. 3, at 8.   [64] COM(2005) 382, above n. 55, at 4.

[65] E.g. most recently in Cyprus, C. Markides, 'By-election Voting Rights Sorted Out But Too Late for Peyia Residents', http://www.cyprus-mail.com, 18 September 2005; see also, in relation to Greece, 'EU Citizens Finding It Hard to Cast Their Ballot', *Athens News*, 14 June 2002, http://www.athensnews.gr.

[66] In order to tackle this problem the Commission has asked the Member States to provide registration figures for their ten largest municipalities concerning participation and candidates.

[67] Interview, Berlin, May 2000.

local elections. One such initiative was the 'Dialogue on Europe', launched by the Commission in February 2000. Its goal was to:

> Encourage public debate about the future of Europe between European and national political leaders and the people of Europe . . . This initiative is in parallel to the Intergovermental Conference on the reform of the institutions that will run throughout 2000 and then continue in 2001.[68]

Whilst the Commission has considered the legal implementation of Directive 94/80/EC to be satisfactory, the Parliament's response to the Commission's Third Report on Citizenship of the Union asserted that the implementation of Directive 94/80/EC has been very unsatisfactory, that with the exceptions of Austria and Ireland participation has been low, and that there has been no substantial change in participation by Community voters in relation to the past.[69] The disappointment of both the Parliament and the Commission over the practical implementation of both Directives stands in contrast to the optimism with which the Parliament, in particular, originally approached the right to vote in local and European elections. However, the low levels of participation on the part of EU nationals cannot be divorced from the general political context of declining turnouts and general apathy towards political parties. Moreover, the profoundly contested nature of these rights in relation to national sovereignty now seems to have faded into the distance in comparison to the efforts of both the Parliament and the Commission to overcome the more banal problems of opacity of registration and voting procedures and of the language and cultural barriers within electoral campaigns which restrict non-national participation in practice. Political parties also continue to engage only partially with the opportunities offered by the electoral rights.

VIII Political freedoms

Neither Article 19 EC nor the implementing directives explicitly address the question of other political freedoms which are essential for effective

---

[68] 'Dialogue on Europe: The Challenges of Institutional Reform: The First Public Debate on 8 March 2000', IP 00/219. There have also been calls from national parliamentarians for governments to do more. In the UK, Roger Casale (Labour) called upon the government to launch a national campaign to inform people of their rights. European Communities Bill, Hansard, 12 November 1997, col. 964.

[69] 'European Parliament Report of the Committee on Citizens' Freedoms and Rights on the Commission Report on Citizenship of the Union', A5-241/2002.

enjoyment of electoral rights, in particular the right to join or found a political party. Enjoyment of freedom of association and expression on the part of foreign residents is enshrined in the Council of Europe Convention on the Participation of Foreigners in Public Life at the Local Level.[70] Article 3 provides:

> Each Party undertakes, subject to the provisions of Article 9, to guarantee to foreign residents, on the same terms as to its own nationals:
>
> a. the right to freedom of expression; this right shall include freedom to hold opinions and to receive and impart information and ideas without interference by public authority and regardless of frontiers. This article shall not prevent States from requiring the licensing of broadcasting, television or cinema enterprises;
> b. the right to freedom of peaceful assembly and to freedom of association with others, including the right to form and to join trade unions for the protection of their interests. In particular, the right to freedom of association shall imply the right of foreign residents to form local associations of their own for purposes of mutual assistance, maintenance and expression of their cultural identity or defence of their interests in relation to matters falling within the province of the local authority, as well as the right to join any association.

However, this Convention does not address directly the right to join a political party but rather refers to 'local associations' for foreign residents.[71] For that reason, not to mention the fact that only a minority of the Member States have signed and ratified this Convention,[72] this provision does not provide the essential legal basis for finding such a right in EU law.

Article 12 of the Charter of Fundamental Rights does expressly provide for freedom of association, in particular in political matters, and Article 21(2) of the Charter prohibits discrimination on grounds of nationality in the field of application of EU law. As Article 19 EC explicitly extends the scope of EU law to cover electoral rights, it can safely be assumed that Article 21(2) of the Charter would indeed guarantee non-discrimination in relation to national measures on joining or founding political parties as covered by Article 12 of the Charter, at least as regards the participation of EU citizens. However, this clarification of

---

[70] ETS No. 144; opened for signature in Strasbourg on 5 February 1992.

[71] See the cautionary comment of the EU Network of Independent Experts on Fundamental Rights in its 'Opinion Regarding the Participation of EU Citizens in the Political Parties of the Member State of Residence', CFR-CDF Opinion 1/2005, March 2005, at 8.

[72] See Tables 3.1 and 3.2 in Chapter 3 above.

the position may make no difference thus far legally, as the Charter merely has a declaratory status in EU law and until recently had never been referred to by the Court of Justice in its case law. It is nonetheless arguable that the right to join or found a political party is implicit in a combination of Articles 12 and 19 EC, when read in conjunction with the fundamental rights which form part of the general principles of law protected under EU law, as laid down in Article 6(2) EU and in a consistent line of case law in the Court of Justice.[73] All of the Member States are bound by a number of key provisions of the ECHR affecting political freedoms, including Article 10 (freedom of expression), Article 11 (freedom of association) and Article 14 (right to non-discrimination in the enjoyment of freedoms under the Convention). While it is true that Article 16 ECHR states that 'nothing in Articles 10, 11 and 14 shall be regarded as preventing the High Contracting Parties from imposing restrictions on the political activity of aliens', in *Piermont* v. *France*[74] the European Court of Human Rights stated that Article 16 could not be raised by one EU Member State to restrict the political activity of a national of another Member State in the territory of the former (including overseas territories). Thus it is strongly arguable that restrictions on EU citizens joining and founding political parties in the Member State of residence is contrary to EU law, as an impermissible restriction of fundamental rights associated with the effective exercise of a right guaranteed by the Treaty (Article 19 electoral rights). This is the conclusion supported by the Commission in its 2002 report on the application of the local elections Directive[75] and by the EU Network of Independent Experts on Fundamental Rights, which has issued an Opinion on this issue.[76]

This latter Opinion provides a detailed review of the position in what were then the twenty-five Member States of the EU, and a summary of concerns in relation to a surprisingly high number of states, either because there are elements of discrimination between nationals and non-nationals in relation to political parties (such as provisions in Germany which treat nationals and non-nationals differently by stating that a political organisation cannot be a 'party' within the meaning of the law if it has

---

[73] In Case 29/69 *Stauder* v. *Ulm* [1969] ECR 419, the Court first referred to 'the fundamental rights enshrined in the general principles of Community law and protected by the Court'.

[74] [1995] IIHRL 28, 27 April 1995.   [75] COM(2002) 260, above n. 3.

[76] 'Opinion Regarding the Participation of EU Citizens in the Political Parties of the Member State of Residence', above n. 71.

a majority of non-nationals on its executive committee) or because – more drastically – there are national rules which prohibit non-nationals from both joining and founding political parties. This was the case in the Czech Republic, Estonia, Greece, Lithuania, Malta, Poland and the Slovak Republic. There is thus ample potential for the Commission to bring enforcement actions under Article 226 EC against these states for breach of the Treaty if it considers that the legal argument outlined in the previous paragraph is sufficiently solid and likely to be supported by the Court of Justice, and if it judges this to be politically expedient.

The Report also noted practical difficulties in the exercise of the right to join or found a political party even in the eighteen Member States where one or both of these actions is permitted. One issue which arises may be where the party is a private association and it in turn claims the freedom of association including the right to determine its own members free from state interference. However, this too could be construed as a restriction on the free movement of workers within the meaning of Article 39 EC, as it would be covered by a line of case law in which the Court of Justice has held that Article 39 EC applies to restrictions imposed by private parties as well as public authorities.[77] However, the reality of electioneering means that in many cases even those allowed membership of a political party and standing on a party ticket are likely to be unsuccessful unless they are standing in a locality with a large pool of potential non-national voters (e.g. some municipalities in the south of Spain where non-nationals have been very active) or where there is some element of cross-national party reciprocity fostering wider identification with a non-national candidate. The small pool of votes available to, for example, a UK citizen in Rome appealing to votes from other UK citizens, means that electoral success is unlikely. In Italy, Dr James Watson was the first Briton to take advantage of the right to stand in another Member State at municipal level. During the 1997 Rome elections, he stood as an independent on the list of the Democratic Party of the Left (PDS) and in return British Labour Party activists canvassed for the PDS.

IX The Charter of Fundamental Rights and the Treaty establishing a Constitution for Europe

It was noted above that the electoral rights first introduced into EU law by the Treaty of Maastricht were subsequently also included in the

---

[77] Case C-281/90 *Angonese* [2000] ECR I-4139.

Charter of Fundamental Rights of the European Union adopted as a declaratory instrument by the institutions in 2000. The electoral rights provisions are to be found in Articles 39 and 40 in a form which is very similar to Article 19 EC, along with an amplification of the existing commitment in Article 190(1) EC that the European Parliament is elected by direct universal suffrage, which adds a further reference to the need for a 'free and secret ballot'. The relevant provisions read as follows:

Article 39

Right to vote and to stand as a candidate at elections to the European Parliament

1. Every citizen of the Union has the right to vote and to stand as a candidate at elections to the European Parliament in the Member State in which he or she resides, under the same conditions as nationals of that State.
2. Members of the European Parliament shall be elected by direct universal suffrage in a free and secret ballot.

Article 40

Right to vote and to stand as a candidate at municipal elections

Every citizen of the Union has the right to vote and to stand as a candidate at municipal elections in the Member State in which he or she resides under the same conditions as nationals of that State.

In the Treaty establishing a Constitution for Europe (the 'Constitutional Treaty' or 'CT') which was drafted between 2002 and 2004 by the Convention on the Future of Europe and then an intergovernmental conference, the Charter of Fundamental Rights was included in essentially unchanged form as Part II of that Treaty to provide the fundamental rights backbone of the EU's constitutional framework. Articles II-99 and II-100 CT contain the unchanged text of Articles 39 and 40 of the Charter.[78]

However, these are not the only provisions on electoral rights in the Constitutional Treaty. Somewhat confusingly for the ordinary reader of the text, Article 19 EC on electoral rights is also, separately, readopted in the Constitutional Treaty in the sections dealing with citizenship (Article I-10 CT and Articles III-125 to III-129 CT). One objective which the drafters of the Constitutional Treaty sought to achieve was

---

[78] OJ 2004 C310/1.

to separate constitutional principle from detailed implementation rules. Thus Article I-10(2)(b) sets out the basic principle on voting in European Parliament and municipal elections, and Article III-126 contains the implementing clauses. The Constitutional Treaty is also intended to simplify the text of the existing Treaties, where this is possible, often without changing its meaning. Thus Article I-10(2) states that: 'Citizens of the Union ... shall have ... (b) the right to vote and stand as candidates in elections to the European Parliament and in municipal elections in their Member State of residence, under the same conditions as nationals of that State.' Because of the way it is drafted, if one omits the final subordinate clause of the sentence, it seems possible to infer, as did Spain in the case it brought against the UK in respect of the latter's decision to grant voting rights in European Parliament elections to Commonwealth citizens resident in Gibraltar, that the Constitutional Treaty makes 'the link between the right to vote in elections to the European Parliament and citizenship of the Union ... no longer merely understood, but explicit'.[79] In other words, Spain sought to read directly into Article I-10 CT the implication that voting in European Parliament elections is an EU citizenship right. This may be a correct conclusion to reach on a reading of the Constitutional Treaty text as a whole, but the better interpretation of the text of Article I-10 CT as it stands must be that, just like Article 19 EC, it confers an equal treatment right, not a right to vote (and stand) as such (and certainly not an exclusive right). In any event, Article I-10 is not in force, and is unlikely to come into force given the doubts about the ratification of the Constitutional Treaty.

Although another of the objectives of the constitution-building process was intended to be the introduction of changes in the legislative process, making co-decision between the Council and the Parliament and qualified majority voting in the Council of Ministers the 'ordinary', default, legislative procedure (Article I-34 CT), this is not extended to electoral rights. By way of derogation from that general legislative procedure, the implementing legislation for electoral rights must be adopted unanimously by the Council, and the European Parliament only has the right to be consulted once on the text:

> A European law or framework law of the Council shall determine the detailed arrangements for exercising the right, referred to in Article I-10(2)(b), for

---

[79] Case C-145/04, *Spain v. United Kingdom (Gibraltar)*, 12 September 2006, at para. 45.

every citizen of the Union to vote and to stand as a candidate in municipal elections and elections to the European Parliament in his or her Member State of residence without being a national of that State. The Council shall act unanimously after consulting the European Parliament. These arrangements may provide for derogations where warranted by problems specific to a Member State. The right to vote and to stand as a candidate in elections to the European Parliament shall be exercised without prejudice to Article III-330(1) and the measures adopted for its implementation.

This is essentially unchanged from the existing EC Treaty, and this approach can presumably be explained by reference to national sensitivities involved in the adoption of measures relating to electoral rights. This might explain the retention of unanimity in the Council of Ministers, but it works less well as an explanation for limiting the European Parliament to consultation rights alone. In a parallel scenario concerning the adoption of measures intended to combat discrimination based on sex, racial or ethnic origin, religion or belief, disability, age or sexual orientation, where many national sensitivities are likewise evident, Article III-124(1) adopts a different solution to Article III-126, providing for unanimity in the Council of Ministers, but also consent in the European Parliament. In this case, the drafters of the Constitutional Treaty chose to depart from the parallel text in the EC Treaty, namely, Article 13 EC, which currently uses the same legislative process for implementing measures as Article 19 EC.

The purely consolidatory approach to electoral rights in the Constitutional Treaty reflects, however, the treatment of citizenship as a whole within that text. Although a very early draft of Part I of the Constitutional Treaty in October 2002 produced by the Praesidium of the Convention on the Future of Europe[80] contained a reference to dual citizenship (European/national), this text disappeared from a later February 2003 draft in favour of a return to a text which reproduced the notion of European citizenship as 'additional' to national citizenship.[81] This was the text which survived into the final version of the Constitutional Treaty approved in June 2004. Article I-10(1) declares: 'Every national of a Member State shall be a citizen of the Union. Citizenship of the Union shall be additional to national citizenship and shall not replace it.' Article I-10(2) goes on to articulate the four basic rights currently contained in Part Three of the EC Treaty: the right

[80] CONV 369/02, 28 October 2002.
[81] CONV 528/03, 16 February 2003 (Articles 1–16), Article 7.

to move and reside freely within the territory of the Member States; the electoral rights set out above; the right to enjoy diplomatic and consular protection when in third states; and the right to petition the European Parliament, to apply to the European Ombudsman, and to address the institutions of the Union in any of the Constitution's languages and receive a reply in the same language. Each of these rights is to 'be exercised in accordance with the conditions and limits defined by the Constitution and by the measures adopted thereunder'.

Provision for implementing measures is found in Articles III-125 to III-129, with only two changes of note in comparison to Articles 18–23 EC. The first of these concerns a further revision of the legal basis for adopting measures to implement the right of EU citizens to move and reside freely within the territory of the Member States. Article 18 EC had already been amended by the Treaty of Nice to provide for the adoption of any measures required to attain the objective of the free movement of persons within the territory of the Member States using the legislative procedure of Council–European Parliament co-decision under Article 251 EC. This means that qualified majority voting will be used in the Council of Ministers, and the European Parliament is fully involved in the legislative process. However, measures concerned with passports, identity cards and residence permits, and provisions on social security and social protection are excluded from the ambit of this legal basis (Article 18(3) EC). The Constitutional Treaty takes this a step further, consolidating the use of the ordinary legislative procedure in Article III-125(1) CT for the purposes of most measures implementing the right to move and reside freely, and adding a specific, but more restricted, legal basis precisely addressing the question of measures concerned with passports, identity cards, residence permits or any other such document, and measures concerning social security or social protection. Article 18(3) EC simply proceeds by excluding this group of measures relating to sensitive issues close to the concerns of national sovereignty. Article III-125(2) CT contains a specific but restrictive legal basis to allow the institutions to adopt measures in those fields, with the Council acting unanimously after consulting the European Parliament. The second change envisages that the internal measures necessary to secure the provision of consular and diplomatic protection in third countries to citizens of the Union, from any Member State which has a mission in those countries, will be adopted by the institutions, with the Council acting by a qualified majority after consulting the European Parliament. Article 20 EC takes an intergovernmental line on this question inviting the *Member States* to establish the necessary rules amongst themselves, and excluding the institutions from taking a role in this matter.

While harbouring doubts that these provisions, even with the changes highlighted, would make any quantifiable difference to the trajectory of European citizenship, it is also important to note that the Constitutional Treaty process has now run aground. The warning shot provided by the Danish referendum on the Treaty of Maastricht in relation to the logic and trajectory of elite-driven treaty reforms was commented upon in Chapter 4. The first Irish referendum on the Treaty of Nice in 2002 likewise suggested that national acceptance of the process of European integration driven on a top-down basis could not be taken for granted, albeit that this referendum result, like the Danish one earlier, was reversed in a subsequent referendum which allowed the entry into force of the amending Treaty.

A much more fundamental reversal occurred in 2005 with the rejection of the Constitutional Treaty in referendums by the voting populations of two of the founding Member States, France and the Netherlands. These votes cast severe doubts upon whether the Constitutional Treaty would ever be ratified, given that the possibility of renewed referendums leading to a different outcome within those two countries seemed a doubtful way of proceeding, especially given the strength of feeling in the Netherlands where the vote went 62%–38% against the Constitutional Treaty on a 63% turn-out. Furthermore, the political bargain between Member States embodied in particular in the final outcome of the IGC in June 2004, after delicate negotiations by the Irish Presidency, could begin to unravel once the Member States return to look closely at the Constitutional Treaty after the nominated period for 'reflection' settled upon by the European Council in June 2005. This extended until early 2007 when the German Government began to press for agreement on a smaller version of the Constitutional Treaty. In a number of Member States, the political forces which agreed the Constitutional Treaty are no longer in power, and it cannot be taken for granted that successor governments, for example in Poland, will take the same view as those who agreed and signed the original text. While it is unlikely that any future disagreements about the text of a putative amending Treaty would centre on the question of citizenship, it is also equally unlikely that the citizenship provisions will be further developed through Treaty amendment in the short or medium term. Consequently, as has been the case throughout the phases of European integration charted in this and the previous chapter, with the salient exception of the Treaty of Maastricht, future changes are likely to be incremental and diffuse in nature. It would also be appropriate to anticipate that they will be deeply contested between and amongst the various national and institutional forces affected.

X Conclusions: limited impacts, hyphenated reforms and the impact of enlargement

The story of EU electoral rights up to the present day is one of limited impact. The electoral rights do display a certain constitutional symbolism in relation to both the EU's own constitutional framework and the constitutions of the Member States. The latter instruments have all had to be adapted, whether or not formal constitutional amendments have been necessitated, to the requirements of allowing EU citizens to vote *as nationals* in a number of elections. However, the evidence reviewed in this chapter indicates that the Commission has encountered some reluctance on the part of the Member States to comply in all respects with the requirements of Article 19 and the implementing directives. In 2004, it commented that for the most part the problems identified stem from 'bad application and incorrect practices rather than ... [from] failure of national legislation to comply with Community legislation'.[82] Moreover, there is no evidence that the EU electoral rights have had a major impact upon electoral politics in relation to either the European Parliament elections in which they have been applied or most of the local elections. The very diffuseness of the local elections across so many Member States militates against a major impact in the latter domain.

On the other hand, as we saw in the later sections of Chapter 2, there has been an incremental development in the legal and constitutional significance of citizenship of the Union more generally since the inception of the Treaty of Maastricht (Kostakopoulou, 2005). Stephen Weatherill has commented that 'the law of [the free movement of] persons is in a remarkably dynamic state' (Weatherill, 2005: 435). Much of this development can be attributed to the line of case law on the equal treatment of EU citizens resident in other Member States in relation to entitlements to welfare and social benefits, which began with *Martínez Sala*.[83] This case law has seen the Court applying the non-discrimination principle in Article 12 EC to protect the equal treatment rights of persons falling within the personal scope of the citizenship provisions (i.e. all nationals of the Member States lawfully resident in

---

[82] COM(2004) 695, above n. 4, at 10.
[83] Case C-85/96 *Martínez Sala* v. *Freistaat Bayern* [1998] ECR I-2691.

another Member State), wherever they are seeking access to a benefit covered by the material scope of the EC Treaty. With the case of *Bidar* in 2005,[84] moreover, the Court moved onto terrain which it had previously expressly said was a matter for national law, namely, the provision of financial assistance to students in higher education, arguing that developments in the law since the 1980s allowed it to reconsider earlier cases such as *Lair*[85] and *Brown*.[86] In *Bidar*, invoking a concept of migrant integration, the Court held that UK rules which made it effectively impossible for a national of a Member State who had completed a considerable proportion of his secondary education in the UK to satisfy the 'ordinary residence' test for the purpose of accessing subsidised grants and loans facilitating access to higher education in the UK would infringe the non-discrimination principle under Article 12 EC. Pertinent developments justifying such a change in approach in its case law cited by the Court *included* the establishment of a concept of citizenship of the Union in the EC Treaty by the Treaty of Maastricht. Thus citizenship of the Union provided both the legal framework within which the judgment could be reasoned and the basis for arguing that the case fell within the scope of EU law altogether, which is an interesting circular outcome for the Court (Dougan, 2005). If we focus on these cases, it is not hard to conclude that citizenship of the Union has made a dramatic difference compared to the legal situation before its establishment, at least in relation to the 'de-nationalisation' of the territorial welfare state (van der Mei, 2005).

In addition, in another development which was not necessarily widely anticipated, the Court confirmed in the *Baumbast* case that the right of every citizen of the Union to move and reside freely within the territory of the Member States under Article 18 EC is directly effective, in the sense that it gives rise to rights for individuals which national courts must enforce.[87] This has left the national courts and the Court of Justice in the position of being able to assess the lawfulness of limitations and conditions upon the exercise of free movement which can be imposed under Article 18. Such limitations and conditions must be both proportionate and reasonable. Writing in an extra-judicial capacity, Advocate General Kokott has suggested that the free movement of EU citizens

---

[84] Case C-209/03 *R* v. *London Borough of Ealing, ex parte Bidar* [2005] ECR I-2119.

[85] Case 39/86 *Lair* v. *Universität Hanover* [1988] ECR 3161.

[86] Case 197/86 *Brown* v. *Secretary of State for Scotland* [1988] ECR 3205.

[87] Case C-413/99 *Baumbast and R* [2002] ECR I-7091; see also Case C-408/03 *Commission* v. *Belgium* [2006] ECR I-2647.

under Article 18 EC is a new fifth fundamental freedom, alongside the free movement of goods, services, persons and capital, as guaranteed in the original EC Treaty (Kokott, 2005).

There have also been limited legislative and Treaty-based developments in the citizenship field. Reference was made above to the amendment to Article 18 EC contained in the Treaty of Nice. Article 18 was one of the legal bases used when, in 2004, the European Parliament and the Council adopted Directive 2004/38/EC,[88] largely replacing and consolidating the previous piecemeal legislation governing the exercise of free movement rights by Union citizens, including workers, jobseekers, the self-employed, students, retired persons, the economically self-sufficient, and members of their families. Not all of these groups have the same entitlements to equal treatment, and moreover it is possible that there is already some dissonance between the provisions of the Directive and some of the Court's more adventurous case law[89] on the equal treatment rights of marginal groups who have traditionally had less protection than the economically active groups, such as workseekers (Golynker, 2005: 118). Although Directive 2004/38/EC is largely consolidatory rather than innovatory, it is in general intended to foster a closer sense of integration between the host state and the migrant Union citizens. Thus in Article 16 a general rule is instituted which did not previously exist, whereby a Union citizen who has been continuously resident in another Member State for a period of five years or more is given the right of permanent residence. The reference in the Preamble to the right of permanent residence refers to the fact that this will 'strengthen the feeling of Union citizenship and [be] a key element in promoting social cohesion'. Even so, there are limits to the cohesion. Even EU citizens enjoying the right of permanent residence can still be expelled from the host state, if only on 'serious grounds of public policy and public security'.[90] The retention of this provision matches the continued refusal of the Member States to remove from the Treaties the provisions relating to the right to expel EU citizens on grounds of public policy, public health and public security (e.g.

---

[88] Council Directive 2004/38/EC on the right of citizens of the Union and their family members to move and reside freely within the territory of the Member States, OJ 2004 L158/77. The Directive came into force on 30 April 2006.

[89] E.g. Case C-138/02 *Collins* v. *Secretary of State for Work and Pensions* [2004] ECR I-2703; see Oosterom-Staples, 2004.

[90] Directive 2004/38 on Citizens' Free Movement Rights, OJ 2004 L158/77, Article 28(3).

Article 39(3) EC), which were also retained in the Constitutional Treaty (Article III-133(3) CT).

The story of Union citizenship since 1993 is hardly one of unmitigated success. For example, in the context of the May 2004 enlargement of the European Union, it is arguable that a new category of second-class Union citizenship has been created, even though 'officially' all the citizens from the new Member States are indeed in principle 'full' EU citizens (Kochenov, 2003, 2006). In practice, their rights are more limited. Given that there have been restrictions placed on the free movement rights of nationals of eight of the ten new post-2004 Member States (the 'EU8 states'[91]), in practice there will be a more restricted number of nationals from the new Member States resident in other Member States who would be able to benefit from the Article 19 electoral rights than if market forces were allowed free reign. This is not least because there are many in the EU8 Member States (as indeed from Bulgaria and Romania after 2007) who take advantage of mobility, and their right to enter the other Member States as EU citizens, at the very least for a period of three months as a 'tourist', but who then enter the informal labour market and thus have only unofficial and unauthorised residence in the host state. They are therefore unable to take advantage of 'official' rights such as the Article 19 rights, although doubtless given their precarious status in the labour market and within society generally this is perhaps the least of their worries. All of this is especially ironic in view of the strenuous efforts made by the European Commission to ensure that new groups of 'Community voters' could benefit from Directive 93/109/EC in the June 2004 European Parliament elections.[92]

Although there is unrestricted freedom of movement in relation to services and establishment (i.e. the self-employed), most of the fifteen 'old' Member States placed transitional restrictions after 2004 on free movement of labour in respect of the nationals of the EU8 states, as authorised under the Act of Accession (Adinolfi, 2005). Only Ireland,

---

[91] Prior to enlargement, these were referred to as the 'A8 states'; they are the Czech Republic, Estonia, Hungary, Latvia, Lithuania, Poland, Slovenia and Slovakia. Only Cyprus and Malta are excluded from these special arrangements, and in any event these are states with tiny populations. Post-enlargement, it is more correct to refer to them as the 'EU8' states, although some UK documentation, for example, still refers to 'A8'. The terminology of 'EU8 states' is used here.

[92] See above text accompanying n. 37.

Sweden and the UK allowed the free movement of labour. Moreover, even in the these cases the rights are not unconditional. In the case of the UK, a Workers' Registration Scheme was established, and the access of nationals of the EU8 states to welfare benefits was severely restricted by a transitional scheme, for a minimum of one year after taking up employment. There are considerable doubts whether the UK's restrictions are in fact compatible with the status of EU8 nationals as EU citizens. In Ireland, a habitual residence test has been used to restrict access to welfare benefits. All of these restrictions, whether total or partial, were imposed ostensibly because of fears of a flood of migrants from east to west, and fears of welfare benefit 'tourism'. It seems probable that, rather than stopping or restricting mobility, many of the restrictions have in fact merely pushed workers from the EU8 states to enter the informal economy in many Member States, thus depriving them of effective employment protection, allowing evasion of minimum wage regulations by employers, and reducing the contribution of the migrants to the tax base of the host state. This is certainly the case in the UK, where it is estimated that only a small proportion of workers from the EU8 states have actually registered under the Scheme established in 2004.[93] Indeed, in many of the old Member States, anecdotal evidence suggests that there are very large numbers of EU8 nationals living and working informally.[94]

Alternatively, EU8 nationals can also reside and work officially in the other Member States if they are able to obtain work permits, granted in the same way as if they were third country nationals.[95] That there are considerable numbers of EU8 citizens falling into this category is evident from the quite high numbers of 'new' European citizens post-2004 charted in Table 5.2 above. Moreover, numbers will doubtless rise as the restrictions imposed by the Member States are gradually removed

---

[93] P. Wintour, 'Tories Drop Hardline Stance on Migration in New Policy Shift', *Guardian*, 29 December 2005.

[94] D. Rennie, 'Sorry, Minister, But You Can't Keep EU Citizens Out of Here', *Daily Telegraph*, 23 August 2006.

[95] The openness of the various Member States to the EU8 workers, even on the basis of work permits, varies greatly. A report in the French newspaper *Libération* commented on the small number of work permits, with fewer than 10,000 being granted by France during 2004 to A8 workers, in comparison to 32,000 in Austria and more than 500,000 in Germany. It put this difference down to the openness and attractiveness of the respective economies, amongst other issues. C. Lamotte, 'La France, terre de rejet pour les travailleurs de l'Est', *Libération*, 7 February 2006.

through the course of the transitional period.[96] However, can we call EU8 nationals (or indeed those of Bulgaria and Romania after 2007, whose labour market rights have been further restricted, including in Ireland and the UK) genuinely 'new' European citizens? Strictly speaking, of course, they are Union citizens within the meaning of Article 17 EC, by virtue of having the nationality of a Member State, and they can and do benefit from the general right to non-discrimination on grounds of nationality (Article 12 EC), but they are denied one of the most fundamental rights under the EC Treaty, namely, the free movement of labour.

Thus one interim conclusion to be drawn from this chapter, read in the light of the wider evidence about citizenship of the Union, is that there remain tensions at the heart of the EU electoral rights, concerning their scope and effects, and concerning the question of what contribution, if any, they can make either to developing concepts of European identity and belonging, to integrating citizens of other Member States more effectively into the host state, or to fostering a democratic culture within EU law-making. These tensions are reflected in a broader uncertainty about the trajectory of European citizenship more generally, regarding the mixed messages emerging from recent developments especially in the context of enlargement (Reich, 2005). However, these tensions come out particularly clearly when we turn to look, as we shall in the following two chapters, at the various arguments which exist for consolidating the nature of European Parliament elections as truly 'European' elections, and for extending EU electoral rights to cover either new categories of election (e.g. national elections) or new groups of beneficiaries (e.g. third country nationals).

---

[96] Commission Memorandum, 'Transitional Measures for the Free Movement of the Workers Forming the Subject of the Accession Treaty of 2003, Second Phase 2006–2009', MEMO/06/176, Brussels, 28 April 2006.

6

Electoral rights for Union citizens: looking
to the future

I Introduction

This is the first of two chapters which explore the developmental potential of the existing EU electoral rights. The chapters cover the material scope of the rights (what elections are covered, what is the nature of the rights available and under what conditions can they be exercised?) and the personal scope (who has the electoral rights?). The discussion is set against the backdrop provided by the political conditions affecting citizenship issues at the national and European levels in the mid-2000s, and specifically the question of electoral rights. As the earlier chapters have shown, the original preoccupations within the debate about electoral rights with the democratisation of the Union's institutions and the special rights of nationals of the Member States are still relevant considerations. It is intriguing to note that the EU in the mid-2000s has been in the grip of a crisis of identity about its role and purpose in the modern world, and about what relationship there should be between citizens and residents and the Union institutions, which has been as intense as any in its history. There was a clear manifestation of this crisis in the debate about the future of the Union in the light of the rejection of the Constitutional Treaty in referendums in France and the Netherlands, but this crisis of identity affects not only the possible future development of the founding treaties, but also the ongoing work of the Union and its institutions.

It is important to be sanguine about the achievements of the European Union thus far in relation to citizenship issues. Even the most basic goals of free movement under the EC Treaty appear not to have been entirely achieved. Why else would 2006 have been declared European Year of Workers' Mobility? And why else would the realisation of employment mobility be made central to the goal of boosting productivity and growth under the Lisbon Agenda?[1] Not all of this desired mobility is necessarily *transnational* mobility, but coincidentally 2006 also marked the date by which Directive 2004/38/EC,[2] adopted by the Council and the European Parliament to facilitate the right of citizens of the EU and members of their families to move and reside freely within the territory of the Member States, should have been duly implemented by the Member States. One of the main aims of the legislation was codification and simplification of the existing measures which had been constructed piecemeal since the 1960s, read in conjunction with a significant body of case law from the Court of Justice which has interpreted those earlier measures. However, it also creates an important new category of 'permanent resident' in the Member States which could have significant consequences in the longer term as a genuine alternative to naturalisation or other forms of citizenship acquisition (Carrera, 2005a: 711–17). In certain respects, the Directive also improves the position of third country nationals, so far as it removes any visa requirements which might be imposed on third country national spouses of EU citizens when travelling across the internal borders of the Union, provided they have a residence permit in their Member State of residence, and also allows them to travel across those borders without a passport, provided they have a valid state-issued ID (e.g. a driving licence) and evidence of family affiliation to the EU citizen with whom they are travelling.[3]

As we saw in Chapter 5, moreover, enlargement provides an important new context in which free movement rights are still being restricted (and continue to be contested), while at the same time – at least on paper – European citizenship is being extended (Krūma, 2004). From the date of accession, citizens of the EU8 states were in the position of being EU citizens in a general constitutional sense, while being subject to restrictive transitional measures in respect of their movement as workers to other Member States, although they have enjoyed free movement as self-employed persons from the date of accession.

---

[1] '2006 – European Year of Workers' Mobility, the Importance of the Mobility of Workers to the Implementation of the Lisbon Strategy', MEMO/05/229, 29 June 2005; Krieger and Fernandez, 2006.

[2] Council Directive 2004/38/EC on the right of citizens of the Union and their family members to move and reside freely within the territory of the Member States, OJ 2004 L158/77. The deadline for implementing the Directive was 30 April 2006.

[3] 'The Directive on the Right to Move and Reside Freely in the Union: Seven Million European Citizens Already Live in Another Member State', MEMO/06/179, 2 May 2006.

In certain respects, however, political conditions do differ sharply from those prevailing in the 1960s and 1970s. For example, the debate about migration in the context of globalisation and some of the cultural and political issues associated with multicultural societies have become issues for the EU and its Member States in ways which could not have been anticipated thirty years ago, and perhaps not even fifteen years ago. That is not to say that the issues raised are necessarily new, but rather that they have a political salience which they did not have in earlier years. This is well illustrated by the conflicts generated in Europe around the US-led war in Iraq and the tensions between radical Islamic sentiments expressed by some Muslims resident in EU Member States and the predominantly secular and liberal societies of those states. As Muslim groups often point out, even in these nominally secular societies, Christianity often remains the dominant religion in terms of visibility and public ideology, and publicly the Judeo-Christian heritage is acknowledged much more openly and extensively than Europe's Islamic heritage (Davies, 1997: 251–8; Menocal, 1990). The debates about free speech and respect for religions engendered by the infamous Danish Cartoons affair in late 2005 and early 2006 highlight the challenge for European states posed by their increasingly diverse and multi-cultural societies (Hansen, 2006). Immigration played a role in the Dutch referendum on the Constitutional Treaty (Taggart, 2006), not least because of well-publicised incidents of intercultural violence such as the murder of the controversial and outspoken Dutch film-maker Theo van Gogh by a young Dutch Muslim, and the issue of enlargement (in particular, possible future enlargement to include Turkey) was raised in both the Dutch and the French referendums. The challenges faced by the French model of integration of immigrants were brought starkly into focus by the riots by unemployed youth in the Parisian suburbs in November 2005. Although the children and grandchildren of immigrants, including those from North Africa, have usually acquired French nationality, typically they find themselves discriminated against in the labour market, and suffer above-average levels of youth unemployment.

Against the background provided by these changed conditions, this and the following chapter will look at three challenging issues for the European Union in terms of the development of electoral rights. The first focus is upon the nature of the European Parliamentary *demos*, and the question of who should define who should vote in European Parliament elections, and how that definition should be framed, now and in the future. Is the right to vote in European Parliament elections an implicit citizenship right under Part Two of the EC Treaty? This will provide some important insights into the truly *supra*national potential for political citizenship in the EU which encompasses and goes beyond the electoral rights in Article 19 EC.

Thereafter attention turns to the question of whether (and how) electoral rights for EU citizens should, and could, be extended to cover a wider range of elections, notably national and regional elections within the Member States. Such a development could be a logical consequence of understanding the existing rights under Article 19(1) EC as fostering something like a new form of European denizenship which challenges nation state citizenship more immediately than does Article 19(2). With the coming into force of Directive 2004/38/EC, a new status of permanent resident is created, under Article 16, for those Union citizens and their family members who have resided legally in another Member State for a continuous period of five years or more. This seems to offer a clear alternative to acquiring the citizenship of the host polity, and raises the serious question of what rights ought properly to attach to this civil status. Should it include the right to vote in regional and national elections?

It remains a moot point whether the conferring of such rights upon EU citizens by virtue of residence in another Member State, as an incident of EU law, in fact makes such citizens more *European*, or rather more *French*, or *German*, or *Polish*, depending upon the state of residence. This is, arguably, a contribution to *transnational* not to *supranational* or *postnational* citizenship, even if it is EU law which has conferred the relevant rights. Indeed, Heather Lardy has argued that viewing the question of electoral rights through the prism of a set of horizontal relationships operating between interlocking national citizenships represents less of a challenge to the connection between national citizenship and the right to vote and thus to national citizenship, than does an approach which endorses above all the contribution of electoral rights to an emerging supranational European citizenship, even if this form of citizenship remains yet to be fully realised (Lardy, 1996: 612–13). In particular, she suggests, the position taken on what constitutes the rationale for EU electoral rights will affect the approach to the issue of extending these rights, in particular to include rights for EU citizens to vote in the national elections of the Member States, which at the present time is a matter of Member State competence. However, given the weaknesses of the current arrangements, and the still highly speculative possibilities of further development, it is arguable that taking a pragmatic position and accepting that the development of

Union citizenship will occur essentially on the horizontal plane is the most that can reasonably be hoped for at the present time.

The final question requires separate attention in the following chapter, and this concerns the broader global migration context within which the EU is operating, and, in the particular context of this book, the personal scope of Union citizenship. Who should be Union citizens, and – conversely – what rights should EU law confer on those who are resident in the Member States but who are not, under the present definition, Union citizens? In Chapter 7, we will examine initiatives to grant third country nationals electoral rights within the context of evolving EU policies in relation to the so-called 'Area of Freedom, Security and Justice', which includes policies on immigration and the integration of immigrants from third countries in the Member States. Here there is a clear interface with national policies, national legislation and indeed national constitutions, given in particular the limited scope of EU competence in this field and the weaknesses of the instruments which it has adopted. Moreover, while under national law there have been very few initiatives to give *national* electoral rights to *resident EU nationals* to supplement their EU-law-based local electoral rights (and the only significant example concerns the now reciprocal arrangements between the UK and Ireland for voting in national parliamentary elections), more than half of the Member States do in fact already give *local* electoral rights to *at least some third country nationals*. To that extent, the discussion in Chapter 7 presages the material covered in Part III of the book which will examine electoral rights debates from the point of view of their nestedness within national policies governing matters such as nationality, citizenship and immigration.

Conclusions on these two chapters are reserved for the end of Chapter 7, which seeks to draw together some of the issues raised.

II The scope and nature of the 'right to vote' for the European Parliament

What is a 'European' Parliament and who should vote for it?[4] Should it be the 'citizens' of the European Union alone? If so, should it be all EU citizens, or only those who are resident in the Member States? Or should the electorate include potentially all residents in the Member States

---

[4] There is very little written on the interaction between European Parliament elections and the notion of Union citizenship: see Rambour, 2004.

which comprise the EU? Does anyone have a 'right' to vote for the European Parliament? Certainly, Article 19(2) EC does not expressly create such a right, but is merely limited to creating an obligation on Member States to accord equal treatment to resident nationals of other Member States. And who should decide who votes for the European Parliament – the Member States, or the European Union itself? In other words, is there a single European concept of the European Parliamentary *demos*, or twenty-seven separate, but overlapping, national concepts?

To put this in legal terms, under the Treaty of Maastricht, EU law now requires all Member States to accord to nationals of the other Member States resident in their territory the right to vote for the European Parliament on the same basis as nationals (i.e. a non-discrimination right). It is therefore pertinent to ask whether this creates an exhaustive framework for a 'European' definition of the European Parliamentary *demos*, or whether it merely creates a facilitative framework within which Member States may add to, but not take away from, the basic rights laid down in Article 19(2). If the Member States may add to the categories of voters for the European Parliament, such as by allowing voting by resident third country nationals, are they subject in that context to any constraints under EU law? In a similar vein, what is the territorial scope of the European Parliamentary *demos*? To what extent is it circumscribed by the outer geographical boundaries of the European Union, as set by Article 299 EC, or can those covered by the personal scope of Union citizenship also quite properly vote for the European Parliament when they are resident in a third state, or in some associated territory which is not fully part of the European Union? If so, is that a matter for decision by the EU institutions under the Treaties or for the Member States, and – if the latter – is their discretion on expatriate voting entirely unfettered or subject to general principles of EU law?

An initial trigger for some interesting reflections on this question came from the action brought before the European Court of Human Rights by a Gibraltarian aggrieved at not having the vote in European Parliament elections. This situation arose as a result of Annex II of the 1976 Act on Direct Elections, which provides that: 'The United Kingdom will apply the provisions of this Act only in respect of the United Kingdom.'[5] Denise Matthews, a resident of Gibraltar, complained that she was not permitted to register as a voter for the European Parliament elections of 1994, even

---

[5] Council Decision 76/787/ECSC, EEC, Euratom relating to the Act concerning the election of the representatives of the Assembly by direct universal suffrage, OJ 1976 L278/1.

though she is a UK citizen and thus an EU citizen. This, she alleged, was a breach of Article 3 of Protocol No. 1 to the European Convention on Human Rights (ECHR), which obliges states to hold free and fair elections ensuring the free expression of the people in the choice of the legislature.

Gibraltar has been a dependent territory and Crown Colony of the UK since the early eighteenth century, when it was ceded to the British Crown by the King of Spain under the Treaty of Utrecht. Gibraltar's situation with regard to the EU is rather anomalous. As a Crown Colony, it is not part of the United Kingdom, but it is part of the European Union by virtue of Article 299(4) EC, as a European territory for whose external relations a Member State is responsible. However, it is not part of the customs territory and is treated as a third country for the purposes of the common commercial policy. On the other hand, many EU legislative acts in areas such as the free movement of persons, services and capital and the protection of the environment and consumers do apply to Gibraltar and become part of the legal order of Gibraltar in the normal way. Since the Act on Direct Elections did not appear to be reviewable before the Court of Justice, Matthews turned to the institutions of the ECHR in order to seek a remedy. By virtue of a declaration made in 1953 by the UK, the ECHR is applicable to Gibraltar.

The Court of Human Rights found that the UK was in principle responsible for any violation even though the infringement originated in the Act concerning the Election of the Representatives of the European Parliament by Direct Universal Suffrage. The fact that the EU electoral machinery is decided at the EU level and not at the national level does not in principle absolve a state of responsibility under the ECHR. Furthermore, Article 3 could be applied to elections to the European Parliament even though this was not envisaged when the ECHR was originally drafted. The European Parliament should now be viewed as at least part of the 'legislature' of the European Union, this being an essential precondition for applying Article 3. Especially since the Treaty of Maastricht, the Parliament has played an important role within the EU's legislative process for many if not all legislative acts, and its role in general can be connected to the task of ensuring an effective political democracy in the EU. Finally, the UK could not invoke its 'margin of appreciation' in deciding that in order to apply its European Parliamentary electoral system it had to exclude Gibraltar, just because its population was too small to be a full European Parliament constituency (at the time there was single constituency, first-past-the-post voting in the UK for European Parliament elections).

The UK's initial reaction was to seek an amendment to Annex II to the 1976 Act on Direct Elections in order to include Gibraltar, but this avenue (which would require unanimity amongst the Member States) was blocked by Spain on the basis of its sovereignty dispute with the UK. As a result, the UK caused the following statement to be included in the minutes of a meeting of the Council of Ministers on 18 February 2002:[6]

> Recalling Article 6(2) of the Treaty on European Union, which states that 'Union shall respect the fundamental rights, as guaranteed by the European Convention for the Protection of Human Rights and Fundamental Freedoms signed in Rome on 4 November 1950, and as they result from the constitutional traditions common to the Member States, as general principles of Community law', the United Kingdom will ensure that the necessary changes are made to enable the Gibraltar electorate to vote in elections to the European Parliament as part of and on the same terms as the electorate of an existing United Kingdom constituency, in order to ensure the fulfilment of the United Kingdom's obligations to implement the judgment of the European Court of Human Rights in [*Matthews*], consistent with European law.

Accordingly, in 2003, the UK adopted legislation enabling elections for the European Parliament to take place in Gibraltar from 2004 onwards in the form of the European Parliament Representation Act 2003, and it incorporated the voters of Gibraltar into the South West of England multi-member constituency for the June 2004 elections, on advice from the Electoral Commission.[7] In addition to any EU citizens entitled to vote under Article 19(2) EC, in line with the general position on the suffrage in the UK, certain qualified Commonwealth citizens resident in Gibraltar were entitled to register and vote. This admittedly small group of Commonwealth citizens (around 100–200 persons, most of whom are from South Asia) would inevitably be third country nationals and not EU citizens, unless they were Maltese or Cypriot and thus entitled to vote as EU citizens.

Spain has long contested the UK's claim to sovereignty over Gibraltar, especially during the Franco era when the land border was closed.[8] Since

---

[6] This procedure is detailed by Advocate General Tizzano in his Joint Opinion in Case C-145/04 *Spain* v. *United Kingdom (Gibraltar)* and Case C-300/04 *Eman and Sevinger* v. *College van burgemeester en wethouders van Den Haag (Aruba)*, 6 April 2006, paras. 32–4.

[7] 'Gibraltar Should Join South West for Elections to European Parliament', 28 August 2003, www.gibnet.com/eurovote/ec_aug.htm.

[8] See Ho, 2004; 'The Issues Explained: Gibraltar', 4 August 2004, http://www.guardian.co.uk/theissues/article/0,,602017,00.html.

Spain became a member of what were then the European Communities in 1986, some of the disputes between Spain and the UK over Gibraltar have been filtered through the prism of the application of EU law in Gibraltar. In this instance, the extension of votes to Commonwealth citizens became the focal point of Spain's objections.[9] Spain filed a complaint with the European Commission in July 2003, stating that the UK measures violated EU law, in particular Articles 17, 19, 189 and 190 EC, and Annex II to the Act on Direct Elections, because the franchise to vote in European Parliament elections as determined under the UK legislation was not confined to persons who are EU citizens. In October 2003, the Commission held an oral hearing involving Spain and the UK, and concluded that there was no violation by the UK. In the absence of specific rules in the franchise in the EU measures which provide for direct elections, the Commission concluded that there was 'no general principle of Community law according to which the electorate in European Parliament elections cannot be extended beyond EU citizens'.[10] Arguing – as indeed is obvious after the *Matthews* case – that Annex II to the 1976 Act on Direct Elections must be interpreted in the light of the ECHR, the Commission furthermore concluded that this was a provision which was sufficiently open to allow the UK to assimilate Gibraltar to the electoral territory of England and Wales in order to comply with its obligations under the ECHR. It suggested that Spain and the UK find a friendly resolution to their dispute without recourse to law, and declined the Spanish request that it adopt a reasoned opinion stating violations of EU law on the part of the UK. Since the Commission refused to take action under Article 226 EC, Spain decided to take the unusual step of starting an enforcement action itself in the Court of Justice, under Article 227 EC, moreover without the support of the Commission.[11] Advocate General Tizzano's Opinion in this

---

[9] 'Spain Says Gibraltar Vote illegal', BBC News, 5 July 2005, http://news.bbc.co.uk/1/hi/uk_politics/4651815.stm; 'Fears over Commonwealth EU Voters', BBC News, 6 April 2006, http://news.bbc.co.uk/1/hi/uk_politics/4882790.stm.

[10] 'Right to Vote in EP Elections in Gibraltar', IP/03/1479, 29 October 2003.

[11] The decision to take up the complaint was made by the People's Party government of Prime Minister José María Aznar. However, even after the March 2004 General Election victory of the Socialist Party led by José Luis Rodríguez Zapatero, the new government decided to continue with the action before the Court of Justice, although its policy on Gibraltar is somewhat more constructive than the previous government's, allowing the Government of Gibraltar, which it does not recognise, to be a partner in discussions over the territory's future.

politically highly sensitive case was handed down on 6 April 2006, and the Court of Justice gave judgment on 12 September 2006.[12]

Before looking in more detail at the legal issues raised in the *Gibraltar* case, it is useful also to consider the related issues concerning EU citizenship and the right to vote in European Parliament elections which have arisen in another case proceeding on a parallel track through the Court of Justice. Indeed, the Advocate General issued a single Opinion for the two cases and they were decided on the same day by the Court of Justice, in terms which rely upon two related sets of propositions about the current state of the law in relation to European Parliament elections.

Unlike the *Gibraltar* case, the case of *Eman and Sevinger (Aruba)*[13] arose originally in the national courts, and it arrived in the Court of Justice on a reference for a preliminary ruling under Article 234 EC from the Dutch *Raad van State* (the highest administrative court). It raised the right to vote in European Parliament elections of citizens of the Kingdom of the Netherlands who are resident in the island territory of Aruba, which is just off the coast of Venezuela. Aruba is part of the Kingdom of the Netherlands, but is a self-governing overseas territory (OCT) and as such is not part of the EU under Article 299 EC.[14] As an OCT, only very limited aspects of EU law apply to Aruba, either directly or indirectly by virtue of Dutch law, or in some cases voluntarily because the Aruban legislature has chosen to align itself with EU law.[15] The Euratom Treaty does apply there, as, arguably, does Part VI of the Treaty on European Union (third pillar on police and judicial cooperation in criminal matters) which has no territorial scope but merely binds the governments of the Member States. As citizens of the Kingdom of the Netherlands benefiting from a single national citizenship for the Kingdom (which extends also to the Netherlands Antilles) but with permanent residence in Aruba, the applicants, Eman and Sevinger, argued that they were citizens of the Union. However, so long as they were resident in Aruba, under Dutch law they were denied the right to vote in European Parliament elections. They could vote if they moved to reside in the Netherlands itself (but only after satisfying a qualifying

---

[12] Case C-145/04 *Spain* v. *United Kingdom (Gibraltar)*, 12 September 2006.

[13] Case C-300/04 *Eman and Sevinger* v. *College van burgemeester en wethouders van Den Haag (Aruba)*, 12 September 2006.

[14] For political background on Aruba, see Sharpe, 2005.

[15] Case C-300/04, Opinion of the Advocate General, 6 April 2006, para. 159.

residence period of ten years), or if they moved to live in a third country. In the latter case, their rights would be based on the general Dutch expatriate voting arrangements which make no distinction in respect of Dutch nationals who are resident in third countries as to whether they have previously been resident in the Netherlands itself, or in Aruba or the other non-European territory of the Netherlands, the Netherlands Antilles. It is noteworthy that Article 1(2) of Directive 93/109/EC explicitly preserves the power of Member States to determine whether nationals who reside outside its electoral territory may vote or stand as a candidate in European Parliament elections, which means that across the Member States there are very different sets of rules governing the expatriate voting rights of citizens in these elections. The Netherlands is one state which does preserve the voting rights of its citizens when they reside in third countries.

The Advocate General's advice to the European Court of Justice was that:

- it should declare, in the *Gibraltar* case, that the UK has failed to fulfil its obligations under the EC Treaty, and in particular the Decision relating to the Act on Direct Elections, by allowing Commonwealth citizens resident in Gibraltar to vote in European Parliament elections; and
- it should rule, in the *Aruba* case, that it is contrary to EU law for a Member State to withhold (without objective justification) the right to vote in European Parliament elections from citizens residing in another part of the state other than the European territory, when it grants that right to vote to citizens when they are resident in the European territory and when they are resident in a non-Member State. This would leave it open to the Member State to provide such an objective justification, but in this case the Netherlands had failed to satisfy that requirement.

The Court of Justice differed slightly in its approach to the two cases from the Advocate General. In the first place, its judgment does not contain an extended discussion of the citizenship and constitutional issues which are raised by the cases. To that extent, it is hard to say with certainty whether it might approve of some of the more general statements made by the Advocate General. Furthermore, while adopting essentially the same ruling as proposed by the Advocate General in the *Aruba* case on the rights of the Arubans, it found in favour of the United Kingdom in the *Gibraltar* case, concluding that in the arrangements that it made it had not exceeded its discretion under EU law as it stands. The discussion which follows presents first the broader approach presented by the Advocate General, and then highlights the narrower solutions offered by the Court of Justice. Of course, the approach of the former is not the definitive statement of the law as it stands, but is merely an advisory Opinion, but it is interesting to study this Opinion because it may provide some pointers as to how EU law in this field might develop in the future.

The Advocate General's Opinion offers the first extended considera-tion by a judicial authority in the EU of the political rights of Union citizens. It does not, however, directly address the equal treatment standard articulated in Article 19 EC, which has been the focus hitherto of the discussion of EU law in this book, but rather the nature of European citizenship as a political status. It is interesting that the Advocate General chose to begin his discussion by a general meditation on whether a right to vote in European Parliament elections is one of the EU citizenship rights guaranteed under the EC Treaty. Such a reflection was not strictly essential for the task of deciding the case (as the omission of any such discussion from the Court's judgment clearly shows), but it provides vital background for understanding the underlying position on the nature of EU citizenship which the Advocate General chose to take, as his argument focuses on the legitimate extensions and restrictions which Member States may grant or impose, taking as a baseline a premise that the right to vote in European Parliament elections is indeed an incident of citizenship of the Union.

The Advocate General's first finding was that:

> it can be directly inferred from Community principles and legislation as a whole, thus overriding any indications to the contrary within national legislation, that there is an obligation to grant the voting rights [in European elections] to citizens of the Member States and, consequently, to citizens of the Union.[16]

He reached that conclusion even though no provision of EU law expli-citly includes the right to vote for the European Parliament amongst the list of rights inherent in citizenship of the Union, although Article 19(2) 'in any event takes it for granted that the right . . . is available to citizens of the Union'.[17] He argues that the right is based on

---

[16] Para. 67. Further standalone references to paragraphs in the footnotes to this section refer to the Advocate General's Opinion of 6 April 2006 in Case C-145/04 and Case C-300/04.

[17] Para. 68.

the principles of democracy on which the Union is based,[18] and in particular, to use the words of the [European Court of Human Rights] the principle of universal suffrage, which 'has become the basic principle' in modern democratic states.[19]

In the arena of EU law, this finding can also be derived from the references to universal suffrage in Articles 189 and 190 EC, and Article 1 of the 1976 Act on Direct Elections, which militate 'in favour of recognition of a right to vote attaching to the largest possible number of people'.[20] The Advocate General finally supported the argument by reference to Article 3 of Protocol No. 1 to the ECHR, which was the foundation for the *Matthews* judgment, protecting 'the free expression of the opinion of the people in the choice of the legislature'.

The Advocate General then considered whether there was a 'strict link' between citizenship of the Union and the scope of the electorate for the European Parliament, as argued by the Spanish Government, as the basis for contesting the extension of the suffrage to Commonwealth citizens in Gibraltar. The Advocate General concluded that the reference to 'peoples' of the Member States in Articles 189 and 190 should be treated as largely coterminous with the citizens or nationals of the Member States (thus avoiding alternative 'ethnic' rather than 'civic' connotations of the term 'peoples'), but that the people/citizens, so defined, and the electorate for the European Parliament should not be treated as automatically coextensive. He based that approach on the fact that Member States can and do place restrictions on the right to vote, even for citizens (e.g. age or competence criteria), and that – albeit less often – they can also deploy a more generous approach to the suffrage, including certain categories of non-nationals within it. This is the case in the UK with Commonwealth citizens. Interestingly, the Advocate General also referred to the fact that EU law does not itself treat the rights it ascribes to citizens of the Union as exclusive, citing Articles 194 and 195 EC as examples of rights (to complain to the Ombudsman or to petition the European Parliament) which are ascribed also to natural and legal persons resident in the Member States,[21] and he noted that it

---

[18] Article 6(1) EU provides that: 'The Union is founded on the principles of liberty, democracy, respect for human rights and fundamental freedoms, and the rule of law, principles which are common to the Member States.'

[19] Para. 69. In the ECHR case law, see, for example, *Hirst v. United Kingdom (No. 2)*, App. No. 74025/01, judgment of 5 October 2005, at para. 60.

[20] Para. 69. [21] Para. 91.

would be paradoxical if the Member States were to remain the ultimate gatekeepers of the personal scope of Union citizenship, by virtue of the link between Union citizenship and nationality of a Member State in Article 17 EC, whilst not at the same time being free to ascribe at least some of those rights of Union citizenship to non-nationals.[22] In other words, it would be odd if the Member States were in an all-or-nothing situation where they could extend all the rights of Union citizenship to a person by allowing them to acquire national citizenship, but they could not, acting autonomously, ascribe a subgroup of those rights to non-citizens.

Rejecting the Spanish argument, the Advocate General denied that allowing the extension of Union citizenship rights to non-nationals of the Member States would '"dismember" the unicity of the concept of citizenship'.[23] He also appeared (albeit implicitly) to refer approvingly to the general principle of alien suffrage by commenting positively upon how the principle of universal suffrage seems to demand voting rights for the largest possible number of persons including 'possibly also for foreigners established in a particular State, who, like citizens, are effectively subject to the measures approved by the national and Community legislative authorities'.[24] The Advocate General also accepted, pragmatically, that in the absence of a uniform electoral procedure there was indeed no consistency among the Member States as to the rules which govern the entitlement to vote for the European Parliament.[25]

It might have been expected, given the conclusions he reached, that the Advocate General would find in favour of the UK's extension of the franchise to allow Commonwealth citizens resident in Gibraltar to vote in European Parliament elections, even though that group of persons *cannot* vote in legislative elections for the Gibraltar Assembly.[26] However, the Advocate General insisted that there are limitations upon the freedom of the Member States to determine the scope of the right to vote for the European Parliament, in particular because such elections are not one-off affairs affecting only one Member State, but rather are matters which affect all the Member States.[27] Consequently, he stressed that the power may be exercised 'only exceptionally' and 'within limits and under conditions which are compatible with Community law'.[28] He cited

---

[22] Para. 82. [23] Para. 92. [24] Para. 93. [25] Para. 100.
[26] Government of Gibraltar, House of Assembly Ordinance, 1950-19, s.3, available from www.gibraltarlaws.gov.gi.
[27] Para. 102. [28] Para. 103.

an example of extensions to persons who had no actual link with the Community (which surely cannot cover the Commonwealth citizens in Gibraltar, who are affected in the same way as other residents by EU legislation) which would not be permissible, and also referred to the principles of reasonableness, proportionality and non-discrimination as governing the compliance of the national rules with EU law. In that sense, the Advocate General saw the situation quite differently to the UK which referred, in its declaration on this matter, to the extension of the right to vote to Gibraltar 'on the same terms' as the electorate of an existing UK constituency.[29]

The reference to compatibility with EU law guided the Advocate General to a consideration of the specifics of Annex II to the Act on Direct Elections.[30] This is a text which, as noted above, originally excluded Gibraltar from the scope of European Parliament elections and a text which remains, to this day, unamended. It was in relation to compliance with Annex II that he found support for the Spanish case, for in effect all of the measures adopted by the UK to give Gibraltarians the vote were adopted in breach of the formal text of Annex II. The Advocate General rejected the contention that in implementing the *Matthews* judgment by facilitating the participation of Gibraltarians in the European Parliament elections the UK should not have included Gibraltar in another UK-based constituency, provided for the establishment of the necessary electoral register, made it possible physically to vote in the dominion, or allowed for legal proceedings to be possible in Gibraltar to contest the elections should an irregularity have occurred.[31] However, as the UK was adopting the relevant unilateral measures essentially in order to comply with a fundamental rights imperative as established in the *Matthews* case, he concluded that it should not take any measures in relation to Gibraltar which did not necessarily follow from this mandate or imperative. He argued that the

> extension [of the franchise to Commonwealth citizens] does not stem from the need to ensure the exercise of a fundamental right and ... therefore a derogation from Annex II is not justified.[32]

---

[29] See above n. 6.
[30] For the latest version of the Act on Direct Elections, see Council Decision amending the Act concerning the election of the representatives of the European Parliament by direct universal suffrage, annexed to Council Decision 76/787/ECSC, EEC, Euratom, OJ 2002 L283/1.
[31] Paras. 125–6.   [32] Para. 128.

On this point, therefore, the Advocate General suggested that the Court should find in favour of Spain. He made that finding notwithstanding his conclusion that there was nothing in the general principles concerned with citizenship and democracy embodied in Articles 17, 19, 189 and 190 EC which precluded the UK adopting the measures that it chose to adopt. Interestingly enough, the Advocate General appeared to find a pathway through the relevant legal provisions allowing him to conclude that, while it was permissible for the UK to give Commonwealth citizens the right to vote in European Parliament elections in the 'mainland' UK (and indeed Spain had not sought to argue this), it was in breach of its EU obligations by so doing in Gibraltar.

The Advocate General's coverage of the issues in the *Aruba* case is somewhat briefer, and draws upon the general principles articulated in the first part of the Opinion about the nature of the right to vote in European Parliament elections under EU law, the role of Member States in this respect, and the scope of limitations and restrictions which they may impose. The case concerned limitations on the right to vote of Union citizens in European Parliament elections, specifically a limitation imposed upon Dutch nationals resident in Aruba. Arubans share a single national citizenship with all other Dutch nationals (whether resident in the Netherlands or in third countries), but they are denied the right to vote in either 'domestic' Dutch or European Parliament elections. The Advocate General concluded that, while normally speaking a Member State may withhold the right to vote in European Parliament elections from certain groups of citizens, where this can be objectively justified, here there was no objective justification for the distinction drawn. The relevant distinction was not between Dutch nationals resident in the Netherlands and those resident in Aruba, but rather between Dutch nationals resident in Aruba and those, previously resident in Aruba, who had moved to another Member State or indeed a third state, without having previously established a connection with the Netherlands (i.e. the European part of the state) itself. The latter group are given, on *leaving* Aruba, the right to vote in national and European Parliament elections under Netherlands law, an outcome which the Advocate General saw as 'not comprehensible'.[33] It undermines completely the basis for arguing that Arubans, although Netherlands nationals and therefore EU citizens, are denied the right to vote in European Parliament elections on the grounds that they lack a relevant

[33] Para. 167.

connection with the EU. It should be noted that Aruba has a different status in relation to the EU and the EU Treaties from that ascribed to Gibraltar, and is not directly affected by EU legislation in the same way as Gibraltar. Thus, in relation to Aruba, the European Parliament could not be described as a legislature, within the meaning of Article 3 of Protocol No. 1 to the ECHR, which was the basis for the reasoning in the *Matthews* case and thus the starting point for the entire saga underpinning the *Gibraltar* case.

While the Advocate General's Opinion is a productive source of provocation about the future of European citizenship, it ultimately leaves unresolved the tension between internal inclusivity and external exclusivity which invades all concepts of citizenship, so long as the bounded nature of citizenship is treated as its central facet. He seems instinctively to want to develop the exclusive aspects of European citizenship, not least because this would help to strengthen European integration, and his conclusions in the *Gibraltar* case seem to indicate a preference for European Parliament elections to be elections by 'European' citizens unless the Member States can demonstrate very good reasons why non-Europeans should be involved. On the other hand, there are several points in the Opinion where the Advocate General appears simultaneously to recognise the attractiveness of an argument which opens out electoral rights to non-nationals on the basis of a principle of affectedness. He notes that:

> the democratic principle of universal suffrage upon which the European Union is based ... militates ... in favour of recognising voting rights for the largest possible number of persons, and therefore possibly also for foreigners established in a particular State, who, like citizens, are effectively subject to the measures approved by the national and Community legislative authorities.[34]

If it is applied the principle of affectedness can, of course, challenge the bounded conception of citizenship.

In the *Gibraltar* case, the Court opted for a narrower approach to the texts and arguments placed before it. It noted from the beginning that Spain was looking for some means of establishing 'a link between citizenship of the Union and the right to vote and to stand as a candidate for the European Parliament, the consequence of that link being that only citizens of the Union can have that right'.[35] However, contrary to the contentions of Spain, it confirmed that Article 19(2) is 'confined to

---

[34] Para. 93.   [35] Case C-145/04, para. 59.

applying the principle of non-discrimination on grounds of nationality[36] to the exercise of the right to vote for the European Parliament. Nor did it find anything in either Article 190 EC or the 1976 Act on Direct Elections defining 'expressly and precisely who are to be entitled to the right to vote and to stand as a candidate in elections to the European Parliament'.[37] It could derive no clear conclusion that there was a clear link between citizenship of the Union and the right to vote in European Parliament elections in Articles 189 or 190 EC or in the provisions on citizenship of the Union. It repeated its favoured phrase from *Grzelczyk*,[38] whereby citizenship of the Union is 'destined to be the fundamental status' of nationals of the Member States, but then went on to state that this statement 'does not necessarily mean that the rights recognised by the Treaty are limited to citizens of the Union'.[39] Thus, to a greater extent than the Advocate General, the Court appears to opt for an open and outward-looking concept of citizenship for the European Union, under which citizenship rights may be constitutive of the status of the nationals of Member States, but the rights themselves are not necessarily confined to citizens alone. However, a warning note should also be sounded for those who seek to derive a stronger concept of Union citizenship from these words, for later in the judgment the Court noted the highly segmented nature of European Parliamentary elections. Because of the way in which the elections are currently organised, 'an extension by a Member State of the right to vote at those elections to persons other than its own nationals or other than citizens of the Union resident in its territory affects only the choice of the representatives elected in that Member State, and has no effect either on the choice or on the representatives elected in the other Member States'.[40]

In conclusion, the Court confirmed that it was 'within the competence of each Member State in compliance with Community law' to define the persons entitled to vote and stand in European Parliament elections, a conclusion which it bolstered also by a reference to the 'constitutional traditions' of the UK in this matter, which include the extension of rights to vote in all UK elections to Commonwealth citizens.[41] It should be noted that the Advocate General himself did not find

---

[36] Case C-145/04, para. 66. [37] Case C-145/04, para. 70.
[38] Case C-184/99 *Rudy Grzelczyk* v. *Centre Public d'Aide Sociale d'Ottignes-Louvain-la-Neuve (CPAS)* [2001] ECR I-6193.
[39] Case C-145/04, para. 74. [40] Case C-145/04, para. 77.
[41] Case C-145/04, paras. 78 and 79.

any problems in the general context of EU law with the principle of Member States extending the right to vote to non-EU citizens, so on this matter the Advocate General and the Court are broadly at one. However, unlike the Advocate General, the Court found no impediment in the detailed text of the Act on Direct Elections and the commitments made by the UK to organise European Parliament elections including the territory of Gibraltar, consequent upon the judgment of the European Court of Human Rights in the *Matthews* case. Rather, given the imperative upon the UK, the Court concluded that, in applying its legislation to the specific case of Gibraltar, the UK 'cannot be criticised for adopting the legislation necessary for the holding of such elections under conditions equivalent, with the necessary changes, to those laid down by the legislation applicable in the United Kingdom'.[42] This includes, of course, the definition of the franchise, which is the same in Gibraltar as it is for the rest of the UK. It is worth noting that, even in its newest version, which moves some way towards a uniform electoral procedure by at least requiring the representatives to be elected on the basis of proportional representation, Article 8 of the Act on Direct Elections continues to provide that, 'subject to the provisions of this Act, the electoral procedure shall be governed in each Member State by its national provisions', and the first recital in the preamble to the 2002 amendments provides that Member States remain free 'to apply their national provisions', subject to the limited restrictions in the Act.

The *Aruba* case concerned not the extension of the right to vote beyond the scope of Union citizenship, but rather its restriction, in this case on the basis of the place of residence of the citizens in question. It is significant that the Court does expressly confirm that as nationals of one of the Member States (sharing Dutch nationality with those resident in the Netherlands) 'citizens' of Aruba are indeed citizens of the Union. It seems to limit its conclusion to those who 'reside or live in a territory which is one of the OCTs referred to in Article 299(3) EC',[43] but would seem equally logical to argue that citizenship of the Union is a personal status of nationals of the Member States which they carry with them wherever they are. How else, logically, could the principle of consular and diplomatic protection for Union citizens while in third countries enacted in Article 20 EC actually apply? It should surely not extend only to those who are temporarily in third countries, but must also extend to those with settled residence in third countries.

---

[42] Case C-145/04, para. 95.   [43] Case C-300/04, para. 29.

However, the Court also confirmed that, as the Treaty contains no rules expressly stating who is to be entitled to vote and stand as a candidate for the European Parliament, it remains a matter, in the current state of Community law, for the competence of the Member States.[44] There is no unconditional right on the part of nationals of the Member States to vote for the European Parliament. In particular, the Member States may choose the criterion of residence to determine who votes. However, the exercise of national competence must occur in compliance with Community law. This led the Court to consider whether an OCT was in the same situation, with regard to Community law, as Gibraltar. It concluded that, unlike the case of Gibraltar, the European Parliament cannot be regarded as a legislature with regard to the OCTs. Hence the *Matthews* doctrine at issue in the *Gibraltar* case does not apply. Moreover, Article 19(2) and Directive 93/109/EC are of no assistance to the applicants in this case, as they concern only the application of the principle of non-discrimination on grounds of nationality. Where the Court does support the applicants is, as with the Advocate General, in relation to the application of the equal treatment principle as between different groups of Dutch nationals. It confirmed that the principle of equal treatment or non-discrimination is a general principle of Community law,[45] and concluded that 'the relevant comparison is between a Netherlands national resident in the Netherlands Antilles or Aruba and one residing in a non-member country'. As the general principle of equal treatment includes the duty not to treat differently those who are in like situations, and since the two groups identified have in common that they are not resident in the Netherlands, there is a *prima facie* case that they should be treated alike. In fact, the latter group can vote in European Parliament elections (on the argument that this helps to maintain their connection to the Netherlands), whereas the former cannot. However, this rationale breaks down when it becomes apparent that Dutch nationals resident in Aruba *gain* the right to vote if they leave Aruba for a third country, since they are then covered by the same general Dutch expatriate voting legislation. The Court concluded that the Netherlands was under an obligation to provide an objective justification for its difference in treatment, and that given this irrationality in the legislative scheme, it had failed to do so.[46]

---

[44] Case C-300/04, para. 45.   [45] Case C-300/04, para. 57.   [46] Case C-300/04, para. 60.

What is notable is the willingness of both the Court of Justice and the Advocate General to extend the protection of the general principles of Community law to a group of citizens of the Union on a personal basis, notwithstanding that they are not 'connected' in any way to the EU as single market, and they are not residing in another Member State. This is the true innovation of the case, and is in many respects far more significant for citizenship as a whole than it is for the narrower question of the right to vote for the European Parliament. The equal treatment principle from which the Arubans benefit is not the general principle of non-discrimination on grounds of nationality which has pervaded the cases hitherto on EU citizenship, such as *Martínez Sala*[47] and *Bidar*,[48] but rather a general principle of equal treatment which protects persons from irrational and unjust legislative outcomes without reference to some physical or social characteristic which they may have (like gender, age or nationality). It is hard to see how the Court could reach that conclusion if it did not have in its mind, notwithstanding its failure to state this explicitly as the Advocate General chose to do, that the right to vote in European Parliament elections is indeed an important incident, or right, of Union citizens.

It would seem that the Court has concluded, in a gloss upon the apparently clear statement in Article 1(2) of Directive 93/109/EC that 'nothing in the Directive shall affect each Member State's provisions concerning the right to vote or stand as a candidate of its nationals who reside *outside its electoral territory*' (emphasis added), that in fact other provisions of EU law *may indeed* constrain such provisions. Clearly, the EU, at its present state of integration, lies some way away from a situation in which there could be a harmonisation of national rules on expatriate voting, but a challenge to general exclusionary expatriate voting rules applicable to European Parliament electoral rights at the national level (e.g. in Ireland) could be regarded as a logical next step of the reasoning in the *Aruba* case. In addition, it is possible to contemplate an attack upon the variable electoral registration arrangements which exist across the Member States which mean that in some cases applications to vote have to be made very far ahead of the actual election, thus discouraging in particular non-national voters, on the grounds that these likewise contravene general principles of EU law, such as proportionality.

---

[47] Case C-85/96 *Martínez Sala* v. *Freistaat Bayern* [1998] ECR I-2691.
[48] Case C-209/03 *R* v. *London Borough of Ealing, ex parte Bidar* [2005] ECR I-2119.

On the same basis, a challenge could also be envisaged in the future to the derogation for Luxembourg in Directive 93/109/EC allowing the imposition of qualifying residence periods for EU citizens seeking to vote or stand in European Parliament elections because of there being a certain percentage of non-national EU citizens of voting age resident in that state, even though such whole state derogations are explicitly provided for in Article 19(2). However, at the very least, the Court may be asked to assess whether the solution chosen in Directive 93/109/EC is proportionate and appropriate to the specific situation of Luxembourg as a Member State with a very small overall population and a high population of non-national EU citizens.[49]

It is thus interesting to note that, while neither the *Gibraltar* nor the *Aruba* cases addressed directly the meaning of the provisions in Article 19, other than to confirm that they are narrow equal treatment rules, the two cases have added somewhat to our broader understanding of Union citizenship, and how political rights fit within this broader status. It is clear from the *Aruba* case in particular that combining the organisation of European-wide elections to the European Parliament, albeit thus far on a segmented national basis,[50] with the creation of a Europe-wide personal status of citizen of the Union can result in quite substantial intrusions into the national electoral sovereignty of the Member States. It seems possible that it is this case, rather than the more immediately politically sensitive *Gibraltar* case, that may have the greatest long-term repercussions for the development of EU citizenship.

III The extension of the electoral rights granted to EU citizens

At the beginning of Chapter 1, I referred to Eurobarometer findings that Union citizens would regard the institution of the right to vote in all elections in the Member State in which they are resident as one of the best ways in which European citizenship could be strengthened.[51] Reflecting these concerns, the question whether EU citizens should

---

[49] A significant point of comparison concerns the Court of Justice's willingness to impose restrictions upon the EU legislature's attempts to structure the exercise of rights under the Treaty: see Dougan, 2006.

[50] One mechanisms for overcoming the segmented and isolated nature of the 'national' elections to the European Parliament would be for a proportion of European Parliament seats to be reserved for election on an EU-wide basis, from transnational party lists. See generally Day and Shaw, 2006.

[51] Eurobarometer Special 251, *The Future of Europe*, May 2006, at 45–6.

have voting rights in national elections has been a consistent theme in written questions posed by MEPs to European Commissioners. For example, in a reply to a question about UK citizens losing voting rights in national elections after fifteen years outside the UK, without acquiring them in the host state,[52] Commissioner Antonio Vitorino commented that:

> The right to vote of own nationals of a Member state in elections of that Member State belongs fully to the competence of the Member States, independent of whether those citizens reside in its territory or outside of its territory. This is explicitly confirmed in the relevant Directives 93/109/EC and Directive 94/80/EC, which provide that nothing in those Directives affects each Member State's provisions concerning the right to vote or to stand as a candidate of its nationals who reside outside of its territory . . . Because of the lack of the competence the Commission does not plan to take any actions relating to the right to vote of nationals of a Member State residing outside of its territory.[53]

Notwithstanding this negative conclusion, the Commission did devote some attention to this question in its Fourth Report on Citizenship of the Union in 2004, raising the matter effectively for the Member States' attention. In so doing, it was picking up a theme it had begun several decades before. As was noted in Chapter 4,[54] back in 1975 it argued that 'complete assimilation with nationals as regards political rights is desirable in the long term from the point of view of *a European Union*' (emphasis added).[55] Returning to this theme in 2004, it noted with regret that:

> Recurrent petitions, parliamentary questions and public correspondence reveal the concerns of many Union citizens regarding a gap in electoral rights at the present level of Community law: Union citizens may still be deprived of important civic rights as a result of the exercise of the right to free movement, namely the right to participate in national or regional

---

[52] Voting by expatriates from the UK was originally introduced by the Representation of the People Act 1985, with a limit set at five years. This was increased to twenty years in the Representation of the People Act 1989, and then reduced to fifteen years by s.141 of the Political Parties and Referendums Act 2000.

[53] Written Question E-1301/02 by Michael Cashman (PSE) to the Commission on *Voting Rights of EU Citizens*, OJ 2003 E92/44. This conclusion might, of course, have to be revisited in the light of the *Aruba* case.

[54] Chapter 4, Section III. The text which follows draws, with permission on Shaw 2007.

[55] Bull. EC Supp. 7/75, point 3.1.

elections. The Member States do not grant electoral rights at national or regional elections to nationals of other Member States residing in their territory.[56]

This comment about recurrent complaints on this matter, it should be noted, is in stark contrast to the Commission's statement in other reports that it has received few complaints over the years about the workings of the right to vote in local elections.[57] The lack of complaints in the latter area could suggest that these work well; it could also provide a message about the comparative salience of local and national elections for voters, and specifically for voters who find themselves resident in a Member State other than the one of which they are a national. What 'special rights' – to reapply the terminology of the early citizenship debates – need to be granted for there to be effective integration of mobile EU citizens into the host state? 'Complete assimilation as regards political rights' is the solution according to the Commission.

In the conclusion to the report, the Commission returned to the same topic, commenting, however, that 'decisions concerning possible measures to be adopted under Article 22(2) of the EC Treaty still require careful consideration'.[58] Article 22 allows for amendments to be adopted to the citizenship provisions using a truncated amendment procedure which avoids the need for a full intergovernmental conference, but still requires any amendments to be ratified by all the Member States following a unanimous agreement in the Council of Ministers, as with other amending treaties. The Commission has yet to make use of its power of proposal in Article 22, and, while it is conceivable that it might make a proposal, it would be highly unlikely for any such proposal to be adopted unanimously by the Council of Ministers. It is notable that, since 1993 and the institution of EU citizenship, the provisions have already been amended in small ways twice – by the Treaties of Amsterdam and Nice.[59] However, in both cases, the provisions adopted formed part of a larger trade-off between the Member States. Without

---

[56] 'Fourth Report on Citizenship of the Union (1 May 2001–30 April 2004)', COM(2004) 695, 26 October 2004, at 8–9. See also the personal (but wholly anonymised) testimonies appearing on the European Year of Workers' Mobility website, http://ec.europa.eu/employment_social/workersmobility_2006/index.cfm?id_page=140/.

[57] 'Commission Report on the Application of Directive 94/80/EC on the Right to Vote and Stand as a Candidate in Municipal Elections', COM(2002) 260, 30 May 2002, at 7.

[58] COM(2004) 695, above n. 56, at 11.

[59] The Treaty of Amsterdam added a phrase to Article 17(1): 'Citizenship of the Union shall complement and not replace national citizenship.' This was part of a set of

the capacity to make such trade-offs against other amendments, it is hard to see Article 22 ever being used.

The Commission returned again to the question of national voting rights for EU citizens in its Communication evaluating the effects of the Tampere Programme in the area of justice and home affairs policy,[60] a programme which is discussed in more detail (at least as pertains to the implications for third country nationals) in Chapter 7. In its Communication, the Commission invited the Member States to open up a dialogue in this area. This is an invitation which they failed to take up when formulating the Hague Programme, which succeeded the Tampere Programme. Instead, the European Council declared that it

> encourages the Union's institutions, within the framework of their competences, to maintain an open, transparent and regular dialogue with representative associations and civil society and to promote and facilitate citizens' participation in public life.[61]

This vague statement hardly seems to presage a collective major initiative from the Member States in this area, and there is nothing in the practical programme for action which refers to electoral rights for non-nationals, even though the possibility of adopting a measure with unspecified contents under Article 22 EC is referred to.[62] In any event, it seems very unlikely that the Member States would demonstrate the collective will at present to adopt a measure under Article 22.

Support for the proposal to extend electoral rights to national elections has come from within the European Parliament in relation to the

---

trade-offs between Denmark and the other Member States. In part, it was retrospective in nature, as the phrase is drawn from the 1992 Conclusions of the Edinburgh European Council which followed the first (failed) Danish referendum on the Treaty of Maastricht, and was agreed as part of a package to persuade the Danish Government and political elite to try, once more, to 'sell' the Treaty to the electorate. In terms of the Treaty of Amsterdam itself, it was also part of a complex trade-off related to the incorporation of Schengen within the framework of the EU Treaties, which included also an 'opt-out' for Denmark in relation to the nature of Schengen law within the domestic legal order, and its continued development, which Denmark has not participated in.

[60] 'Commission Communication on the Area of Freedom, Security and Justice: Assessment of the Tampere Programme and Future Orientations', COM(2004) 401, 2 June 2004, at 8.

[61] Presidency Conclusions, Brussels European Council, Doc. 14292/04, 5 November 2004, Annex 1, at 16.

[62] 'Council and Commission Action Plan Implementing the Hague Programme on Strengthening Freedom, Security and Justice in the European Union', OJ 2005 C198/1, point 2.1, (e).

question of EU citizens voting in national elections. In a somewhat con-
fused and controversial report on the Commission's Fourth Report on
Citizenship which was approved by the Committee on Civil Liberties,
Justice and Home Affairs,[63] several references were made to this question:

> 16. [The Parliament] Calls upon the Member States to discuss forthwith
> the possibility of granting European citizens the right to vote and to stand for
> election in municipal, local and regional elections of the Member State in
> which they are resident, irrespective of nationality; [and]
>
> 17. Calls upon the Member States to discuss forthwith the possibility
> of granting EU citizens the choice of voting and standing for election in
> national elections either in the country in which they are resident or in
> their country of origin (though not in both), irrespective of nationality.

Picking up a text contained in the earlier Opinion given by the Committee
on Constitutional Affairs, the report goes on to suggest that:

> the conferring on European citizens who are not nationals of their
> Member State of residence of the right to vote and to stand for election
> in national and regional elections would make a tangible contribution to
> the feeling of belonging to the Union which is indispensable for genuine
> European citizenship.

However, it is not necessarily obvious why a citizen of one Member State
who is given additional rights of political participation in another
Member State where she is resident should feel more *European* in these
circumstances, as opposed to feeling more attached to the state (generously) conferring these rights upon her. Perhaps the latter is a necessary
precondition for the former? In any event, the report as a whole was
rejected by the European Parliament in plenary in January 2006, largely
because it was opposed by the centre-right majority party grouping of
the European People's Party–European Democrats, and thus this text
should be treated with caution as expressing at most the view of a
particular committee.[64]

A more sophisticated link between European citizenship and electoral
rights for non-nationals in national elections is developed by Heather
Lardy, who argues for voting rights in national elections in terms of the

---

[63] European Parliament Report on the Commission's Fourth Report on Citizenship of the
Union (1 May 2001–30 April 2004), Committee on Civil Liberties, Justice and Home
Affairs, Rapporteur: Giusto Catania, A6-0411/2005, 15 December 2005.

[64] In a vote held in plenary on 17 January 2006, the report was rejected by 276 votes in
favour to 347 against with 22 abstentions.

link between citizenship and self-government and democracy: 'If citizens are denied full voting rights, they are deprived of one of the most effective mechanisms available to them for exerting political power' (Lardy, 1996: 625). Furthermore, she goes on:

> The denial of full voting rights to European Union citizens effectively creates within each Member State two sub-groups of European citizens: those who happen to be national citizens of that state, and those who are not. Only the former group is granted the right to vote in national elections.
>
> (Lardy, 1996: 626–7)

To those who would argue that ascribing wider electoral rights to EU citizens within the Member States would undermine national sovereignty, she argues trenchantly that 'it should be remembered that the primary purpose of democratic principle is not to prescribe the conditions which will protect national sovereignty, but to set out the precepts designed to further and sustain democratic government' (Lardy, 1996: 632). In other words, she invites us to look more critically at the relationship between the defence of national sovereignty and the development of European citizenship as a political and democratic project. Those seeking to defend national sovereignty as they see it by excluding certain groups of residents from the franchise should also have to justify the damage to democracy done by excluding those residents in terms of limiting the scope and compass of democratic *self*-government. Lardy's argument is that, having now breached the boundary which a traditionally exclusive conception of national citizenship places around the boundaries of the suffrage by introducing at least limited electoral rights in the form of Article 19 EC, the Member States consequently must base any rejection of the argument for subsequently extending those rights on something more than the defence of national sovereignty.

The normative issue here is how to prevent the EU free movement space becoming a space of negative democratic impetus. To put it another way, if the impulse of the EU Treaties is positively to encourage EU citizens to exercise their free movement rights, then how are they to be protected against the negative consequences of moving without acquiring the host state citizenship (such as the loss of the right to vote in national elections unless they are protected by expatriate voting rights from their home state), and indeed how are the EU and its Member States as a whole to be protected from losing the democratic input of migrants into national elections? While this number is not necessarily significant at the present time, at around 1.5 per cent of the total population of the Member States, if the exercise of free movement rights under EU law consistently coincides with the loss of democratic participation rights, then this must have negative consequences for the Member States as democratic polities. It is arguably wholly inconsistent for the EU and the Member States to preserve those participation rights by means of non-discrimination rights instituted at EU level under Article 19 EC in relation to *local* and *European* electoral rights, whilst ignoring the impact upon democratic participation in *national* elections.

It seems plausible to argue not only that this is a live issue – as demonstrated above – but also that so long as the EU exists in its current form it is likely to become an ever more acute challenge both to the EU as an emergent polity, and to the Member States as more established polities. Consequently, it is useful to consider the various mechanisms by which the Member States, separately or together, in conjunction with the EU institutions or alone, might address this challenge, even if the political omens regarding decisive action at the present time are poor. The objective here is not to make a plea for one particular outcome, in particular a generalised extension of national electoral rights to EU citizens, but rather to illustrate the richness of the legal instruments available to the Member States at the present time, and to indicate how they might be developed in the future.

Under EU law as it stands, the Member States enjoy full and unlimited discretion as to the groups upon which they may confer the franchise in national elections, subject only to the strictures of the European Convention on Human Rights such as Article 3 of Protocol No. 1. This means an unlimited power to restrict the franchise to national citizens alone, and an unfettered discretion as to whether, and under what conditions, to grant the right to expatriates to vote in national elections, and to how to deal with issues of voter registration and absentee ballots. This is the *status quo*.

Clearly, if each and every migrant EU citizen became a citizen of the Member State in which they resided, then there would be less of a difficulty, although this would still not deal with issues raised by differences of rules on expatriate and absentee voting. However, citizenship acquisition is unlikely to be the answer. As things stand, a resident non-national EU citizen may be unable or unwilling to acquire the nationality of the host Member State for one or more of the following reasons: failure to satisfy a qualifying residence period; failure to satisfy other citizenship acquisition conditions requiring applicants to pass language or cultural tests, to relinquish other nationalities (if dual nationality is not tolerated), or to state long-term future residence intentions; or unwillingness to acquire the host state nationality on grounds of a future intention to return to the home state or to move to a third state. There is presently nothing like a system of automatic or ascriptive citizenship acquisition for resident non-nationals (without prejudice to home state citizenship). Thus each and every national of a Member State resident in another Member State will have to satisfy whatever conditions are imposed by the host on nationality acquisition. Ruth Rubio-Marín argues in favour of a system of automatic or ascriptive citizenship acquisition by resident non-nationals, making the argument precisely in order to find a normatively satisfactory method for promoting democratic inclusion in the context of migration: she sees 'immigration as a *democratic* challenge' (Rubio-Marín, 2000).

In terms of what such a shift in approach might mean for the development of a more intensive multi-level system of federal-type citizenship in the Union, it is useful to make the comparison with the US. In combination with the gradual development and hardening of a concept of national citizenship over many years, a matter on which the original constitution itself was remarkably silent (Smith, 1997: 115–28), the United States has developed a form of state citizenship which links to residence alone, rather than any other marker of belonging. However, this was imposed from above through the Fourteenth Amendment's Citizenship Clause, which provides that US citizens are citizens of the state 'in which they reside' (Schuck, 2000: 223). It did not result from the separate or even collective decision of the states. Such a decision would be required in the Union at its present stage of development. In the Union, Directive 2004/38/EC does at least (and – some might say – 'finally') create a status of permanent resident, which removes any further conditions upon the right of residence of the Union citizen, thus potentially smoothing the pathway for a Union citizen who does in fact seek naturalisation in the host state by establishing a framework for establishing settled residence. It also seeks to ensure that EU citizens are granted equal treatment with nationals so far as pertains to any matter falling within the scope of EU law. But it does not directly interfere with national citizenship status, or matters such as electoral rights at the national level. However, it is perhaps arguable that the status of permanent residence should be regarded as a form of 'citizenship-of-residence-lite' for resident non-national EU citizens. In that case, could it be seen as a sufficient condition for the granting of electoral rights to vote in national elections in the host state, as the next step towards integration?

Alternatively, we could shift the focus from looking at rights within the *host state*, to consider the case for Member States to facilitate *home state voting* for expatriates resident in other Member States. Home states could do this without changing the rules on the right to vote simply by relaxing registration arrangements to allow the loosest of connections with the home state to suffice as the basis for registration in the former district of residence. Alternatively, Member States could look more closely at expatriate voting arrangements. In the latter case, this could be either with specialist arrangements for direct representation of expatriates in the legislature (as in France and now, most recently and controversially, Italy where expatriates effectively decided the outcome of the 2006 General Election), or with participation of expatriate voters in the normal elections of home-based representatives, as in the case of the UK (where expatriate votes are reallocated back to the constituency where the expatriate most recently resided). This may be hard to sustain in the longer term, as indeed may the alternative of allowing flexible arrangements for voter registration in their former domicile, as the connections between the expatriate (and even potentially their children and grandchildren) and their state of origin become ever looser. In turn, of course, that very looseness of the connection undermines the case for arguing that expatriate voting is an adequate form of democratic representation, since it can easily be argued that the expatriate voter may always be a relatively disconnected and ill-informed voter, and thus hardly one who adds to the democratic quality of the electoral process (López-Guerra, 2005).

In any event, wherever there is a possibility that an expatriate EU citizen resident in another Member State could have two votes (in the home and the host state), the question arises as to the desirability and acceptability of dual voting. Under Directive 93/109/EC,[65] both dual voting and dual candidatures are emphatically ruled out in respect of European Parliament elections. Article 4(1) provides that:

> Community voters shall exercise their right to vote either in the Member State of residence or in their home Member State. No person may vote more than once at the same election.

It is, of course, clearly wrong that any person should have two votes in a single election, even one that is still conducted along essentially segmented

---

[65] Council Directive 93/109/EC laying down detailed arrangements for the exercise of the right to vote and stand as a candidate in elections to the European Parliament for citizens of the Union residing in a Member State of which they are not nationals, OJ 1993 L329/34.

national lines. However, it is not so clearly problematic that a person should have two votes in separate national elections. Persons with dual nationality may already be able to vote in general elections in two Member States, depending upon the national rules in place. Interestingly, Maarten Vink comments upon a trade-off within Dutch parliamentary politics. The case for extending electoral rights in national elections to non-nationals (building upon the right to vote in local elections introduced in the 1980s) was traded off between the two governing parties, the Christian Democrats (who were against) and the Social Democrats (who were in favour), to produce an outcome which supported greater toleration of dual nationality instead (Vink, 2005: 5). This emphasises the intimate link between policies on expatriate voting and voting rights for non-nationals and citizenship policies. Meanwhile, in Belgium in the 2000s, expatriate voting rights were traded against local voting rights for third country nationals.

Under EU law at present, any formal change to the rights and status of EU citizens within the Member States will need to be driven forward by national action. What role could the EU be given or acquire in this domain?

The Member States could always choose to act together, by changing the EU Treaties to institute an equivalent to Article 19 EC in the domain of national elections and thus oblige themselves to secure national implementation of the EU citizen's right to equal treatment in relation to national elections, just as they did with local and European Parliamentary electoral rights. This would require a formal extension of existing powers and competences either under Article 22(2) EC by way of a free-standing addition to the citizenship provisions under this truncated amendment procedure (and initiating that process would require an initiative from the Commission), or as part of a generalised treaty amendment process. While I have already commented on the unlikelihood of the Council and the Commission in practice applying Article 22(2), the latter proposal for generalised treaty amendment is the type of change to the EU Treaties which looks ever more unlikely in the wake of the failure of the Constitutional Treaty to achieve ratification in 2005 and 2006. Even under more propitious political circumstances than those pertaining in the mid-2000s, the need to achieve unanimous agreement around and unanimous ratification of a measure which would necessarily involve an intrusion into national sovereign choices elections militates against such a major change in the scope of the EU Treaties.

Marginally more conceivable is a Treaty provision which merely encourages the Member States to adopt electoral rights in national elections. This could be along the lines of Article 41 EC, which states that: 'Member States shall, within the framework of a joint programme, encourage the exchange of young workers.' Any such reference to voting in national elections in the Treaty, even if it did not include a dispositive element such as that which can be found in Article 19 EC, would open the way for the Commission to propose various forms of action promoting convergence or benchmarking as between the Member States in relation to electoral rights practices, so long as such action fell short of proposing formal harmonisation of national laws. Even without such a reference, in the interests of promoting EU citizenship, the Commission could doubtless already encourage forms of soft law action on the part of the Member States such as, for example, a Council Recommendation on electoral rights for EU citizens. As will be seen in Chapter 7, these types of measures have been much used in recent years in the field of policy-making in relation to the integration of immigrants from third country nationals, where such policy action lies at the margins of the EU's formal competences. There have even been references in some policy documents to encouraging the Member States to institute local electoral rights for such immigrants. However, such measures do not impose enforceable obligations upon the Member States.

An alternative way forward could be to use a mechanism of international law outside the formal legal framework of the EU Treaties, which would have the advantage of providing a flexible structure into which the Member States could opt, as politics and circumstances dictated. Using the mechanisms of international law to promote flexible policy-making in the EU is a form of 'old-fashioned' flexibility, not least because this mechanism has always existed and makes use of the external resources of international law, and in particular the principle of reciprocity of obligations (de Witte, 2000). Thus, instead of just adopting recommendations or guidelines which the Member States take little notice of, and which it cannot formally enforce, the Commission could try to encourage the Member States to follow the line taken by at least some Member States with the Schengen Agreement in the 1980s. Namely, some or all of the Member States could explore the possibilities for further integration or for a laboratory of integration offered by an international agreement developed outside the framework of the European Union, without prejudice to the possibilities of future Union action or Union competences in the field. Such a Convention negotiated between all the Member States could lay down a consensual framework for reciprocal recognition of voting rights in national elections to non-nationals on a bilateral and possibly multilateral basis, and provide a roadmap to achieving mutual recognition in this field, and thus encourage the development of the requisite trust and common action between the Member States needed for developments to occur in this area. The Convention could be developed such that it comes into force as soon as a minimum of two Member States have formally signed and ratified it, thus creating a dispositive framework that states could gradually opt into as they developed bilateral arrangements with their partners within the Union. The level of detail in the Convention should at the minimum outline the issues relating to registration and mutual recognition covered in the two electoral rights directives of 1993 and 1994.

It may be objected that there already exist many international instruments in the field, including ones which are much less far-reaching in nature, such as the Council of Europe Convention on the Political Participation of Foreigners in Local Life,[66] which the majority of the Member States have declined to adopt and ratify. Why should they proceed with a convention along the lines suggested? The reply to this objection would presumably point to the incentives on the Member States resulting from a convention which is clearly reciprocal in nature, offering the possibility for Member States creating bilateral or possibly multilateral arrangements of reciprocity in the first instance for which there may be genuine pressure from their respective citizens (e.g. Portugal/Spain; Germany/France; Sweden/Finland/Denmark; Czech/ Slovak Republics; Baltic states; Benelux; and so on). Only after trust has been built up in the context of such relationships might Member States move on towards generalising the ascription of voting rights in national elections. The downside of such alliances, of course, could be the increasing fragmentation of EU law, and the danger that some European citizens may find themselves excluded from access to what is regarded as the 'gold standard' of political rights, just because the Member State where they reside and the one of which they hold the national citizenship do not belong to the same alliance.

On the other hand, one advantage of this manner of proceeding, which stresses reciprocity, is that it could build in interesting ways upon the few examples of the ascription of voting rights to non-nationals in *national* elections within the Member States of the

---

[66] ETS No. 144; opened for signature on 5 February 1992; entered into force 1 May 1997; www.conventions.coe.int.

European Union at the present time. The UK is the most substantial case, giving rights to Irish citizens, and to Cypriot and Maltese citizens as Commonwealth citizens, to vote in all UK elections,[67] subject only to satisfactory immigration status.[68] They may also stand for election, but again subject to satisfactory immigration status.[69] The franchise for Irish citizens and Commonwealth citizens is a legacy of the British Empire and the slow emergence of a concept of 'citizenship' as opposed to 'subjecthood' (to the Crown) in the UK.[70] In that sense, neither Irish citizens nor Commonwealth citizens were treated as 'aliens', that is, as persons whose influence on domestic politics should be prevented.

From time to time, the case for extending the suffrage is canvassed in the UK Parliament. The views of the various political parties presented in a 1998 Home Affairs Select Committee of the House of Commons Report on Electoral Law and Administration[71] give a flavour of the range of views, and how these map onto the political landscape:

> [I]t has been suggested that the right to vote in parliamentary elections could be extended to all EU citizens or, further still, that the right to vote in all elections could be given to all foreign residents after they had been

[67] The Representation of the People Act 1918 established the first truly modern franchise for the UK Westminster Parliament, abolishing property qualifications for men and introducing the franchise for (some) women for the first time. At the time it posited the franchise for 'British subjects', and, when Ireland and what are now the countries of the Commonwealth became independent states, the franchise arrangements were preserved and updated, for example in the Ireland Act 1949. The relevant consolidating legislation laying down the general entitlement to vote is the Representation of the People Act 1983, as amended. For a review of the current scope of the franchise, see House of Commons Library Standard Note, 'Electoral Franchise: Who Can Vote?', SN/PC/2208, 1 March 2005.

[68] House of Commons Library Standard Note, 'The Franchise and Immigration Status', SN/PC/419, 11 October 2005. There is now a requirement that to be registered a person must have leave to enter and remain in the UK: ss.1, 2 and 4 of the Representation of the People Act 1983, as substituted by s.1 of the Representation of the People Act 2000. Such a person is a 'Qualifying Commonwealth Citizen'.

[69] It is s.3 of the Act of Settlement 1700 which prescribes the basic contours of the right to stand for election in the UK, although its requirement that a person be born in England, Scotland or Ireland or one of the dominions thereto in order to stand for election does not apply to Irish and Commonwealth citizens. However, until the adoption of the Electoral Administration Act 2006, s.18, the immigration status of the candidates had not been dealt with in like manner to the immigration status of non-national voters. See House of Commons Library Research Paper 05/65, 'The Electoral Administration Bill 2005', October 2005, at 74.

[70] In Case C-145/04 *Spain* v. *UK (Gibraltar)*, 12 September 2006, at para. 79, the Court recognised this position as one of the constitutional traditions of the UK. The issue is discussed in more detail in Chapter 8, Section IV.

[71] HC 768-I, Session 1997–8, at para. 118.

in this country for a set period of time. The representatives of the political parties were not at one on this point, with Lord Parkinson for the Conservatives reluctant to extend the current exceptions, Mr Gardner for Labour recognising there might be a case – particularly on the basis of reciprocity – for some extension, and Mr Rennard for the Liberal Democrats suggesting that the present distinctions were artificial and that *prima facie* those who were resident here and paying taxes should have some form of right to vote ... [W]e do not think the present voting entitlements for non-UK citizens need extension.

From the UK perspective, the franchise for EU citizens is already one step closer to being universal since, unlike other Member States of a federal or proto-federal character, the UK allows EU citizens to vote in the elections for the devolved Parliaments/Assemblies of the component nations of the UK.[72] Moreover, the degree of openness to this question in the UK is further illustrated by the fact that, prior to the publication of the draft European Union Bill, which would if passed have provided for the UK's referendum on the Constitutional Treaty, there was some speculation in political circles about whether the government would propose extending the franchise to EU citizens resident in the UK.[73] However, in the event, the Bill proposed that the franchise should be based on that for general elections in the UK, and thus included only Irish, Cypriot and Maltese citizens resident in the UK. Since Irish citizens would not have had an expatriate electoral right in relation to voting in the Irish referendum, they would not have enjoyed double representation. Interestingly, however, in a nod in the direction of the Gibraltar saga detailed above, the Bill also included the Gibraltar European Parliament electorate in the franchise.[74]

Ireland is the only other EU Member State which gives rights to vote in national elections to nationals of any other EU Member State.[75] It gives the right to vote, but not stand, in *Dáil* elections to UK citizens. It

---

[72] See further on this Chapter 8, Section VI.

[73] Conspiracy theorists suggested that the Labour Government of Prime Minister Tony Blair might try to extend the franchise in this way to increase the chances of a 'yes' vote in the referendum, on the (perhaps misplaced) assumption that EU citizens from other Member States resident in the UK might be more likely to vote 'yes'. The possible options for the franchise (local or national) are canvassed in 'Proposals for a Referendum on the New European Constitution', House of Commons Library, Standard Note, SN/PC 3064, 27 May 2004.

[74] European Union Bill 2005, clause 7.

[75] Ireland also grants electoral rights to all non-nationals in local elections (voting and standing), and has done so since 1972. This is discussed further in Chapter 8.

does not give UK citizens the right to vote in referendums or Presidential elections.

The text of the Ninth Amendment to the *Bunreacht na hÉireann* (Irish Constitution) which was passed by referendum in 1984 gives a general power to the *Oireachtas* (Irish Parliament) to legislate to extend rights to vote in *Dáil* elections to non-citizens. These provisions were only introduced after a case had been brought before the Supreme Court which contested a 1983 Bill which would have originally extended the franchise to UK citizens to vote not only in *Dáil* elections, but also in elections for the President and in referendums.[76] This Bill was intended to extend the existing legal position which already gave UK citizens the right to vote in local elections (along with all resident non-nationals) and in European Parliament elections (in the latter case, of course, in advance of the introduction of Article 19 EC). A primary motivation for the 1983 Bill was to introduce some element of reciprocity in relation to the electoral rights granted under UK law to Irish citizens.

In finding that the Bill violated the Constitution, as it stood, the Supreme Court concluded that Article 16 of the Irish Constitution in the form in which it then existed provided a complete code limiting the electorate for the *Dáil* elections to Irish citizens, and Irish citizens alone. There could be no possibility of extending by ordinary legislation the franchise to other groups of electors, as had been contended by the Attorney General,[77] who was tasked with arguing the case for a Bill which had been piloted through Parliament by the Fine Gael/Labour coalition government before being challenged before the Supreme Court. The Supreme Court based its argument on a conception of the national suffrage oriented around a concept of national popular sovereignty. It found that this conception of sovereignty underpins the Irish constitution:

> Article 6 [of the Constitution] proclaims that all powers of government derive under God from the people and, further, that it is the people's right to designate the rulers of the State and, in final appeal, to decide all questions of national policy. There can be little doubt that 'the people'

---

[76] *In the Matter of Article 26 of the Constitution and in the Matter of the Electoral (Amendment) Bill, 1983 [SC No. 373 of 1983]* [1984] IR 268. UK citizens continue to be excluded from voting in Presidential elections and referendums. These are powers reserved under the Constitution to citizens alone, by interpretation of Article 6 of the Constitution.

[77] Interestingly, the Attorney General of Ireland at the time was Peter Sutherland, later to become Irish Commissioner and Director General of the WTO, and an important proponent of closer European integration.

here referred to are the people of Ireland by, and for, whom the Constitution was enacted. In short, this Article proclaims that it is the Irish people who are the rulers of Ireland and that from them, under God, all powers of government derive and that by them the rulers are designated and national policy decided. It is not possible to regard this Article as contemplating the sharing of such powers with persons who do not come within the constitutional concept of the Irish people in Article 6.

The Court went on to distinguish between a provision regarding the basic political organisation of the state, such as Article 16 on the suffrage, and provisions on fundamental rights such as freedom of association and expression, granted ostensibly under the Constitution to citizens alone, but which the courts had interpreted in certain circumstances as protecting the rights of non-citizens also. Consequently, Article 16 was interpreted as providing an exhaustive definition of the suffrage, which meant that the introduction of electoral rights for UK citizens (and any other non-citizens) would require a constitutional amendment.

After the referendum adopting the Ninth Amendment to the Constitution, the Electoral (Amendment) Act 1985 was passed amending the suffrage for *Dáil* elections to cover British citizens, and to create a power for a minister to extend this on the basis of reciprocity in the event that other EU Member States confer the right to vote in their parliamentary elections on Irish citizens. Thus:

(1B) Where the Minister is of opinion that—

(a) the law of a Member State relating to the election of members of, or deputies or other representatives in or to, the National Parliament of that Member State enables citizens of Ireland, by reason of their being such citizens and being resident in that Member State, to vote at such an election, and

(b) the provisions of that law enabling citizens of Ireland who are so resident so to vote are the same, or are substantially the same, as those enabling nationals of that Member State so to vote,

the Minister may by order declare that Member State to be a Member State [whose citizens may vote in *Dáil* elections].[78]

This is an interesting development on two counts: first, because, while the political act of extending the suffrage to UK citizens can be regarded as

---

[78] S.2 of the Electoral Amendment Act 1985 inserting a new s.1B into s.5 of the Electoral Act 1963 (now Electoral Act 1992, s.8(2)–(7)).

recognising the historical connection between, and the overlapping citizenships of, the two states of the UK and Ireland, as well as the rights granted by the UK to Irish citizens,[79] only the condition of reciprocity is applied for the future to other EU Member States. The second curiosity is that it requires only a ministerial order to extend the suffrage beyond its current boundaries, the relevant parliamentary consent having already been given.

As it stands, with the reciprocity requirement in s.8(3) of the Electoral Act 1992, the trigger for action must in principle come from another Member State, or from common action amongst the Member States. The debates in the Irish Parliament on this question looked

> forward to the day when member states will be prepared to confer on each other's citizens the right to vote at parliamentary elections. [The Irish Government] would welcome this development and, in anticipation of it, this Bill proposes to enable the Minister by order to extend the *Dáil* vote on a reciprocal basis to nationals of other member states.[80]

While the issue of extending electoral rights to EU citizens has not recently been actively debated in Irish politics, it is supported within a number of opposition parties, notably Sinn Féin and the Labour Party, even as an issue which should be taken up unilaterally by Ireland, in the absence of common action amongst the Member States.[81] The logic of

---

[79] Introducing the original Electoral (Amendment) Bill 1983 into the *Dáil*, the Minister stated that 'the aim of this Bill is to give a further measure of practical expression to what has been referred to as the unique relationship which exists between this country and our nearest neighbour, and to acknowledge and reciprocate the voting rights enjoyed by Irish citizens. It is my hope that measures such as this, reflecting close ties between neighbouring peoples, will make their contribution to promoting peace and reconciliation throughout these islands.' Debates *Dáil Éireann*, vol. 345, 19 October 1983, col. 251. The case for excluding British citizens from the right to vote in Presidential elections, *Seanad Éireann* (upper house) elections and referendums was highlighted by the speaker from Fianna Fáil, Bobby Molloy TD, precisely because there cannot be reciprocity in the UK with a non-elected Head of State and Upper House, and (at that time) no tradition of referendums, Debates *Dáil Éireann*, vol. 345, 19 October 1983, col. 253. As was noted, text accompanying n. 74 above, the franchise for the UK referendum on the Constitutional Treaty would have included all those entitled to vote in general elections in the UK, including Irish citizens.

[80] Minister for the Public Service (Mr Boland), Debates *Seanad Éireann*, vol. 108, 27 June 1985, col. 1193.

[81] Interviews conducted in the *Oireachtas* on 3 March 2005 with TDs (Irish MPs) representing Sinn Fein and the Labour Party; a TD representing the Green Party was broadly supportive of the suggestion in the light of wider Green Party policy, some of which is highly critical of developments within the EU notably in the defence field, but a Senator from the Progressive Democrats, the junior coalition partner of the Fianna Fáil government, was much more sceptical.

EU electoral rights does seem to point in the direction of extension along these lines, and there is certainly some bottom-up pressure from those affected, yet it does not seem likely that there will be legal developments aimed at extending electoral rights to non-nationals to vote in parliamentary or general elections at the EU level in the near future, and there is currently no evidence that any Member State is ready to take the initiative.

What the combined examples of the existing franchises in the UK and Ireland show is that there are many conceivable routes within political argument towards the extension of the franchise in national elections to resident non-national EU citizens. In Ireland, a mechanism such as an international agreement between the Member States could be a trigger for developing the reciprocity necessary to extending the existing scope of the franchise whilst preserving flexibility of response for the Member States.

In the UK, it would be only a small shift from acknowledging that the degree of integration of and trust in resident non-national EU citizens which makes them part of the electorate for elections to the devolved authorities of the non-English parts of the UK, to acknowledging that the same principles of integration and trust should also mandate the possibility that an EU citizen, perhaps having served a qualifying residence period, should be able to participate in Westminster elections as well as elections to institutions based in Edinburgh, Cardiff or Belfast. This argument might particularly be made in respect of EU citizens resident in *England* who do not currently enjoy the opportunities for democratic participation given to their EU citizen peers in Scotland, Wales and Northern Ireland to vote for the authorities which hold powers in fields such as education, agriculture, transport and health and, in the case of the Scottish Parliament, at least, the power to make primary legislation. In any event, the existing anomalies in relation to the UK's asymmetric federal arrangements are enhanced by the differences in the franchise between these two types of elections, and any attempt to review the UK's current constitutional settlement should surely take that question into account.[82] A Convention mechanism could create, as for Ireland, the institutional structure in which the necessary trust and reciprocity between the Member States could gradually be seeded and then developed.

---

[82] There is a further discussion of EU citizens voting in devolved or 'regional' elections in Chapter 8, Section VI.

However, one final note of caution needs to be sounded, and this concerns possible constitutional obstacles at the national level which may be faced by this type of innovation in the broad context of European integration. While the UK clearly knows no constitutional obstacle to including non-nationals within the franchise for the purposes of national elections, since it already allows Irish and Commonwealth citizens to vote and stand in Westminster elections, and since Ireland has already successfully amended its constitution to make it possible in practice to enfranchise non-national EU citizens, it can be assumed that these two states would not encounter a significant difficulty. However, for Ireland to go beyond what has already been established in order to enshrine, for example, a right to stand for election, or the right to vote in Presidential elections or referendums, would undoubtedly require a further amendment to the Constitution. Equally, it can be assumed that constitutional changes would be required in most if not all of the other Member States. Rights to vote in national and regional elections cut closer to the heart of national sovereignty than do local (or indeed European parliamentary) electoral rights, and the latter set of electoral rights already required national constitutional adjustment in many Member States (O'Leary, 1996: 218–33; Oliver, 1996: 476–8).

However, there may in some cases be a further problem beyond the feasibility and political possibility of such a sensitive constitutional amendment, and that concerns its very possibility in constitutional terms, given that it would be proposed to include non-nationals within the group of persons tasked with electing the sovereign legislature. It may simply be legally impossible to amend some of the national constitutions of the Member States to allow for non-national EU citizens to vote in national elections, as to do so would violate their fundamental self-conceptions as nation states, where power flows from the 'people' and the 'people' is the national citizens, bound together in a community. The rulings of the German Federal Constitutional Court in 1990 annulling *Land* level legislation put forward by Hamburg and Schleswig-Holstein to introduce electoral rights for non-nationals were discussed briefly in Chapter 3, and will be the subject of close attention in Chapter 9.[83] Extrapolating from those rulings to the question as to whether a constitutional amendment would be possible to give non-national EU citizens the right to vote in German national elections raises some obvious problems, in so far as the Federal Constitutional Court

---

[83] BVerfGE 63, 37 (Schleswig-Holstein); BVerfGE 63, 60 (Hamburg), 31 October 1990.

demonstrates a clear constitutional preference for a bounded concept of the *demos* calculated by reference to the limits of formal legal nationality, with some indications in the text that it has a preference for a concept of a national legal community involving strong societal bonds (of language, culture, and so on). This goes to the untouchable core of the German constitutional framework, in so far as the *Staat*, which is the basis for calculating the *Staatsvolk* (literally, the 'state's people'), is defined in the Basic Law as a democratic, federal and social state based on the rule of law, and in so far as the Court seems to indicate its support for the principle that there can be no democracy without a *demos*, a legally defined group which in turn wields state power (Rubio-Marín, 2000: 205). One does not need to be deploying an ethno-cultural reading of the concept of *Volk* in the German Basic Law for it to be possible to envisage difficulties with an attempt to amend the text to allow nonnationals to wield state power, even in the liberal and increasingly pluralistic society which Germany is today, just because of the tight conception of political responsibility which the Court gave in the 1990 judgments. In its rulings, it did explicitly recognise the possibility of EU citizens being given the right to vote in the future in local elections, as this was already under discussion at the time (1990). This required an amendment to Article 28 of the Basic Law, as part of the package of measures introduced to give effect to the Treaty of Maastricht. However, it remains a moot point in German constitutional law whether the Basic Law can be stretched first to accommodate local electoral rights of third country nationals and secondly to accommodate national electoral rights of non-national EU citizens.

7

Electoral rights for third country nationals: what role for the European Union?

I Introduction

In the previous chapter, we examined two key aspects of the debate about the material scope of EU electoral rights, highlighting where the potential might lie for an EU citizen to gain additional electoral rights when resident in a Member State other than the one of which he or she is a national, and emphasising the as yet untapped potential for European Parliament voting rights to reinforce the vertical dimension of Union citizenship. The focus shifts in this chapter to the debate regarding the personal scope. What scope is there for measures to be enacted at EU level to enhance the political participation of nationals of third countries resident in the Member States? Can, for example, the Member States be *obliged* under EU law to institute local electoral rights for third country nationals? Does the EU already have the relevant competence under the Treaties, and – if not – is it likely or even conceivable that the Treaties will be amended to make it possible for such measures to be adopted? More broadly, what is the scope for EU citizenship itself to be widened to encompass third country nationals as EU citizens, a change which would automatically have the effect of bringing them within the scope of Article 19 EC and its implementing directives? Would there be any prospect for change in that direction under the Constitutional Treaty, or by virtue of the application of the Charter of Fundamental Rights? In the absence of any powers of compulsion, whether now or in the future, to what extent does the EU already encourage Member States to adopt such rights by merely persuasive means?

This chapter will examine the manner in which these matters have thus far been debated across the EU institutions, the Member States, and – to a lesser extent – the associations and bodies of civil society (NGOs) which frequently intervene in the debate to argue for the extension of migrants' rights. One key question is whether, if the EU did have the competence to adopt such a measure, it should actually do so. Alternatively, would it be more appropriate, and more in accordance with the principle of subsidiarity, for the matter to remain with the Member States allowing them to adopt measures which are appropriate to local conditions? Presently, twelve Member States allow all third country nationals to vote in local elections (of which most accord also the right to stand for election), and three give rights to some third country nationals.[1]

II Third country nationals and the European Union

Some background is necessary in this context, both to present the figures regarding resident third country nationals within the Member States and to highlight the limitations upon EU competence in relation to third country nationals. Any statistics, and comparisons with the figures for non-national EU citizen voters, should always be treated with caution, not least because it is notoriously difficult to assess accurately the number of resident non-nationals present within a state at any one time as many (non-EU – and indeed EU8 Member State) foreigners are resident without lawful permits, or are resident for a brief period of time or on a seasonal basis (Salt, 2005). In addition, there is a marked diversity of rules on nationality acquisition across the Member States, whether by naturalisation for first-generation migrants or by birth or registration for second and subsequent generations. This diversity is one reason why patterns of immigration, integration into the host state, and nationality held do not map neatly across each other.

Interestingly, from the very beginning writers appreciated the link between the development of European Community law and the evolution of patterns of migration in the Member States. Commenting on figures showing that after establishment of the European Communities the percentage of nationals of the Member States amongst the total number of migrants within the Member States declined over a period of around fifteen years from 75 per cent in 1959 to 25 per cent in 1973, Richard Plender observes that this is no coincidence:

> In ensuring that nationals of the several member States, employed within the same enterprise in the Communities, will enjoy equally with nationals of the State in which the enterprise is situated the same pay, the same social security entitlements and the same conditions of employment the organs of the Communities seem to have made nationals of the Member

---

[1] See Tables 3.1 and 3.2 in Chapter 3 above.

States less attractive to employers within the Communities than are
nationals of Third Countries, to whom those rights have not yet been
applied.

(Plender, 1976: 40)

Today, around 1.5 per cent of EU nationals are resident in another
Member State at any one time – a proportion which has hardly changed
for more than twenty years.[2] In the short term, the impact of enlargement in 2004 has changed the scale of the free movement of EU citizens
to a limited degree, and certainly distorted the patterns. Longer term,
however, there is no reason to believe that the level of free movement
will not revert to the pre-2004 levels right across all the Member States,
as standards of living rise in the new Member States and both the push
and the pull factors decline. Despite the best efforts of the Commission
in particular to promote the benefits of workers' mobility, there do
not appear to be either the psychological or practical factors in place
to give rise to the types of high levels of mobility of workers or other
categories of migrants such as students which are more familiar in the
US where intra-country migration is at much higher levels than intra-
EU migration.

While much larger numbers of third country nationals are now
resident in all of the Member States than nationals of other Member
States, this has not always been the case. In 1994, the average of third
country nationals as a proportion of the population of the fifteen
Member States was 2.7 per cent; in 2003, the average (including what
were then the ten accession states) was 3.76 per cent.[3] In Germany, by
2000 the proportion of foreign residents altogether had risen to 8.9 per cent
of residents, or 7.3 million foreigners, a figure which stayed steady until
2004, when it dropped to 6.7 million, or 8.1 per cent of residents.[4] This
drop can presumably be attributed at least in part to the effects of the
new nationality law which came into force on 1 January 2000.[5] Only a
quarter of foreign residents were from the EU Member States in 2003,[6]

---

[2] *Migration News*, July 2005 vol. 12 No. 4, http://migration.udavis.edu/mn/.
[3] 'Integration of Third Country Nationals', MEMO/05/290, 1 September 2005. This
document gives comprehensive figures for the then twenty-five Member States regarding
the percentages of third country nationals resident in 2003, but does not compare these
figures with the numbers of EU citizens.
[4] *Migrationsbericht des Bundesamtes für Migration und Flüchtlinge im Auftrag der
Bundesregierung (Migrationsbericht 2005)*, at 172.
[5] This is discussed in more detail in Section II of Chapter 9.
[6] *Trends in International Migration*, Paris: OECD, 2003, at 201.

although this percentage rose somewhat after enlargement in 2004, as the overall numbers of foreign residents dropped slightly and the large group of nearly 300,000 Poles resident in Germany moved into the category of EU citizens.[7]

The patterns demonstrated by these figures are replicated across the EU Member States. According to 2001 figures, there were 764,300 foreigners in Austria, accounting in total for 9.4 per cent of the population. However, EU citizens made up just 1.3 per cent of the population. Thus third country nationals constitute around 8 per cent of the total population.[8] In the Netherlands in 2001, 30 per cent of the foreigners were from the European Union, with foreigners themselves representing 4.2 per cent of the population. However, because of the relatively unrestrictive conditions for naturalisation and nationality acquisition in the Netherlands, this gives a rather misleading picture of the current Dutch population, since a total of 18.5 per cent of the population in 2001 had at least one parent born outside the Netherlands.[9]

Moreover, in some Member States (particularly those with higher growth rates), the situation is changing fast. The situation in Spain is illustrative of this. Official figures released in Spain in January 2006 indicated that the number of foreigners in Spain in 2005 rose to 8.5 per cent of the total population, or 3.7 million out of a total population of 44.1 million,[10] and it was expected to continue rising rapidly above 4 million on the basis of projections using current trends. This was against a foreign population of just over 1.1 million reported in the OECD's 'Trends in International Migration' report in respect of 2001.[11] No specific figure for non-EU citizens as a proportion of the overall foreign population are provided, but figures are given for different national groups highlighting the dominance of third country nationals: Ecuador: 475,698; Morocco: 420,556; Colombia: 248,894; Romania: 207,960; UK: 174,810. Ireland, traditionally a country of emigration, had just 26,000 non-EU nationals in 1998, but this had grown dramatically to over 80,000 by 2002.[12] According to 2006 census results, net inwards migration of 46,000 per year was recorded during

---

[7] *Statistisches Bundesamt*, 'Über 30% der Ausländer stammen aus der EU', Press Release, 2 May 2005.

[8] *Trends in International Migration*, above n. 6, at 160.   [9] *Ibid.*, 239.

[10] Press Release of the Instituto Nacionale Estadística, 17 January 2006, http://www.ine.es/prensa/np403.pdf.

[11] *Trends in International Migration*, above n. 6, at 269.

[12] *Trends in International Migration*, above n. 6, at 214.

the period 2002–6, compared to 26,000 per year during the previous census.[13] Ireland is slightly unusual, in that the number of resident UK nationals in a country with a small population of 4.2 million, according to the 2006 census, somewhat distorts the overall figures. Nonetheless, non-EU nationals represented nearly 50 per cent of the total foreign population of around 180,000. Ireland, like the Netherlands, has reasonably generous rules on citizenship acquisition, as legally resident non-nationals may be eligible for naturalisation after residence of four years, and – at least until 2004 when the rules were changed for the children of parents who lack a connection with Ireland – had a general rule whereby children born on the island of Ireland (i.e. including Northern Ireland) automatically acquired Irish citizenship by birth.[14]

In some of the new Member States which acceded to the Union in 2004, there are also quite high proportions of third country nationals, although not generally for reasons relating to recent migration. For example, non-citizens constitute around 22.8 per cent and 20 per cent of the total population in Latvia and Estonia respectively, but in both cases this high figure is related to an inflow of citizens from other parts of the Soviet Union into the Baltic states in the period from the Second World War up to 1989.[15] In contrast, in Poland, in 2002, just 0.13 per cent of the population (less than 50,000 people) were foreigners, of whom 25 per cent originated elsewhere in the EU.[16] At the present time, Poland is both a transit country for East–West migration, and a country of emigration suffering a brain drain and a drain of unskilled (young) labour towards other EU Member States (and elsewhere). In the longer term, as with Ireland's patterns of emigration/immigration, this can be expected to change as the economy develops, as it should with the other EU8 states. Shorter term, it is looking to reverse the depopulation trends by considering opening its frontiers to workers from states to the East such as Belarus and Ukraine. Already, commentators identify a high level of diversity in the migration patterns across, into and out of the new Member States (Szczepaniková et al., 2006).

What both the 'new' and the 'old' Member States share in common are negative birth rates, with a cross-EU average of 1.5 babies per

---

[13] Government of Ireland, 'Preliminary Report for Census 2006', July 2006, at 9, available from http://www.cso.ie/census/Census2006Results.htm.
[14] Birthright citizenship in Ireland is discussed in more detail in Chapter 8.
[15] Trends in International Migration, above n. 6, at 165.
[16] Focus Migration, Country Profile, No. 3, Poland, July 2005, available from http://www.focus-migration.de.

woman, where 2.1 is regarded as necessary for replacement fertility.[17] Although some of the most acute problems are arising in Germany, where 30 per cent of women do not have children,[18] across the EU the figures indicate lower than average fertility rates in most new Member States. The lowest on the 2004 Eurostat figures is the Czech Republic, with a fertility rate of just 1.22. Women are also choosing to have their children later in life, with an EU25 average for first-time motherhood in 2004 of 28.2 years. In that context, immigration is seen by some political commentators and politicians as a necessary corrective for negative demographics, as well as labour shortages in both high-skill (e.g. IT and medical professions) and low-skill industries (e.g. in the UK in the hospitality and food processing industries), and in recent years many states, as well as the EU so far as it has policy tools, have altered their positions on migration issues.[19]

III Union policies and third country nationals

On the basis of these figures and trends, and bearing in mind the increasingly widely recognised context of global migration as an issue affecting economic growth and welfare,[20] it is not hard to argue that the legal status and treatment of third country nationals within the territory of the Member States is a matter of legitimate and growing concern for the European Union, as are more general questions about population mobility and immigration. However, the Member States have worked hard to ensure that they retain control both over the numbers of third country national immigrants arriving in their territories, and the precise conditions of admission. Although the EU only has very limited powers to engage with these issues at the Union level, not least because of the limited personal scope of the EU Treaties, this has not deterred the Commission from issuing a Green Paper and subsequently a Policy

---

[17] Eurostat News Release, 29/2006, 6 March 2006, 'A Statistical View of the Life of Women and Men in the EU25'; C. Murphy, 'The EU's Baby Blues', BBC News, 27 March 2006, http://www.guardian.co.uk/germany/article/0,,1695850,00.html.

[18] L. Harding, 'Germany Agonises over 30% Childless Women', *Guardian*, 27 January 2006, http://www.guardian.co.uk/germany/article/0,,1695850,00.html.

[19] European Commission, 'Green Paper: On an EU Approach to Managing Economic Migration', COM(2004) 811, 11 January 2005.

[20] '*Migration in an Interconnected World: New Directions for Action*', Report of the Global Commission on International Migration, October 2005.

Plan on Legal Migration.[21] Under consideration at present is a proposal for a Green Card system covering highly qualified workers, modelled on the US system, with proposals expected from the Commission in 2007. However, the Member States have shown a greater willingness to work together (in both policy and operational terms) on issues of irregular migration, or illegal immigration as it is normally termed in political debates, and indeed to work constructively with third countries on these questions as well, especially where such activities have had a repressive content – i.e. preventing so-called illegal immigrants from reaching the EU Member States in the first place or seeking the repatriation of those who do.[22] It is this willingness to cooperate, albeit not always to the satisfaction of states which are the most common first destinations (such as Italy, Malta and Spain), which has attracted the criticism that the EU is becoming a 'Fortress Europe', with a collective embrace of the repressive aspects of a common citizenship which excludes third country nationals.

The issue of the treatment of third country nationals once they are resident in the Member States, often referred to as policies on the integration of immigrants, has become a more intensively debated subject within the context of EU policy-making, as new and more diverse patterns of migration and migration flows have become established. Such policies have to engage with a multitude of countervailing forces and pressures, including the diversity of the Member States themselves as receiving states, as well as the common challenges which they face, such as the rise in the number of applications for asylum during the 1990s, which was one factor which triggered a sharper delineation of the line between wanted and unwanted migration (Geddes, 2005). The 'regularisation' of illegal immigrants, as practised periodically hitherto in states such as Spain and Italy (Zincone, 2006), has generated concerns in other states because of the knock-on effects which will occur and because such regularisations can operate as a pull factor for other migrants. Indeed, Justice Commissioner Franco Frattini has moved several times to remind Italy that such a regularisation should be preceded by a process formal consultation with fellow Member States and should only be carried out with appropriate checks.[23]

---

[21] Green Paper, above n. 19; European Commission, 'Policy Plan on Legal Migration', COM(2005) 669, 21 December 2005.

[22] 'EU Policy to Fight Illegal Immigration', MEMO 06/296, 19 July 2006.

[23] 'Frattini: Regularisation of Immigrants Is an EU Matter', Euractiv, 29 May 2006, http:// www.euractiv.com/en/justice/frattini-regularisation-immigrants-eu-matter/article-155602/; 'Italy Warned over Immigrant Amnesty', EU Observer, 31 May 2006.

Some states such as France and Germany have been managing the longer term consequences of immigration under post-Second World War post-colonial and guestworker programmes, whilst at the same time experiencing very high levels of domestic unemployment since the 1990s. There are often problems of social exclusion amongst certain immigrant communities, especially amongst younger people, and such matters have been complicated in some cases by the rise of radical and fundamentalist Islamic ideologies. In the UK, even where problems of social exclusion amongst the children and grandchildren of immigrants were thought to be lower, some adherents to fundamentalist Islam have shown themselves to be prepared to use terror methods such as suicide bombings to attack Western liberal societies in an indiscriminate way. Developments such as these have destabilised a number of Member States, both because repressive measures to deal with terrorism are resented within immigrant and many host communities, and also because there has been an unprecedented rise in equally indiscriminate verbal and, less often, physical attacks upon Muslim communities and individuals.

As was noted in Chapter 1, the right to non-discrimination on grounds of nationality in Article 12 EC protects only those with the nationality of a Member State, and not third country nationals. This is derived from the Court of Justice's approach to the interpretation of what is now Article 39 EC (formerly Article 48 EEC), which sets out the basic principle of freedom of movement for workers within the context of the provisions on the single market, which has been limited to workers with the nationality of one of the Member States. However, an argument was made in the past that the Court could have interpreted these provisions more broadly to encompass third country nationals within their scope (Böhning, 1973: 83; Plender, 1990: 605; Hervey, 1995: 97). Even so, the third country national was never a complete stranger to EU law. So far as he or she was a member of a family of an EU national taking advantage of free movement rights, third country nationals were protected under secondary legislation (now Directive 2004/38/EC[24]), and there has been an important line of case law from the Court of Justice protecting third country nationals and their derivative rights under the free movement rules even where there has been quite a weak

---

[24] Council Directive 2004/38/EC on the right of citizens of the Union and their family members to move and reside freely within the territory of the Member States, OJ 2004 L158/77. The Directive came into force on 30 April 2006.

link with the scope of EU law.[25] Also protected were the nationals of states with which the EU has contractual relations such as an Association Agreement (e.g. Turkey or Morocco). Such agreements would not give third country nationals rights of entry into the Member States, but would protect their right to equal treatment once admitted under national law.[26]

In terms of positive integration measures which could be adopted under the Treaty, in a 1987 case, *Germany et al. v. Commission (Migration Policy)*,[27] the Court acknowledged that, within the framework for the development of EU social policy as it then existed (Article 118 EEC), the Commission had a limited power to request information from the Member States regarding the integration into the workforce of third country nationals within their territories. However, so far as the Commission had requested information regarding the cultural integration of third country nationals, this had exceeded its powers. This began to raise the visibility of third country nationals within the framework of EU law and policy-making (Kostakopoulou, 2001a: 182; Kostakopoulou, 2001b), but the possibilities for measures to be adopted actively regulating the situation of third country nationals within the Member States was limited until the 1990s.

The Treaty of Maastricht issued rather mixed messages about the status of third country nationals. On the one hand, the strict limitation of Union citizenship by reference to the nationality of the Member States, 'calcifies Member State nationality as a badge of exclusion still further' (Nic Shuibhne, 2003: 279). The Member States also rejected the possibility of extending the derived rights of third country nationals under the EC Treaty, specifically in the area of electoral rights. A new provision was proposed by the Danish Government in February 1991, which would have been added to the Title on the free movement of persons (now Articles 39–42 EC):

> Citizens in the Member States and members of their families who are legally resident in one of the Member States of the European Community shall have the right to vote and be eligible to local councils in their State of

---

[25] Case C-413/99 *Baumbast and R* [2002] ECR I-7091; Case C-200/02 *Chen* v. *Secretary of State for the Home Department* [2004] ECR I-9925; Case C-60/00 *Carpenter* v. *Secretary of State for the Home Department* [2002] ECR I-6279; Case C-503/03 *Commission* v. *Spain*, 31 January 2006.

[26] Case C-192/89 *Sevince* v. *Staatssecretaris Van Justitie* [1990] ECR 3461.

[27] Cases 281, 283, 284, 285 and 287/85 *Germany* v. *Commission* [1987] ECR 3203.

residence provided they have been resident in that State for three years prior to the election. To that end the Council, acting by a qualified majority on a proposal from the Commission and in co-operation with the European Parliament, shall adopt the necessary Directives.[28]

This would have made the citizens of the Union the primary benefici-aries of such electoral rights, with members of their families as secondary beneficiaries. It would thus have added an additional layer of benefits to the group of privileged third country nationals, namely, those who are members of the families of EU citizens. The text is ambiguous as to whether movement to another Member State is first required to trigger the equal treatment rights, but given its proposed location within the EC Treaty this has to be assumed to be the case. However, this suggestion was not adopted, with the Member States preferring to use the option of inserting electoral rights for EU citizens alone into Part Three of the Treaty, on Union citizenship, thus leaving all non-EU citizens out in the cold.

However, at the same time the Treaty of Maastricht created the Justice and Home Affairs 'Third Pillar', which was supposed to lead to the adoption of measures addressing the status of third country nationals within the EU. In practice, this innovation proved to be a false dawn, as the third pillar in its Maastricht form was seen largely as an ineffective regulatory framework of an intergovernmental nature leading at most to some weak soft law measures and a number of conventions which never came into force (Peers, 2000: 84). Partly to correct these failures, the Treaty of Amsterdam installed the pursuit of the so-called 'Area of Freedom, Security and Justice' as an objective for the European Union under Article 2 of the EU Treaty, and offered new policy instruments by remodelling the legal framework for regulating the external and internal borders and the movement of third country nationals around a new Title IV of Part Three of the EC Treaty and changing the third pillar to focus on police and judicial cooperation. The Treaty of Amsterdam also saw the Schengen *acquis* incorporated into the EU legal framework. The various Schengen Conventions and implementing measures have been the basis for frontier-free travel amongst all of the pre-2004 EU Member States apart from the UK and Ireland since 1995, and they originated in an

---

[28] Conference of the Representatives of the Governments of the Member States, Political Union, CONF-UP 1777/91, 21 February 1991, copy of a letter from Ambassador Riberhold, Danish Delegation to the IGC on Political Union to Mr Ersbøll, Secretary General of the European Council of Ministers.

Agreement drawn upon between France, Germany and the Benelux countries in 1985 (Peers, 2000: 66).

Under Title IV of the EC Treaty, the Council can now adopt measures in a number of fields of justice and home affairs policy: the crossing of internal and external frontiers; immigration policies relating to conditions of entry and residence, as well as illegal immigration; and the definition of the rights and conditions under which third country nationals resident in one Member State may reside in other Member States (Article 63(3) and (4) EC). In a separate development, the Council was also empowered to adopt measures to combat discrimination based *inter alia* upon race and ethnic origin under Article 13 EC; this has a clear relevance to third country nationals. In the reworked social policy section of the EC Treaty, the Council was given a power to enact measures governing the conditions of employment for third country nationals legally residing in the territory of the EU (Article 137(3) EC). Both these new powers under the EC Treaty and the incorporation of much of the old third pillar into the body of the EC Treaty saw a shift in the balance of power within the policy-making process away from an essentially intergovernmental model into one which largely resembled the traditional 'Community' method. Thus the balance of power in initiating policy-making has shifted away from the Member States towards the Commission (Uçarer, 2001), although in practice it remains shared in many areas. Moreover, the European Council still holds the all-important political power to give impetus to new developments and proposals. In addition, many measures under Title IV still require a unanimous vote in the Council of Ministers for adoption, thus giving a veto to each of the Member States. Thus the anticipated body of EU immigration and asylum law has been quite slow to develop.

At Tampere in 1999, the European Council approved a programme of regulatory and programmatic measures, which gave the Commission considerable agenda-setting powers in relation to policy development.[29] The Tampere Programme attempted to balance out the sometimes countervailing concerns of 'freedom, security and justice'. It included a commitment to the '*fair treatment* of third country nationals' and 'a more vigorous integration policy [which] should aim at granting them rights and obligations *comparable* to those of EU citizens'; 'the legal status of third country nationals should be *approximated* to that of Member

---

[29] Presidency Conclusions, Tampere European Council, 19–20 October 1999.

States' nationals'[30] (emphases added). Such comments acted as triggers to a considerable volume of focused NGO activity aimed at making concrete suggestions on what a policy of 'fair treatment' for third country nationals might look like (Niessen, 2000; ILPA and Migration Policy Group, 2000[31]). One of the most important measures to be adopted under the Tampere framework was the Council Directive on the status of third country nationals who are long-term residents,[32] a measure by which neither the UK nor Ireland are bound. Both countries enjoy an opt-out from measures adopted under Title IV unless they specifically choose to opt into particular measures and they have not opted into the long-term residence Directive, or indeed any of the Title IV measures which are concerned with securing protection of legal immigrants, especially those with long-term residence. The long-term residence Directive, and the discussions which have taken place regarding the possibility of including electoral rights for third country nationals amongst the rights to be guaranteed for long-term residents at national level, are discussed in more detail below.

The question of the successful 'integration' of immigrants into the Member States has become a central topic within EU justice and home affairs policy after Tampere. The factor which has mainly driven the process of policy formation has been the recognition of the reality of immigration. Not only is there the historical legacy of post-war immigration into many of the 'old' Member States, but also the more recent waves of immigration into almost all of those states, whether as a result of economic and political upheaval in certain areas of the world or the demand for cheaper labour (unskilled and skilled) within the increasingly globalised economies of the Member States. The recognition that there are large numbers of apparently 'unintegrated' nationals and non-nationals (both the immigrants themselves, and their children, grandchildren, and so on) in many of the Member States has posed a severe challenge to policy-makers especially at the national level and, to a lesser

---

[30] *Ibid.*, paras. 18–21.

[31] The ILPA/MPG proposals – especially the proposed Directive on long-term residents which bears considerable similarities to a March 2001 proposal from the Commission discussed in the text below – did not explicitly deal with voting rights (or indeed any political participation rights) for long-term residents, although one general provision (Article 6(3)) did provide for 'equality with Union citizens'. However, this appears to have been limited in scope to security of residence, mutual recognition of qualifications, protection from expulsion and social and cultural rights.

[32] Council Directive 2003/109/EC of 25 November 2003 concerning the status of third country nationals who are long-term residents, OJ 2004 L16/44.

extent, at the EU level. However, in addition to such an instrumental logic, the Commission has also adopted the powerfully symbolic language of 'civic citizenship' to signal the development of an enhanced status for third country nationals, which it articulated in its initial reaction to the Tampere Programme. It argued that:

> The legal status granted to third country nationals would be based on the principle of providing sets of rights and responsibilities on a basis of equality with those of nationals but differentiated according to the length of stay while providing for progression to permanent status. In the longer term, this could extend to offering a form of civic citizenship, based on the EC Treaty and inspired by the Charter of Fundamental Rights, consisting of a set of rights and duties offered to third country nationals.[33]

In its 2003 Communication on Immigration, Integration and Employment, the Commission[34] referred to the Charter of Fundamental Rights as a reference point for the rights inhering in a concept of civic citizenship for third country nationals:

> The Charter of Fundamental Rights establishes a basic framework for civic citizenship, some rights applying because of their universal nature and others derived from those conferred on citizens of the Union.

The language of civic citizenship has reappeared in numerous Commission documents, but does not appear as such in European Council or Council of Ministers documents, indicating that it may be a contentious phrasing for at least some of the Member States (Bell, 2007).

The five-year time period for the Tampere Framework, and also for certain transitional arrangements relating to the legislative process under Title IV, elapsed towards the end of 2004, and at that point, while recognising that not all the aims of the Tampere Programme had in fact been achieved, the Member States agreed amongst themselves a new programme: the Hague Programme.[35] Perhaps unsurprisingly in view of supervening events, including the terrorist attacks of 11 September 2001 in the United States and of 11 March 2004 in Spain, as well as continuing concerns over illegal migration, so-called 'bogus' asylum-seekers, and organised cross-border crime including people-trafficking, the major emphasis of the Programme was upon security

---

[33] 'Communication on a Community Integration Policy', COM(2000) 757.
[34] COM(2003) 336, 3 June 2003, at 23.
[35] Presidency Conclusions, Brussels European Council, Doc. 14292/04, 5 November 2004, Annex 1, at 16.

issues, the fight against terror, and instrumental concerns relating to managing immigration for the benefit of the Member States, rather than focusing on fairness and equity issues as such. Fundamental rights are emphasised, but the general impression is given that the primary concern is with the fundamental rights of the citizens of the Union, and not with those of non-nationals or immigrants. Issues relating to the fight against racism, xenophobia and anti-semitism are emphasised under the heading of citizenship of the Union, rather than in relation to the integration of legal immigrants, where once again it is the term 'fair treatment' which is used.

However, both the Hague Programme itself and the Commission's May 2005 Action Plan implementing the Hague Programme[36] highlighted the concept of 'integration' (of immigrants) as one of the EU's policy priorities. The same language was evident in the initiatives taken by the Commission in mid-2006 to persuade the Member States that, even in the absence of the changes to justice and home affairs policy-making structures which would have been introduced by the stalled Constitutional Treaty, the Member States should consider using the potential of the existing provisions in order to place the policy-making processes on a footing which would make it easier for the agreed objectives of Tampere and Hague to be implemented.[37] In other words, in the future, integration issues will not be regarded as solely matters of national concern, although the extent to which the EU policy-making processes could actually effect practical change in national policies may remain doubtful for the foreseeable future (Carrera, 2006a).[38]

IV The question of political participation

One of the key questions is whether the development of this status of fair treatment (and the concept of integration) is, in a legal sense, fundamentally a matter for the EU institutions, or for the Member States. In other words, what is the scope of EU competence in this field since the Treaty of Amsterdam? And what are the implications of this for electoral

---

[36] 'Communication on the Hague Programme: Ten Priorities for the Next Five Years – The Partnership for European Renewal in the Field of Freedom, Security and Justice', COM(2005) 184, 10 May 2005.

[37] 'Implementing the Hague Programme: The Way Forward', MEMO/06/254. 28 June 2006.

[38] A further discussion of the concept of integration, especially as applied at the national level, can be found in Section II of Chapter 8.

rights for third country nationals? Would they be included in a concept of 'civic citizenship'?

There have been some initiatives which have emphasised the interface between the EU's competences in relation to third country nationals in the field of justice and home affairs and the important role of third country nationals in relation to the achievement of the economic and growth objectives of the EU under the so-called Lisbon process, in particular a 2003 Communication on Immigration, Integration and Employment.[39] This involved collaboration between two Directorates General of the European Commission: that concerned with justice and home affairs, and that concerned with employment and social affairs. The two Directorates General have not always had identical views on how the Commission should proceed in this area.

Developments in relation to integration have mainly taken the form of 'soft' policy; only to a very limited extent have 'hard' law measures requiring harmonisation of national laws played a role in this area. In 2002, the Commission established National Contact Points on Integration, bringing together officials within the national governments actively dealing with integration issues to examine on a comparative basis how policies are developed and implemented, and since 2003 the European Council has invited the Commission to submit Annual Reports on Migration and Integration.[40] The principles on which EU policy on integration of immigrants is based have been developed by both the Commission and the Council. The 2003 Communication on Immigration, Integration and Employment emphasised the need for greater efforts at the national level in this area, emphasizing that integration is a two-way process involving both those 'being' integrated, and the societies into which they are expected to integrate.

Working with the National Contact Points within the context of the funding programme INTI,[41] DG Justice and Home Affairs collaborated with the Migration Policy Group, an NGO offering expertise in the area, to produce a Handbook on Integration for policy-makers and

---

[39] COM(2003) 336, 3 June 2003.

[40] See COM(2004) 508, 16 July 2004 and SEC(2006) 892, 30 June 2006 for the first two reports.

[41] See http://europa.eu.int/comm/justice_home/funding/inti/funding_inti_en.htm: 'This is an EU funding programme for preparatory actions promoting the integration in the EU member states of people who are not citizens of the EU. Its aim is also to promote dialogue with civil society, develop integration models, seek out and evaluate best practices in the integration field and set up networks at European level.'

practitioners, which seeks to establish best practice, drawn from examples across the Member States, in areas such as initial reception of immigrants and civic participation.[42] This Handbook encourages Member States to extend political rights to third country nationals:

> The representativeness and democratic legitimation of policies is enhanced by extending formal political rights to immigrants. Where political rights exist, they need to be put into practice with commitment from all sides including political parties ... At the local level in particular, electoral rights provide immigrants with political representation in decisions that affect their most immediate interest ... Governments should grant electoral rights to all residents at least at local level and minimise obstacles to the use of these rights, such as fees or bureaucratic requirements. Immigrants can be encouraged to make use of electoral rights through information campaigns and capacity building, relying in particular upon the networks offered by immigrant organisations.

More diffuse support along the same lines can be found in the Common Basic Principles for Integration adopted in the form of Council Conclusions in November 2004.[43] Principle 9 states:

> The participation of immigrants in the democratic process and in the formulation of integration policies and measures, especially at the local level, supports their integration.

This stops short of explicitly recommending that the Member States institute local electoral rights for third country nationals. Amplifying these Common Basic Principles in a subsequent Communication on the integration of third country nationals,[44] the Commission repeated some of the text of the Handbook on Integration regarding the benefits of democratic participation and encouraging immigrants to use electoral rights, but likewise stopped just short of explicitly encouraging the Member States which do not have such rights to adopt them.

There has been plenty of encouragement elsewhere, from within civil society and academia in particular, for the EU institutions and the

---

[42] DG Justice, Freedom and Security, *Handbook on Integration for policy-makers and practitioners*, (Brussels: European Communities, 2004).

[43] Conclusions of the Council and the Representatives of the Governments of the Member States on the establishment of Common Basic Principles for immigrant integration policy in the European Union, Doc. 14776/04 MIGR 105, 18 November 2004.

[44] 'A Common Agenda for Integration Framework for the Integration of Third Country Nationals in the European Union', COM(2005) 389, 1 September 2005.

Member States to pursue more vigorously the concept of civic citizenship. A 'European Civic Citizenship and Inclusion Index' was published in 2005 (and is intended to be updated annually), explicitly encouraging the benchmarking of civic citizenship rights for all non-nationals within the Member States against the standards set by EU citizenship, including electoral rights in local and European Parliamentary elections.[45] A Green Paper for the Council of Europe on the Future of Democracy urged progress in this area, arguing that 'giving voice to *denizens* offers an opportunity for dealing with potential ethnic and cultural conflicts through democratic procedures' (Schmitter and Trechsel, 2005). Thus the practice of granting voting rights to denizens

> should be encouraged and improved. In particular, measures to make registration and subsequent access to voting (and hence participation) easier for long-term foreign residents should be introduced. Normally states and municipalities grant voting rights after a fixed number of years of residence in a country (this normally varies between two and eight years). A proposal could be that denizens who participate in programmes of citizen mentorship . . . or demonstrate a proficiency in civic education, constitutional matters and political history of the receiving country could be rewarded by gaining access to the vote after a shorter period of residence.
>
> (Schmitter and Trechsel, 2005: 94)

The general theoretical issues regarding the extending of electoral rights to migrants were canvassed fully in Chapter 3.[46] There have been few attempts to apply such approaches to the specific case of the EU. However, Heather Lardy has argued that the exclusion of third country nationals from the scope of EU electoral rights also contradicts 'norms of democratic theory which are widely accepted and respected in the Member States and which the European Union is committed to respecting' (Lardy, 1996: 613). In the absence of clear guidance from international law, where, she argues, voting is effectively treated as a 'concession' rather than as a 'right of citizenship' (Lardy, 1996: 628), she argues instead in favour of EU citizenship being extended to third country nationals. That is, she would 'broaden the mechanisms by which Union citizenship is distributed' (Lardy, 1996: 628). This

---

[45] British Council Brussels, Foreign Policy Centre and Migration Policy Group, 'European Civic Citizenship and Inclusion Index', British Council: Brussels, 2005, at 3.

[46] See Sections II, III and IV in particular.

approach has been supported by a number of other writers, such as Dora Kostakopoulou (2001b) and Andreas Føllesdal (1999), who have argued for the limits of EU citizenship to be extended to include third country nationals (with the necessary implication that this will also give them electoral rights). Effectively, such an argument about a (European) citizenship of residence would match the internal inclusivity of the EU in relation to citizens of the Member States to an external inclusivity. It also presents a vision of EU citizenship which does not adopt the patterns of national citizenship, and which uses the external border in order to select those who are in, and those who are out. However, of course the negative side of extending EU citizenship to third country nationals would be a corresponding loss of internal diversity, so far as the current diverse patterns of electoral rights for non-nationals respond to a variety of impulses of inclusion and exclusion from within and without the national polities. However, the argument runs that this loss of diversity is the price of a more just solution to the challenge of ensuring fair treatment of third country nationals.

At the present time, the Commission is clear that it believes there is no competence in the EC Treaty as it exists for the adoption of measures requiring the Member States to institute electoral rights for third country nationals. In its proposal for a directive on the status of third country nationals who are long-term residents in the Member States, it stated that, 'although the importance of voting rights and access to nationality for the integration of third country nationals who are long-term residents is now generally acknowledged, the EC Treaty provides no specific legal basis for it'.[47]

Article 63(3) and (4) EC, on which the Directive which was finally adopted by the Council was based, provide for the adoption of

> measures on immigration within the following areas: conditions of entry and residence, and standards on procedures for the issue by Member States of long term visas and residence permits … [and]
>
> Measures defining the rights and conditions under which nationals of third countries who are legally resident in a Member State may reside in other Member States.

---

[47] 'Proposal for a Council Directive Concerning the Status of Third Country Nationals Who Are Long-Term Residents', COM(2001) 127, para. 5.5 of the Explanatory Memorandum, OJ 2001 C240E/79.

On the Commission's view, this does not go as far as justifying measures with a view to promoting the integration of immigrants into the Member States. This view is at odds with Norbert Reich's suggestion to use Article 63 as the basis for developing a 'quasi-citizenship' for third country nationals by thickening out the concept of 'legal residence' in the Member States (Reich, 2001: 18–19).

It is worth referring in this context to Article III-267(4) of the Constitutional Treaty which would provide the following legal basis, if it is ratified and enters into force:

> European laws and framework laws may establish measures to provide incentives and support for the action of Member States with a view to promoting the integration of third country nationals residing legally in their territories, excluding any harmonisation of the laws and regulations of the Member States.

However, it is hard to see how this text in fact goes any further than merely codifying the current practices of the Commission in encouraging the exchange of best practice between the Member States as well as the coordination of national policies, as described above.[48]

The Commission has not made a firm proposal that the Member States should amend the EC Treaty to institute a competence to adopt electoral rights for third country nationals, although it has referred in its Fourth Report on EU Citizenship to the extension of the existing rights in Article 19 EC to nationals of the Member States of the European Free Trade Area states (Norway, Iceland and Liechtenstein) who already benefit from full free movement rights under the arrangements for the European Economic Area (EEA):[49]

> The next step could be to establish the right to vote and stand as a candidate in local elections, through agreements between the Member States and the third countries concerned. Currently, the right to participate in local elections in the country of residence exists between some Member States and the EFTA countries on the basis of bilateral agreements.

This would do nothing, of course, to help the third country nationals resident in the Member States.

---

[48] For an analysis of other negative implications of the 'loss' of the Constitutional Treaty in the field of Justice and Home Affairs, see Guild and Carrera, 2005.

[49] COM(2004) 695, at 8.

V The case of the Directive on the status of long-term resident third country nationals

To see how that limited view of EU competence plays out in practice, it is necessary to look in a little more detail at the debates surrounding the Commission's proposal for a directive governing the status of long-term resident third country nationals which is one of the flagship measures underpinning the evolving Area of Freedom, Security and Justice. This is because it seeks to create a single legal status for third country nationals resident in the Member States and, in an important innovation, brings about the harmonisation of national laws to this effect. An important feature of the legislative process for the Directive on the status of long-term resident third country nationals was that it involved a formal consultation of the European Parliament, under the legislative procedure laid down for the adoption of measures under Article 63(3) and (4) EC, giving the Parliament for the first time a specific policy context in which to consider the question of the electoral rights of third country nationals. This built upon more 'abstract' statements of policy which have emerged from that institution over the years, such as support for the extension of electoral rights to third country nationals in the parliamentary resolution on the 1996 Intergovernmental Conference[50] and in a resolution on the 'Barcelona Euro-med' process.[51] Since the adoption of the 2003 Directive, this general policy orientation has been reiterated in the July 2006 resolution on the Commission's 2005 Communication on the integration of third country nationals.[52] The Parliament called

> on Member States to encourage the political participation of immigrants and discourage their political and social isolation; . . . [and called] on the Commission to carry out a legal review of existing provisions relating to EU civic citizenship in the various Member States as well as of current

---

[50] European Parliament Resolution on the convening of the Intergovernmental Conference and evaluation of the work of the Reflection Group, 13 March 1996, para. 4.16, http://europa.eu.int/en/agenda/igc-home/eu-doc/parlment/opinion.html.

[51] European Parliament Resolution on the Commission Communcation to prepare the fourth meeting of Euro-Mediterranean foreign ministers 'reinvigorating the Barcelona Process', 1 February 2001, para. 49. It was voted in at plenary by a narrow majority (235 votes to 222, with 56 abstentions), on a proposal from the far-left GUE/ NGL group.

[52] COM(2005) 389, above n. 44.

Member State practices regarding the right of long-term resident immigrants to vote in local and municipal elections.[53]

As the report which formulated the resolution made clear, the concept of
citizenship lies within the sovereign domain of the Member States, but it
lies within the power of the EU institutions to seek the development of
the concept of *civic citizenship* for third country nationals.[54]

The competence argument advanced by the Commission for omitting
electoral rights from the proposal was broadly accepted in the report on the
proposed Directive on third country nationals for the European
Parliament's Committee on Citizens' Freedoms and Rights, Justice and
Home Affairs, drawn up by Sarah Ludford, a British Liberal Democrat
MEP.[55] Adopted by a majority of nineteen to eleven in the Committee, the
report proposed for adoption by the European Parliament plenary session a
substantial number of amendments to the Commission's proposal, quite
a number of which were clearly motivated by the increased political salience
of the security agenda following the events of 11 September 2001.
Even though the report was prepared with the aid of key migration policy
NGOs,[56] in certain respects the proposed amendments appeared less
generous in terms of rights for resident third country nationals, proposing
only that their rights should be 'similar' to those of EU citizens, rather
than 'as near as possible' (Article 1). The Committee noted in its justification that:

> Although the Tampere conclusions provide for an *approximation* of the
> legal status of third country nationals to that of Member State nationals
> (paragraph 21), *harmonisation* in the form of equal status would do away
> with any incentive to seek citizenship of the host Member State, a step
> which third country nationals should be encouraged to take with a view
> to fostering integration.
>
> (emphasis in the original)

In similar vein, several amendments referred to the need for skills
in the host nation language(s) needing to be acquired by the resident

---

[53] European Parliament Resolution of 6 July 2006 on strategies on means for the integration of immigrants in the European Union, para. 22.
[54] 'Report on Strategies and Means for the Integration of Immigrants in the European
Union', A6-0190/2006, 17 May 2006, at 14.
[55] 'Report on the Proposal for a Council Directive Concerning the Status of Third
Country Nationals Who Are Long-Term Residents', A5-0436/2001, 30 November 2001.
[56] The Migration Policy Group, the Welfare Council for Immigrants, the European
Network Against Racism and the Immigration Law Practitioners Association.

non-national, to foster integration, although these came not from the Rapporteur, but from the Conservative/Christian Democrat grouping on the Committee. In other key respects, the amendments proposed by the Committee did extend the draft Directive, and electoral rights were a crucial heading under which extensions were proposed, albeit through the medium of national law. Thus the proposal was made for an amendment that encouraged the Member States themselves to adopt electoral rights for third country nationals.

Before adoption of the report and a legislative resolution on the proposal in plenary, the amendments went through a further process of revision, based on the need to reconcile various political factions. Eventually the Parliament adopted by a large majority (but with the UK Conservative group voting against) a text adding to the list of areas under which third country nationals were to be guaranteed equal treatment by the host Member State a new heading of 'participation in community life at local level' (new Article 12(1)(b) of the draft directive).[57] This presumably refers to institutions of civil society rather than to formal political participation rights such as voting rights, for in the very next paragraph voting rights are added as a specific example of an area in which Member States may *choose* to accord equal treatment, but are not *obliged* so to do:

> Member States may extend the benefit of equal treatment to matters not referred to in paragraph 1, *such as active participation in political life, including voting rights at local and European level.*
>
> (Article 12(2); italics indicate amendment proposed)

Only voting, and not standing rights, are referred to here. The statement of justification in the report refers to the competence argument, in the following terms:

> Whilst there is no competence under the Treaties to provide for voting or other political rights in a Member State this should not preclude Member State governments using their prerogative to provide such within their national legislation.

The Rapporteur's Explanatory Statement elaborates a little further:

> The proposal does not grant voting rights as the Commission considers this is not covered by the legal base. The rapporteur understands that this

---

[57] OJ 2002 C294E/184.

is a politically sensitive issue for some Member States, although she considers that the grant of voting rights at least at local and European level ought to be encouraged as a factor of responsible integration. She therefore recommends a reference to an option for Member States to grant long term resident third country nationals the right to vote in municipal, national and European elections.

Voluntarism on the part of the Member States and the recognition of national competence were thus the order of the day. Notably, the proponents of the extension of electoral rights to third country nationals themselves appeared to regard this as a merely symbolic statement, one which was unlikely to find its way into the final legislative text and therefore one of minimal practical impact.[58] Indeed, their predictions were correct, and no reference to electoral rights was included in the final text of the Directive. The text suggested by the Parliament was removed by the Member States in Council at a later stage of the negotiation process.[59] The final text referred, on the one hand, to a list of areas where the Member States *must* accord equal treatment to long-term residents under Article 11(1), most of which are concerned with issues of employment and public services, and combined this with a bare reference in Article 11(5) to the possibility that 'Member States may also decide to grant equal treatment with regard to areas not covered in paragraph 1'. It does not specify in what areas this might be desirable. Ultimately, therefore, the story of the adoption of the Directive on the status of long-term resident third country nationals amounts to a missed opportunity to reinforce in legislative form at least the general overall direction of the Common Basic Principles on integration as regards the question of political participation, and to give specific encouragement to the Member States to consider facilitating the participation of immigrants in the democratic process in order to support their integration into the host society.

It seems clear that, on the basis of the accumulated *acquis* in this area, whether this takes the form of the rather narrowly drafted Directive 2003/109/EC or the largely rhetorical Common Basic Principles of integration, the Member States have yet to live up to the principles articulated by the Commission in the concept of civic citizenship for

---

[58] Interview with Julia Bateman, European Parliamentary research assistant to Baroness Sarah Ludford, MEP, 21 February 2002. I am very grateful to Anthea Connolly for sharing this interview data with me.

[59] Council Directive 2003/109/EC, OJ 2004 L16/44.

third country nationals. The lack of competence is often raised as the argument for the failure to adopt measures, but it is clear that in this area it is the absence of political will to enact such measures which is just as great a problem. That is apparent from the parallel story of the evolution of electoral rights for EU citizens, where it was political will as much as legal conditions which altered between the mid-1980s (when nothing happened) and the mid-1990s (when electoral rights were implemented under Article 19 EC).

Less attention has been paid to another constitutional principle of the European Union which could perhaps be of significance in this context, namely, the principle of subsidiarity. Formally speaking, this principle restrains action at the EU level under Article 5 EC, to circumstances where a comparative efficiency argument mandates that 'the objectives of the proposed action cannot be sufficiently achieved by the Member States', but on the contrary can be better achieved by the Community. More generally as a political principle one could suggest that subsidiarity allows and encourages the Member States to design integration policies which are appropriate to local conditions. Some of those local conditions will be exposed in more detail in the chapters which follow.

The by-product of the institution of electoral rights under the EC Treaty for EU citizens and not for third country nationals is that it perpetuates a degree of discrimination against third country nationals, by treating them as entitled to a lesser range of rights as immigrants than the nationals of the other Member States (Kostakopoulou, 2002). This outcome may not be sustainable in the long term, both on fairness grounds and on grounds of the effectiveness of policies on the integration of non-nationals and the political urgency of dealing with the consequences of having non-integrated minorities within the European Union. However, at the present time, the impetus for that change seems more likely to come from the national level rather than the EU level.

VI Conclusions

This chapter has brought to a conclusion a lengthy and wide-ranging section of this book which has looked in detail at all aspects of the European Union's direct engagement with the question of electoral rights for non-nationals. Through four chapters we have reviewed the story of electoral rights under EU law from inception to implementation, and, in the latter two chapters, discussed some of the pressure points which may in the future see further development of these rights, as EU citizens' rights or as rights ascribed to residents in the Member States. The chapters have charted the institutional struggles which have shaped the evolution of the limited EU electoral rights under Article 19, and highlighted why it proved necessary, for such an innovation to take hold, for there to be amendments to the founding EU treaties. The general objective was to enhance the understanding of the emergence of the electoral rights by placing them in the broader context of the evolution of EU citizenship more generally, with reference where appropriate to the wider context provided by the development of the EU as a system of economic integration based on a single market and – more incrementally – as a polity with more general, if still limited and shared, sovereign powers.

Thus far, there has been no substantial case law discussion of the Article 19 electoral rights. Hence any interpretations of the significance of these rights within the framework of the EU Treaties must be derived directly from the text of the Treaties themselves, from the secondary legislation, and from the practice of the Member States, with no authoritative guidance from the Court. Where the Court has had the opportunity so far to discuss 'electoral rights' has been in relation to the right to vote and stand for the European Parliament, but not in the context of the Article 19 equal treatment provision (although it did confirm, as an aside, that Article 19 is limited to an equal treatment guarantee). The *Gibraltar* and *Aruba* cases[60] challenged the Court of Justice to look directly at the nature of the right to vote for the European Parliament. Unlike Advocate General Tizzano,[61] the Court did not attempt to view the right to vote for the European Parliament via the prism of citizenship rights, in particular the rights attaching to citizenship of the Union. Even so, it seems implicit in its judgment that the right to vote for the European Parliament, which is not an absolute and unconditional right, is implicitly a citizenship right. However, the Court explicitly preserved the discretion of the Member States in setting the precise boundaries of that right, both by limiting when citizens can exercise the right (e.g. by reference to place of residence) and also by granting the right also, in appropriate cases, to persons who are not citizens of the Union. Thus, if

---

[60] Case C-145/04 *Spain* v. *United Kingdom (Gibraltar)*, 12 September 2006; Case C-300/04 *Eman and Sevinger* v. *College van burgemeester en wethouders van Den Haag*, 12 September 2006.

[61] Para. 82 of the Opinion of Advocate General Tizzano of 6 April 2006.

the right to vote for the European Parliament is a citizenship right, it is certainly not an *exclusive* right of citizens. This reinforces a message that citizenship of the Union is an open-textured and outward-looking concept, and could – perhaps – embolden the European Commission to make proposals in the future for the EU institutions formally to extend more EU citizenship rights to third country nationals, including the right to vote in local elections in the Member States on the basis of residence, which was the topic of the present chapter. The *Gibraltar* case, with its affirmation that it is acceptable for Member States to confer European Parliament electoral rights on third country nationals, also opens up the political space within which campaigns could be developed in other Member States by groups representing third country nationals, or by political parties, to exploit this opportunity. Pressure could be placed upon Member States which already recognise *local* electoral rights for third country nationals to extend this also to *European Parliament* elections, thus aping the parallelism which exists in EU law for EU citizens.

Most significant for understandings of EU citizenship was the approach the Court of Justice took in the *Aruba* case to the discretion of the Member States in limiting the right to vote of their nationals who are not resident on the national territory (or at least not in a part of the national territory that is in practice fully part of the European Union). The willingness of the Court to extend the protection of the general principle of equal treatment, as one of the rights enjoyed by citizens of the Union under Article 17(2) EC, to a group of persons whom it had confirmed are indeed citizens of the Union, that is, Dutch nationals resident in Aruba, could foreshadow some interesting developments. Moreover, it compared one group of citizens against another *within the boundaries* of national citizenship, rather than making the comparison *across the boundaries* of national citizenship. In future, the Court could intervene to uphold the EU law rights of EU citizens in more situations which are not directly or even indirectly linked to the inter-state and market dimensions of the EU, as was the case here. In this case, the only connection between the citizens who were given the protection of the general principles of law and the scope of EU law was the fact that they were citizens of the Union, and the fact that they enjoyed a putative right to vote for the representatives who sit in one of the Union's institutions. The protection of the equal treatment principle forced the Member State in question to justify its actions and demonstrate that they were objectively justified and proportionate (which the Court clearly doubted was the case).

The second part of Chapter 6 departs somewhat from the generally descriptive and analytical tenor of this book by articulating a specific proposal which could be adopted to develop the electoral rights of EU citizens resident in a host Member State in relation to a range of elections from which they are normally excluded by national law, namely, national and regional elections. This is done not in order to defend that particular proposal, but in order to highlight the potential legal resources which the Member States and the Union institutions could exploit in the field of electoral rights, if the political conditions were to allow this. Using the example of the limited national developments in relation to national elections which do exist, namely, in the UK and Ireland, the proposal suggests taking advantage of the flexibility of EU law by encouraging the Member States to negotiate and conclude an international agreement alongside the EU Treaties where they could develop the requisite mutual trust and understanding which could underpin the extension of the right to vote in national elections, without the need for the resident non-national to acquire the national citizenship of the host state. Such a development could do much to reverse the democratic deficit that occurs as a consequence of a system of regional economic and political integration which encourages nationals of the Member States to leave behind their state of nationality and to live, study and work in other Member States, but then condemns them in effect to lose most of their democratic citizenship rights. Indeed, what is the logic of a system of economic and political integration which guarantees rights to participate in local and European Parliamentary elections, and which guarantees extensive market and socio-economic rights, but which stops at the point of national elections, on the grounds that this is a step too far for national sovereignty?

Chapter 6 paints a picture of the potentially elastic limits of the electoral rights which are conferred upon EU citizens, indicating the scope for EU citizens to step outside the treaties as currently constituted and to seek to persuade the Member States to use other mechanisms of international cooperation so as eventually to reach a situation where electoral rights in national elections are available for all resident EU citizens. In contrast, Chapter 7 suggests that in respect of electoral rights for third country nationals under EU law, the situation may currently be rather comparable to that regarding the situation of EU citizens in the 1970s. That is, the primary 'citizenship' resources which structure the equality and fairness claims of third country nationals are all 'soft law' or informal in nature, and do not create a binding legal framework of rights for third country nationals as residents of the Member States. Although the Member States have begun, bit by bit, to develop a framework of protection for the rights of third country nationals, for the most part the action which they have taken has been either highly restricted, such as the Directive on long-term resident third country nationals, or soft law in nature, consisting of the mutual learning and the benchmarking of good practices between the Member States which does not necessarily lead to any tangible changes. There is an argument to be made that as a single market, backed up by a system of political integration and autonomous institutions, the EU should do more to equalise the rights of the different groups who experience both new opportunities but also a certain loss of rights as a result of residing in a state which is not the one of which they hold the nationality. That argument can be extended as readily to nationals of third countries as it can to nationals of the EU Member States. Both experience similar forms of dislocation when they reside in a state where they lack the nationality, but EU citizens enjoy a much higher level of protection because of the reach of EU law than do nationals of third countries. Perhaps in the longer term, these informal resources may be developed into formal resources, as happened, eventually, with EU citizenship and Article 19 in the late 1980s and early 1990s, as we saw in Chapter 4.

However, viewing the treatment of third country nationals in relation to issues of political participation solely from the perspective of EU law offers a far too one-dimensional picture. On the contrary, the conclusions on the findings in this chapter need to be revisited in the light of the rather different set of lenses applied in the final substantive section of this book in order to review cases of electoral inclusion and exclusion. Since, as we shall see, there is widespread debate about the extension of local electoral rights to third countries across the Member States (if not necessarily in absolutely every Member State at the present time), and since it seems widely agreed that giving *local* electoral rights could be a useful tool in the context of *developing* integration and assimilation (rather than just *rewarding* it after the fact), then it may be in the future that the EU Member States will decide that the most rational route to develop this area of policy would be through a common decision at the EU level, rather than merely through dispersed national action, as at present.

Of course, rights are not the only important element of citizenship. Citizenship also comprises elements of access and belonging, which make up the idea – if not the reality – of 'full' membership of a community. The interest provided by the cases of the Article 19 rights – discussed in relation to their emergence, implementation and possible development in these four chapters – lies in their distinctly ambiguous relationship to those other elements of citizenship. How do the rights to vote in European Parliament and local elections accorded to citizens of the Member States resident in other EU Member States relate to the notions of a European *demos* and of a set of overlapping and interacting national (and subnational and local) *demoi*? Clearly, those relationships are multifaceted, as the complex nature of the various electoral rights demonstrates, once we strip away the superficial similarity of the two clauses of Article 19 EC. What makes for meaningful access to citizenship in circumstances where the political domains of the Member States remain substantially segmented, despite evidence of an increasingly Europeanised media based on internet communications? Political parties still rarely engage directly with transnational concerns except in order to argue about the *national* impact of such concerns.

The picture painted thus far in this book, so far as it seeks to uncover the complex nestedness of EU electoral rights within the evolving EU and national constitutional frameworks, is incomplete. It could be argued that what is needed now for a fuller understanding of the EU electoral rights is more information about their impact in practice in the Member States, which goes beyond the top-down perspective on effective implementation sketched in Chapter 5 in particular. Thus, the last substantive section of this book takes a rather different turn. It turns the focus towards the national citizenship regimes, understood in the widest possible sense, looking at cases where electoral rights for non-nationals have been debated, both positively and negatively, within the Member States, thereby building up a more complex picture of the multiple approaches to these questions which are visible across the Member States. It shows, moreover, how the contestation of electoral rights can be not just a 'national' issue, but also one which engages the emerging regimes of subnational territorial, electoral and constitutional politics which distinguish many of the Member States.

PART III

The contestation of electoral rights in the Member States of the European Union

8

National politics of immigrant inclusion: the extension of electoral rights to resident non-nationals

I Introduction

As part of a general discussion of electoral rights for non-nationals, Tables 3.1 and 3.2 in Chapter 3[1] highlighted the states in which electoral rights have, and have not, been granted to some or all resident third country nationals. In this and the following two chapters, some of the stories behind those tables are picked up and discussed in more detail to draw out the processes of transformation and institutional forms which any reconfigurations of citizenship and citizenship practices have taken in that context. However, while the presentation is focused on the processes of transformation which have occurred at the national level, the discussion should not be seen in isolation from the developments that have occurred within EU law, which have been presented in the previous four chapters. Many of the same themes on immigration and immigrant inclusion picked up from the perspective of EU policy-making in Chapter 7 recur when the issues are viewed from the perspective of the Member States. Thus electoral rights at the national level should not be seen in isolation from the influence of EU law, including EU policies on the treatment of both EU citizens and third country nationals. Where appropriate, the contrast is made in this chapter and the two which follow between the specific case of Article 19(1) EC local electoral rights for *EU citizens*, and the broader cases of local electoral rights for *all non-nationals* as enacted in some states under national law or as denied in others. Certainly, there are many cases of the direct and indirect influence of the EU electoral rights upon the development of electoral rights under national law, as well as evidence of the influence of national law upon EU law.

In Chapter 3, I outlined some of the arguments typically used to provide a grounding in democratic theory or theories of rights for the extension of the boundaries of the suffrage beyond national citizens

---

[1] Section VII of Chapter 3.

alone to include resident non-nationals. Many claims promoting the extension of electoral rights have been premised upon a view of electoral rights as both a political element within the framework of human rights law (including a putative right to political participation) and more specifically as part of an evolving set of migrants' rights, designed to incorporate non-nationals into the polity on the grounds that their interests are as greatly affected by political decisions as are those of nationals. More instrumentally, as the following section on integration seeks to show, electoral rights are used in some cases as interim rewards given in return for the gradual adoption of the norms and codes of the host society. Normative arguments for alien suffrage, meanwhile, typically downplay the significance of citizenship as a formal marker of national membership, and concentrate instead upon looser concepts of membership premised on a patchwork of rights, access and belonging, where memberships are rarely exclusive and often overlap and intersect.

In this chapter, I shall examine some of the key cases where electoral rights have been extended to cover some or all third country nationals within EU Member States, although this is often only after lengthy periods of struggle and debate amongst interested parties. When these stories are examined in more detail, they help to reveal the sites (laws, institutions, practices, etc.) where citizenship and notions of belonging are contested between the various stakeholders in the debate. In practice, the extension of electoral rights to non-nationals never involves smooth, inevitable progress towards greater inclusion of immigrants, or other non-nationals, especially when the issue of electoral rights is placed in a wider context of other policies on immigration, nationality acquisition and social inclusion (including the broader array of mechanisms which states can, and often do, make available for immigrants and their descendants to participate in the host polity, whether with or without the host polity nationality).

The examples given in this chapter focus on developments in the fifteen pre-2004 Member States. Many of these states are now facing similar challenges relating to immigration, and what is commonly termed the 'integration' of immigrants, that is, the question of how immigrants and their host society 'fit' together. In some cases, the immigration processes date back to the period of post-Second World War economic boom and the phases of guestworker immigrants or immigrants from former colonies; in other cases, the debate about immigration and immigrants is of much more recent vintage, as emigration rather than immigration has, until recently, been the main social and political issue.

That is not to say, of course, that immigration (either the reality of it, or the anticipation of it) is not a live issue right across the Union and all of its twenty-seven Member States at the present time. As I noted in Chapter 7, patterns of migration affecting Central and Eastern Europe are likely to change dramatically over the coming years as economies develop, especially given that some of the post-2004 Member States are seeing highly unfavourable demographics (and consequently a shrinking domestic labour force), as a result of emigration, low birth rates and higher life expectancy. At the same time, these same states are gradually coming under immigration pressure especially from states further to *their* east or south, in the same way as has happened with the 'old' Member States. The issue has already been raised in states such as the Czech Republic where the government has started to do forward projections on migration right up to 2050, by which time it expects that 1.4 million foreigners will live in the Czech Republic, whereas at the present time there are something over 0.25 million.[2] In that context, integration policies will clearly become a priority.[3]

However, in practice, as Chapter 10 will show, many of the cases where electoral rights have thus far been extended to third country nationals in the EU10 of post-2004 Member States (in particular the eight new Member States from Central and Eastern Europe) need to be viewed in the context of other pressing concerns specific to the nature and evolution of those polities. To put it another way, the presence of substantial populations of third country nationals in these Member States has often resulted from recent (and in some cases not so recent) boundary changes (e.g. the division of former empires, multinational states, or federations, and the creation of new states[4]) rather than from labour migration or asylum-seeking. These changes themselves have also

---

[2] 'Updated Concept of Immigrant Integration', http://www.cizinci.cz/files/clanky/329/Concept_of_II.pdf, at 1.

[3] In January 2006, the estimated population of the Czech Republic was 10.25 million (http://www.cia.gov/cia/publications/factbook/geos/ez.html). The information about immigration is derived from a report in a Czech newspaper, *Hospodarske Novinyô* in February 2006, digested in English by *Euro-topics*, 14 February 2006, http://www.eurotopics.net/en/presseschau/archiv/archiv_results/archiv_article/ARTICLE2594/.

[4] In total twenty-two new states (after the referendum confirming the break-up of Serbia and Montenegro in May 2006) have been created in the arena of the former Soviet Union and its 'satellite' states since 1989, and within those states the scale of ethnic minorities amounts to around 29 per cent of the population on average (figures presented by M. Kovács, Presentation at the Central European University, 31 May 2006).

necessitated the formal redefinition of citizenship and nationality and the divisions between insiders and outsiders, citizens and aliens.

In this chapter, I look first at the broad terrain within which the issue of electoral rights for non-nationals is generally debated, and that is the question of immigrant 'integration'. Since 'integration' is itself a contested term, it deserves closer examination, as do related issues such as the 'inclusion' (and exclusion) (civic, social, political, etc.) of immigrants. I move on then to consider a number of sites of contestation, where policies on the extension of electoral rights to non-nationals have intersected with other broader issues implicating the national polity in some manner. These include the scope and forms of national citizenship acquisition, the role of political parties both in terms of debates about the extension or restriction of the suffrage and in terms of parties' orientations towards the political opportunities opened up by widening the suffrage, and the question of disaggregating the 'state' into a variety of subnational or regional units in relation to certain questions of citizenship and belonging.

II Immigration, integration and electoral rights

What is meant by 'integration' in the context of immigration? Most often, the concept is premised upon a notion of the immigrant as outsider, and as different from the indigenous population (Penninx and Martiniello, 2004: 140–2), not to mention the supposed prior existence of an integrated society, into which newcomers are themselves then integrated. Sergio Carrera (2005b: 1) describes integration as 'a *compendium of processes of inclusion* tackling social exclusion' (his emphasis). Rinus Penninx and Marco Martiniello (2004: 141) define integration as 'the process of becoming an accepted part of society'. However, both these definitions seem to suggest integration is a one-way track towards inclusion, whereas in practice, as Carrera himself notes elsewhere, some actual concepts and practices of integration, especially those involving instituting an ever more juridified concept of integration dependent upon enforceable citizenship or affiliation programmes, for example, are actually '(mis)using the device of 'integration' as a tool to put in practice a restrictive policy' (Carrera, 2006b: 1). According to Carrera (2005b: 1), there were traditionally three main national models for the integration of immigrants:

- The 'multicultural model', based on 'respect and protection of cultural diversity' and aimed at 'explicitly guaranteeing the identity of the immigrant community'.

- The 'assimilationism model' (also called republican or universalistic), with 'equality at its root', but only for those individuals who fall within 'the privileged category of "citizens"'. It is 'based on the complete assimilation of the immigrant into the dominant, traditional national values and perceived common identity'.

- The 'separation or exclusionist model', characterised by 'restrictive and rigid immigration legislation and policies', referring in this context mainly to the 'legal conditionality that must be satisfied in order to have access to and reside in the territory'. It consists of 'policies aimed at artificially maintaining the temporary character of an immigrant's settlement'.

These models, while useful as a starting point for analysing national models and policies as we shall see in this and the following chapter, in reality do not reflect either the complexity or the swiftly changing toolkit of policy instruments being used by EU Member States either separately, or now, in a tentative way, collectively, to address the issues flagged under the integration heading. There is certainly diversity amongst the Member States, in relation to values pursued, the practices adopted and the outcomes achieved, and it is not clear that substantial convergence is occurring, notwithstanding the attempts by the Commission to foster mutual learning through initiatives such as INTI.[5] This diversity is also evident from the 'European Civic Citizenship and Inclusion Index' prepared by groups including NGOs and the British Council (British Council Brussels, 2005). There are, in broad terms, three areas in which issues of integration most urgently arise, reflecting key elements of the concept of citizenship as membership itself. These are the legal-political, the socio-economic and the cultural and religious (Penninx and Martiniello, 2004: 141).[6] Under every heading, divergences persist. Perhaps the only exception lies in the increased tendency amongst the Member States, described in more detail below, to use mandatory programmes based upon national legislation as the basis for integration programmes (Carrera, 2006b: 6). Such programmes are often applicable not only as a condition for the acquisition of national citizenship, but also to all newcomers in a polity. Thus, despite the fact that the Common Basic Principles for Integration adopted in the form of Council

---

[5] See Chapter 7, Section IV.

[6] British Council Brussels (2005) focuses on five areas of concern where issues of inclusion/exclusion are concentrated: 1. Labour Market Inclusion; 2. Family Reunion; 3. Long Term Residence; 4. Naturalisation; and 5. Anti-Discrimination.

Conclusions in November 2004[7] by the Member States state in Principle One that 'Integration is a dynamic, two-way process of mutual accommodation by all immigrants and residents of Member States', in practice it seems most often that the demand is that the immigrant, and his or her family if appropriate, 'integrate'. That is, they must adjust to the new conditions of life in the host polity, if necessary by passing mandatory tests of integration, with little evident sign that the dominant host society wishes to adjust to accommodate the newcomers.

Some scholars of immigration and citizenship have argued that 'generally speaking, countries that are reluctant to make immigrants into nationals are also those that differentiate most between the rights of foreigners and of nationals' (Koopmans et al., 2005: 45). Of course, what such a generalisation about the apparent double burden carried by non-nationals in certain polities and societies in relation to patterns of exclusion actually conceals is that, on closer inspection, supposedly contrasting stories of inclusion in other polities and societies actually demonstrate less rosy-coloured outcomes than might be expected. This trend is becoming increasingly apparent as we have moved into the twenty-first century; as the same writers comment, 'the apparent benefit of multiculturalism, both as an idea and as a policy, no longer appears self-evident to policy-makers across Europe' (Koopmans et al., 2005: 243). The terrorist attacks in the US in 2001, in Madrid in 2004, and in London in 2005, have each contributed in substantial ways to a situation in which 'the loyalty of many Muslims to their societies of settlement has been placed in question by governments and public across Europe' (Koopmans et al., 2005: 243). These questions have been raised at the same time as hostility has grown in many Member States towards other groups of immigrants, such as so-called 'bogus asylum-seekers', who have found themselves squeezed between restrictive regimes from the 1970s onwards which reduced the options for economic migration and cumbersome and inefficient regulatory systems governing the treatment of those who need the protection of refugee status, as defined in international law, which have been increasingly narrowly interpreted by many states.

Increasingly across the Member States, we are seeing a shift towards a 'civic-universalist policy' (Koopmans et al., 2005: 244), in which

---

[7] Conclusions of the Council and the Representatives of the Governments of the Member States on the Establishment of Common Basic Principles for Immigrant Integration Policy in the European Union, Doc. 14776/04 MIGR 105, 18 November 2004.

measures like 'integration contracts' have been mooted not only for those who seek the formal badge of citizenship through nationality acquisition, but also for all 'new entrants' (and possibly even retrospectively for those who have previously entered before such tests were in place, and who are judged to be insufficiently integrated). Citizenship tests at the point of nationality acquisition are becoming increasingly common (e.g. in the UK, Germany and Austria), building upon well-established traditions in countries of immigration such as the United States and Australia. In some cases these tests are adopting much more challenging questions which require very substantial levels of education and knowledge on the part of the would-be citizen, putting in place much higher barriers to entry, selecting out from access to nationality those whose educational attainment, for whatever reason, is low. They are also becoming more culturally specific, aiming to tease out what are perceived to be the socially conservative views of many Muslim communities.

The Netherlands has so far gone furthest with integration tests at a variety of different points in a would-be immigrant's process of integration into Dutch society. Much of the Dutch policy has been developed in the context of an ongoing reaction to the perceived failures of a multicultural model emphasised throughout the post-war years, and especially in the 1980s and 1990s, which crystallised in substantive policy reactions to the religiously motivated murder of the Dutch filmmaker Theo van Gogh in November 2004 by a young Dutch man with radical Muslim beliefs, who was the child of immigrants from Morocco (Penninx, 2005). In common with many states, the Netherlands now has a naturalisation test for new citizens covering competence in the Dutch language, as a second language, and questions about Dutch culture, history, politics and society.[8] The fee for this test is €260 in total. It has also implemented a pre-entry citizenship test to be taken by would-be new entrants before they leave their home country in the

---

[8] The most high-profile case of a would-be citizen failing the naturalisation test is that of Solomon Kalou, a talented football player from the Ivory Coast, who had been playing successfully for the Dutch team Feyenoord in 2005. Expressing the wish to adopt Dutch citizenship, with a view to playing for the Dutch national team, Kalou failed a naturalisation test in November 2005. Thereafter, the Dutch Minister of the Interior refused to exempt him from the test, and provide a fast track to nationality acquisition, and the Dutch courts refused to overturn the Minister's decision. In the end, Kalou decided his future in international football lay with his country of birth and nationality, the Ivory Coast, although he did not play in the 2006 FIFA World Cup. See 'Kalou's World Cup Hopes Dashed', http://news.bbc.co.uk/sport1/hi/football/africa/4755303.stm, 9 May 2006.

Dutch consulate or embassy, which incorporates the compulsory viewing of a film about the Netherlands and Dutch lifestyles (including famously scenes of a topless woman bathing and a gay couple kissing, meant to reinforce the liberal nature of Dutch society). The fee to take the examination is €350, and it tests knowledge of Dutch language and culture, and would require a would-be immigrant to have studied for several hundred hours prior to taking the test. This was instituted as of 15 March 2006. It is widely thought that one of the policy objectives of the Dutch Government in instituting this test is to reduce the numbers of new immigrants who are entering the Netherlands for family formation purposes – that is, in order to marry. It is openly discriminatory, since it does not apply to nationals of high-income countries, such as Canada, the United States, Australia, New Zealand and Japan, and, of course, the EU Member States, which are protected by the principle of non-discrimination. It is also exceptionally difficult to obtain Dutch language teaching in many of the target states such as Turkey or various African states. It is viewed by many commentators as a measure targeted at reducing immigration, not promoting integration, and especially reducing the immigration of Muslims.[9] However, a very early report indicated that almost all of those actually taking the test were passing it: 101 out of 106 by mid-May 2006, although the total figure remained at that time remarkably low.[10]

Most controversially, a further addition to the policy on integration tests was announced in December 2004.[11] This comprises a very stringent set of courses and integration tests to be applied to any person wishing to settle permanently in the Netherlands, which would be applied retrospectively to immigrants already settled in the Netherlands, including those who have been resident for up to thirty years, who would be required to pass the test within five years, or face fines of around £700 per annum and possible revocation of their residence permits. The only exceptions would be in respect of those who had attended school for eight years or more in the Netherlands (who would be presumed to be integrated), and in its initial form it was proposed that the test would also apply to naturalised Dutch citizens in certain cases: immigrants who are unemployed, parents

---

[9] 'EU: Netherlands Leading Trend to more Stringent Immigration Rules', RFE/RL, 5 April 2006.

[10] 'Would-Be Immigrants Almost All Passing Language Exam', NIS News Bulletin, 25 May 2006, http://www.nisnews.nl/public/250506_1.htm.

[11] 'Government Adopts New Integration System', http://www.government.nl/actueel/nieuwsarchief/2004/12December/07/0-42-1_42-51591.jsp.

caring for children, and religious workers such as imams.[12] The costs of the courses and the tests would be very high – around £4,000 per person – but immigrants would be able to reclaim up to 70 per cent of the costs from local authorities. Subject to parliamentary approval, the Dutch Government planned to introduce the tests as of 1 January 2007. Other proposals mooted by the Dutch Government, and in particular its hardline Justice Minister Rita Verdonk, include the banning of the wearing of the *burqa* by Muslim women in public and a Code of Conduct requiring that only the Dutch language should be spoken on the streets.[13]

It is becoming increasingly clear that, while the Netherlands may be the current laboratory for measures which many liberals claim are intended to discriminate against Muslim residents and immigrants, with choices posed along the lines of 'learn the language of the host state and accept its dominant social norms or risk being expelled',[14] these initiatives will not necessarily always remain confined either to this particular state, or to the national level alone. An initiative aimed at an integration contract applicable across a number of countries was discussed amongst the interior ministers of the so-called 'G6' countries, that is, the six largest EU Member States, at an informal meeting in March 2006.[15]

On the other hand, a society which is simultaneously hostile towards (unintegrated) immigrants, but recognises certain rights as a *quid pro quo* for assimilation or integration is not as contradictory as it appears at first sight. The case of Spain, which has seen a rapid increase in immigration in recent years, is instructive.[16] In early 2006, a report in the newspaper *El Pais* reviewed a November 2005 public opinion survey conducted by the Madrid-based Centre for Sociological Research (CIS), which showed that, while 60 per cent of respondents felt that there were

---

[12] N. Smith, 'Pass This Test, Dutch Tell Immigrants', *The Times*, 18 June 2006.

[13] '"Dutch-Only" Bid Stirs Angry Debate', Deutsche Welle World, 25 January 2006, http://www.dw-world.de/dw/article/0,2144,1870753,00.html.

[14] H. Williamson, 'EU Ministers Consider Immigrant "Contracts"', *Financial Times*, 23 March 2006; R. Watson and A. Browne, 'EU Leaders Want All Immigrants to Take an Entry Exam', *The Times*, 24 March 2006.

[15] Meeting of the Interior Ministers of France, Germany, Italy, Poland, Spain and the United Kingdom, Heiligendamm, 22 and 23 March 2006, Conclusions, available at http://www.statewatch.org/news/2006/mar/06eu-interior-minister-conclusions.htm and as Appendix Five to a Report of the House of Lords Select Committee on the European Union, 'Behind Closed Doors: The Meeting of the G6 Interior Ministers at Heiligendamm', Session 2005–6, 40th Report, 19 July 2006, at 25.

[16] In Italy, there is a similar dissonance between public opinion and actual policy which has involved, over the years, a number of regularisations of the status of immigrants who entered originally with permission: see Zincone, 2006.

too many immigrants in Spain, the same percentage nonetheless felt that those who are resident in Spain should have the right to vote in local elections. Indeed, 53.4 per cent of respondents wished to extend this to the right to vote in national elections.[17] At the present time, Spain grants electoral rights only on the basis of reciprocity and where an international agreement has been concluded, and in practice this only covers Norway, amongst non-EU Member States. Unlike Portugal, Spain does not (yet) have any reciprocity arrangements with former colonial territories or those to which it has historical connections resulting from Spanish emigration.

As we saw in Chapter 7,[18] the Handbook on Integration for policy-makers and practitioners, produced under the auspices of the INTI programme, seeks to establish best practice, drawn from examples across the Member States, in areas including the civic and political participation of immigrants. In relation to the latter, under the heading 'citizenship', the first edition of the INTI Handbook comments (DG Justice, Freedom and Security, 2004: 40):

> Participation in political processes is one of the most important elements of active citizenship. Political participation of immigrants provides opportunities for integration and should be supported in its different forms, including acquisition of nationality, local electoral rights and consultative structures.

It is clear that this text is nested under the heading of 'citizenship' in its broader 'membership' sense, not in the narrower sense of nationality (acquisition), since that issue is referred to separately. On the contrary, it refers to the question of political participation rights specifically for those who have not (yet) acquired the badge of nationality. The remainder of this chapter will explore in more detail some of the ways in which electoral rights can and have intersected with issues of citizenship, immigration, and political power and behaviour more generally. The discussion begins with the case of Ireland, a Member State which is picked out in the INTI Handbook as being an important reference point in the context of benchmarking and identifying best practices. In this context, we shall look at the intersection between the boundaries of citizenship (as nationality) and the boundaries of suffrage.

---

[17] H. Elkin, 'Number of Registered Immigrants Climbs 23 Per Cent in 2005', reprinted February 2006 at http://www.iht.com/getina/files/303736.html. Details of the CIS survey (which is repeated regularly) can be found at http://www.cis.es/cis/opencms/Archivos/Marginales/2620_2639/2625/e262500.html.

[18] Chapter 7, Section IV.

III The boundaries of political citizenship and the boundaries of suffrage

Ireland has amongst the widest alien suffrage provisions in the Member States. As the INTI Handbook notes (DG Justice, Freedom and Security, 2004: 41):

> Ireland is a country where few limitations are placed with regard to local elections in that the residence requirement is comparatively short (ordinary residence since 1 September 2003 for the 11 June 2004 local election) and asylum seekers as well as recognised refugees and immigrants of all nationalities can register to vote.

Ireland's local franchise is expressed in the Electoral Act 1992, s.10, in the terms of a broad citizenship of residence, with no requirement of prior qualifying residence period other than the requirement to be entered on the annually compiled register:

> A person shall be entitled to be registered as a local government elector in a local electoral area if he has reached the age of eighteen years and he was, on the qualifying date, ordinarily resident in that area.

The requirement that the local elector be an Irish citizen was removed in 1972, by the Local Elections Act 1972, s.5(2)(a), which also effected a number of other changes such as removing a property qualification.

The change to include non-national voters did not engender controversy at the time, not least because there were very few non-nationals affected by the legislation, and most of those were UK citizens. Ireland at the time was overwhelmingly a country of emigration, not immigration, and emigration continued to exceed immigration until well into the 1990s. Indeed, much of the net migration in the late 1990s and right up to 2004 was actually accounted for by return migration by those who had previously emigrated, or by migration from Irish-connected communities in the United States, rather than the immigration of non-nationals with no previous connection to Ireland (Ruhs, 2004). Moreover, since the local government structure in Ireland even in the 2000s has been described as 'centralized, clientalist and weak' (Halfacree, 2003: 187), and as it lacks constitutional status, with little or no tradition of strong local self-government, it is perhaps unsurprising that the definition of the local franchise in those circumstances attracted little controversial attention. Likewise, turnout has been historically lower than in general elections, and had been declining over the years, especially since the 1970s, to reach a historically low point of 51 per cent in 1999 (Forde, 2005). In 2004, when the elections were held on the same day as the European Parliament elections, a further decline in turnout was expected, but did not transpire. One of the reasons for this was that the government held a referendum on the definition of citizenship on the same day as the elections, and this attracted a great deal of press attention (Kavanagh, 2004: 69). In fact, turnout rose again to reach nearly 60 per cent, with a particularly steep rise in the urban constituencies of Dublin from 36 per cent to 53 per cent.

Of marginal impact, perhaps, in terms of the overall turnout of electors, but nonetheless of considerable symbolic political importance, was the fact that in the June 2004 local elections the issue of third country nationals voting *and standing for election* reached political prominence for the first time ever.[19] In that year, not only was there mobilisation by associations representing non-nationals and immigrants, in order to promote electoral registration and hence participation by non-nationals and thus to encourage the political parties to see them as an increasingly important constituency which should be canvassed and engaged with, but in addition, for the first time, a number of non-national candidates stood for election, and two were elected:[20] Rotimi Adebari and Taiwo Matthew were both elected to town councils in Portlaoise and Ennis respectively. Both, like almost all the unsuccessful non-national candidates (such as Benedicta Attoh in Dundalk, and Tokie Laotan and Paul Osikoya in Galway), stood as Independents.[21] Both, again like almost all the unsuccessful candidates, were Nigerian,

---

[19] Information provided by William Stapleton, official in the Franchise Section of the Department of the Environment, Heritage and Local Government to Fidèle Mutwarasibo of the Immigrant Council of Ireland, in emails dated 14 April and 25 May 2005 indicated that 28,257 non-EU electors were registered to vote when the initial Register of Electors was published in February 2004, but a further 8,718 were added before a Supplementary Register was published just before the elections. The total number of electors for the 2004 local elections was 3,176,675, although interestingly only 64,287 of these were included in the Supplementary Register. This indicates that non-EU nationals were disproportionately represented in the late-registering electors.

[20] I am grateful to Fidèle Mutwarasibo of the Immigrant Council of Ireland for providing me with some of the information relied upon in this section, and also for facilitating access to a number of key informants.

[21] José Ospina, a dual Colombian/UK national, stood unsuccessfully for the Labour Party in Skibbereen Town Council; Stanley Airewele, a Nigerian asylum-seeker, stood for Labour in Scarrif, County Clare. The Green Party also had a number of foreign-born candidates, including Parvez Butt, born in Tanzania.

reflecting the fact that, according to the 2002 Irish census,[22] Nigerians represented the second largest community of non-EU nationals in Ireland, with nearly 9,000 persons then resident in Ireland having been born in Nigeria. It is also worth noting that 2004 also saw a slight increase in the number of ethnic minority (e.g. Black Irish) candidates standing in elections, including for mainstream parties such as Sinn Féin and the Labour Party. This represents, perhaps, the first stirrings of a movement towards a more diverse representation of the new, more culturally diverse Ireland in political institutions, building on the pioneering work of Dr Moosajee Bhamjee, who was born in South Africa, of Indian descent, who was elected a TD (member of Parliament) for the Labour Party between 1992 and 1997, and was Ireland's first Muslim TD. Bhamjee has naturalised as an Irish citizen after marrying an Irish woman whom he met when studying medicine in Ireland in the 1960s, and moving to Ireland in the 1980s to settle and work as a doctor.

The campaigns which occurred in and around the 2004 elections, and the experiences of participants and activists, viewed in the wider context of an emergent debate about immigration in Ireland, and the need to develop measures regulating immigration and the status of immigrants and non-nationals, illustrate the multivalent character of inclusion and exclusion in relation to citizenship and membership in Ireland. Thus the emergence of a debate around the participation of non-nationals in local elections, both as candidates and as voters, is closely linked to the dramatic changes in Ireland's immigration/emigration trajectory in the last ten years (Mac Éinrí, 2005), as well as the challenges which this has posed in relation to issues such as racism[23] and immigrant integration. However, a closer look at the policy reveals the intriguing conclusion that Ireland has a gradually emerging policy on 'immigration' (which is overwhelmingly focused on the needs of the labour market and seeks to restrict as much as possible other 'non-chosen' immigrants), but almost no policy at all in relation to the treatment of 'immigrants'.

[22] The results of the census are available online at http://www.cso.ie/census/ Census2002Results.htm. The results of the 2006 census are expected to show that much larger numbers of persons resident in Ireland were born in other states; preliminary results available online at http://www.cso.ie/census/Census2006Results.htm show a significant population increase across Ireland which can be partly explained by primary immigration (although there is also evidence of a relatively high birthrate in Ireland).

[23] NGO Alliance Shadow Report, 'In Response to the Irish Government's First National Report to CERD under the United Nations International Convention on the Elimination of All Forms of Racial Discrimination', November 2004.

Impetus towards strengthening the role of non-nationals and ethnic minorities in the 2004 local elections was provided by the publication of a brief report and call to action by the Africa Solidarity Centre in November 2003: 'Positive Politics: Participation of Immigrants and Ethnic Minorities in the Political Process'.[24] The report was based on contacts with political parties to ascertain their degree of engagement with immigrant and ethnic minority communities, and the charting of developments relating to immigration suggesting 'an urgent need for a debate on ethnic minority under-representation in Irish politics'.[25] It recommended increased responsiveness by political parties to immigrant and ethnic minority communities, good practices to be adopted to encourage members of those communities to become members of political parties, the extension of existing anti-racism commitments by political parties[26] into the field of promoting ethnic minority membership and engagement, including training for potential candidates, and the development by political parties of mentoring schemes aimed at encouraging future candidates to consider standing. The artwork displayed on the cover of the pamphlet reinforced an image of Ireland as an increasingly multicultural society, with potentially all residents participating in the electoral process.

In addition, at a local level, community-based initiatives such as the Tallazens project in Tallaght, an area with a high level of non-national residents in south-west Dublin, sought to encourage local electoral participation as one dimension of a 'municipal citizenship' which built upon the notion that most people's first engagement with public authorities is at the local level.[27] Actions included the holding of a meeting for members of the ethnic minority and non-national communities to encourage engagement with South Dublin County Council, including the possibility of non-national or ethnic minority candidates standing for office, and leafleting in areas where members of the target groups might be found, such as shopping centres, to encourage electoral registration with a view to participating in the 2004 local elections.

---

[24] Researched and written by Bryan Fanning, Fidèle Mutwarasibo and Neltah Chadamoyo, available from www.africacentre.ie.

[25] 'Positive Politics', at 9.

[26] In 2004, all the parties signed the Anti-Racism Political Protocol, sponsored by the National Consultative Committee on Racism and Interculturalism, available at http://www.nccri.ie/elections.html.

[27] Interview with Clemens Esebamen, Tallaght Partnership, 1 March 2005.

Figure 8.1: The cover of the *Positive Politics* pamphlet issued in late 2003.

By the time a follow-up report was published in June 2004 by the same group that had produced 'Positive Politics', this time entitled 'Negative Politics, Positive Vision: Immigration and the 2004 Elections',[28] a new shadow was cast upon the generally more propitious environment for immigrant communities to participate in the 2004 local elections which had been engendered by these campaigns. This was the rather sudden decision of the Irish Government to hold a referendum, coinciding with the local and European Parliamentary elections in June 2004, on amending the Constitution to restrict the acquisition of national citizenship by birth of children born on the island of Ireland to non-Irish parents. Even so, the second report noted a successful campaign to persuade the Progressive Democrats, a small centre-right party, to change its constitution to allow non-nationals to be members,[29] as well as a change made by the Minister to the electoral regulations in April 2004 to enable Temporary Residence Certificates and Garda National Immigration Bureau cards to be used for voter identification in the context of both voter registration and the actual act of voting, rather than requiring passports and driving licences to be shown (thus effectively excluding a large group of immigrants lacking this documentation). This latter change significantly increased the number of potential voters who were able to put their names on the supplementary register which closed just fourteen days before the actual poll. Moreover, a second survey of the political parties seemed to highlight a greater awareness of the need to engage with ethnic minority and immigrant communities through measures such as translating election literature or soliciting members through advertisements in immigrant-read newspapers.

However, underlying the presentation of positive responses was a sense of negativity associated with the referendum on national citizenship, in terms of what it might mean for immigrants currently in Ireland for security of residence and in terms of its overall signal in relation to the 'value' of ethnic minority communities so far as concerns the broader agenda of immigrant integration. It needs to be borne in mind, for example, that Ireland still does not have either a politically coherent or legally enshrined policy on immigration whether for family reunification purposes or for employment, nor does it have a legally enshrined process for achieving the status of permanent non-national

---

[28] Also researched and written by Bryan Fanning, Fidèle Mutwarasibo and Neltah Chadamoyo, and available from www.africacentre.ie.

[29] 'Negative Politics', at 7.

resident, as such matters have historically been dealt with as a matter of executive discretion. In practice, many adult immigrants have relied upon a secondary 'right of residence' (that is, the capacity to resist deportation) parasitic upon the residence rights of Irish-born children who have acquired Irish citizenship by birth on the island of Ireland, under what were, until 2004, Ireland's rather expansive birthright citizenship rules. This right of residence was derived from the case of *Fajujonu* v. *Minister for Justice* in 1990, when a family of immigrants to Ireland, who did not otherwise have a legal residence in Ireland, successfully resisted a deportation order made by the Minister on the grounds that the Minister had failed to give sufficient weight to the interests of the Irish-born citizen children, who were part of the family.[30] As Ciara Smyth and Donncha O'Connell (2006: 127) note:

> The reasoning of the Supreme Court was child-centred in that it attached paramount weight to the entitlement of the Fajujonu children to the care company of their parents and appeared to accept that this was a right exercisable within the state.

However, the Court left open the possibility that a family with Irish citizen children could be removed from the jurisdiction 'for grave and substantial reasons associated with the common good'. This seemed to indicate that a case-by-case consideration of the status of families otherwise lacking legal residence in Ireland would be necessary, but in practice after 1990 the state acted on the assumption that such families could not be deported. This situation was dramatically changed after the 2003 case of *Lobe and Osayande* v. *Minister for Justice, Equality and Law Reform*, where it was held that in respect of two families, where the parents had previously applied for asylum in Ireland and also in the UK where their first applications had been lodged, the fact that there were Irish-born citizen children in each of the families was not a ground, necessarily, for quashing the deportation orders. The Supreme Court placed the strongest weight not upon the best interests of the children, or upon the integrity of the family, which would appear to be mandated by the terms of the Irish Constitution, but upon the interests of the state in relation to the integrity of the process of asylum determination and in relation to the control of immigration more generally.[31] The Irish Government immediately suspended the procedure to give residence rights on application to families with Irish-born children, and as a result

[30] [1990] 2 IR 151.   [31] [2003] 1 IR 1.

a number of people who had withdrawn asylum applications as a result of having an Irish born child, reapplied for asylum as the only basis on which they could achieve legal residence in Ireland.

The only alternative route to stable residence other than that of the Irish-born child or the asylum process was to acquire Irish nationality, either by virtue of naturalisation after marriage to an Irish citizen, or by virtue of a period of residence. However, this latter process remains at the absolute discretion of the Minister under ss.14 and 15 of the Irish Nationality and Citizenship Act 1956, as amended (Handoll, 2006: 295). However, Ireland did not have, and still does not have, a legal process for regularising the long-term residence status of non-EEA nationals, outside either the asylum process or the naturalization process. It has only arrangements for work permits, issued to employers and not employees, which in turn are problematic from a human rights perspective. For example, family reunification is not effectively provided for in that context.

The referendum restricting acquisition of citizenship by birth of children born to some non-Irish parents was passed by a very large majority, and resulted not only in an amendment to Article 9 of the Constitution,[32] but also in implementing legislation which entered into force on 1 January 2005.[33] However, considerable political and legal controversy was generated by the decision to hold the referendum,[34] and by the way in which the government chose to characterise certain legal developments in relation to the status of immigrants which led up to the referendum (Ryan, 2004; Smyth and O'Connell, 2006; Harrington, 2005; Mullaly, 2005). Perhaps it was in response to this controversy that the government chose, after the entry into force of the new legislation which left around 11,000 non-national parents of Irish citizen children in legal limbo regarding their right of residence, to undertake a regularisation exercise in respect of this group of immigrants. For the

[32] The amended Article 9 of the Constitution reads: 'Notwithstanding any other provision of this Constitution, a person born in the island of Ireland, which includes its islands and seas, who does not have, at the time of the birth of that person, at least one parent who is an Irish citizen or entitled to be an Irish citizen is not entitled to Irish citizenship or nationality, unless provided for by law.'

[33] Irish Nationality and Citizenship Act 2004.

[34] For an example of commentary presented during the course of the referendum campaign, see 'The Citizenship Referendum: Implications for the Constitution and Human Rights', papers presented at a conference on the referendum held at the Law School of Trinity College Dublin on 22 May 2004.

future, however, the situation is as follows:[35] a person is only entitled automatically to Irish citizenship if born on the island of Ireland if one of his or her parents was either an Irish citizen or entitled to be an Irish citizen, a British citizen, or a person entitled to reside in Ireland, North or South, without any restriction on his or her period of residence. Those who do not fall into this category are only entitled to Irish citizenship by birth if one of their parents has been lawfully resident in the island of Ireland for three of the four years immediately preceding the birth, although residence as an illegal immigrant, an asylum seeker or a student will not count towards the period of residence.

This needs to be placed in the context of the politics of Irish citizenship and citizenship acquisition, which has been hitherto conditioned to a very great extent by the specific historical features of the emergence and development of the Irish Free State and then the Republic of Ireland, the separation of the six counties of the North which remained part of the United Kingdom, and more recently the Good Friday (or Belfast) Agreement of 1998 which has been a crucial cornerstone of the Northern Irish peace process. Historically, Irish citizenship has had a problematic relationship with the concept of the Irish nation, and with the territorial claims laid to the whole island of Ireland by the Irish Republic, until the 1937 Constitution was decisively changed after the Belfast Agreement. Instead of a territorial claim, what was inserted instead was a clear message of political and civic inclusion to nationalists in the North of Ireland. Article 2 was amended to read:

> It is the birthright and entitlement of every person born on the island of Ireland . . . to be part of the Irish nation. That is also the entitlement of all persons otherwise qualified in accordance with law to be citizens of Ireland. Furthermore the Irish nation cherishes its special affinity with people of Irish ancestry living abroad who share its cultural identity and heritage.

Onto a stage set by these political developments, many associated with issues of Irish identity as well as issues of security, has come the additional factor of Ireland's emergence as a country of immigration, but that in turn has occurred in the context of both a set of wider global

---

[35] Sections 3 and 4 of the Irish Nationality and Citizenship Act 2004, which in turn amend the Irish Nationality and Citizenship Act 1956, providing for a new section 6A, which Act had been subsequently amended in material ways by the Irish Nationality and Citizenship Act 2001.

challenges about migration and asylum and the legal, political and economic effects of Ireland's membership of the European Union.

It has been argued that the amendments after the Belfast Agreement constitutionalised the status of birthright citizenship, or *ius soli*, this principle having previously been enshrined only in legislation. This was the interpretation given to Article 2 by the government in its case in support of the citizenship amendment in 2004,[36] although some commentators have claimed that to argue that this is the effect of Article 2 is to confuse the concepts of Irish national citizenship (as a narrower legal concept) and membership of the Irish nation (as a broader socio-political and cultural concept) (Smyth and O'Connell, 2006: 138–9).

Be that as it may, the case made by the government for the amendment was that 'very large numbers of non-EEA nationals [are] now coming to Ireland to give birth' (and had continued to do so, even after the *Lobe* judgment, it alleged).[37] The government deployed a blend of arguments for change, based on little factual backup. These were 'the shifting sands of the government's campaign against non-EEA national births', according to Smyth and O'Connell (2006: 133–5; see also Harrington, 2005: 443–7). The arguments ranged from the alleged strain these births were placing upon maternity services in Dublin, through a generalised and unspecific allegation that there was some sort of deliberate abuse of Ireland's generous arrangements for birthright citizenship occurring, to a suggestion that Ireland's position on birthright citizenship could have a negative impact upon other EU Member States, a point reinforced by the arguments made in the Advocate General's Opinion in the *Chen* case.[38] This Opinion was handed down on 18 May 2004 and it addressed the residence rights of third country national carers of citizens of the Member States resident in other Member States. The *Chen* case itself concerned the residence right in the UK of the mother of a child who had acquired Irish citizenship by virtue of being born in Northern Ireland, and who was thus a national of a Member State resident in a state other than the one of which she had the nationality. She thus came within the scope of EU law, and her mother was protected, indirectly, as her carer.

---

[36] 'Information Note: Proposal for Constitutional Amendment and Legislation Concerning the Issue of the Irish Citizenship of Children of Non-National Parents', Department of Justice, Equality and Law Reform, March 2004, www.justice.ie, at para. 19.

[37] *Ibid.*, para. 11.

[38] Case C-200/02 *Chen* v. *Secretary of State for the Home Department* [2004] ECR I-9925.

While for the most part both the government, and most of those who actively campaigned for a yes vote, avoided making overtly racist statements in their public pronouncements (thus perpetuating the government's claim that there is no racism problem in Ireland, a claim which is manifestly unfounded: O'Connell, 2005; Fanning, 2002), there are many codes inscribed in the texts surrounding the referendum which highlight a continuing ambivalence about the role of immigrants in Irish society. Certainly, the 'good' immigrant is the migrant worker, filling gaps in the Celtic Tiger economy where growth has largely been fuelled by asset price inflation, low taxation and, more recently, low-cost migrant labour; the 'bad' immigrant, by definition, is the woman who comes to Ireland when pregnant, to take advantage of Ireland's generosity. There is no explicit recognition that these two categories might in fact overlap. Thus the concern is with 'immigration', but with a preference for not dealing with 'immigrants' as the consequences of immigration. There remains a sense of an unsettled sense of (national) identity in Ireland, in the context of the shift from a society of emigration to one of immigration. As Smyth and O'Connell (2006) suggested, the citizenship referendum was a 'solution in search of a problem'. If it was true (and they doubt that it was) that the restriction of birthright citizenship required an amendment to the Constitution, then something so momentous should have been preceded by a proper process of discussion and consultation, including engagement with all the political and civic institutions in Northern Ireland. The human rights relevance of the change should have been fully taken into consideration, bearing in mind other provisions of the Constitution, especially those which give primacy to the family as a social unit which necessarily has implications for how children are constitutionally and legally conceived as subjects of law.

In fact, the government rushed these changes through in a manner which reinforces the point that Ireland has an emergent immigration policy without a true policy on immigrants, except that it wishes them to service gaps in the labour market, in the interests of the Celtic Tiger economy. For a number of years, and in particular since it issued its current Programme for Government in 2002, it had been promising a more constructive policy on immigration and immigrants, and NGOs such as the Immigrant Council of Ireland have pressed, primarily behind the scenes, not only for the development of new legislation putting the legal status of non-EEA immigrants on a sounder basis, but also for a Minister with responsibility for *immigrants* and not just *immigration*. However, the practice of government has been predominantly concerned with issues of control, especially in relation to the asylum system which has been significantly tightened up (in line with European and international practices across many states) over recent years, and in relation to the citizenship referendum and subsequent legislation. Consultation papers were issued in April 2005, trailing an Immigration and Residence Bill,[39] and the Bill itself was finally published at the end of 2006. The consultation papers seemed to indicate a desire on the part of the government to ensure that Ireland, although not bound by the various measures of the EU institutions in relation to long-term resident third country nationals adopted under Title IV of the EC Treaty, should nonetheless comply with the standards of protection inherent in these various provisions. However, despite a reference to integration as a two-way process at the beginning of the Bill and the introduction of a status of long-term resident, there is no substantial evidence in the body of the Bill that it is concerned with issues other than the control of foreign nationals, in a manner which continues to be criticised by human rights groups as repressive.[40] In a slightly different context, the decision of the Irish Government to maintain a work permit scheme in place as a transitional measure for Bulgarian and Romanian workers after enlargement on 1 January 2007, after having an open-door policy to workers from the new Member States after May 2004, indicates a lack of confidence in the underlying role and direction of its immigration policy.

It is also interesting to note, from figures obtained by Irish TDs via parliamentary questions to the Department of Justice, Equality and Law Reform during 2005, that, while the numbers of applications for naturalisation, or citizenship acquisition by marriage via a declaration of post-nuptial citizenship, were rising quite dramatically, from less than 1,500 in 2001 to more than 4,500 in 2005, the number of cases actually dealt with during those years was by no means keeping pace, with less than 1,500 applications accepted in 2005, and a rather smaller number definitely rejected. Thus a huge backlog of applications for citizenship acquisition is building up in Ireland, which exacerbates the problems

---

[39] 'Immigration and Residence in Ireland: Outline Policy Proposals for an Immigration and Residence Bill: A Discussion Document', 12 April 2005, available from www.justice.ie.

[40] For an argument about the importance of the development of concepts of integration as well as security of residence for protecting the human rights of immigrants in Ireland, see Irish Human Rights Commission, 'Observations on the Immigration and Residence in Ireland Discussion Document', July 2005.

relating to the absence of stable arrangements for long-term residence as a non-national.[41]

The contrast between this narrative and the mobilisation of forces pushing for a more holistic approach to the inclusion of non-nationals around the issue of participation in local elections could not be starker. The words of Rotimi Adebari, one of the successful non-national local election candidates in 2004, are pertinent in this context. Adebari was a previous beneficiary of the process whereby residence could be regularised via the birth of an Irish-born child, such that he consequently withdrew an earlier asylum application before it was considered by the Irish authorities and relied instead upon residence as the parent of an Irish-born child. Asked about his feelings, just after being elected, about the result in the citizenship referendum, his response was clear: 'My euphoria was turned into ashes.'[42]

IV Electoral rights and political parties

This section examines the role of political parties in the evolution of electoral rights for non-nationals. In the Scandinavian countries which were pioneers of the move towards the ascription of a general right to vote in local elections for all foreigners, pressure often originated in Social Democratic political parties. The initial drive by the Swedish Social Democrats in the 1970s to extend the franchise stemmed from their belief, according to Zig Layton-Henry (1991: 120), that 'to exclude long-term residents from voting not only violated principles of representative democracy, but would foster divisions between natives and immigrants and would encourage the neglect of immigrants' grievances, thus fostering alienation and bitterness'. In other words, it was associated with a policy of integration.

In the United Kingdom, the extension of the franchise to Commonwealth and Irish citizens appears to be widely seen across political parties as an historical accident.[43] This is probably an unfair conclusion, as in truth it derives from a conference held in 1947 between the United Kingdom and the Dominions (with Ireland also participating) which

---

[41] Answers by the Minister of Justice, Equality and Law Reform to questions put by Sinn Féin TDs Caoimhghín Ó Caoláin and Aengus Ó Snodaigh and Fine Gael TD Bernard Durkan during 2005 and 2006, held on file by author.

[42] Interview with Rotimi Adebari, Dublin, 3 March 2005.

[43] See Home Affairs Select Committee, Fourth Report, Session 1997–8, 'Electoral Law and Administration', paras. 117 et seq.

recognised the freedom of each of the parties to define their own nationality laws, but agreed that such persons should continue to be recognised by the common status of British subject. It followed from this, and an attempt to give substance to this status of British subject, that the UK accorded voting rights to Commonwealth citizens. The UK argued in the *Gibraltar* case that 'the grant of the right to vote to [Commonwealth citizens] is regarded as one of the constitutional traditions of the United Kingdom',[44] and the Court of Justice referred to these 'constitutional traditions' when it upheld the extension of the right to vote to Commonwealth citizens in Gibraltar, against Spain's objections.[45]

The issue of the UK's extended franchise arose in debate in the House of Commons on the proposed extension of the franchise to certain categories of previously excluded persons such as the homeless, those remanded in custody and not yet convicted, and patients resident in mental hospitals who are not detained offenders.[46] According to Douglas Hogg MP (Conservative):

> If we were starting from scratch, we probably would not extend the franchise to citizens of the Commonwealth or Ireland. Their right to vote has happened for historical reasons, but it is quite difficult, if one sets about defining why people should have the vote, to say with any great confidence that citizens of Ireland or the Commonwealth should have it.[47]

His views were quite closely echoed in the views of the Labour Government Minister, George Howarth MP:

> Whatever the historical reasons for their existence, the arrangements with the Commonwealth should not necessarily be taken as a precedent for arrangements with other countries that currently do not apply.[48]

The same debate on the Bill before Parliament in 1999 provided an opportunity for the range of views on the possible extension of the franchise to other non-nationals to be aired. An amendment was moved by a Labour member of the House of Commons, Harry Barnes MP, to extend the franchise to non-nationals resident in the UK, in

---

[44] Case C-145/04 *Spain* v. *United Kingdom (Gibraltar)*, 12 September 2006, at para. 46.
[45] *Ibid.*, paras. 63 and 79.
[46] Representation of the People Act 2000. See Lardy, 2001: 71–3, for a brief discussion of the use of the criterion of citizenship for suffrage.
[47] See Hansard, House of Commons, 15 December 1999, cols. 293–305, for the debate; and for Douglas Hogg MP, see col. 296.
[48] George Howarth MP, *ibid.*, col. 301.

addition to the Commonwealth and Republic of Ireland citizens who already have it. The argument for citizenship based on residence was made on the basis that those who are resident in a given polity are affected by decisions made by political representatives, and should therefore have the right to participate in their election. Finding himself largely alone in the House of Commons in making the argument for alien suffrage and residence-based voting, even within his own party, Harry Barnes MP appealed to cosmopolitanism:

> We now have a cosmopolitan world in which people move in and out of different areas. It is not always clear to people what their nation is. However, it is clear where they are, and the Government and administration responsible for making decisions that immediately affect their lives at that time can be clearly identified. We should develop electoral registration that is based on those circumstances, while recognising that there is sense in terms of citizenship.[49]

Opposition to the amendment, which was eventually withdrawn without a vote, centred on maintaining the reciprocal link between the citizen and the state. According to Robert MacLennan, Liberal Democrat MP:

> the state has the duty to look after its citizens, and the citizen must exercise his or her duty to be interested in how that service is provided. The notion of citizenship would be under challenge, perhaps even under threat, if that very considerable right were partly diminished by being no longer a characteristic of citizenship, but simply the happenstance of residence.[50]

Similarly, for Douglas Hogg MP:

> the right of voting – the duty to vote – runs with citizenship. It is part of that relationship with society that involves affinity and allegiance; it is part of being a member of a society . . . I certainly do not think that [the right to vote] should arise simply from the fact that a person is affected by the consequences of legislation.[51]

The terms of this debate revealed, therefore, a consensus across the mainstream UK political parties which was against any changes to the *status quo*.

---

[49] Harry Barnes MP, *ibid.*, cols. 303–4.   [50] Robert MacLennan MP, *ibid.*, col. 295.
[51] Douglas Hogg MP, *ibid.*, col. 296.

Looking at the varying success and failure stories of campaigns to widen the franchise, commentators such as Dirk Jacobs and Jan Rath conclude that the primary determinant of extensions of the franchise remains the possibility of coalitions between major national political parties (Jacobs, 1998, 1999, 2000a and 2000b; Rath, 1990). Interestingly, in fact, as Jacobs has shown by comparing the cases of the Netherlands and Belgium, arguments about the nature of the national polity can be used – in different settings – both to support (the Netherlands) and to contest (Belgium) the enfranchisement of resident aliens. In the Netherlands, the decision after ten years of parliamentary debate to extend municipal voting rights to non-nationals who had been resident in the Netherlands for at least five years was taken in the context of what he terms a 'discourse coalition' based on a temporary hybrid of different inclusionary and mildly exclusionary discourses coming from different positions on the political spectrum. The step was taken so that the government appeared to be doing something at a key point in time about certain acute inter-ethnic tensions, but this 'something' was in fact based on a secret agreement amongst the principal political actors not to promote open discussion in order to restrict the capacity of the extreme political right to find a platform for its segregationist exclusionary discourse. In Belgium, where the issue remained under political scrutiny over many years, and where an amendment to Article 8 of the Constitution on citizenship was put in place back in 1998 to allow the adoption of a law granting electoral rights to third country nationals, the opportunity for a decisive 'discourse coalition' was much slower to arise.[52]

The issue fell victim in early 2002 to the complexities of the Belgium coalition government system. The Belgian Foreign Minister, Louis Michel, was quoted as making the following statement about the question of electoral rights for non-nationals:[53]

---

[52] See the debate on 'The Voting Rights Issue in Belgium', in Merger, vol. 5, No. 1, www.ercomer.org/merger/vol5no1/Debate.html.

[53] 'Je n'ai pas changé politiquement. J'étais et je reste favourable à l'octroi du droit de vote aux étrangers. Mais je sais aussi que, dans le meilleur des cas, même si l'on devait voter le 12 mars, tout cela n'adviendrait pas avant 2006, année durant laquelle se déroulera le prochain scrutin communal. Dès lors et dans ces conditions, il serait pour le moins inélégant de mettre en difficulté un partenaire du gouvernement.' Author's translation. Belgian Deputy Prime Minister and Foreign Minister Louis Michel on why he intervened to prevent a vote in the Belgian Senate on a vote to institute local electoral rights for third country nationals expected to take place on 12 March 2002, quoted in Le Soir en Ligne, 20 February 2002.

I have not changed politically. I have been, and I remain, in favour of the granting of the right to vote to strangers. But I also know that even in the best case scenario, even if this were to be accepted in the vote on 12 March, nothing would actually happen until 2006, the year in which there will be the next local elections. Consequently, and in those circumstances, it would be quite ungracious to cause difficulties for a coalition partner of the government.

A proposal for the necessary legislative measure had been placed before the Senate and was due to be voted in March 2002, but it faced opposition from Flemish participants in the broadly liberal Belgian coalition government – themselves under electoral and political pressure from the extreme rightwing and nationalist Vlaams Belang (formerly the Vlaams Blok). In contrast, there has been near unanimity across political forces within the Brussels-Capital region and Wallonia about the desirability of extending voting rights to third country nationals. By demonstrating his unwillingness to see a measure adopted at that time, Louis Michel effectively undermined the proposals before Senate. His reasoning was that he did not wish to embarrass a coalition member over an issue which would not become a reality until 2006, when the next local elections would be held. Immigrants' rights were sacrificed to a greater political good, although Michel expressed his intention to see that the issue was made part of the political programme of the next national government. Consequently, on 12 March 2002, a proposal on third country national voting rights was rejected in the Internal Affairs Committee of the Belgian Senate.[54]

The threat to the Belgian coalition, along with vehement right-wing opposition to the extension of electoral rights to third country nationals, resurfaced in early 2004, when the draft law was brought once more before the Belgian legislature. A committee of the Belgian Senate adopted a draft law in late 2003, and it was approved by the Senate in early 2004. The decisive vote was in the lower house of the Parliament on 20 February 2004, leading to a law formally adopted on 19 March 2004. One of the parties of the government coalition, the Flemish Liberal Party (VLD), declined to vote with the rest of its government

---

[54] M. Vandemeulebroucke, 'Le vote des étrangers est mis au frigo. La commission de l'Intérieur du Sénat rejette le projet par neuf voix contre six', Le Soir en Ligne, 12 March 2002. See also P. van Parijs, 'Droit de vote: Perpétuer une distinction infamante?', La Libre Belgique, 7 March 2002. Further press commentary is collected online at http://users.skynet.be/suffrage-universel/be/bevo.htm.

partners, but both the opposition social democratic parties, from both Wallonia and Flanders, voted with the government, thus ensuring a majority. Essentially, the reform was carried by the Francophone parties in Belgium, but, despite dire predictions because the Prime Minister Guy Verhofstadt's own party had voted against, the government did not fall. The new rules require that resident third country nationals must have been resident for a minimum of five years before they can register to vote, and they must also be on the population register in the commune in which they wish to vote. In addition, unlike EU electors under Belgian law, non-nationals must make a formal declaration, in the application for registration, that they will observe the Belgian Constitution and its sovereign laws, and the European Convention on Human Rights.[55]

The law was applied for the first time in the local elections held throughout Belgium on 9 October 2006, with a deadline for registration of 31 July 2006. In early July 2006, Belgian media outlets were reporting that after months of stagnation the number of third country nationals applying to be registered was finally starting to rise, from around 1 per cent of eligible persons at the beginning of June to nearly 4 per cent at the beginning of July. The percentages were higher in Wallonia and Flanders, but much smaller in Brussels itself where just 786 of the 42,872 persons thought eligible to register had done so by early July 2006.[56] The final figures for third country nationals saw just 15.7 per cent of qualified voters registering to vote for the October 2006 elections, alongside 20.9 per cent of the eligible EU voters. The total of 128,000 registered non-national electors amounted to just 1.6 per cent of the overall electorate of some 7.5 million persons.[57] It was broadly felt that the obstacles to becoming registered as a voter were a disincentive to many. This rather disappointing (but not necessarily surprising) outcome of the long-running campaign pushed primarily by Francophone and social democratic parties, and backed up by associations representing the interests of immigrants and their descendants, presents an

---

[55] 'Je déclare m'engager à respecter la Constitution, les lois du peuple belge et la Convention de Sauvegarde des Droits de l'Homme et des Libertés fondamentales.' For further details see the website of the Institut Emile Vandervelde, also carrying further links to public information sites set up in Flanders and in Brussels, http://www.iev.be/index.php?id=130.

[56] 'Elections: augmentation des inscriptions d'étrangers hors UE', 4 July 2006, http://www.7sur7.be/hlns/cache/fr/det/art_228743.html.

[57] 'Vote des étrangers: tous les chiffres', Le Soir, 17 August 2006.

interesting contrast with the outcome of the October 2000 local elections in terms of *their* impact upon the level of participation and representation of *Belgian* citizens of immigrant origin. In that election, without there being any legal change in the participation rules, patterns of representation began to change in marked ways. 20–25 per cent of the representatives elected to the municipal councils in a number of Belgian municipal areas with large numbers of citizens of immigrant origin (Schaarbeek, St-Josse and Molenbeek) were of Turkish or Moroccan origin (Jacobs, Martinello and Rea, 2002). Thus the ethnic composition of Belgian local politics, at least in some municipalities, was decisively altered already in 2000, even in advance of the possibility for the non-nationals to vote.

V After the vote: elections, electors, candidates and parties

As noted above, it is not surprising that relatively low numbers of non-nationals registered to vote in the Belgian local elections of October 2006. As Lise Togeby (1999: 665) comments, 'the general impression is that immigrant participation in elections is relatively low in all countries, but information about voter turn-out is rather haphazard and scattered'. Certainly, the case of third country nationals voting in the local elections in Ireland discussed in Section III of this chapter and the evidence gathered on the effects of the EU's own local electoral rights for non-nationals in Chapter 5 both seem to support that general finding.

However, there are some interesting cases where voter participation appears to be higher than expected. For example, it is higher in Denmark than in Sweden, despite the fact that the general environment regarding multiculturalism and immigrant incorporation policies is more contested and – arguably – more hostile to foreigners in Denmark than in Sweden. Togeby concludes that the main reason for higher levels of non-national voter turnout in Danish than in Swedish local elections relates to differences in the relevant political opportunity structures (1999: 683):

> the Danish local government electoral system creates far better opportunities for collective mobilisation than the Swedish one.

More specifically, the electoral system for local government in Denmark means that, if immigrants mobilise effectively and use the system strategically, they can encounter success, in terms of getting candidates elected who directly represent their interests. Even if immigrant candidates are placed rather low down the lists of the big mainstream parties, in practice a small group of focused voters can often achieve the election of one or more of those migrant candidates off the party lists, especially in the larger urban areas, because of the small number of mandates needed at the bottom of the lists. In further work comparing the situations in Copenhagen, in Denmark, and Oslo, in Norway, Bergh and Bjørklund (2003) concluded that in both cities, in comparison to their share of the general population, non-national communities of immigrants are over-represented amongst municipal councillors, indicating a high level of ethnic mobilisation amongst immigrant communities as voters, resulting in an effective exploitation of the preferential voting systems used in both cities.

In Oslo, the greatest power stems from the individual voter's capacity to indicate a 'plus' or a 'minus' next to any individual (or indeed all individuals) on the party's list. Likewise, in Copenhagen, voters can indicate not only the choice of a party, but also the choice of a particular candidate. If non-national groups mobilise in the two cities to take advantage of those possibilities, and if – in contrast – many others in the general population do not take advantage of them, then effective mobilisation amongst non-national voters can deliver, as has indeed occurred, over-representation of the minority population amongst those elected to local office in comparison to their share of the general population.

However, Bergh and Bjørklund warn that this situation may not be permanent. They point out that, in the 1970s in Norway, preferential voting was used as one element of a set of policies to enhance the representation of women at the municipal level. While this increased the numbers of women elected in the short term, in the longer term women have been systematically disadvantaged by voters placing a 'plus' next to the name of male candidates, and a 'minus' next to the names of the female candidates. Thus, in the longer term, non-national candidates may suffer 'minuses' from the general population, as resentment of their presence within society and ethnic tensions grow. This is clear from the reaction of the Danish People's Party to the increasing awareness amongst non-national communities of the availability of the right to vote. The *Copenhagen Post* reported in 2003:

> Since the 1989 local elections, when 77,253 foreigners exercised their right to vote, voter turnout in local elections has more than doubled, topping 155,880 in 2001. But rather than considering surging voter turnout as a sign that immigrants in Denmark are taking democracy to heart,

the Danish People's Party is concerned ... 'The government has shar-pened its requirements for citizenship, demanding a reasonable level of Danish proficiency and a familiarity with Danish culture, together with loyalty to Denmark. If the government is willing to put its money where its mouth is, these new demands should also count for voting rights', said party justice spokesman Per Dalgaard.[58]

The People's Party supports a policy of repealing foreigners' voting rights, seeing voting – as it makes clear in this statement – as a reward for integration, rather than a pathway towards integration.

Up to the present time, it would appear that mainstream parties have remained largely indifferent to electoral rights being accorded to third country nationals, although one of the arguments of the Flemish VLD (a liberal party) in Belgium which was used to oppose the widening of the suffrage to include third country nationals was that the presence of third country nationals on the register of voters would have the effect of driving 'old' Belgians into the arms of the far-right parties such as the Vlaams Belang. These parties have enjoyed rather high levels of electoral success especially in Flanders in recent years, particularly in the context of increased polarisation about the politics of racial and religious iden-tity, by making a policy of opposing immigration, and supporting the repatriation of immigrants, one of their main platforms. However, although the Vlaams Belang did well in some parts of Flanders in the October 2006 local elections, they did not enjoy a sharp rise in support across the board. On the contrary, the governing VLD did extremely badly in the election, often suffering at the hands of social democratic parties which had consistently supported electoral rights for non-nationals.

The evidence from the Dutch local elections of 2006 confirms that local electoral success can be achieved in circumstances where a party specifically embraces a policy of attracting immigrant non-national voters, and indeed voters who are the descendants of immigrants who have acquired national citizenship. As we noted in Chapter 7,[59] a very high percentage of the population of the Netherlands – approaching 20 per cent – has one or more parent born outside the Netherlands. The so-called 'allochtoonen' voted disproportionately for the Dutch Labour

---

[58] 'Party Anxiety over Voting for Foreigners', *Copenhagen Post*, 21 February 2003, http://www.cphpost.dk/get/65766.html.
[59] Chapter 7, Section II.

Party,[60] which recouped many of the losses which it had suffered in the 2002 local elections, for example in Rotterdam where it had lost out to the Leefbaar Rotterdam party founded by the late Pim Fortuyn, a prominent anti-immigration Dutch politician. However, a fuller assessment of the questions raised by elections such as these, which involve interactions between the votes of non-national immigrants and immigrants and their descendants who have acquired national citizenship is beyond the scope of this review, as it raises broader questions about the political engagement of immigrants and their descendants more generally, and the role of political parties in that context (see Martiniello, 2005).

VI Creating a space for migration and integration within the polity

In this chapter thus far, and indeed throughout much of this book, the 'state' has generally been treated as a unitary entity. In reality, as was argued in Chapter 2,[61] issues around migration and citizenship are subject to pressures within polities, both from sub-state regions which often view themselves and/or are treated as stateless nations within wider multinational states and from cities which regard themselves as transnational rather than national actors. Cities, in particular, may be the chosen destinations of immigrants, rather than countries as such, not least because newly arrived immigrants often wish to join an established community in the host state of co-ethnics or co-nationals (DeVoretz, 2004; Bauböck, 2003). A range of questions about migration and citizenship policies and practices can thus arise once the state is disaggregated in this way, particularly but not only in federal states, and especially in relation to the implementation of national, state-level policy decisions on immigration (Green, 2004: 12–18).

These trends are clearly visible in relation to asylum where a policy of dispersal of asylum applicants has been pursued in a number of states, including Germany, Ireland and the UK, in the name of sharing the costs and the 'burdens' (Boswell, 2001). In practice, this has also meant that

---

[60] 'Migrants Vote Massively for the PvdA', Press Release, University of Amsterdam Institute for Migration and Ethnic Studies, http://www2.fmg.uva.nl/imes/verkiezingen.htm; see B. Delemotte, 'Pays-Bas: forte mobilisation des électeurs d'origine étrangère aux élections municipales de mars 2006-07-11', *La Lettre de la Citoyenneté*, July–August 2006, http://perso.nnx.com/marion/lettre.htm.

[61] Chapter 2, Section IV.

there have been some differences in the politicisation of asylum questions across states. In Scotland, for example, while immigration (and asylum) questions are reserved matters for the Westminster Parliament under the Scotland Act 1998, certain issues about the treatment of asylum seekers, and especially the forced removal of those who have been refused asylum, have been more heavily contested than in other parts of the UK. Since policy on children falls within the remit of the Scottish Parliament, moreover, political conflict has arisen as to whether so-called dawn raids to remove those who have been refused asylum from the United Kingdom are traumatic experiences which infringe the rights of the child, and whether such removal, however effected, would also deny the children certain basic rights, such as the right to an education.[62] The issue has led directly to conflict between the Scottish Executive, involving a Labour Party-led coalition, and the Westminster-based UK Government, likewise led by the Labour Party. When the Scottish First Minister Jack McConnell sought some type of dispensation from the Home Office in London regarding the involvement of Scottish education and social service agencies in the decision regarding deportation and also its implementation,[63] he was firmly rebuffed. In a political commentary in the *Sunday Herald*, a senior Scottish political commentator noted somewhat gloomily:

> If anything, McConnell's brush with the Home Office has confirmed that Holyrood's attempt to project Scotland as a welcoming place for foreigners is increasingly out of step with the clampdown implemented at Westminster.[64]

It is arguable that in other fields of immigration policy, while restricted in what it can do, the Scottish Executive has been a little more successful. Historically, like Ireland, Scotland has been a nation of emigration. This has involved principally emigration to the rest of the British Isles (including the island of Ireland, especially Ulster) and to North America and elsewhere in the British Empire/Commonwealth. According to David McCrone (2001: 101):

---

[62] 'Protest over refugee dawn raids', *BBC News*, 17 September 2005, http://212.58.240.36/1/hi/scotland/4254490.stm.

[63] 'McConnell Seeking Asylum Protocol', BBC News, 22 September 2005, http://news.bbc.co.uk/1/hi/scotland/4269894.stm.

[64] 'Holyrood vs Westminster: The Battle over Asylum', *Sunday Herald*, 27 November 2005, http://www.sundayherald.com/53116/.

Some two million people have left Scotland in the twentieth century, and at least similar numbers have done so in the previous century.

Immigration was largely confined to inward flows from Ireland (especially Catholics, whereas it had been principally Protestants who had left Scotland for Ireland), Poles and Lithuanians especially after the Second World War, Italians, and in more recent years the English. Scotland's population has declined severely as a proportion of the overall population of the United Kingdom (as Scotland's has dwindled to around 5 million, England's has continued to grow), and its population (and population profile) has continued to decline (and to age) because of declining fertility and insufficient immigration to match the continuing emigration.

One of the major initiatives of the Scottish Executive in the early years of managing devolved government after the first Scottish Parliament elections in 1999 was to promote positively the image of Scotland as a migration destination. This has included some specific initiatives which can be understood as exceptions to the generally restrictive UK policy, such as the Fresh Talent initiative giving overseas students who have completed university courses in Scotland two-year visa extensions to work in Scotland, without the need to seek a work permit.[65] Clearly, this is hardly a radical departure from broader UK policy which likewise promotes a selective migration policy, focusing on migrants with specific skills especially in shortage areas or those with entrepreneurial tendencies, but it is a broader and less restrictive programme, aimed at ensuring that highly qualified migrants remain in Scotland, perhaps long enough to acquire personal reasons to stay there permanently. In contrast, most UK-wide schemes permitting the employment of non-nationals are either limited to specific shortage occupations, where it is much easier for the employee and employer to obtain a work permit, or are limited to very narrow categories of 'Highly Skilled Migrants'. Furthermore, with its promotional and informational website, 'Scotland Is the Place',[66] which is also available in a Polish version under a separate '.eu' domain name,[67] in recognition of the important role which Polish migrants have been playing in the Scottish economy since EU enlargement in 2004, the Scottish Executive is offering warm encouragement to migration to Scotland which is not matched by the equivalent UK-wide

---

[65] See the statement of First Minister Jack McConnell to the Scottish Parliament, 25 February 2004, http://www.scotland.gov.uk/News/News-Extras/191/; Scottish Executive, 'New Scots: Attracting New Talent to Meet the Challenge of Growth', February 2004.

[66] http://www.scotlandistheplace.com.   [67] http://www.szkocja.eu.

websites.[68] On the contrary, the public face of the UK in relation to employment-related mobility often demonstrates the increasing 'fortress mentality'[69] which now appears to pervade much UK policy in relation to immigration, border controls and the treatment of foreigners more generally.

While making electoral rights available to non-nationals is rarely likely to affect any migrant's decision-making in relation to choosing a destination (the 'Scotland Is the Place' website promoting mobility to Scotland does not mention at all who can vote for the various political institutions it briefly describes), policy-makers may well regard them, as we have seen in this and the previous chapter, as useful parts of the broader toolkit of integration mechanisms. It is interesting to note that the UK already gives electoral rights to EU citizens to participate in 'regional' elections, notably the elections to the devolved political institutions in Northern Ireland, Scotland and Wales, as well as in the direct elections for the Mayor of London. Technically, this is because such elections are governed within a framework analogous to local elections for the purposes of the franchise and so the right to vote flows naturally from that conclusion.[70] Moreover, EU citizens were able to vote in the regionally based referendums in Scotland and Wales held to ascertain whether the people of these 'region-nations' wanted new forms of representation or political authority, and they have had the right to vote in every other referendum held since 1997 (e.g. the one held in London to decide whether to have a Mayor of London and a London Assembly) apart from the one held on the establishment of devolved institutions in Northern Ireland.[71]

---

[68] Compare the tone and focus of the Home Office's 'Working in the UK' website, http://www.workingintheuk.gov.uk/working_in_the_uk/en/homepage.html. A warmer tone is struck by a website of the British Council specifically focused at encouraging the mobility of researchers: http://www.britishcouncil.org/eumobility-networkuk-working-in-the-uk.htm.

[69] D. Orr, 'Open Borders Are the Only Alternative to the Erection of a Repressive Fortress State', *Independent*, 26 July 2006.

[70] S.3(1) of the Local Government Elections Regulations 1995 (SI 1995 No. 1948) provides the basic amendments to the local electorate to incorporate the requirements of EU law, and in relation to the inclusion of EU citizens in the 'regional' franchise, see s.17 of the Greater London Authority Act 1999; s.11 of the Scotland Act 1998; para.10 of Schedule 1 to the Government of Wales Act 1998; s.2(2) of the Northern Ireland (Elections) Act 1998.

[71] Ss.1(2) and 2(2) of the Referendums (Scotland and Wales) Act 1997. The parliamentary electoral register was used to determine the franchise in the Northern Ireland referendum, doubtless given the sensitivities of the issues attaching to this referendum, which followed on from the Belfast Agreement of Easter 1998. See generally House of

No other EU Member State proceeds in this manner in relation to electoral rights in 'regional' elections, although electoral rights are extended in a number of states, such as Hungary, Denmark and Sweden, to 'county' or 'provincial' level assemblies which are regarded, like the municipalities covered by Article 19(1) EC, as part of local self-government (Waldrauch, 2005). In other Member States with federal systems of government, such as Germany and Austria, voting at the regional level is strictly reserved to nationals. The restrictive approaches in these states, which are grounded in a constitutional approach to the notion of the 'people', are charted in more detail in Chapter 9.

Two questions might arise from this. One is whether other Member States with federal or quasi-federal arrangements might in the longer term choose to follow the UK in relation to the scope of EU citizens' rights. Clearly, this question is closely related to that of EU citizens' possible future voting rights in national elections canvassed in Chapter 6. Here, the case of Spain seems to offer some potential for future developments, and Spain is examined at the end of this section, with reference back to how the UK case has developed.

The other question is whether, and if so how, the devolved parts of the UK might see a further widening of the suffrage to include third country nationals generally voting for the devolved Parliaments/Assemblies (or indeed local elections), even in the absence of more general UK-wide developments. I shall deal with this question first, with particular reference to the situation in Scotland.

A subnational territorial unit with autonomous or semi-autonomous powers and institutions of government, such as Scotland, the German or Austrian *Länder*, the Spanish autonomous communities, or indeed the municipal authorities anywhere in the Member States, could seek to push the boundaries of the suffrage wider than they stand at national level for a variety of principled and instrumental reasons. In some cases, it may be because the party or parties controlling the relevant territorial unit differ sharply in ideology and approach to the national government, and they seek to use the opportunity of legal reform at the local or regional level in order either to emphasise their local 'difference' or to try to push for reform at the national level by offering an example of good practice. A form of intergovernmental intra-state competition can consequently emerge, and in that context it may well be decisive how

Commons Library Standard Note, '*The Franchise for Referendums*', Standard Note SN/PC/2583, 18 August 2003.

exactly powers are divided according to the relevant constitutional settlement regarding local self-government or devolution, and which organ of the state has the decisive power to determine who decides. As we shall see in Chapter 9, competition between different levels of government has been a characteristic feature of struggles over electoral rights for non-nationals in at least three states of the European Union, namely, Germany, Austria and Italy. In no case, as yet, has the franchise been widened beyond the requirements laid down in the EC Treaty for EU citizens. That does not mean to say it will not happen in the future.

The politicisation of debate about immigration and non-nationals in Scotland, as illustrated earlier in this chapter, demonstrates that Scotland offers the type of environment in which arguments about developing a different franchise might occur. The *status quo* does not look positive, however. Section B3 of Schedule 5 to the Scotland Act 1998 lists the powers reserved to the Westminster Parliament after devolution, so far as pertains to elections. The list reads:

> Elections for membership of the House of Commons, the European Parliament and the [Scottish] Parliament, including the subject-matter of—
>
> (a) the European Parliamentary Elections Act 1978,
> (b) the Representation of the People Act 1983 and the Representation of the People Act 1985, and
> (c) the Parliamentary Constituencies Act 1986,
>
> so far as those enactments apply, or may be applied, in respect of such membership.
>
> The franchise at local government elections.

This leaves very little competence at all for the Scottish Parliament in electoral matters, although the reference in the last line to local government elections means that the Scottish Parliament can make arrangements for local elections which deviate from the UK norm, and indeed it has done so recently in order to introduce proportional representation for Scottish local elections as of 2007.[72] A broader commission (the Arbuthnott Commission) to look at the conduct of elections more generally in Scotland, including voter participation and the existence of several systems of voting, was established not by the Scottish Ministers, but by the Secretary of State for Scotland – that is, a Minister

---

[72] Local Governance (Scotland) Act 2004.

responsible to the Westminster Parliament. In sum, the Scottish Parliament is not permitted to change the franchise for any elections in Scotland, and could only be empowered to do so if the Scotland Act were amended. But at present there is no active political debate on this question, whether in Scotland or the wider UK, and so it is not foreseeable that this might occur in the near future; longer term, it is conceivable that it could become coupled to the wider migration debate likely to develop under the framework of one or both of the Scottish Executive's Futures Project,[73] or the Scottish Parliament's Futures Forum.[74]

While any change would require primary legislation from the UK Parliament, there is no other constitutional bar to a wider franchise in Scotland. This point is reinforced by the fact that the current arrangements permitting EU citizens to vote in such 'regional' elections in the UK are simply laid down in primary legislation making reference to the local government register. Section 11 of the Scotland Act provides:

> (1) The persons entitled to vote as electors at an election for membership of the Parliament held in any constituency are those who on the day of the poll—
>
> (a) would be entitled to vote as electors at a local government election in an electoral area falling wholly or partly within the constituency, and
>
> (b) are registered in the register of local government electors at an address within the constituency.

From the point of view of electoral administration, this offers a certain degree of simplicity, especially since in 1999, 2003 and 2007 the Scottish Parliament elections were held on the same day as the Scottish local government elections. However, Scottish Parliament elections need not necessarily coincide with Scottish local government elections.

In fact, the current arrangement differs from that laid down in the Scotland Act 1978 for the abortive Scottish Assembly, an initiative which failed to win sufficient electoral approval in a referendum held in early 1979. Section 4 of the Scotland Act 1978 provided that the persons entitled to vote as electors at Assembly elections would be those who had their names on the register of parliamentary electors, plus peers (i.e. members of the House of Lords) on the local government electoral register. Peers are not entitled to vote in Westminster elections but they are entitled

---

[73] http://www.scotland.gov.uk/Topics/Government/futures/.
[74] http://www.scotlandfutureforum.org.

to vote in local government elections.[75] Schedule 17 to the same Act laid down that the same groups of electors could vote in the referendum.

One might question why a changed definition of the franchise was used after 1997, both for the referendum and for the Scottish Parliament elections,[76] and indeed the issue of the franchise was much discussed in both the House of Lords and the House of Commons in 1997, especially in relation to the question of who should vote in the referendum, as they would be the group effectively determining Scotland's constitutional status for the foreseeable future.[77] Two key developments in relation to the local government and parliamentary registers between 1978 and 1997 should be noted: first, the presence of EU citizens on the former since 1993, and, secondly, the presence of overseas (i.e. expatriate) voters on the latter. The latter were enfranchised by the Representation of the People Act 1983, as amended most recently by the Representation of the People Act 2000, to allow British nationals living overseas to register for up to fifteen years after leaving the UK in the constituency in which they were last registered as residents.

Choosing the local electoral register as the basis for the franchise for elections in Scotland focused on residence rather than any other form of affinity with Scotland. It not only avoided the question of the affinity and belonging of those 'expatriates' who had moved outside the UK within the last fifteen years, but also avoided the question of the participation 'rights' of the very much larger Scottish diaspora comprising those who had left Scotland within the last fifteen years in order to reside elsewhere in the UK. To what extent should the 'Scottishness' of either group of expatriates give them a say? Should the expatriates born in Scotland, who have chosen to emigrate whether within or outside the UK, be given a stake in the future of Scotland? Do they have a better right to participate, as indeed some might argue, than those English 'incomers' (i.e. those born and formerly resident in England, but now resident in Scotland)? It is not hard to see that such questions of affinity

[75] The Scotland Act 1978 was immediately repealed by the newly elected Conservative Government in 1979 after the failed referendum of 1 March 1979 contributed to the fall of the Labour Government soon thereafter.

[76] The issue of who should be able to vote in devolved Scottish elections was not discussed in the Kilbrandon Report of 1973 (*Royal Commission on the Constitution, 1969–1973*, Cmnd 5460), which was one of the main sources of inspiration when the devolution scheme of 1997 came to be put in place.

[77] For examples of debates, see House of Commons Committee stage of the Referendums (Scotland and Wales) Bill, House of Commons Hansard, 3 June 1997, cols. 247–78; House of Lords Hansard, 3 July 1997, cols. 321–44.

would be precisely those which a government committed to pushing through a referendum on a rather limited and localised concept of devolution in 1997 would want to avoid, given the presence of an active political movement for independence in Scotland. The parliamentary debates in 1997 reveal that the issue about expatriate voters was principally raised by members of the opposition Conservative party in order, perhaps, to muddy the waters about what the significance of a devolution referendum might be for the future of 'Scottishness' and of Scotland. Labour government ministers instead stressed that devolution was about residence and localism. It is clear from those debates that issues about the scope of the franchise are clearly linked to questions of identity. This is also the case, as we shall see, in Spain.

In contrast to the UK, with its *sui generis* constitutional arrangements, if other states were to grant electoral rights in regional elections, whether to EU citizens or to other third country nationals, this would normally require amendments to constitutional provisions. Some consideration has been given in Spain to widening the franchise in elections to assemblies in Spain's seventeen regions or autonomous communities, but there exists a constitutional bar to extending electoral rights which would first need to be removed. Article 13(2) of the Spanish Constitution provides:

> Only Spaniards shall have the rights recognized in section 23 [i.e. the right to vote], except in cases which may be established by treaty or by law concerning the right to vote and the right to be elected in municipal elections, and subject to the principle of reciprocity.

This text includes the constitutional reform adopted in August 1992 to give effect to Article 19 EC; this reform merely added the words 'and the right to be elected' to the paragraph.

It has been suggested by academics studying this issue at the University of Malaga that the constitutional limitation, allowing non-national voters only in municipal elections and not in elections in the autonomous communities, could be eliminated by removing the relevant words referring to municipal elections, thus leaving the matter to the various units of territorial governance to decide what approach they might like to take by adopting specific legislation under their various powers.[78] However, in practice, any constitutional amendment

---

[78] Participación política de los Extranjeros Residentes en Andalucía (PPERA). Propuestas de reformas constitucionales y estatutarias, http://campusvirtual.uma.es/in_en/ppera.htm.

is likely to face difficulties in Parliament. This is in large measure because the final territorial constitutional settlement in Spain, and especially the status of Catalonia, remains unclear. The conservative opposition Popular Party (PP) has expressed its opposition to any amendments to the Constitution, including an amendment to Article 13, at the present time; it remains unhappy about developments in relation to Catalonia, particularly in the wake of a referendum on 18 June 2006 which expressed clear public support for greater autonomy. In the absence of a constitutional change, the regional governments are blocked from extending the range of electoral rights for non-nationals. Thus, for example, the regional government in Andalusia, which has expressed some interest in facilitating the political participation of non-nationals in regional political institutions, whether EU citizens or third country nationals, would be limited to other types of political participation initiatives such as elected foreigners' representatives with the right to make representations to the elected regional politicians.

However, assuming that the constitutional obstacle could be overcome, notwithstanding this negative prognosis, it is possible that regional electoral rights could be extended in the future to EU citizens at least in places like Andalusia; such a development would be most likely to garner broad public support, since it could be linked into the generally still positive view in Spain about the role of 'Europe' generally. This positive view was expressed most recently in the lukewarm, but nonetheless positive, result of the Spanish referendum on the Constitutional Treaty in March 2005. In terms of political prestige, it still carries weight for politicians and policy-makers to be seen as putting themselves in the vanguard of European developments, and from that point of view the possibility of pointing to the UK examples of EU citizens voting for representatives in devolved regional bodies represents a good example of 'best practice' which can be referred to in public debate.

Moreover, there are also some examples of the mobilisation of EU citizens in the Spanish local elections, particularly amongst the retired communities in the south, not only in Andalusia, but also in nearby Murcia (Mendez Lago, 2005) which could indicate an 'appetite' amongst such communities for the possibility of regional political representation. One group of EU citizens, including Spanish, British, German, Dutch, French and Belgian nationals, has sought to establish a new political party in one municipality, precisely for the purpose of promoting cross-national representation at the local level taking advantage of the availability of the EU electoral rights.[79] However, UK-based political parties such as the Labour Party have also sought to foster political mobilisation at a local level in Spain, and John MacKay, the Secretary of the Labour International Costa Blanca North, wrote to a local expatriate newspaper to express his concerns about the dangers of 'ethnic-based' politics if this sort of single-issue party takes hold. His call was for the established Spanish parties to become more involved with the expatriate communities.[80]

The issue of third country nationals voting in regional elections would inevitably be a much more contested political issue in Spain. As regards local elections, it is already possible for third country nationals to vote under Article 13, provided treaties are negotiated (at the national level) with the relevant third countries (so far this is only the case with Norway), and local electoral rights are granted on a reciprocal basis. There are moves to extend this on a piecemeal basis, in support of a relatively broad consensus across both the PP and the PSOE (the Socialist Party, in government since 2005) that local electoral rights could be an important element of a national integration programme for third country nationals. However, any move to remove or amend Article 13 of the Constitution to allow third country nationals to vote in regional elections could easily be interpreted by conservative political forces such as the PP as opening the door to allow Islamic voters to elect Spanish representatives.

While an Islamophobic cultural and political trend in the public sphere is undoubtedly visible in Spain, and is often associated with the increased recent immigration into Spain of Muslims especially from North Africa, this is not a unitary phenomenon, especially in the south of Spain. On the contrary, there are some political trends, especially associated with processes of subnational identity formation in southern Spain, which seek to embrace more fully Spain's Islamic heritage. Gunther Dietz (2004: 1088) argues, for example, that:

> Andalusia is undergoing a hasty process of sub-national identity building, which is motivated by an ethnicised tug-of-war of asymmetrical devolution and federalisation. Simultaneously, however, Andalusian regional society *de facto* is quickly 'multiculturalising' and pluralising in religious terms; this is mainly induced by North African immigration and the immigrant-support activities of local civil society movements and organisations.

---

[79] See details of the new political party, Nueva Javea, at http://www.nuevajavea.com/en/index.html.

[80] Letter, Costa Blanca News, Issue 9–15 June 2006, http://www.costablanca-news.com/.

In broader 'European' terms,

> Andalusian identity has always been tempted to bridge the Mediterranean divide. Oscillating throughout different epochs between identifying itself as the 'top' of the African and/or Oriental world or the 'bottom' of the Occident, its still recent integration into the European Union and its subsequent role as a European 'gate-keeper' at the margins of the continent is ambiguously re-defining the region's self-perception.
>
> (Dietz, 2004: 1088)

This is complicated by the internal dynamics of Spanish devolution, where Andalusia looks for a space to define itself regionally and subnationally as not Castilian (and therefore different from Madrid), even though as a region it lacks the clear subnational identity focus which has driven the autonomy demands of the three northern regions of Galicia and, especially, the Basque country and Catalonia. The latter regions tend to see themselves as historic but currently stateless nations, mirroring a widespread view in Scotland. Andalusia cannot make such a claim, but it has at least been able to identify some limited features of its Maghrebian heritage, at least up to and probably beyond the reconquest of Spain around 1485, and reincorporate these into the construction of a notion of Andalusian-ness, as part of its ultimately successful attempt to gain recognition as a historic region. Consequently, the process of devolution has proceeded in Andalusia at approximately the same pace as in the Basque country and Catalonia. In that context, the extension of electoral rights could operate in a positive synergy with the cultural encounters occurring on a continuing basis in the region between pro-immigrant NGOs, the immigrant communities, and more mainstream civil society organisations; this could not only bolster the possibility of integration, as defined and critiqued in this chapter, but also hold out prospects for a more multicultural and hybrid regional or subnational identity. Thus an identity-based approach could be a different way of conceiving of citizenship-related reforms such as electoral rights for non-nationals at the regional level as a form of intra-state, inter-regional or intergovernmental political competition.

VII Conclusions

In contemporary Europe, it is clear that there is no definite 'dividend' in terms of democracy-building or the strengthening of the legitimacy of political regimes stemming from the extension of electoral rights to non-nationals. The stories as they emerge from the various Member States of the EU demonstrate rather different orientations to the overall question of inclusion, and its interplay with matters such as citizenship acquisition, the role of political parties, and intra-state political competition with regard to migration and citizenship issues which has often played to the gallery of regionally defined identities. Such differences exist, even where the states in question have relatively similar structures of electoral opportunity for non-nationals. But cases of electoral inclusion do not seem to be capable of being read as straightforward vindications of the types of normative, or even instrumental, arguments which are generally used to justify the extension of electoral rights in principle. On the contrary, these narratives demonstrate the need to pay close attention to the detail, legal and political, of transformational processes occurring in relation to the different dimensions of citizenship and membership, as was argued in Chapter 3. To that end, it is perhaps wise not to draw any firm conclusions in advance of taking a closer look at the related issue of exclusion from the electorate. I shall turn to this question in the next chapter.

9

Electoral exclusion, models of citizenship
and the contestation of belonging

I Introduction

The restriction of electoral rights (especially but not only the right to vote in national elections) exclusively to those holding the national citizenship of a given state remains a rather common state practice, as we saw in Chapter 3. The most substantial 'exception' stems, of course, from the equal treatment rights granted to EU citizens in relation to local and European Parliamentary electoral rights under Article 19 EC, which now extend to twenty-seven Member States. In addition, as we have observed in the previous chapter, there are a number of important exceptions to the restriction of electoral rights to non-nationals, especially in relation to local electoral rights. Perhaps it is precisely because the denial of rights remains the *status quo* that the arguments in favour of the restrictive position tend to be less sharply defined in both political and academic discourse than the arguments for opening up the franchise. Where such arguments are explicitly articulated, they tend to concentrate on emphasising the normative and instrumental desirability of maintaining the incentive for non-nationals to acquire national citizenship. Voting rights, at every level, are seen on that argument as a reward for achieving a sufficient level of integration in terms of residence periods, affinity with the new state, and passing of all conditions such as naturalisation tests, especially those concerning language. They cannot be seen as part of the gradual process whereby non-nationals are made to feel 'at home' and thus acquire the inclination to seek national citizenship.

It is perhaps unfortunate that some of the states which have the most restrictive rules on the acquisition of nationality have also been the most restrictive in relation to expanding the boundaries of the suffrage. Germany and Austria, for example, have both had ethno-culturally driven definitions of national citizenship acquisition principally by descent (*ius sanguinis*) and restrictive rules on citizenship acquisition by naturalisation. In terms of the relationship between citizenship and nation state, each broadly conforms to Rogers Brubaker's model of the 'ethnic' nation (Brubaker, 1992). Equally, both have seen initiatives from the subnational level of government to extend the local franchise to third country nationals decisively ruled out by constitutional court judgments which concentrate on the centrality of the *national* 'people' for the purposes of defining the boundaries of suffrage. These initiatives are the primary focus of discussion in this chapter.

While restrictive national policies and restrictive regimes of citizenship acquisition may frequently intersect, they do not necessarily coincide with negative public attitudes. A survey of public attitudes towards electoral rights was undertaken in 2000 on the initiative of the NGO La Lettre de la Citoyenneté, which supports a citizenship of residence for non-nationals under which electoral rights would automatically follow. Percentages in favour of according electoral rights in *European Parliament* elections varied across the EU Member States (then fifteen), from a low of 15% in Denmark to a high of 62% in Spain. In Germany, 42% were in favour, as were 55% in Italy.[1] The average was 45% across the EU. More substantial in nature are the recurrent surveys on public attitudes to migration and citizenship questions undertaken on behalf of the Fondazione Nord Est and La Polis University of Urbino in Italy, which cover various Member States (of the EU25). Of the six states included in a survey conducted in late 2005, only Hungary granted electoral rights to third country nationals. The others were France, Germany, Italy, Poland and the Czech Republic.[2] The results showed the following percentages of the population in favour of electoral rights at the *local level* for third country nationals who also pay taxes: France, 82%; Italy, 74%; Germany, 62%; Poland, 56%; Czech Republic, 45%; Hungary, 32%.

In relation to the right to vote in *national elections*, even more surprising results were obtained. Those expressing themselves in favour of extending the right to tax-paying foreigners were: France, 67%; Italy, 65%; Germany, 58%; Poland, 47%; Czech Republic, 39%; Hungary, 27%. Yet trends in, for example, Germany are towards decreasing trust between citizens and non-nationals, so that, while 33% of Germans

---

[1] *La Lettre de la Citoyenneté*, No. 49, January/February 2001, http://perso.nnx.com/marion/menu49.htm.

[2] *Migration and Citizenship Rights in Europe: European Citizens' Attitudes*, Quaderni FNE, Collana Osservatori, No. 21, November 2005, at 13.

regarded foreigners living in Germany as posing a 'threat of foreign infiltration' five years ago, this figure had risen to 54% in early 2006.[3] One way of reconciling these trends could be that citizens already regard 'tax-paying foreigners' as a wholly different group in their minds to the broader group of 'foreigners' in general, and view them as being on a progressive pathway to integration that certain foreigners, the dangerous ones, the ones to be distrusted and hence excluded, eschew altogether.

Thus, notwithstanding the problems raised by constitutional restrictions, it can be anticipated that, even in those Member States where there is comprehensive electoral exclusion of third country nationals at the present time, political claims to develop electoral inclusion will still continue to be heard for the foreseeable future. This chapter will investigate some of the ways in which the line between exclusion and inclusion is contested in Germany and Austria, two federal states where the respective Constitution Courts have 'blocked' the development of electoral rights, in both cases at the initiative of subnational units of government.

We start with the case of Germany, where the arguments about electoral rights have been widely rehearsed in many political and legal forums over the years. Discussions in Austria are less well developed, but an additional element in Austrian politics, not present in German politics, has been the role of a radical right-wing party in the governing coalition with an explicitly anti-immigration rhetoric at the heart of its political standpoint. However, in both cases, the link between the constitutional framework of the state and the definition of the 'people' has offered a reference point for political contestation. It is worth noting that the 'status' of these two states within the EU is rather different: Germany is a large founding Member State; Austria is a smaller state, which joined the EU only in 1995 after the opening up of the European geopolitical realm that occurred with the end of the Cold War.

Before we move on to look at these cases in detail, however, it is worth taking a brief glance at two other large founding Member States of the EU where local electoral rights for third country nationals have likewise not been granted, but both of which are now – like Germany and Austria – grappling with large, and in some cases quite 'unintegrated', populations of immigrants or their descendants: France and Italy. In the case of France, central to the definition of citizenship is a republican

---

[3] efms Migration Report, May 2006, http://web.uni-bamberg.de/~ba6ef3/main_e.htm.

conception, linked to the nation defined in civic rather than ethnic terms (Brubaker, 1992; Lefebvre, 2003). Because of France's approach to citizenship acquisition, large numbers of immigrants have either acquired citizenship through naturalisation, or seen their children and grandchildren acquire it by birth. Thus when events such as the riots in the Parisian suburbs in 2005 and 2006 by unemployed young men of North African descent protesting their exclusion from the labour market are characterised by politicians as being problems generated by out-siders, this construction operates in denial of the fundamental legal principle that such persons, many of them French by nationality, are in fact already within the golden circle of the polity as nationally defined, with the right to vote. Hence, citizenship acquisition which gives the reward of full political membership does not always operate in practice to bring about socio-economic inclusion and membership. Meanwhile, the necessary constitutional amendment to start the process of bringing about local electoral rights for third country nationals remains on the table within the French legislature. It is consistently supported by forces of the political left,[4] but it has not so far been adopted. Initiatives within municipalities to organise local referendums on giving the right to vote to third country nationals have, like other subnational initiatives exam-ined in this chapter, been declared illegal as outwith the competence of the relevant subnational authorities,[5] but held on a consultative basis at the municipal level nonetheless.[6]

In Italy, meanwhile, although national citizenship acquisition is primarily framed by a model of family affinity (Arena, Nascimbene and Zincone, 2006), commentators postulate that problems of nation-building and political and economic modernisation have left a weak residual link between citizenship and national identity (Koenig-Archibugi, 2003). In relation to immigration policy development in Italy, commentators have frequently observed paradoxical moves: a broad

---

[4] See the Socialist Party 'manifesto', *Réussir ensemble le changement: Le projet socialiste pour la France*, Part III, at 21: 'We will grant the right to vote in local elections to resident non-nationals who have been paying taxes for more than five years in our country', 1 July 2006, www.projet.parti-socialiste.fr.

[5] Judgment of the *Tribunal Administratif* Cergy Pontoise (1st Chamber), 23 February 2006, *Préfet de la Seine-Saint-Denis*, Req. No. 0511415, reported and briefly noted in *Bulletin Juridique des Collectivités Locales* No. 4/06, 257.

[6] A local consultative referendum was held on 26 March 2006 in the town of Saint-Denis: 31 per cent of the electorate participated, and 64 per cent voted in favour of extending the right to vote to third country nationals.

public hostility both to immigration and to immigrants, but at the same time a willingness at various times to develop a more open immigration policy through recourse to mechanisms such as the regularisation of the status of those already residing in the state (Zincone, 2006). Italy also displays an interesting example of the intra-state competition emerging between different levels of government, again – as in France – involving political forces of the left. Local initiatives to give electoral rights to non-nationals developed in parti-cular during the years of the centre-right coalition government of Prime Minister Silvio Berlusconi (2001–6), which saw few developments at national legislative level in relation to the rights of non-nationals and immigrants. On the contrary, it saw a notorious tightening of immigra-tion policy in the form of the Fini–Bossi law of 2002. However, these have come into conflict not only with less generous national policies on immigrants' rights but also with the limits of legal possibility as the law stands at the present time. Thus, in August 2005, a Presidential decree struck down an amendment to the statute of the municipality of Genoa which would have allowed electoral rights to third country nationals, following advice provided by the *Consiglio di stato* in July 2005 to the effect that there was currently no legal basis in Italian law for such a development (Bencini and Cerretelli, 2005: 6). Nonetheless, in an unli-kely development in October 2003, the same Gianfranco Fini of the Fini–Bossi law put his political weight behind the proposition that third country nationals should have the right to vote in local elections in Italy, perhaps knowing that this was very unlikely to come to fruition under Berlusconi's right-wing government.[7] Indeed, it did not.

In an interesting twist, at the general election held in April 2006, Italy's large *expatriate vote* was crucial in tipping the balance in a close election in favour of the centre-left coalition led by former European Commission President Romano Prodi. It will be interesting to see whether this centre-left coalition will be any more open to suggestions for legislative change in relation to the electoral rights of non-nationals and *immigrants* at the national level. There would be a nice symmetry if the Italian expatriates were, in effect, to assist those expatriated from other states. The first signs were positive, with the Italian cabinet in summer 2006 approving a draft law, to be put before Parliament, reducing the waiting time for naturalisation from ten years to five, and

[7] E. Povoledo, 'Immigrants in Italy Get Unlikely Aid on Voting', *International Herald Tribune*, 17 October 2003.

introducing birthright citizenship, following a similar model as that adopted in Germany in 2000, for the children of immigrants with settled residence in Italy. This followed a regularisation of illegal immigrants earlier in the summer based on a quota of 350,000 non-EU workers, and, in a related move concerning the transitional measures imposed on the workers from the EU8 Member States after May 2004, in mid-July 2006 the Prodi government reversed the decision of the Berlusconi government to continue the transitional restrictions after the initial two-year period, and opened Italy's labour markets fully to the EU8 workers.[8]

II Constitution, citizenship and integration: the case of Germany

'Not a country of immigration' (*kein Einwanderungsland*) was the epithet used by successive German governments, almost to the present day, to describe a country which nonetheless has received large numbers of immigrants, especially since the Second World War. However, for generations, German policy persisted in describing Turkish immigrants, even where they stayed long term, with their families and descendants, as 'guest workers' or '*Gastarbeiter*', rather than immigrants. The implication was that their stay was temporary, not permanent. As Christian Joppke notes (Joppke, 1999: 62), 'this discrepancy between *de facto* immigration and its political denial is the single most enduring puzzle in the German immigration debate'. Germany has raised 'the no-immigration maxim to a first principle of public policy and national self-definition'.

A second, closely linked maxim relates to the treatment of the 'alien' or '*Ausländer*'. The fundamental principle of the German *Ausländergesetz*, the law which regulated the status of non-nationals until 2005, was the core definition of the alien as 'not German', and indeed this principle continues in the new *Aufenthaltsgesetz* under a different guise. This contrasts with an approach to alienage which constructs the non-national as an 'immigrant', that is, as someone who may be an incomer but who is subject to, and is benefiting from, a set of reciprocal duties and rights, incumbent upon both the incomer herself and the receiving state in terms of a developing relationship. Instead, the alien is constructed as the stranger – a potential danger to German society (Schmid-Drüner, 2006).

---

[8] 'Italy Drops Barrier on EU Labor', *International Herald Tribune*, 21 July 2006. In January 2007 the Italian government approved measures on local autonomy allowing local authorities to extend voting rights to third country nationals.

The relationship between these two principles is cemented by a third maxim, namely, the ethno-cultural concept of German citizenship (Preuss, 2003), which has traditionally made the acquisition of German nationality by non-national immigrants, however they are defined or recognised in national law and politics, rather difficult, whilst at the same time facilitating access to national citizenship (and to the national territory) of those 'ethnic' Germans excluded by boundary changes at various points through the twentieth century (and even earlier).[9] The requirements for citizenship acquisition were made rather less restrictive by a new nationality law which entered into force on 1 January 2000 (Hailbronner, 2006b).[10] However, it remains relatively difficult for resident non-nationals to naturalise on the basis of residence (an eight-year qualifying period and renunciation of a former nationality except in very limited circumstances are required, as is the completion of other tests on language, etc.) and German law remains generally hostile to dual nationality except in limited circumstances where another state makes it literally impossible to renounce nationality, thus effectively cutting down the choices which can be made in relation to nationality acquisition by the descendants of those who have earlier migrated to Germany but who wish to retain ties with the state of origin. The children of settled non-nationals do now acquire German nationality automatically if they are born in Germany (*ius soli*), but when they reach maturity such children must positively declare their intention to keep German nationality, or otherwise it will be lost when they are 23 (unless this renders them stateless). Even though the figures for non-nationals resident in Germany have shown a slight decline in numbers since 2000, from around 7.3 million to 6.7 million in 2005 (that is from 8.9 per cent to 8.1 per cent of inhabitants), it remains extremely high.[11] This suggests only limited use of the naturalisation opportunities offered by the new law, although there has also been a decline in the number of non-nationals entering Germany in recent years.

---

[9] Around 15 million persons of German origin have settled in the Federal Republic of Germany since the Second World War. They are not *Ausländer* in the sense of being 'not German', but rather *Aussiedler* (those from outside Germany settling in the historic motherland) and *Übersiedler* (literally, 'settlers moving across' from the former German Democratic Republic): Green, 2004: 4–5.

[10] *Staatsangehörigkeitsgesetz* (StAG) of 15 July 1999, *Federal Law Gazette*, vol. I, p. 1618.

[11] See *Migrationsbericht des Bundesamtes für Migration und Flüchtlinge im Auftrag der Bundesregierung (Migrationsbericht 2005)*, at 172.

Opinions remain divided amongst commentators about the political significance of one of the *causes célèbres* of the constitutionally based distinction between Germans and aliens. These were the rulings handed down in 1990 by the German Federal Constitutional Court, annulling as unconstitutional two legislative schemes introduced at the level of the *Land* by the states of Hamburg and Schleswig-Holstein which would have given electoral rights in local municipalities to non-nationals who satisfied certain types of criteria regarding residence and attachment (Rubio-Marín, 2000: Ch. 8; Benhabib, 2004: Ch. 3; Joppke, 1999: 104–19; Neuman, 1992; Béaud, 1992).[12]

However, legally speaking, the significance is clear. The Court relied upon a concept of popular sovereignty as the basis for political legitimacy, and linked this to a principle of a bounded *Staatsvolk* (or 'state people'), limited by reference to the holding of national citizenship. It explicitly rejected the principle of affected interests as the basis for a claim to political equality and access to the franchise. The key phrase reads:

> The principle [of popular sovereignty] in Article 20(2) of the Basic Law does not mean that the decisions engaging state authority must be legitimated by those who are affected by them; rather state authority must be based on a people understood as a group of persons bound together as a unity.[13]

It extended its conclusion about 'state' authority also to the level of local democracy, holding that municipalities, like the elected authorities at the state and federal level, wield state power. Not only did this rule out the Hamburg and Schleswig-Holstein initiatives, but it also meant that the implementation of Article 19 EC subsequently required an amendment to Article 28 of the Basic Law. It makes it clear that any conceivable further steps towards the political inclusion of non-nationals would require further constitutional amendments. How far such amendments could go, and in particular whether EU citizens might conceivably be included in the national or even *Land*-level electoral franchise, is not obvious, since the ruling is premised on the central and unalterable norms of the German constitution about the nature of the state and its democratic legitimacy linked to the people. In any event, that latter issue is not a live one in Germany at present, but the question of enfranchising third country nationals certainly is, as we shall see below. In the shorter

---

[12] BVerfGE 63, 37 (Schleswig-Holstein); BVerfGE 63, 60 (Hamburg), 31 October 1990.
[13] BVerfGE 63, 37, at 50 (my translation).

term, the Federal Constitutional Court pointed in the direction of the loosening of the rules on citizenship acquisition as the means of ensuring that pluralist political representation and voice is assured in a more diverse Germany, with large numbers of persons not qualifying for German nationality under the historically restrictive conceptions which applied up to, and beyond, the date of reunification.

This is what prompted Seyla Benhabib to understand the Court's judgments as a 'swan song to a vanishing ideology of nationhood' (Benhabib, 2004: 207), but equally as the trigger for a set of 'democratic iterations' involving other political and legal forces such as political parties, groups representing immigrants in Germany, and the legislative organs of the state which have resulted in changes to the rules on the acquisition of nationality which came into force in 2000. This perhaps understates the rather fraught nature of the domestic political debates about the amendments to the laws on citizenship and national citizenship acquisition, which resulted in a more limited compromise law being adopted. More recently still, in rules which came into force in 2005, Germany belatedly adopted something approximating to an 'immigration law' for the first time, although it did so using not the term '*Einwanderung*', but rather a neologism developed for the purpose of avoiding that contested term: '*Zuwanderung*' (Bast, 2006: 3). This term literally means 'movement towards', rather than 'into'. 'Migration', rather than '*immigration*'. The *Zuwanderungsgesetz* of 2004 was delayed from 2002 because an earlier text was annulled by the Federal Constitutional Court for reasons relating to the procedure followed in the *Bundesrat*, the upper house of the German Parliament where the *Länder* are represented. The limitations of the texts which comprise the *Zuwanderungsgesetz* package and the difficulties which attended their adoption will be examined in more detail below. Germany's 'democratic iterations' have indeed been extremely fraught at every turn in relation to issues of citizenship and immigration.

While Benhabib's understanding of the significance of the Court's judgments may be evocative of the role of law in wider societal and political processes, it is not shared by all commentators. Certainly, Christian Joppke echoes her broad premise in commenting that 'the German debate over alien suffrage was a foundational debate over the meaning of membership and citizenship in the nation-state' (Joppke, 1999: 195). But Simon Green takes a different line about where the late 1980s and early 1990s controversy about voting rights for non-nationals should be understood as leading. He interprets the debate as a form of 'issue spillover' from related debates occurring in the 1980s about the treatment of non-nationals under German law, and the emerging debate about integration (Green, 2004: 56). He highlights the role of the Kühn Memorandum of 1979 (Green, 2004: 41–3), drawn up by the Federal Commissioner for the Integration of Foreign Workers and Their Families, Heinz Kühn, which first placed the issue of treating guest-workers not as temporary residents but as permanent immigrants on the table for German policy-makers. The Memorandum proposed that non-nationals be granted such rights, in order to encourage their political participation at the local level. The idea provoked political controversy, of course, engaging support from immigrants' groups, trades unions and the social democratic left, but encountering hostility from the centre-right Christian Democrats (CDU[14]), as inimical to the notion of the sovereignty of citizenship. The CDU insisted throughout the debate that any institution of local electoral rights for non-nationals, including for EU nationals, would first require constitutional change, and intimated that it would not be agreeable to facilitating such change, which requires a two-thirds majority in the *Bundestag*. Overall, Green felt that:

> The issue was therefore a poor choice with which to champion the interests of foreigners, as it not only detracted from the more pressing issues of residence and naturalisation, but also received little sympathy from the public.

> (Green, 2004: 57)

Because the matter was brought to a head by the actions of the Hamburg and Schleswig-Holstein governments, led by the social democrats of the SPD,[15] followed by the judgments of the Federal Constitutional Court of 1990, this effectively 'closed off the avenue of granting suffrage independently of nationality ... and graphically illustrated the formidable ability of the constitutional court to limit the range of options available to policy-makers' (Green, 2004: 57). For Green, unlike Benhabib, the judgments are about closure of options, not the opening of a phase of democratic iterations between political and legal actors.

The constitutional court judgments of 1990 certainly did not close off the possibility of Germany doing its European integration duty by implementing the provisions of Article 19 EC, which were already under

---

[14] Christliche Demokratische Union. [15] Sozial-demokratische Partei Deutschlands.

consideration by the date of the judgment (October 1990).[16] Indeed, it explicitly stated that its conclusions were without prejudice to this possibility, although implementing Article 19 did require an amendment to Article 28 of the Basic Law to open a constitutional window for EU citizens to take their place alongside German voters in local elections. It would therefore seem to follow that a constitutional amendment could be enacted to open up the possibility of local electoral rights for third country nationals, if the political will to make this happen is matched to the political will to effect a necessary amendment to the Basic Law. What was lacking in the case of the two isolated *Länder* in 1989 and 1990 was a broadly based political consensus across the federal and state levels about the desirability of this step towards inclusion. What the constitutional court's judgments ruled out was the possibility of bottom-up pressure for change developing because such a policy is enacted in certain areas of the country, but not in others.

Article 19 EC was introduced in Germany without a great deal of either constitutional or political fanfare (Dill, 1999: 13). A new sentence was added to Article 28(1) of the Basic Law:

> In county and municipal elections, persons who possess citizenship in any member state of the European Community are also eligible to vote and to be elected in accordance with European Community law.

Nothing like the public debate engendered by pre-1990 discussions about electoral rights for non-nationals (Sieveking *et al.*, 1989; Joppke, 1999: 195–9) (which have picked up again in the years since 2000) attended even the amendment of the Basic Law. This was subsumed into a bigger debate about the Treaty of Maastricht more generally. The implementation, which was the responsibility of the *Länder*, was not always smooth, and the Commission did have to take steps to ensure that registration requirements were not unduly harsh.[17] For example, the *Land* authorities cannot require EU nationals to register afresh each time the electoral register is renewed. However, by 1999, everything, legally speaking, was fully in place (Zuleeg, 2001), and the registration and voting systems had been used in each *Land* at least once (Dill, 1999).

---

[16] As we saw in Chapter 4, Section VI, the prospect of including a concept of citizenship of Union including electoral rights for EU citizens in the texts which were eventually agreed at the IGC on political union in November 1991 was already clear by the autumn of 1990. This fact was obviously communicated to the Federal Constitutional Court and is incorporated in its reference to the European Community at the end of its judgment.

[17] See Chapter 5, Section VII.

In legal terms, the only issue beyond that strictly mandated by Article 19 which has received close attention concerns whether the amendment to Article 28(1) of the Basic Law introduced in order to accommodate the requirements of EU citizens voting in local elections could also extend to allowing EU citizens to vote in local referendums. This point is contested amongst academics (Burkholz, 1995; Meyer-Teschendorf and Hofmann, 1995).

Politically, the impact of Article 19 has not been judged to be particularly substantial even though there are nearly 2 million EU citizens in Germany. In the absence of country-wide statistics, estimated rates of participation lie between 15 per cent and 30 per cent of those entitled to vote.[18] As regards the right to be elected, detailed figures for the 1997 local elections in the *Land* of Hessen are illustrative of the problem: 560 EU citizens stood for election to community councils (*Gemeinderäte*) and 56 stood for election to municipal councils (*Kreistagsräte*). Of these, 115 were elected to the *Gemeinderäte* and 19 to the *Kreistagsräte*. Thus, overall, 0.9 per cent of all those elected were EU citizens, although EU citizens made up 4 per cent of the electorate.[19]

The intervening period has also seen limited engagement on the part of German political parties with the electoral possibilities of Article 19, despite the fact the active engagement of parties is seen by many observers as a vital catalyst to raising participation levels and success rates in relation to the active and passive electoral rights respectively.[20] There have been some examples of mobilisation. Thus the SPD engaged in a local campaign in the state of Hessen, with the party actively seeking the electoral support of EU nationals. It organised meetings with other social democratic sister organisations such as the Greek socialist party PASOK, and it translated leaflets into various Member State languages. However, in the words of one social democratic party official: 'There is no national policy though, it differs from town to town.'[21] There is no hard evidence on what the political preferences of EU citizens resident in Germany might be, and indeed this topic is only just starting to be investigated in relation to naturalised citizens, given that naturalisation by groups other than ethnic Germans (*Aussiedler*) who had immigrated

---

[18] *Bericht der Beauftragten der Bundesregierung für Migration, Flüchtlinge und Integration über die Lage der Ausländerinnen und Ausländer in Deutschland (Ausländerbericht 2005)*, Berlin, August 2005, at 307.

[19] *Ibid.*, 308.   [20] *Ibid.*, 308.

[21] Interview with official at the Sozialdemokratische Gemeinschaft für Kommunalpolitik in der Bundesrepublik Deutschland, 16 May 2000.

from the former Soviet Union, Poland or elsewhere in Eastern Europe or Germans who emigrated from the former German Democratic Republic (*Übersiedler*) was very restricted until recent years (Wüst, 2004; Hunger, 2001). However, this latter research does seem to indicate that natural-ised citizens who do not fall into the group of ethnic Germans are most likely to vote for the SPD and the Greens (*Bündis 90/Die Grünen*) rather than the CDU and its Bavarian sister party, the CSU,[22] which were the favoured political homes of the *Aussiedler* and the *Übersiedler*. Even so, it does not seem sensible to extrapolate automatically from this group of voters to the very different group of EU citizen voters. Equally, just as there is no hard evidence about the influence of naturalised citizens on political parties and other political structures themselves,[23] so this evidence is lacking in the context of the application of Article 19 EC.

Finally, it has been argued that the enfranchisement of EU citizens by means of a top-down constitutional and legislative change in Germany has had a regressive impact upon the ongoing struggles regarding the political participation rights of third country nationals. While the case for electoral rights foundered in 1990 upon the constitutional rock of the constitutional court's approach to the notion of the 'people', bottom-up pressure for political participation of non-nationals had been diverted into the framework provided by the consultative foreign-ers' councils, which operate at the level of cities and the *Länder*. However, Brett Klopp suggests that (Klopp, 2002: 252):

> As EU political integration suddenly lurched another step forward, it incorporated EU foreigners locally, at their place of residence, in one fell swoop. This top-down move inadvertently split the emerging representa-tion solidarity practiced in the foreigners' councils. Non-EU foreigners suddenly became third-class citizens.

Despite this warning, the political salience of the debate about electoral rights for non-nationals, diverted since 1993 into the debate about electoral rights for third country nationals, has continued to rise and fall, notwith-standing the constitutional blockage imposed by the constitutional court. It remains clear that constitutional change is required, and since the 1980s the CDU had made it clear that it would not facilitate such constitutional

---

[22] Christliche Soziale Union.
[23] Federal Office for Migration and Refugees, *The Impact of Immigration on Germany's Society*, the German Contribution to the Pilot Research Study 'The Impact of Immigration on Europe's Societies' within the framework of the European Migration Network, October 2005, at 40.

change (at least not other than for EU citizens where the dynamics of European integration demanded a different approach); thus it has been 'cheap talk' for the SPD to support electoral rights for third country nationals, knowing that they would not be able in practice to take steps to make these a reality (Kempen, 1989). However, it can be assumed that the SPD, like the Greens also, would in principle support electoral rights for third country nationals because this would be a popular policy amongst a group which precisely would not benefit from such rights if they were to be extended, namely, naturalised Germans of third country national, especially Turkish, origin.

When the SPD/Green coalition came to power in 1998 (and when talk could finally become action), it set as a priority not the introduction of electoral rights for third country nationals, but a reformed national citizenship law. The 1998 Coalition Agreement between the SPD and the Greens did declare that 'to promote integration, those foreigners living here who do not possess the citizenship of an EU Member State *shall also receive the right to vote in district and local elections*'.[24] In practice, however, the issue did not receive political prominence in comparison to the lengthy debates on the regulation of citizenship and, later, the issue of immigration.

The issue was in fact never pushed by either the SPD or the Greens during the period when the coalition existed between 1998 and 2005. According to an SPD spokesperson: 'Politicians are agreed that the topic was simply not one in which the party could engage even with its own members let alone society at large.'[25] The view of the Greens was that the constitutional barrier meant there could be no realistic chance of change at the present time:

> The fact that a two-thirds majority would be needed to amend the constitution means that without CDU support it was simply pointless attempting to pursue this issue. There are no victories if you struggle too hard.[26]

On the other hand, the changes to the citizenship law were already a significant change, and should not be underestimated, especially according to the Greens. Meanwhile, maintaining its opposition to electoral rights for third country nationals, the CDU continued to refer back to

---

[24] SPD–Green Coalition Agreement, 20 October 1998 (*Aufbruch und Erneuerung – Deutschlands Weg ins 21. Jahrhundert*), Chapter IX(7), http://www.boell.de/downloads/gedaechtnis/1998_Koalitionsvertrag.pdf.

[25] Interview with Martin Hantke, advisor to Dr Sylvia-Yvonne Kaufmann, MEP, Berlin, May 2000.

[26] Interview with Malti Tanja, Office of Claudia Roth, MdB, Berlin, May 2000.

the symbols and 'perks' of citizenship: 'citizenship rights are a privilege for those who belong', and 'if such rights are proliferated for the many then they are no longer special for the few'.[27] The rhetoric sometimes comes rather close to a form of narrow ethnocentrism:

> A child's connection to his or her parents is the most important issue, not the political community and this is something that needs to be cherished. While a child of Turkish parents can join the political community via the *ius soli*, his or her language and culture are Turkish.[28]

These comments highlight the intimate connection between the debate on electoral rights and the contested revision of the citizenship law brought about after 1998.[29] This reform, to a greater extent than the later immigration law reform, was connected to the hangover from the reunification of Germany, and the need to modernise German citizenship law now that there were no longer two German states. For the existence of two states had always been available as an argument to justify referencing nationality entitlements back to earlier legislation pre-dating not only the division of Germany but also earlier territorial losses after the First World War.[30] However, in terms of effects, both of the two substantial legislative reforms discussed in this section concern the challenge of immigration and of multiculturalism for Germany and German society. The basic premise of the citizenship legislation, which was supported by SPD/Green coalition partners, was to facilitate access to national citizenship both by immigrants, and by their children who had been born in Germany (Hailbronner, 2006b). But a restrictive position on dual nationality was maintained, even though this meant forcing young people to opt between German and another nationality.

Thomas Faist highlights the paradox of Germany now having one of the most liberal nationality laws in Europe in terms of the birthright citizenship (*ius soli*) of children born in the territory, including those born to non-nationals, and yet one of the most restrictive positions on dual nationality, and argues that this can be understood in large measure via the differing positions taken by political parties and their relationships to concepts of the nation (Faist, 2005). In particular, the Christian Union parties (the CDU and the CSU) catered to a national conservative

---

[27] Interview with CDU representative, Berlin, May 2000.   [28] *Ibid.*

[29] *Gesetz zur Reform des Staatsangehörigkeitsrechts* (StARG) of 15 July 1999 (BGBl. I, p. 1618). On this see generally Green, 2000; 2001.

[30] *Reichs- und Staatsangehörigkeitsgesetz* of 1913.

ethnically focused concept of the nation and a suspicion of the impossibility of owing loyalty to two sovereigns simultaneously, and were able to carry this through during the citizenship reform. After 1999, the results in *Länder* elections started to give increased power to the CDU/CSU in the *Bundesrat*, the upper chamber of Parliament where the states are represented. Thus the SPD/Green coalition had by no means a free hand in designing the legislation, despite its majority in the *Bundestag*, the lower chamber of Parliament. During the legislative process, the CDU/CSU managed to campaign quite successfully to restrict the proliferation of dual nationality, by presenting what was proposed by the SPD/Green coalition as amounting to the granting of a special right particularly benefiting the Turkish population. In contrast, the Greens welcomed the basic changes made by the citizenship reform such as a more standardised procedure lessening discretion given to public officials in each of the *Länder*, and in particular the weakening of *ius sanguinis*: 'The principle of *ius soli* was the most important element of the new law.'[31] However, their concerns surround the requirement to opt at the age of 23 for German or another citizenship so that dual nationality could be avoided: 'All agree especially the first generation that they don't want to lose their Turkish passport. It's like a picture of your family in the bedroom. They feel that the new citizenship is like forcing them to hand over this picture.'[32]

One part of the citizenship law which proved very controversial was a provision decreeing that a person who acquired another nationality would normally automatically lose their German nationality. This hit particularly hard upon a number of Germans of Turkish descent who acquired German nationality in the 1990s, but who subsequently re-acquired a Turkish passport without declaring this to the German authorities. The nationality law reform which came into force in 2000 decreed that those who re-acquired another nationality after taking German nationality automatically lost their German citizenship, and this came to public prominence when this group were unable to vote in the 2005 General Election.[33]

From 2000 onwards, the focus of most of the political debate moved away from citizenship as such. In the first place, there was no evidence that all non-nationals were likely to take the route of naturalisation, or indeed opt for German citizenship after acquiring it at birth, alongside a nationality of descent. Thus Germany was likely to retain a substantial

---

[31] Interview with Cem Ozdemir, MdB, Berlin, May 2000. [32] *Ibid.*
[33] 'Thousands of Turks Barred from Voting', *Deutsche Welle*, 17 September 2005.

population of non-nationals on a continuing basis for the foreseeable future. Secondly, as Merih Anil puts it, 'acquisition of formal citizenship is only a necessary, not a sufficient, condition for full integration of the immigrant population' (Anil, 2005: 466). Thus the German political class and German society needed to dedicate additional thought to the issue of integration. Finally, economic and demographic imperatives in relation to continued (if controlled) immigration had begun to acquire increased political prominence, not least as a result of a well-publicised campaign by the IT sector regarding skills shortages and the role of immigration (Schmid-Drünner, 2006: 193). Proposals were brought forward in mid-2001 by the SPD/Green coalition for a new immigration law which would foster the immigration of skilled and highly qualified foreigners into Germany, in particular in order to address skills shortages in the German labour market. Part of the political controversy which the draft law attracted was the contrast which it provided with a soaring domestic unemployment rate of over 10 per cent in January 2002, rising to 12.6 per cent of the working age population (5.2 million people) in March 2005,[34] and dropping back to around 10.5 per cent in mid-2006.

2002 was also an election year, and, although the SPD/Green coalition was eventually returned to power (not least because of the Iraq war effect with Chancellor Gerhard Schröder's well-publicised opposition to the invasion proving particularly useful to the coalition), there was considerable controversy during the early part of the campaign regarding the coalition's immigration policy. Conservative Chancellor candidate Edmund Stoiber epitomised the debate when he declared that 'with 4.3 million unemployed, we can't have more foreign workers coming to Germany ... [W]ho is going to pay for integrating these workers? I've not heard the chancellor saying he'll give the billions it will cost to pay for this. Will industry pay?'[35] The draft law originated in a report from an independent Commission appointed by the Interior Minister, Otto Schily, which was published in July 2001. The Commission was chaired by a member of the CDU, Rita Süssmuth, and the report, 'Managing Immigration, Promoting Integration', arguably laid to rest the assertion that Germany is not an *Einwanderungsland*.[36] The report made the case for

---

[34] 'German Jobless at New Record', BBC News, 1 March 2005, http://news.bbc.co.uk/1/hi/business/4307303.stm.

[35] *Migration News*, vol. 9, No. 2, February 2002 (http://migration.ucdavis.edu).

[36] Report of the Independent Commission on Immigration, *Zuwanderung gestalten. Integration fördern*, 4 July 2001.

planned and targeted immigration matching skills shortages and bringing in persons with high levels of skills and qualifications – moving away from the rather more haphazard admission of some 200–300,000 newcomers per year which has occurred up to now on the basis of a mixture of family unification, asylum seekers and others seeking temporary protection, and ethnic Germans. However, it followed the lead of other EU Member States, notably the Netherlands, by arguing for more proactive integration policies alongside an immigration policy. Even so, this did not satisfy the CDU/CSU opposition, with one senior CDU politician commenting that the 'law would completely change German society within a few years'.[37]

Progress through the legislative process was not smooth. By March 2002, the draft law was in serious trouble in the German parliament, particularly in the upper house, the *Bundesrat*, where the representatives of the *Länder* sit. In view of the impending national elections in September 2002 to the *Bundestag*, the SPD/Green coalition was unwilling to see the draft immigration law mired in a joint commission of the two houses, as that would be likely to prevent its adoption. This seemed a likely outcome, given problems not only with the CDU/CSU conservative parties, but also with the liberal Free Democratic Party. Hence, in March 2002, despite concerns about the compromise text, the government pushed the issue to a vote, first in the *Bundestag*, where it was carried with the votes of the ruling coalition, and then in the *Bundesrat*, where the outcome was expected to be very close and hinged on the vote of the Brandenburg delegation, which was led at the time by a CDU/SPD coalition. Since the two representatives of the *Land* contradicted each other when they spoke, the chair of the chamber counted that as a vote in favour of the draft law and declared it adopted, by the narrowest of majorities. After some hesitation, the measure was signed into law by the German President Johannes Rau, but was successfully challenged by the CDU/CSU opposition – on the procedural technicality of Brandenburg's vote in the *Bundesrat* – before the Federal Constitutional Court in December 2002, forcing the whole debate on the substance to be reopened (Becker, 2003).

Put back on the agenda in March 2003, by a renewed vote in the *Bundestag* by the re-elected SPD/Green coalition, it proved very difficult for the government to secure passage of the *Zuwanderungsgesetz* through the *Bundesrat*, even though it offered to compromise on a number of elements relating to the selection system for the prospective highly skilled immigrants and in relation to demands from the CDU/CSU to

---

[37] *Migration News*, vol. 9, No. 1, January 2002 (http://migration.ucdavis.edu).

include more security-related elements in the law in the wake of the Madrid bombings in March 2004. The final negotiation process effectively excluded the SPD's coalition partners, the Greens, and involved the CDU/CSU instead, thus foreshadowing the Grand Coalition which eventually took power after the 2005 election (Schmid-Drüner, 2006: 196). The law was adopted in July 2004, and came into force on 1 January 2005.

The *Zuwanderungsgesetz* is in truth a package of measures, comprising two main Acts – the Residence Act (*Aufenthaltsgesetz*) which replaces the *Ausländergesetz* in force since 1990, and the Freedom of Movement Act (*Freizügigkeitsgesetz*) which applies only to the mobility of EU citizens (Bast, 2006: 3). There are also a number of measures – executive orders – which have been put in place by the federal government to give effect to the two main Acts. While, in some respects, the immigration law does simplify the arrangements for securing the legal status of non-nationals living and working in Germany, by reducing the number of different types of residence permits that are in existence, remarkably it precisely fails to do the task which the original immigration law was supposed to do, namely, to regulate through a selection procedure the process of bringing chosen groups of immigrants to Germany in areas where a labour market need is discerned. Thus the situation is essentially as it was before, with officially no new immigrant workers, but with exceptions allowed in areas where economic migration is deemed desirable, for example seasonal workers on temporary permits. There are certain mechanisms in the *Aufenthaltsgesetz* to distinguish between the qualifications and skills sets of certain groups of potential migrants, who are given 'red carpet' treatment, and given accelerated access to full permits allowing settled residence and employment. Moreover, in an echo of the Scottish Fresh Talent scheme discussed in Chapter 8, overseas students who have completed university studies in Germany are now allowed a further residence period of one year, to seek employment.[38]

The most substantial and innovative part of the *Zuwanderungsgesetz* concerned measures relating to the integration of immigrants. For Germany even to take steps along the road towards instituting measures relating to the integration of non-nationals implied, of course, the recognition, in official discourse, of the reality of the permanency of immigration (Davy, 2005). This is, in itself, a paradigm shift. Of course, it should not be forgotten that the EU itself has been engaging with the issue of integration, and, while it has not required Member States to

---

[38] Chapter 8, Section VI.

introduce any specific types of measures, it has considerably raised the profile of integration policies on a cross-EU basis, through soft law measures such as the Common Basic Principles for Integration adopted in the form of Council Conclusions in November 2004.[39] This provides a set of exogenous pressures upon Germany, to move its policy base closer to an emerging EU norm. The *Zuwanderungsgesetz* package dealt with integration issues for the first time at the federal level, rather than leaving these matters for local regulation at the level of the *Land*. The new law instituted courses for newcomers, which should also in principle be accessible to those who are already settled in Germany and may in fact become compulsory for some settled non-nationals if they are drawing state benefits, which are primarily concerned with language (600 hours of courses) and to a lesser extent with society and culture (30 hours). Migrants must pay for the courses, but only at the rate of €1 per hour, and thus it can be seen that there is a degree of state subsidisation of the courses. Participation in the courses reduces the waiting period for naturalisation from eight years to seven, and non-participation could have negative consequences in relation to the acquisition of settlement permits, and could even potentially lead to expulsion.

Germany's embrace of integration policies has been notably one-sided in the first instance. The crucial element of protecting the migrant against racial or ethnic prejudice through a right to non-discrimination has been missing. In relation to the implementation of the EU's race equality directive of 2000,[40] Germany has lagged many years behind the other Member States and has greatly exceeded the directive's implementation period, which expired in July 2003. Despite a judgment of the Court of Justice in April 2005,[41] it took Germany until the summer of 2006 to introduce implementing legislation.[42] Moreover, the integrating measures of the *Zuwanderungsgesetz* were in the end more than matched by repressive measures, facilitating the expulsion of those suspected of terrorist offences.

---

[39] Conclusions of the Council and the Representatives of the Governments of the Member States on the establishment of Common Basic Principles for immigrant integration policy in the European Union, Doc. 14776/04 MIGR 105, 18 November 2004. For commentary, see Urth, 2005.

[40] Council Directive 2000/43/EC implementing the principle of equal treatment between persons irrespective of racial or ethnic origin, OJ 2006 L180/22.

[41] Case C-329/04 *Commission* v. *Germany*, 28 April 2005.

[42] *Allgemeine Gleichbehandlungsgesetz* of 14 August 2006; came into force on 18 August 2006. For commentary, see http://www.allgemeines-gleichbehandlungsgesetz.de.

Overall, the evaluation of the *Zuwanderungsgesetz* must be that, while it recognises the interests of immigrants as a group in German society, it is nonetheless highly instrumentalist in its approach. Thus it is heavily focused on the security of the state, on the integration of immigrants (with the greatest onus very clearly on the immigrant herself), on the protection of the German labour market, and on seeking to offset demographic change by encouraging, for example, overseas students to stay on and seek employment (Schmid-Drüner, 2006: 207–8). Marion Schmid-Drüner describes the

> downward slide from the liberal, open-minded and forward-thinking pro-posals of the Süssmuth Commission through the already much more restricted first and second Bills, to the law which was adopted in the end.
>
> (Schmid-Drüner, 2006: 211)

She phrases her criticism of the outcome of the process, which sees the implementation of the law now in the hands of the CDU/SPD Grand Coalition which took power in late 2005, in trenchant terms:

> The review of the law's implementation in its first year of existence makes it clear that the new government has built more obstacles to immigration and longterm settlement, which corresponds to their 'secret will' to make immigration more difficult. Integration is seen as the task of immigrants and implemented mainly through coercive measures such as fines, and despite the integrationist rhetoric, public funds for integration courses have been reduced considerably.
>
> (Schmid-Drüner, 2006: 211)

This seems, therefore, to be an unlikely environment in which one might anticipate a revival of interest at the political level in electoral rights for non-nationals, particularly since the Interior Minister for the new coalition is a member of the CDU, not the SPD.

Even so, the question of electoral rights never completely disappears from the German political scene, and statements in favour of extending electoral rights can regularly be found in both the declarations issued by the various *Ausländerbeiräte*, or foreigners' councils, which are attached to many local municipalities,[43] and in the reports on integration issues

---

[43] Ausländerbeirat der Landeshauptstadt München, *Politische Partizipation und Kommunalwahlrecht für Nicht-EU-Ausländer*, Decision No.147, 1 December 2003. On the role of these councils, see *Ausländerbericht 2005*, above n. 18 at 309.

put out by the *Länder*, especially those governed by the SPD.[44] Indeed, the Coalition Contract between the CDU and the SPD commits the government to take another look at the question of local electoral rights for third country nationals.[45] In more definitive terms, a July 2006 SPD party document on integration called explicitly for third country nationals to be given local electoral rights.[46] This document was prepared in advance of a cross-coalition 'summit' on integration (*Integrationsgipfel*), held on 14 July 2006, which brought together eighty-six stakeholders from across government, politics, society and the economy, including representatives of migrants' organisations, to discuss a national 'integration plan'.[47] While press reports of the summit revealed some differences of opinion across the leadership of the CDU/CSU parties in relation to some aspects of integration, with Chancellor Angela Merkel markedly more open both to the possibility of greater numbers of immigrants in the future to engage with Germany's demographic problems and also to a more inclusive approach to integration through support and promotion of immigrants and non-nationals than some of her colleagues,[48] the Conservative parties nonetheless have stuck firmly to their traditional opposition to electoral rights for non-nationals. 'This is what naturalization is for' is a typical statement.[49] If this is the case, then the chances of any progress being made on the vague commitment of the CDU/SPD Coalition Contract seem almost nil, and it would seem that the SPD's support for the proposal becomes once more the 'cheap talk' which it was during the years before the SPD/Green coalition, when the CDU dominated in national government. It is a mechanism to enhance their electoral standing amongst the group of German voters most closely linked to the target group who would benefit from any electoral rights, namely, naturalised voters, especially those of Turkish heritage.

---

[44] *Zuwanderung und Integration in Nordrhein-Westfalen*, 3rd Immigration Report of the *Land* Government, March 2004, at 180.

[45] *Gemeinsam für Deutschland. Mit Mut und Menschlichkeit. Koalitionsvertrag von CDU, CSU und SPD*, 11 November 2005.

[46] *Leitlinien zur Integrationspolitik: Faire Chancen, klare Regeln*, SPD, 11 July 2006, at 5.

[47] 'Deutschland: Erster Integrationsgipfel', *Migration und Bewölkerung*, Newsletter, Issue 6, August 2006.

[48] S. Fischer and A. Reimann, 'Angriff auf den eigenen Reihen', *Der Spiegel*, 17 July 2006, http://www.spiegel.de/politik/deutschland/0,1518,427204,00.html.

[49] C. Baldauf, 'Es is Zeit zum Handeln', Newsletter 218/2006 of the CDU Rheinland-Pfalz, 14 July 2006.

III Electoral rights against the backdrop of radical right politics: the case of Austria

Political opposition to immigration entered the Austrian political mainstream in recent years, especially since the formation of the controversial right-wing coalition government involving the People's Party (ÖVP) and the Freedom Party (FPÖ) in early 2000. While the ÖVP is a mainstream European Christian democratic party, which had largely shared political power for more than forty years with its social democrat counterpart (the SPÖ), the FPÖ, since the controversial figure Jörg Haider had become its leader, had left behind its more liberal roots and become a party of the radical and populist right, making opposition to immigration and hostility to foreigners one of the central planks of its political programme (Gärtner, 2002: 17). Its 1999 election manifesto referred to Austria as being 'swamped by foreigners', and it made use of the discredited Nazi term *Überfremdung* in a description of the state of Vienna. Somewhat moderated after it entered government, the FPÖ's rhetoric remained determinedly anti-multiculturalist:

> I don't see why we must be multi-cultural. You see what kind of difficulties it makes in most countries. Our country has more [immigrants] [in proportion to size] than other countries. They should become more Austrian those who want to say here – learn German, enter into our culture – but we don't want to have more of them.[50]

Eschewing radical language, the Austrian Government's official position took pains to reaffirm Austria's position within the European political mainstream, declaring its future to be at the 'heart of Europe'.[51] 'Modern' Austria is, of course, a relatively young state, and some of its post-war self-image has been constructed on the basis of a sense of Austria more as victim than as perpertrator of Nazi atrocities. However, the Government Declaration likewise committed Austria to a self-critical scrutiny of its National Socialist past. This type of statement seemed to satisfy the three 'wise men' appointed in order to effect a climbdown after the somewhat sensationalist step taken by Austria's fellow EU Member States of imposing diplomatic 'sanctions' on the new

---

[50] John Gudenus, FPÖ Deputy, quoted in 'Head to Head: Is Haider a Threat?', BBC News, 29 February 2000, http://news.bbc.co.uk/1/hi/world/europe/628410.stm.

[51] See Declaration by the Austrian Government, 'Responsibility for Austria – A Future in the Heart of Europe', Vienna, 3 February 2000, www.undp.org/missions/austria/r040200a.htm.

Austrian Government in February 2000.[52] Ostensibly, the sanctions, intended to reduce diplomatic contacts with Austria to a minimum, were measures taken because the other fourteen Member States needed to 'continue to defend the essential values that underpin the European construction and which are also the reference framework for the way the European Union behaves in its external relations'.[53] The wise men reported that there was little to fear from the new coalition, and accordingly the sanctions were dropped, although not without hardening attitudes somewhat in Austria about its fate as a small state within the European Union.

The FPÖ (and indeed the splinter party formed in 2005 by FPÖ defectors including Haider himself, the Alliance for the Future of Austria, or BZÖ) represents an example of the rise of social-nationalism. Advocates of social-nationalism shun external influence, use a traditional social democratic language in relation to the materialist sphere (full employment, welfare states, etc.) and an extremist language *vis-à-vis* the cultural/social sphere which is dominated by a collectivism based on exclusion, intolerance and emotion. For social-nationalists, Europe represents a monolith that is determined to 'subsume national identity and a country's history', and hence has to be resisted at all costs.[54] The FPÖ of Haider reflected a classic populist approach, with the adoption of a Janus-like position, presenting different faces to different audiences. As Governor of the Austrian *Land* of Carinthia, for example, Haider's rhetoric against the Slovene minority appealed to the FPÖ's core support. In other areas, though, which have brought about improved relations with Slovenia, Haider was able to portray himself as a responsible and reasonable person. At the same time, while Haider was careful (at least since he and his party entered government) to steer clear of controversial statements, others within the party, such as Ernest Windholz (FPÖ leader in Lower Austria), have been less circumspect. He used the SS motto – 'Our honour is called loyalty' – and then

---

[52] 'Report by Martti Ahtisaari, Jochen Frowein, and Marcelino Oreja', adopted in Paris on 8 September 2000, http://www.mpil.de/shared/data/pdf/report.pdf.

[53] Portuguese Secretary of State for European Affairs, Francisco Seixas de Costa, speaking for the Council Presidency, as quoted in Merlingen, Mudde and Sedelmeier, 2001: 65.

[54] György Márkus, 'Social Democracy – The Alternative to Social Nationalism', *European Forum for Democracy and Solidarity Newsletter*, June 1997. Examples of successful social nationalist forces include: elements within the Fidesz–MPP (Alliance of Young Democrats–Hungarian Civic Party); István Csurka's MIÉP (Party of Hungarian Truth and Life) in Hungary in 1998; and elements of the AWS (Solidarity Electoral Action) in Poland in 1997.

subsequently claimed not to have known about its origins. Similarly, one of the FPÖ defectors to the BZÖ, Siegfried Kampl, a long-time associate of Haider and a member of the Austrian legislature, caused outrage when he described denazification as 'brutal persecution of Nazis'.[55]

Furthermore, the FPÖ presented itself as fighting for the ordinary person against the forces of conservatism. The policy of selling cheaper petrol in Carinthia in May 2000 was a classic example of fighting for ordinary people against the multinational oil companies that were increasing the price at a time when they were making record profits. It also opposed the cosy system of *Proporz*, a form of political patronage, presided over by the Social Democrats (SPÖ) and the ÖVP for forty years, allowing them to carve up all major positions in government and the public sector. Finally, the FPÖ succeeded in elevating the leader above the day-to-day business of party politics. Haider stood down as party leader in February 2000, partly – it was thought – to appease international opinion, but also as part of an attempt to increase his standing by elevating himself above everyday politics. Despite remaining the *de facto* leader (his successor, Susanne Riess-Passer, was generally seen as a puppet), this also, rather conveniently, put him above responsibility for the difficulties associated with governing, or indeed above responsibility for the FPÖ's subsequent decline in the opinion polls.

Perhaps equally predictably, in terms of the typical trajectory of a radical right party entering into government on a populist platform, the FPÖ subsequently self-destructed. A bitter row between Haider and Riess-Passer contributed in large measure to the calling of early elections in 2002, where the FPÖ collapsed, and the ÖVP benefited with additional seats. Although the coalition continued in a renewed form after 2002, in truth the FPÖ was in trouble. Subsequently, the party splintered in 2005, with the BZÖ separating off (although the two parties still sit together in the federal legislature). However, since then, both the FPÖ and the BZÖ have performed exceptionally badly in *Land* elections.[56] However, Kurt Richard Luther attributes the (electoral) decline of the FPÖ not only to its internal squabbles, but also to the changed

---

[55] 'Haider-Abgeordneter kritisiert "brutale Naziverfolgung"', *Tagesschau*, 18 April 2005, http://www.tagesschau.de/aktuell/meldungen/0,1185,OID4266908_REF1,00.html.

[56] In the General Election of October 2006, the FPÖ and BZÖ achieved a combined vote of nearly 15 per cent, which commentators regarded as surprisingly high, indicating a solid measure of support for the radical right in Austria. However, the SPÖ recovered votes primarily at the expense of the ÖVP and was returned as the largest single party, and entered into Grand Coalition negotiations with the ÖVP.

behaviours of the mainstream parties, especially the ÖVP, which effectively removed some of the platform on which the FPÖ had appealed to the popular vote (Luther, 2003). A substantial part of this concerned the issue of political management of immigration and of the integration of immigrants, where the ÖVP in particular moved onto the terrain of the FPÖ in terms of not only the restriction of immigration, but also increasingly disciplinary approaches to the integration of immigrants. This is the background against which the relatively few attempts to mobilise political forces to extend electoral rights to non-nationals in Austria should be viewed.

Austria shares a number of characteristics in common with Germany in the field of nationality, citizenship and immigration. Not least amongst these have been the pervasive denial that Austria is an 'immigration country' (König and Perchinig, 2003: 1; Jandl and Kraler, 2003), a basic attachment to an ethno-cultural concept of nationality, where the most common form of citizenship acquisition is via descent (*ius sanguinis*), rather restrictive and often quite discretionary conditions on naturalisation, and hostility to dual nationality. This latter point was actively supported by the ÖVP/FPÖ government:

> People with double citizenship can only be loyal with reservation. Double citizenship discriminated against Austrians, because they only had one citizenship, which will increase the danger of political conflict. Those who apply for Austrian citizenship should want to be integrated fully and not attach more importance to another land and there is no possibility of deportation for convicts. In my opinion two identities are impossible.[57]

Post-war reconstruction involved the development of Austria into a federal republic in which the nine *Länder* rather than the federal authorities administer nationality law. There are strong discretionary elements in the naturalisation process, and amendments introduced in 1998 were concerned with tidying up weaknesses in the current laws resulting from anomalies, such as whether a language test was required, and were not attempts to liberalise the laws. The amendments also confirmed the regular waiting period of ten years before naturalisation and contributed to restricting the possibilities for more lenient application of discretionary naturalisation which had been practised in Vienna (which is a *Land* as well as a City) and which had led to higher rates of

---

[57] Interview with Dr Peter Mak, *Ministerialrat*, Austrian Ministry of the Interior, Vienna, June 2000.

naturalisation in this part of the country. In contrast to Germany, Austria has not introduced the *ius soli* principle for children born in Austria. Citizenship at birth is transmitted by descent, not by place of birth, and the children of non-nationals born in Austria must wait six years for naturalisation, although this is granted by entitlement not discretion. It is these dimensions of its nationality and naturalisation law and policy which marks Austria out as an exception to any putative European trend towards 'the harmonisation and liberalisation of citizenship acquisition by immigrants and their descendants' (Bauböck and Çinar, 2001: 267). Even so, Rainer Bauböck and Dilek Çinar still maintained that it was not a conception of the nation as an ethnic community which drove such restrictive policies, but rather an attempt to close the Austrian welfare state off from 'strangers' to the maximum degree possible. This argument is harder to sustain after further amendments to nationality legislation which came into force in March 2006, which also instituted a test requiring 'basic knowledge' of the 'democratic order and history of Austria and the respective federal province' (Çinar and Waldrauch, 2006: 53). Dilek Çinar and Harald Waldrauch (2006: 35) conclude that the most recent amendments, which also include higher fees for naturalisation, restrictions on the naturalisation of foreign spouses, and changes to the conditions for facilitated naturalisations for certain groups, are 'inspired by the principle of "integration before new immigration" that has been asserted since the late 1990s'.

Until the 1990s, Austria experienced waves of migration that were partly associated with its geographical and geopolitical position as a transit country situated on the Iron Curtain, and partly a result of its labour market requirements. Thus Austria, like Germany, recruited 'guestworkers', principally from the former Yugoslavia (SFRY) and Turkey. From the early 1990s onwards, labour migration was restricted, with quotas imposed; these were gradually decreased, and, after 2002, effectively abolished except for very highly paid workers, whose salary exceeded a minimum threshold. Immigration continued, throughout the 1990s and into the 2000s, on the basis of asylum applications, and also requests for family reunification, in particular as earlier waves of migrant workers who acquired Austrian citizenship through naturalisation subsequently sought to bring in non-national spouses and other family members. After the creation of the first ÖVP/FPÖ coalition in 2000, the rhetoric moved to 'zero immigration', and to an emphasis on integration obligations upon non-nationals. Accordingly, since 2002 and an amendment to the Aliens Act (*Fremdengesetz*), all non-nationals who have entered Austria since 1998 are required to comply with an 'integration agreement', which means following courses especially in language skills which involve, since January 2006, some 300 hours of attendance. There was also a strong emphasis on security issues, and the ÖVP/FPÖ coalition agreement dealt with immigration and security issues under a joint heading (König and Perchinig, 2003: 3–5).

Against such a policy and legislative background, it is hardly surprising that electoral rights for non-nationals, beyond the confines of EU law, have rarely been on the political agenda in Austria. According to the SPÖ in 2000: 'Today there is simply not the political will to address the issue of voting rights at the national level.'[58] Nominally, the SPÖ might be expected to be in favour of widening the suffrage. Indeed, they admit that: 'Our theoretical goal is close to the Greens, but in practice in the world of politics it is necessary to make compromises.'[59] As the same interviewee indicated, the fear of losing political capital has restricted debate: 'Between 1989 and 1993, with over 120,000 immigrants in Vienna, no one within the SPÖ continued to talk about voting rights for third country nationals.' However, the SPÖ in Vienna was responsible for a more limited project to support the rights of third country nationals, in the form of the so-called Integration Fund. This latter body developed a model for the city whereby immigrants can vote for a representative body which is then able to *consult* with the municipal council. The Steering Committee for the Fund is the *Kuratorium*, established by the city. It issues guidelines for the Fund and determines its tasks and goals. The *Kuratorium* is a body with eighteen seats, of which three are reserved for migrants and NGOs. The Greens and the Liberals had wanted this to be seven. The Fund focuses on a diversity approach, rather than the management of minorities, and its principal work is in the areas of social work, youth programmes and language courses (Krahler and Sohler, 2005: 21–7 and 50–6).

Matters changed somewhat in Vienna after the election of a new SPÖ *Land* and city government in 2002, which reached an agreement with the Greens on a number of matters including a commitment to introduce electoral rights for third country nationals (Perchinig, 2005). This brought to centre stage Renate Brauner, an SPD member who had

---

[58] Interview with Robert Leingruber, International Secretary of the Austrian Social Democratic Party, Vienna, June 2000.

[59] Franz Jerabek, Office of the Fund for Integration, and assistant to SPÖ City Councillor and Member of the City Government, Renate Brauner, Vienna, June 2000.

long campaigned on the issue of electoral rights as city councillor for integration matters, but who had previously been a more marginal figure. Furthermore, an opinion poll amongst potential third country national voters conducted on behalf of Brauner and her colleagues indicated that 70 per cent of potential third country national voters said they would use the vote if granted it (Krahler and Sohler, 2005: 52, referring to Jenny, 2002). This suggested that the vote in municipal elections for third country nationals could effectively be seen as part of a larger integration strategy, binding the non-nationals closer to the Austrian state and public authorities. Amendments were introduced to the relevant Viennese electoral laws to allow for voting by third country nationals with five or more years of residence in the *Bezirksvertretungen*. These community councils are the level at which EU citizens also participate in municipal governance within Vienna, since the Viennese city council doubles as a *Land* parliament and thus is excluded from the scope of the Article 19 voting rights.[60] Such councils below the level of the city do not exist elsewhere in Austria, and indeed they are not mentioned at any point in the Austrian Constitution. This raised the question of whether third country national voting in these elections was possible under Austrian constitutional law, since it is clear from the Constitution that voting for *Gemeinderäte* (the normal level of municipal councils) is reserved for Austrian citizens, with an exception being made for EU citizens pursuant to an amendment to implement the Treaty of Maastricht (Article 117 of the Austrian Constitution).[61] It is universally agreed, moreover, that voting in national and *Land*-level elections is also reserved for citizens.

In seeking to exploit this constitutional 'space', the Viennese city government found support for its approach from senior constitutional lawyers in Austria, including Professor Heinz Mayer of the University of Vienna (Mayer, 2002). He concluded that, as the Viennese *Bezirksvertretungen* are regulated by law at the level of the *Land* rather than the federal state and exercise no legislative competences, they should not be regarded as general representative bodies, and as such are not subject to the principle under the Constitution of the 'homogeneity of the franchise', which restricts the right to vote in all elections to Austrian citizens. After the

---

[60] Judgment of the Austrian Constitutional Court of 12 December 1997, B3113/96, B3760/96.
[61] For brief notes on the application of Article 19 in Austria, see the regular national country reports for the EU Network of Experts on Fundamental Rights (CFR-CDR), most recently Nowak *et al.*, 2005: 113.

Figure 9.1: Campaign poster of the FPÖ displayed in Vienna during the summer of 2003. Photograph by Alfred J. Thomas.

law was adopted in December 2002, it was subjected to a constitutional challenge before the Austrian Federal Constitutional Court by a number of members of the ÖVP and FPÖ parties sitting in opposition in the Viennese legislative body. The FPÖ, in particular, mounted a political campaign against the amendment, arguing that 'a registration form (i.e. proof of residence) is too little' for the right to vote, which should be reserved only for citizens. Its campaign included the use of posters displayed prominently in Vienna, indicating that as a party it does indeed have a multicultural view of the scope of Austrian citizenship, a view which does not necessarily chime happily with some of its other political pronouncements. However, the point of the campaign was to emphasise that to be a true 'Wiener' or 'Wienerin', regardless of colour or ethnic background, an immigrant had to become an Austrian citizen.

In the event, the constitutional court adopted a narrow interpretation of the constitutional possibilities under Austrian law, cutting off what had been put forward by proponents as a promising experiment to see whether third country national voting could contribute to the integration process in Austria (Nowak and Lubich, 2005: 80). As a matter of constitutional text and interpretation,[62] the Court had no difficulty in first confirming that the electorate for national elections to the lower house of parliament (the National Council, or *Nationalrat*), for regional elections to the legislatures of the *Länder* (*Landtag*), and for local elections to the municipal councils (*Gemeinderat*), is restricted in principle to Austrian citizens alone, subject to the requirements of Article 19 EC which are referred to in Article 117 of the Constitution. However, this is not really an exception built into the Constitution as such, but rather a recognition of Austria's internal national perspective on European Community law, which is to recognise its supremacy *vis-à-vis* Austrian law, even the Austrian Constitution. It emphasised the principle of the 'homogeneity of the franchise' in this context, whereby each level of government should be voted for by an identically defined electorate. Drawing upon what might be described as the ethos of nineteenth-century nationalism (Perchinig, 2005: 10), the Court decreed that the rules on the franchise for the national, provincial and municipal levels of government are merely a specific example of the general principle stated in Article 1 of the Constitution whereby 'Austria is a democratic Republic. Its law stems from the people.' This 'people' is the Austrian people, defined by citizenship.[63]

Recognising that Vienna's *Bezirksvertretungen* are not regulated by the Constitution but by state law, the Court nonetheless found that they are general representative bodies, in the sense that they are established by law to deal with matters in the public interest, not in the interests of particular groups or professions, and fulfil a function as representative organs of a defined territorial entity. Consequently, the principle of the homogeneity of the franchise must apply to them, even though in reality the 'people' or *Volk* which can vote for the *Bezirksvertretungen*, like the *Gemeinderäte* in the rest of the country, is constituted by Austrian citizens plus resident EU citizens from other Member States. Thus the Court gave no intrinsic weight to the redefinition of the 'people' in terms of the impact of EU law, other than to recognise the single exception mandated by Article 19 EC. It stated that the exception to Article 1 brought about in order to give effect to Austria's membership of the EU, whereby the law stems not only from 'the people', but also from the 'organs of the (European) Community', was 'irrelevant' in this

---

[62] VfGH 30 June 2004, G218/03.   [63] VfGH 30 June 2004, at 47.

context.[64] Consequently, the Court annulled as unconstitutional the amendments to the Viennese law on municipal elections which would have allowed third country nationals with five years' settled residence to vote in elections to the *Bezirksvertretungen*.

Of course, as Manfred Nowak and Alexander Lubich (2005: 80) point out, the Court was not bound to have limited itself to defining the 'people' for the purposes of the elections to the *Bezirksvertretungen* by reference to Article 1 of the Constitution, but rather it could have taken a different line in relation to the fact that these local bodies, which have very few powers, are not covered explicitly by the Constitution. If it had not concluded that these bodies are general representative bodies, it would not have felt itself obliged to apply the narrow concept of (Austrian) people to them. It is also notable that the Court hardly makes any reference to the contribution of EU law to undermining a unitary concept of 'the people', but rather it simply dismisses the relevance of EU law to deciding the issue in relation to other groups of 'non-people'. Bernhard Perchinig deplores the failure to refer to the development of concepts of citizenship in the EU context, including the notion that the rights and status of third country nationals resident in the Member States should be approximated as closely as possible to those of EU citizens resident in another Member State. This idea was first articulated in the Tampere Programme in 1999, and was a principle that the Commission in turn sought to develop into a conception of 'civic citizenship' for third country nationals (Perchinig, 2005: 10; Perchinig, 2004: 180).[65] However, for the Austrian Constitutional Court to take these essentially declaratory developments as a reference point for a judgment in 2004 would have been a revolutionary step for it to take, going way beyond the preparedness of the Member States together under the *aegis* of EU law to implement their grand declarations of Tampere. In any event, the Court's narrow conclusion on the reach of a nationality-defined concept of the 'people' as sovereign means that the *Bezirksvertretungen* elections cannot become a laboratory within which the city authorities in Vienna could experiment with different participatory mechanisms to promote the integration of non-nationals, in addition to naturalised citizens who are already included in the franchise. Indeed, naturalisation – however difficult it remains – is the

---

[64] VfGH 30 June 2004 at 48.

[65] See further the discussion of civic citizenship and the Tampere Programme in Chapter 7, Section V.

Figure 9.2: Campaign poster of the Green Party displayed in Vienna during the General Election campaign of 2006. Photograph by Wiebke Sievers.

only route to political inclusion in Austria for third country nationals. As Figure 9.2, an election poster issued by the Green Party for the October 2006 general election, shows, the mainstream parties are also capable of seeking to exploit this possibility for political advantage by appealing to the votes of an increasingly large naturalised population by stressing an inclusive concept of the nation.

IV Conclusions

While it remains true, as we saw in Chapter 8, that stories of 'inclusion' can often hide exclusion, it is also possible that stories of exclusion can open pathways, albeit indirectly, to enhanced inclusion. Thus the interpretation given by Seyla Benhabib (2004) to the interactions, or iterations, between politics and law and between political and legal actors, which she saw developing in the aftermath of the German Federal Constitutional Court's alien suffrage judgments in 1990, involves some sort of opening rather than a closure. She related the closure of the avenue to greater electoral inclusion as signalling a first step on the pathway towards easier citizenship acquisition by migrants and their descendants, following reform of the nationality and citizenship legislation in 1999–2000. On the other hand, as recent commentary has shown, legislative change does not necessarily herald societal change. For Germany's immigrants, even though now better recognised as 'immigrants' and not 'guestworkers', the predominant story remains: 'Integration in Theory, Alienation in Practice'.[66]

Looking at the point from a different perspective, this chapter has identified a consistent theme of tensions and struggles between national and subnational authorities, with the latter pushing hard at the limits of the legally possible, both in order to assert aspects of subnational identity in relation to the space of citizenship within and below the state, but also in order to create laboratories for experimentation and thus ultimately to push for national constitutional and legislative change. On occasions, those initiatives have been knocked back by reference to a unitary concept of 'the people' asserted by a national constitutional court (Austria, Germany); on other occasions, the legal message delivered to the subnational authorities has been that they lack the necessary formal legal power to act in this domain (France, Italy). This hardly seems to bode well for the possibilities canvassed in the previous chapter that the UK and Spain could one day see a differentiation of the pattern of electoral rights between different subnational regions of the state. The constellation of political forces in play, and the willingness (or lack of it) at a national level to address the issue of integration constructively and on a participatory basis also appears to be a factor distinguishing the patterns of contestation which have been examined in this chapter. The role of a radical-right party as in Austria may not be unique, and one should not discount also such forces in France and Italy, but it certainly appears to have played a role in the Austrian case in reinforcing restrictive immigration policies which have also stretched into highly disciplinary and securitised approaches to the issue of integration.

None of the stories related in this chapter has involved initiatives for change in relation to electoral rights which have thus far been successful, although time may one day change this outcome. Even in an era where

---

[66] R.-A. Clermont, 'Germany's Immigrants: Integration in Theory, Alienation in Practice', *Spiegel Online*, 23 August 2006, http://service.spiegel.de/cache/international/0,1518,433006,00.html.

citizenship is, as we have seen in earlier chapters, becoming an increasingly complex and fuzzy concept in relation to the operation of many national boundaries, it remains possible within many national polities for change to the boundaries of the suffrage to be decisively resisted by reference to the argument that national citizenship marks the outer limit of the right to vote. What is clear is that the cases studied here demonstrate both variety and complexity in the contestations to which electoral rights give rise, as citizenship concepts are both stretched and restricted, often simultaneously, by a range of political and legal actors within and sometimes across the Member States.

10

Out of Empire: electoral rights, enlargement and the wider Europe

I Introduction

The examples given in the previous two chapters of both inclusion and exclusion have focused on the pre-2004 Member States of the EU. As was explained at the beginning of Chapter 8, there are good reasons for taking a closer look at cases of electoral inclusion and exclusion in the new post-2004 Member States, in particular those of Central and Eastern Europe which were previously part of the broad 'Soviet bloc' (or non-aligned in the case of the former Yugoslavia[1]), because they raise on the whole a slightly different set of issues. That does not mean there is no overlap between what will be discussed in this chapter and the cases examined in Chapters 8 and 9. Spain, for instance, has undergone a relatively recent transition from autocracy to democracy, and (indeed, like the UK) still has a relatively unstable set of territorial governance arrangements; such factors all impact upon questions of citizenship and membership, as we have seen. Equally, Ireland's transition from a country of emigration to a country of immigration, which has occurred in concert with processes of economic and political modernisation, offers some parallels with processes of change occurring in Central and Eastern European states at the present time, not least because the choices of economic policy mix and tax policies made by the respective governments to encourage foreign investment bear considerable similarities. However, at this stage, with enlargement in 2004 a very recent memory, and with the changes triggered in 1989 still very much in mind, it is useful to examine some of the key contestations over the scope of electoral rights in the new Member States in a separate chapter, focusing in particular on the consequences of polity formation and re-formation.

---

[1] To avoid confusion with other manifestations of 'Yugoslavia', the state which was created after the Second World War and existed until it disintegrated in the wars in the 1990s is referred to as the Socialist Federal Republic of Yugoslavia, or SFRY, in this chapter.

This chapter will look at how the Baltic states (Estonia, Latvia and Lithuania) have addressed the issue of the political participation and integration of the large ethnic Russian minorities within their borders and how Slovenia has dealt with the issue of citizenship definition, given its history as a borderland state, situated at the cusp of many empires, states and blocs which have come and gone over the centuries. The common element in both these cases is that, where the issue of electoral rights for non-nationals has arisen, it has done so most often not because there has been a substantial population of non-nationals in the host state created by a process of *migration*, but rather because a state border has moved (or disappeared; or been created), in the recent and/or the more distant past.

Two broad sets of issues provide the background against which these contestations can best be examined: these relate to the break-up of empires and the (re)formation of states, and the role of the European Union and other international organisations in Central and Eastern Europe, in particular the enlargement policies of those organisations. However, the issue of national reawakenings and processes of international integration are ultimately closely intertwined.

Since the beginning of the twentieth century, Central and Eastern Europe has been directly affected by the rise, decline and/or dissolution of successive 'empires': the Ottoman Empire, the Austro-Hungarian Empire, the German Reich and its forerunners, and the Soviet Union and its forerunner, the Russian Empire. A number of forms of national self-expression have contributed to and been unleashed by these changes, and considerable geopolitical instability has been experienced in the region, although there have also been important new opportunities for economic prosperity and political freedom. The most important structural effects have included the creation of new states, with new citizenship and nationality regimes as well as new governance structures, and the creation of diasporas and minorities separated from their so-called 'kin-states' (Tóth, 2003). In addition, the break-up of the Soviet Union and the end of the Cold War contributed directly to the dissolution of two federal states, Czechoslovakia and the Socialist Federal Republic of Yugoslavia (SFRY), the former peacefully and the latter with considerable bloodshed. Of the eight Central and Eastern European countries which acceded to the EU in 2004, all bar Poland and Hungary were 'new' states, constructed or reconstructed since 1989. Each of the six 'new' states, with the exception of the Czech Republic, has significant issues arising around minority groups within its borders:

Russians (especially, but also Poles, Belarussians, Ukrainians and others) in the Baltic states; Hungarians in Slovakia; and citizens of other former Yugoslav republics in Slovenia. More generally, and outwith the system of states as such, a number of Central and Eastern European states have substantial populations of Roma, who experience high levels of discrimination and social exclusion and segregation (Pogany, 2004). Some of these minority groups may have the national citizenship of the host state; others may lack it. Most members of such 'national' groups, whether they have the national citizenship or not, will perceive themselves as part of an ethnic minority group in the host state, and will probably experience certain problems, notably social, economic and political exclusion, as a consequence.

In addition, Hungary also experiences the national minority problem in reverse, with diasporas in a number of countries, mostly as a consequence of the Treaty of Trianon of 1920. Thus, there are substantial minorities of ethnic Hungarians in Slovakia and Romania, with smaller groups in states such as Slovenia, Serbia, Austria and the Ukraine. For Hungary, the question becomes the ongoing relationship which it maintains with such groups outwith its borders, whose members see themselves as still strongly affiliated to Hungary, notwithstanding that they may have the national citizenship of another state. The attempts to regulate the relationship between Hungary and ethnic Hungarians abroad have encountered critical comment from a number of quarters,[2] and suggestions have even emerged that Hungary retains irredentist ambitions (Ambrosio, 2002). More generally, the Council of Europe's European Commission for Democracy through Law (the Venice Commission) accepted a report in October 2001, which represents the first step towards the development of international norms governing kin-state policy towards co-ethnics abroad (Fowler, 2004b).[3]

In many of the cases arising in Central and Eastern Europe, in the new Member States, it is not alienage, i.e. the lack of national membership which has been the focus throughout this book, which is the problem, but rather the issue of the rights of national minorities within host states, and the role of national and international laws in the protection of the

---

[2] For a comprehensive review of the issues, see Kántor et al., 2004.

[3] Council of Europe, 'Report on the Preferential Treatment of National Minorities by Their Kin-State', adopted by the Venice Commission at its 48th Plenary Meeting, Venice, 19–20 October 2001 (Document CDL-INF (2001) 19).

rights and interests of such groups once defined as 'minorities', whether by the host state or by the state of origin.

The second set of issues pertains to the role of supranational and international organisations in relation to the states of Central and Eastern Europe in the post-Soviet constellation. A number of external pressures have driven the speedy economic and political transformation and modernisation processes which have occurred within these states since 1989, and these have included the possibilities of acceding to a number of supranational and international organisations. Central amongst these organisations, of course, is the EU, which has long had an explicit enlargement policy, but accession to other organisations such as the Council of Europe and NATO, which perform rather different types of functions as international organisations in the European sphere, has also proved to be of considerable importance for the foreign policy goals of these states. All of this has reinforced the break with the pre-1989 past, but at the same time has raised questions about how the post-1989 period relates back to earlier periods of history, such as the years leading up to 1914, or those following the 1919 peace settlement, which instituted substantial boundary realignments across Europe. In some cases, the post-1989 reawakening has also created the space for certain types of nationalist sentiment to be given political expression, both through the medium of elections bringing to power populist and nationalist groups and parties, and also through the medium of undemocratic activity including violence. There has, of course, been a substantial amount of ethnic conflict in south-eastern Europe since 1989, much of it historically related to earlier conflicts. However, the process of 'joining Europe', in the formal sense of acceding to the EU, the Council of Europe and NATO, has often involved accepting outside scrutiny of internal processes, although this has obviously been of a very different type to that imposed during the period of Soviet domination of Central and Eastern Europe.

Those processes of adjustment, and scrutiny, continue both for those states from the initial first tranche whose accession to the EU was delayed until 2007 (Romania and Bulgaria), for the next tranche of potential members (candidate countries Croatia and Turkey, with which accession negotiations started in late 2005, and Macedonia, with which they have not yet started), and for the other potential candidate countries identified by the EU in south-eastern Europe (Albania, Bosnia, Serbia, Montenegro and, depending upon final status, Kosovo). These latter states are linked to the EU through a set of stabilisation and association processes and structures. Consequently, it becomes a question of intense interest to the EU and the other Member States how many Macedonians take on Bulgarian national citizenship,[4] or how many Moldovans acquire Romanian national citizenship,[5] to name two pairs of states right at the margins of the EU where substantial numbers of citizens of the state outside the EU are able to qualify, through historical connections, for citizenship of the EU Member State, and thus for EU citizenship, even if not necessarily (yet) full rights to free movement within the EU. Equally, from the perspective of the states in the 'border regions' of the EU, the requirement to implement the Schengen *acquis* from the moment of enlargement, including the imposition of visa requirements on the citizens of states where there are close historical connections or many co-ethnics, can cause severe destabilisation of relations between states (Tóth, 2003). To put it another way, there can be inherent tensions 'between the "re-nationalization" of history in Central and Southeast Europe and the process of European integration' (Iordachi, 2004b: 114). The pressure put on Bulgaria and Romania to restrict access to citizenship in respect of non-resident 'co-ethnics' in the run-up to the 2007 enlargement can be contrasted with earlier efforts made in the 1990s by the European Commission to pressure Latvia and Estonia to adopt more generous access-to-citizenship policies in respect of *resident* Russians (Kochenov, 2004), in particular to avoid the problem of statelessness in the Baltic states (Gelazis, 2004). However, as we shall see in Section III, the three Baltic states have taken rather different approaches to both the citizenship and the electoral rights issues since independence (Kalvaitis, 1998; Chinn and Truex, 1996). In sum, there are many new sites of, and styles of, transnational politics in the post-1989 world. Before looking at these in more detail, we must look at how 'national' minorities have been regulated in Europe, and how the system of minority protection under international law has developed since 1989.

---

[4] 'For Dream Jobs in Europe, the Line Forms in Bulgaria', *New York Times*, 23 July 2006. It is also reported that, in addition to the many Macedonians entitled to Bulgarian nationality, there may be up to 300,000 Moldovans and many Ukrainians who are also qualified through historic connections.

[5] On the intertwining of Moldovan and Romanian nationality, see Iordachi, 2004a; on Moldova as a challenge after the 2007 enlargement, see Berg and Ehin, 2006: 64.

II 'National minorities' and international law in the European political space

The topic of national minorities and their protection under the system of international law needs to be teased out in more detail, as so much of this book hitherto has been premised on the issue of *migration* and *migrants* and the implications for the boundaries of the suffrage, rather than the question of *minorities*. Gwendolyn Sasse and Eiko Thielemann have sought to tease out some of the complex interlinkages between the terms 'migrant' and 'minority', while at the same time searching for common trends in thinking which make it possible to bring the study of migrants and minorities closer together. They note that 'some countries (e.g. the UK) explicitly refer to migrants as "ethnic minorities", thereby adding to the confusion'. In their work, they use the term 'ethnic minority' as subsuming a range of migrant groups, 'while the term "national minority" is reserved for established minorities claiming minority rights (e.g. forms of autonomy) to preserve their distinctive features and status' (Sasse and Thielemann, 2005: 655–6).

Sasse and Thielemann share with many other writers a baseline definition of 'migrants' as those settled temporarily or permanently in a state where they were not born. They also note that in practice the words 'migrant' and 'migration' are often qualified by other terms such as 'long term', 'temporary', 'forced' or 'voluntary', 'irregular'/'illegal', 'labour', 'family', and so on.[6] States and boundaries are indissolubly linked to the issue of migration (Geddes, 2005: 802), but they are also linked, in different ways, to the issue of minorities, especially national minorities, because of the ways in which national minorities might arise, both through population movements, but also because states and boundaries change over the years and because of the claims which they may make against states. A national minority is defined by Sasse and Thielemann as

a numerical, non-dominant group of individuals that combines objective criteria, such as specific cultural characteristics (ethnicity, language, religion) distinct from the majority of the population, with subjective criteria, such as a collective sense of community. The cultural specifics tend to form the basis of these groups' claims to certain rights or autonomy.

(Sasse and Thielemann, 2005: 657–8)

---

[6] For a glossary of terms, largely drawn from the relevant United Nations instruments, see the Migration Policy Institute's material at http://www.migrationinformation.org/Glossary/.

It is the issue of the protection of these claims under national and, in particular, international law which animates this brief review of the question of national minorities. Hitherto, EU law has not placed any specific obligations upon its Member States in relation to standards of protection of national minorities within their borders, other than by reference to the fundamental rights guaranteed under Article 6 of the EU Treaty, and through the measures relating to equal treatment on grounds of racial or ethnic origin and religion adopted by the Council of Ministers on the basis of Article 13 EC.[7] Although Article 6(2) EU in turn refers to the civil rights included in the European Convention on Human Rights, as there is no free-standing right to protection of an individual *qua* a member of a national minority in the ECHR, and the reference to 'association with a national minority' in Article 14 ECHR does not establish a free-standing right to non-discrimination, reference back to the ECHR is of little assistance. Moreover, Member State compliance with fundamental rights standards as norms of EU law is also limited by reference to the scope of EU law. Where there is no EU competence in a specific field, or where national competences are not in any way affected by norms of EU law, Member States are constrained only by *national* standards of fundamental rights protection, and of course by reference to their common commitment to the standards of the ECHR. The only conceivable tool under EU law for ensuring the compliance of Member States with fundamental rights standards in areas outwith the scope of EU competence would be the procedure laid down in Article 7 EU for suspension of the rights of a Member State found to be in serious breach of the principles laid down in Article 6(1), namely, liberty, democracy, respect for human rights and fundamental freedoms, and the rule of law. In practice, this procedure is highly political and is likely never to be invoked in full,[8] and in any event it does not refer to minority rights explicitly.

---

[7] Council Directive 2000/43/EC implementing the principle of equal treatment between persons irrespective of racial or ethnic origin, OJ 2000 L180/22; Council Directive 2000/78/EC establishing a general framework for equal treatment in employment and occupation, [2000] OJ L 303/16; Council Decision 2000/750 establishing a Community action programme to combat discrimination (2001–2006), OJ 2000 L303/23.

[8] The steps taken by the Member States in order to avoid formally invoking the then rather crude procedure in Article 7 EU against Austria in 1990, as a consequence of the establishment of the controversial right-wing coalition government involving the People's Party (ÖVP) and the Freedom Party (FPÖ) is instructive. In practice, the Member States invited three 'wise men' to report on the situation in Austria (see Chapter 9, Section III), and a later amendment to Article 7 EU in the Treaty of Nice incorporated this softer process of reporting into the text of the Treaty.

However, as part of its enlargement policy, the EU has insisted on the satisfactory handling of minority rights issues as a condition of accession, generating considerable controversy in the wake of the policy (Schwellnus and Wiener, 2004). The policy is termed 'conditionality'. One of the so-called 'Copenhagen criteria', formulated in 1993 as political conditions for accession to the EU, is 'respect for and protection of minorities'.[9] However, accession criteria are just that: criteria for *accession*; thus conditionality becomes irrelevant once a Member State joins the EU and is subject only to the obligations of membership (Toggenburg, 2006).

That said, the new Member States have shown some enthusiasm since accession for bringing minority rights more clearly within the scope of EU law, and, as a result of pressure from states such as Hungary, the phrase 'rights of persons belonging to minorities' was included in the final text of Article I-2 of the Constitutional Treaty by the Intergovernmental Conference.[10] Article I-2 provides:

> The Union is founded on the values of respect for human dignity, freedom, democracy, equality, the rule of law and respect for human rights, including the rights of persons belonging to minorities.

Like so much in the Constitutional Treaty, the text lacks precision, and any clear means to secure implementation. There is an equivalent to Article 7 EU in Article I-59 of the Constitutional Treaty, and under the Constitutional Treaty regime the reference to the values which should not be breached by the Member States would include, because the scope of Article I-2 is wider than that of Article 6 EU, a reference to minority rights. However, the same objections to the effectiveness of such a procedure apply as do in relation to Article 7 EU. Moreover, no additional reference to minority rights was added to Part II of the Constitutional Treaty, which enshrines the Charter of Fundamental Rights originally promulgated in a declaratory form in 2000, and no tools of enforcement or relevant legal bases are included in Part III of the Constitutional Treaty. In any event, in the absence of ratification and entry into force of the text of the Constitutional Treaty, the *status quo ante* still applies: no reference to minority rights in the body of EU primary law and consequentially no *policy* mechanisms as such to secure progress in this field, even so far as it falls within the purview of the European integration process. The only

---

[9] On the accession criteria, see http://ec.europa.eu/enlargement/enlargement_process/ accession_process/criteria/index_en.htm.
[10] OJ 2004 C310/1.

exception concerns the policies developed to combat social exclusion amongst the Roma, who are defined as a specific racial or ethnic minority under Article 13 EC; these have been developed under the Community action programme to combat discrimination.[11]

The issue of subsuming minority rights protection under the umbrella of fundamental rights protection is in some ways problematic, because often minority groups are looking for *collective* rather than *individual* protection. They may seek both the right to be left alone and given autonomy as a group, as well as the right, where appropriate, to be exempted on the grounds of cultural or religious specificity from general norms applying to the rest of the population. They may also be asking for specific forms of representation which appear, at first sight, to amount to positive action, such as special representation in legislatures or elected municipal authorities. Such claims may conflict with republican and universalist norms of individual protection, such as those which underpin the French constitution. This is doubtless a contributing factor to France's refusal, alone amongst the Member States of the European Union, to sign the Council of Europe's 1995 Framework Convention on the Protection of National Minorities.[12] This is among the most important international instruments applicable right across Europe, and it is specifically tailored to creating and maintaining standards of protection based on the specificities of national minorities. It deals with minority rights protection as a dimension of fundamental rights protection. Although the majority of the Member States have signed and ratified the Convention, and participate in the monitoring process which involves periodic reports from the states parties and resolutions from the Committee of Ministers of the Council of Europe, assisted by an Advisory Committee, a number of Member States have only signed and not ratified the Convention: Belgium, Greece and Luxembourg. Latvia has only recently (2005) ratified and brought the Convention into force, having signed in 1995.

However, the work done under the aegis of the Framework Convention is just part of a dense (and confusing) network of institutions and activities involving the bodies of both the Council of Europe and the Organization for Security and Co-operation in Europe in the field of national minorities. The list includes, under the aegis of the Council of Europe, the work of

[11] See above n. 7.
[12] ETS No. 157; opened for signature on 1 February 1995; entered into force 1 February 1998; www.conventions.coe.int.

the Commissioner for Human Rights,[13] the work of the European Commission against Racism and Intolerance,[14] and the work of the European Commission for Democracy through Law (the Venice Commission),[15] which is the Council of Europe's advisory body on constitutional matters (including the constitutional protection of minority rights and issues such as political participation), and, under the aegis of the OSCE, the work of both the Office for Democratic Institutions and Human Rights[16] and the High Commissioner on National Minorities.[17]

In relation to the latter institution, so far as pertains to political participation, it is pertinent to cite the 1999 Lund Recommendations on 'Effective Participation of National Minorities in Public Life'. These provide:

> Effective participation of national minorities in public life is an essential component of a peaceful and democratic society ... (1) These Recommendations aim to facilitate the inclusion of minorities within the State and enable minorities to maintain their own identity and characteristics, thereby promoting the good governance and integrity of the State. (2) These Recommendations build upon fundamental principles and rules of international law, such as respect for human dignity, equal rights, and non-discrimination, as they affect the rights of national minorities to participate in public life and to enjoy other political rights. (3) States shall guarantee the right of persons belonging to national minorities to take part in the conduct of public affairs, including the rights to vote and stand for office without discrimination.

It is useful to bear these principles in mind as we work through the specific cases treated in the following sections. However, as Francesco Palermo and Jens Woelk (2003) warn, representation can only follow from 'recognition'. Hence, the crucial starting point remains that a state must first recognise those national minority groups within its borders which require specific protection.

III State re-formation and electoral rights: the case of the Baltic states

All three Baltic states were, of course, obliged to institute electoral rights for EU citizens under Article 19 as a consequence of accession, and

---

[13] http://www.coe.int/t/commissioner/default_EN.asp.
[14] http://www.coe.int/t/E/human_rights/ecri/. [15] http://www.venice.coe.int.
[16] http://www.osce.org/odihr/. [17] http://www.osce.org/hcnm/.

figures released by the Commission in 2004 (Table 3.2 in Chapter 3) indicated the presence of 5,000 Community voters in Estonia, 3,500 Community voters in Latvia, and 1,000 Community voters in Lithuania. However, two out of the three Baltic states have also instituted electoral rights for third country nationals since they became independent in the early 1990s (Estonia (1992) and Lithuania (2002)), with Latvia being the exception.

In March 2005, local elections were held in Latvia at which EU citizens were able to vote, but not the large population of non-citizen ethnic Russians. The controversies surrounding the scope of the electorate in these elections, and the large number of disenfranchised 'aliens' in Latvia, attracted attention in Western European media.[18] Latvia has refused to grant electoral rights to third country nationals even though the citizenship regime established after Latvian independence excluded most non-ethnic Latvians from obtaining citizenship, because a principle of 'inherited citizenship' was applied restricting citizenship acquisition to those who had been citizens of Latvia in 1940 or their descendants. Ethnic Russians form nearly 30 per cent of the total resident population of around 2.3 million, many having moved to Latvia with Soviet encouragement or indeed compulsion during the post-Second World War period of industrialisation. Equally, nearly 23 per cent of that population have neither Latvian nationality, nor indeed that of any other state.[19] Many of these 'non-citizens' (i.e. in practice the ethnic Russians referred to above) are effectively stateless and have to travel on 'non-citizen' passports and need visas to visit almost all EU Member States apart from Estonia, Lithuania and Denmark. They find it hard to access Latvian nationality, because of a combination of residence requirements and challenging language and history tests (Heleniak, 2006). In August 2006, Latvia tightened its arrangements still further, introducing a rule refusing citizenship definitively to anyone who had failed the Latvian language test three times.[20] Only around 11,000 persons are

[18] A. Roxburgh, 'Latvia Bars Its Russian Minority from Voting', *Sunday Herald*, 13 March 2005; A. Roxburgh, 'Citizenship Row Divides Latvia', BBC News, 25 March 2005, http://news.bbc.co.uk/1/hi/world/europe/4371345.stm.

[19] The Office of the Citizenship and the Migration Affairs, 'Public Annual Report 2003 on Statistics on Migration, Asylum and Return', Riga, March 2006; 'The People of Latvia', Latvian Institute Fact Sheet, October 2005, No. 13.

[20] 'Latvia Tightens Citizenship Laws', BBC News, 9 August 2006, http://news.bbc.co.uk/1/hi/world/europe/4776511.stm.

naturalised per year. In total, since 1995, that amounts to just over 100,000 people. Meanwhile, there remain over 400,000 non-citizens in Latvia.[21] Even after acquiring Latvian citizenship, non-ethnic Latvian citizens regularly face language discrimination in both the educational and political domains (Taube, 2003). The Latvian government resists international pressure to extend electoral rights to third country nationals, insisting that the non-citizen problem stems largely from ethnic Russians bearing an attachment to the former Soviet Union, and that the problem of political rights should be solved by the process of naturalisation and assimilation to Latvian culture. Moreover, they argue that to grant political rights in advance of naturalisation would undermine the motivation of non-citizens to apply for naturalisation, and thus to go through the process of integration.[22]

In the accession process, this issue was raised on a number of occasions by various EU institutions, but to no avail. For example, just before enlargement happened in 2004, the European Parliament resolution on the comprehensive monitoring report of the European Commission on the state of preparedness for EU membership of all the ten states which acceded on 1 May 2004 commented that:

> the naturalisation process of the non-citizen part of society remains too slow; [the Parliament] therefore invites the Latvian authorities to promote the naturalisation process and considers that minimum language requirements for elderly people may contribute to it; encourages the Latvian authorities to overcome the existing split in society and to favour the genuine integration of 'non-citizens' ensuring an equal competitive chance in education and labour; [and] proposes that the Latvian authorities envisage the possibility of allowing non-citizens who are long-time inhabitants to take part in local self-government elections.[23]

---

[21] 'More Than 97,000 Persons Obtain Citizenship by Naturalization', BNS 26 July 2005, http://www.mfa.gov.lv/en/news/Newsletters/CurrentLatvia/2005/July/618/. See also the official presentation of Latvian citizenship by the Ministry of Foreign Affairs, 22 May 2006, http://www.mfa.gov.lv/en/policy/4641/4642/4651/.

[22] Union 'For Human Rights Law in Latvia', 'International Recommendations on Voting Rights for Latvian Non-Citizens', background information, available from www.zapchel.lv.

[23] Para. 74 of the European Parliament Resolution P5_TA(2004)0180 of 11 March 2004 on the comprehensive monitoring report of the European Commission on the state of preparedness for EU membership of the Czech Republic, Estonia, Cyprus, Latvia, Lithuania, Hungary, Malta, Poland, Slovenia and Slovakia, based on the Report A5-0111/2004, 25 February 2004.

This was not taken further, and now the opportunity has been lost. After accession, the EU institutions lose all purchase upon the conduct of new Member States, since there is nothing in the current state of EU law, as we saw in Chapter 7, to oblige any Member State to enact electoral rights for third country nationals. Moreover, the thrust of the policy developments that have occurred thus far has been focused on electoral rights as part of the policy programme to support the integration of *immigrants*, not in relation to the situation of those who, because of political transformations in which they may have had no say at all, have become *non-citizens* in the place they reside, having previously been *citizens* of another, now no longer existing state.

In marked contrast to Latvia, both Estonia and Lithuania have proved open to the argument that the right to participate in local elections for such groups of non-citizens could be a useful political element in dealing with the ongoing consequences of the break-up of the Soviet Union and the (re)creation of the Baltic states.[24] However, in terms of their approach to the re-establishment of citizenship in conjunction with independence from the Soviet Union, the two states took markedly different approaches: the 'zero option' (Lithuania) and the 'reference back' option (Estonia).

Lithuania adopted a 'zero option' approach to citizenship in its 1989 law on citizenship, offering citizenship to all residents as of the date of independence, with two years prior residence, provided they opted for this within a period of two years (i.e. by 1991). The boundaries of the polity were thus not drawn on ethnic grounds. Well over 90 per cent of those residents who were not ethnic Lithuanians chose to become Lithuanian citizens. On the other hand, Lithuania is relatively homogeneous, compared to the other Baltic states. The April 2001 census showed that more than 83 per cent of the population was Lithuanian in terms of ethnic origin, with only 6.7 per cent Poles, 6.3 per cent Russians and much smaller groups of other ethnicities such as Belarussians and Ukrainians. Today, around 99 per cent of the population of Lithuania holds Lithuanian citizenship,[25] and citizenship acquisition since the expiry of the two-year period of grace for permanent residents has

---

[24] See further Day and Shaw, 2003; and Smith and Shaw, 2006. Some parts of this section draw directly upon these texts.

[25] Migration Department under the Ministry of the Interior of the Republic of Lithuania, Migration Annual 2004, at 13, available from http://www.migracija.lt.

become as difficult as it is in the other Baltic states, requiring ten years of residence and the passing of language tests.[26]

Estonia, while allowing permanent residents to participate in the independence referendum of 1990 and in certain early elections for the Supreme Council (which was the successor body of the Estonian Supreme Soviet), opted in its 1992 Citizenship Law for a solution in which only those who had been citizens of Estonia on 16 June 1940, and their descendants, could be citizens. This is essentially an identical approach to that taken in Latvia. In turn, political participation was initially strictly limited to Estonian citizens, and that included both the right to vote and the right to be a member of a political party. However, in terms of the figures for ethnic minorities, Estonia is much more similar to Latvia than it is to Lithuania, with 65 per cent of the population being ethnic Estonians, 28 per cent Russians, plus much smaller groups of other ethnicities such as Ukrainians. The 2000 census[27] found that around 80 per cent of residents were Estonians by national citizenship, and only about 6 per cent were Russians, but quite a large figure of nearly 13 per cent were dual nationals (Estonian, plus one other).

It is worth noting that neither Lithuania nor Estonia (nor indeed Latvia) is currently 'restocking' its proportion of foreign-born or non-citizen residents, because neither is experiencing substantial levels of inward migration. Indeed, all three (although particularly Latvia and Lithuania) are experiencing continued emigration in particular to the UK and Ireland since accession to the EU in 2004, and all have a downward demographic trend with low birth rates and an ageing population (Munz, 2006). These three states also share in common the challenge of building a modern democratic polity after fifty years of Soviet domination, not to mention unstable political histories through centuries before that, and Latvia and Estonia in particular have had to deal with the consequences of substantial inward migration of Russians during the period of rapid (and forced) industrialisation after the Second World War. Consequently, Russians tend to be predominantly located in all three states in the urban areas, or in the vicinity of major items of infrastructure, such as nuclear power stations. Thus, as newly (re-)established states, the Baltic states had to deal with issues of instability, from both an internal and an external perspective. They

[26] Smith and Shaw, 2006: 158.   [27] Results are available from www.stat.ee.

have adopted quite different trajectories, especially in the internal sphere. In the external sphere, all three opted for collective security, seeking membership of the Council of Europe, the European Union and NATO, and were in due course successful in all cases. Internally, stability has been sought in very different ways.

The dynamics of regime change in Estonia and the subsequent impact this had upon defining the boundary of the suffrage began with intense interactions between two bodies: the Supreme Council (formerly the Supreme Soviet) and the Congress of Estonia. The former was dominated by the reformist/pragmatic Popular Front (which included Russian and Estonian intellectuals who emerged out of the Communist Party of Estonia) while the latter emerged from the independence movement, which was dominated by the Estonian Citizens' Committees. Crucially for what was to come, the Citizens' Committees were associated with members of Estonia's indigenous cultural elite. According to Taupio Raun:

> the competition between the Popular Front and the Citizens' Committees during 1989 already revealed the basic fault line in Estonian politics between what may be called the *fundamentalists*, who argued on the basis of principle and demanded the strict return to the status quo before Soviet rule, and the *pragmatists*, who proceeded from the concrete situation confronting them and were willing to make compromises in a less than ideal world.
>
> (Raun 1997: 347; emphasis in original)

In both cases, the desire was freedom from the Soviet yoke, but in the latter case this had an added dimension, namely one that equated ethnic Russians with an illegal and unconstitutional occupying force that was associated with the 'Russification' of Estonia. The Congress of Estonia politicised a golden past that advocated the restoration of the pre-war Estonian state based upon the Estonian language, Estonian culture and the 1938 Constitution as the most effective method with which to galvanise support. This had the effect of rendering non-ethnic Estonians unfit for the task of rebuilding the Estonian nation. Supporters of the Congress expected that large numbers of Russians would return to the motherland. The fact that only a small number did so posed a significant problem: what exactly should be done with the rest?

The right to vote for the Supreme Council had been given to *all permanent citizens*, and the right to stand to those of ten years' permanent residency including members of the Red Army. The Congress of Estonia restricted its electorate to Estonian citizens (based on pre-1940 residency) and those ethnic Russians who had signed the independence charter (Kionka, 1993: 90). Although it was the *de facto* legislature, the Supreme Council found that its legitimacy was constantly under challenge. The Estonian Congress argued that its legal status was undermined by the inclusive nature of the 1990 franchise and that it therefore lacked the legitimacy to introduce new legislation. In these circumstances, the idea of readopting the more inclusive citizenship law of 1920, or the proposal to adopt a 'zero option' formula of citizenship as in Lithuania, were dropped in the face of national political realities. This came in the face of opposition from Russia which believed that the 1991 Treaty of Intergovernmental Relations, which acknowledged Estonian independence, ensured recognition of the civil and political rights of the Russian minority.[28] What emerged ultimately was a situation whereby

> From the Estonian point of view, the citizenship laws were a hard-won compromise between two seemingly conflicting goals. First, lawmakers had sought to assure the survival of the Estonian nation by limiting citizenship to those who understood the country's language and culture. Second, the Supreme Council intended the laws to integrate those who had settled in Estonia under Soviet rule and thus to ensure a stable and loyal population.
>
> (Kionka, 1993: 90)

These developments were to have an immediate effect upon the nature of the franchise and in turn the polity. While 1,144,309 people had been eligible to participate in Estonia's 1990 independence referendum, those eligible to vote in the referendum on the Constitution on 28 June 1992 numbered just 689,319. This was because the 1992 Citizenship Law stipulated that only those who were citizens on 16 June 1940 (regardless of their ethnicity), and their descendants, were automatically deemed citizens. The definition of a citizen became the basis for deciding who was to be entitled to the full array of political rights. In addition, only citizens had the right to be a member of a political party, which under

---

[28] Interview with representatives of the Russian Embassy in Tallinn, July 2000. Relations with Russia continue to remain problematic, not least over the retired military personnel.

the 1994 Political Parties Act was defined as 'a voluntary association of *Estonian citizens*'.[29] Despite the fact that this restriction was clearly not in accordance with EU law, the Estonian Government was not quick to make changes.[30] This notion of a 'national' politics clearly conforms to a desire to secure internal stability by restricting participation in the political arena.

The changed nature of the franchise was also to have a significant impact upon the outcome of the 1992 election. According to Vello Pettai (1997: 22):

> the ethnic Estonian share of the electorate went from an approximate figure of 65 per cent in 1990 to well over 90 per cent in 1992. Not surprisingly, the first Estonian parliament elected in 1992, was 100 per cent Estonian.

As the title of Pettai's (1997) article aptly put it, there was 'Political Stability through Disenfranchisement'. According to Graham Smith, Estonia now constituted what he called an 'ethnic democracy', i.e. a situation whereby the titular nation constructs an institutional architecture that consolidates its political dominance (Smith, 1996).

The complete disenfranchisement of the Russian-speaking minority was, according to Kalle Liebert, averted by 'a compromise between political parties and western states, although most of the parties were supportive of this'.[31] The right to vote (but not to stand) in local elections for non-citizens with *permanent residency* status was enshrined, from the outset, in Article 156 of the 1992 Estonian Constitution which provides:

> In elections to local government councils, persons who reside permanently in the territory of the local government and have attained eighteen years of age have the right to vote, under conditions prescribed by law.

---

[29] Emphasis added. Section 1(1) of the Political Parties Act of June 1994, as amended most recently in March 2002. This Act and all subsequent Estonian legislation cited in this paper can be found in English on the website of the Estonian Legal Translation Centre, which is a state agency administered by the State Chancellery: http://www.legaltext.ee/indexen.htm.

[30] 'Opinion of the EU Network of Independent Experts on Fundamental Rights Regarding the Participation of EU Citizens in the Political Parties of the Member State of Residence', CFR-CDF Opinion 1/2005, March 2005, at 13.

[31] Interview with Kalle Liebert (former judicial counsellor to the citizenship and immigration department), Tallinn, 13 July 2000.

Amendments to section 3 of the Local Government Council Election Act introduced in 1999 lay down in more detail the application of this principle by stipulating that an alien has the right to vote in local elections:

1. if he or she has attained eighteen years of age by the election day;
2. if he or she resides permanently in the territory of the local government;
3. if he or she resides in Estonia on the basis of a permanent residence permit;
4. if he or she has resided legally in the territory of the corresponding local government for at least five years by 1 January of the election year; and
5. if he or she has not been divested of his or her active legal capacity by a court.

Actually putting this right into practice proved to be less straightforward than inserting it into the Constitution. Article 156 was first nominally applied in the local elections held in October 1993. Yet, at the time, no legislation had yet been passed to enable non-citizens to register as 'permanent residents'. *Thus there were simply no voters to take advantage of the right to vote.* Indeed, between 1992 and the summer of 1993, non-citizens had no legal status whatsoever in Estonian law. This situation was eventually rectified by the adoption of the highly controversial 1993 Aliens Law which declared that all those living in Estonia without Estonian citizenship would have to apply for residency status, however long they had been resident.[32] It was a decision that caused considerable international consternation. The Estonian President called for national calm while at the same time seeking the opinions of the OSCE and the Council of Europe. The Council of Europe's panel of experts duly found that 'it was wrong to equate the status of those already resident in Estonia with that of non-citizens not currently resident there'.[33] From Russia's point of view, this was not only an attempt to persuade Russians to leave, but it was the 'first time in history that a state set about forcing its own people to get citizenship of another state'.[34]

---

[32] This was to be divided into two categories: permanent residence and temporary residence. The resulting outcome was that Russian-speaking non-citizens were now classified as aliens regardless of whether they had been born in Estonia or how long they had lived there. It also meant that in strict legal terms the state could expel them.

[33] Quoted in Sheehy, 1993.

[34] Interview with representatives from the Russian Embassy, Tallinn, July 2000.

Yet in the minds of many of the Estonian political class the existence of a range of civil and social rights had a significant influence upon the nature of the debate concerning the boundaries of suffrage. Some have argued, for example, that the fact that the Estonian Constitution guarantees a range of civil and social rights, such as the right of peaceful assembly (Article 47) and the right to form non-profit undertakings and unions (Article 48), in some way compensated for the absence of *full* political rights.[35] This is explicitly stated in the 1998 Estonian Human Development Report, which states that:

> activities that rely on economic and cultural interests form quite a substantial counterbalance to political alienation among the aliens which accompanies certain restrictions on the non-citizens' political rights. Yet the participation of non-citizens in local elections integrates non-natives into Estonian society on a wider socio-political level. The alien's passport guarantees for local stateless permanent residents Estonian statehood. All these levels of cohesion expedite the acquisition of political citizenship.[36]

The backlog of permanent residency applications continued to delay the effective implementation of Article 156. Indeed, it was not until 1997 that an amendment to the Aliens Law (section 6(2)) provided *temporary* resident holders with the right to vote at the local level. The amendment enfranchised some 280,000 people. Interestingly, until 2000, those with permanent resident status only accounted for approximately 12 per cent of the overall number of non-citizens.[37] Moreover, residency status is not the only obstacle to political participation. Non-Estonians continue to be denied the right to stand for election, and the language law provisions also continued to have exclusionary effects on Russian-speaking Estonian citizens, notwithstanding international pressure (Day and Shaw, 2003: 226–30; Maveety and Grosskopf, 2004; Hughes, 2005).

[35] The government report entitled 'Integrating Estonia 1997–2000' highlighted the importance of civil society in the following terms: 'the civilizing influence of civil society is expressed in the fact it is founded on democratic norms and values, it increases ... interest and participation', see 'Integrating Estonia 1997–2000', Report of the Government of Estonia, Tallinn, June 2000, at 52.

[36] See United Nations Development Programme, 'Estonian Human Development Report 1998', Tallinn, 1998, at 48. This and additional reports can be found at http://undp.ee/nhdr.php.

[37] At this stage, with Russians accounting for 90.8 per cent of legal aliens, 311,259 had temporary residency permits compared to only 11,728 with permanent residency permits. Changes were introduced in 1997 that enable those who had applied for a temporary residency permit prior to 12 July 1995 to apply for a permanent residency permit from 12 July 1998.

In sum, one of Estonia's big issues since its independence from the Soviet Union in the August coup of 1991 has been that of defining the polity, and hence of defining the suffrage. Although the reasons for excluding Russians from the citizenry, and hence from the suffrage, were understandable in the early years of Estonian independence, the exclusionary arguments in favour have become increasingly hard to sustain both in the face of external political pressure from the OSCE and from the EU, and in the light of greater internal political maturity and experience with democratic practices and the rule of law. Internally, Estonia wished to avoid a 'one country, two societies' scenario. Externally, it found itself more pressured by international norms and organisations than would have been a more established liberal state, both in the form of OSCE recommendations and in terms of the pressure to conform to the *acquis communautaire* and the 'EU mainstream' prior to accession being contemplated. In this sense, there may be a positive synergy between the need to take steps internally with a view to settling the status of the substantial Russian minority, and the need to take steps in view of accession to settle the status of those who would become Estonia's 'second-country nationals', i.e. other EU citizens. Estonia's economic success since the late 1990s is also likely to contribute positively to an integration of the Estonian and Russian communities, both those amongst the latter who have acquired Estonian citizenship, and those who have not. This could contribute to a distinct Estonian-Russian identity.[38]

The story in relation to Lithuania is very different. Having opted for an inclusionary approach in terms of citizenship norms in 1989, it was in no hurry to enact the electoral legislation which would grant rights to the remaining small number of non-nationals. When independence was initially established (1990–3), the number of immigrants from the Commonwealth of Independent States (CIS) declined from 12,031 to 2,302, while the number of emigrants to CIS, mostly to Russia, Belarus and Ukraine, increased: in 1992, emigration to CIS reached its peak and stood at 26,948. Those ethnic minorities who chose not to exercise the right to obtain Lithuanian citizenship in this period left Lithuania to return to their 'home' state. This left behind extremely small numbers of non-citizens resident in Lithuania (regardless of their ethnic heritage). By 2000, Lithuania had more emigration to other foreign countries than

---

[38] I. Kotjuh, 'Varjus loojad', an article in the Estonian newspaper on 8 August 2006, abstracted in English by euro-topics, http://www.eurotopics.net/en/presseschau/archiv/aehnliche/archiv_article/ARTICLE6253/.

immigration: 1,190 against 389.[39] This process has continued, and in 2004, when Lithuania joined the EU, the emigration figure had risen to 15,165 with a net migration figure of minus 9,612.[40]

Furthermore, it is possible that economic considerations were relevant when choosing the 'zero option' route. In order to boost the economic progress of Lithuania as an annexed territory within the Soviet Union, a number of specialists (for instance in industry, and in particular in atomic energy) had been moved there by the Soviet Union. A number of highly skilled workers were therefore not of Lithuanian ethnic descent. Any long-term perspective on the economic stability and development of Lithuania might wish to encourage such highly skilled workers to remain there, rather than to return to Russia (or to go elsewhere such as the United States). Encouraging these highly skilled residents to stay would be all the more difficult if those persons, who were of non-ethnic Lithuanian descent, felt that they might be discriminated against, or lacked the ability effectively to access the same rights as were guaranteed to ethnic Lithuanians. A third factor which, like the pursuit of NATO and European Union membership, has been high on the foreign policy agenda of the independent Lithuanian state is that of good neighbourly relations.[41] Stabilising relations with its neighbouring states, particularly its previously occupying neighbours Poland and Russia,[42] was an obvious concern given the historical instability of Lithuania's borders. According ethnic Poles and Russians the choice as to which citizenship they would prefer was definitely a move in the right direction and reassured the neighbouring states that their 'ethnic'

---

[39] Council of Europe, Framework Convention for the Protection of National Minorities, State Report submitted by Lithuania, October 2001, ACFC/SR(2001)/007, at 12.

[40] Net migration means the difference between the total number of persons arriving and the total number of persons departing. Department of Statistics to the Government of the Republic of Lithuania (Statistics Lithuania).

[41] 'To enable Lithuanians residing abroad and Lithuanian nationals who have left their country lately to develop their ethnic and cultural identity, to maintain contacts with the Motherland, to participate in developing economic and cultural co-operation between Lithuania and foreign states': 'Programme of the Government of Lithuania 2001–2004', under Foreign Policy Objectives, Economic and Cultural Diplomacy, http://www.lrv.lt/main_en.php?cat=17&d=2002/.

[42] Sergey Mironov, Chairman of the Council of Federation of the Federal Assembly of the Russian Federation, on a state visit to meet the Lithuanian President Rolandas Paksas, stated that 'positive bilateral trends can be mainly accounted for by Lithuania's liberal "zero-option" citizenship law, when the citizens could choose themselves, which country's citizenship they wanted to have'. Source: http://www.mironov.ru/english/foreign. phtml?id=63/, June 2003.

citizens would not be discriminated against. This certainly eased tensions,[43] although there have been some difficulties since that time.[44]

At the same time as the citizenship law, a law that protected the cultural development of national minorities was also introduced.[45] Again, this pointed towards a new state which is tolerant of, and indeed which even embraces, a variety of ethnic and cultural heritages. The point was to insulate the ethnic Russians and Poles resident in Lithuania from connecting the choice of Lithuanian citizenship with the obliteration of their cultural identity. This law was the first of its kind in Central and Eastern Europe, and the Lithuanian Government also set up a Department of National Minorities and Lithuanians Living Abroad, responsible for formulating policies on ethnic harmony, whose task was to assist in the preservation of the cultural identity of national minorities. At such a pivotal time in the formation of a new state, when all residents had a two-year window to choose their citizenship, the Lithuanian state authorities were thus adopting relatively inclusive policies, certainly in comparison to the other Baltic states. It should be reiterated that, at the time of independence, the acquisition and holding of national citizenship was the gateway to accessing all rights in Lithuania. Laws relating to minority protection thus focus on protecting the cultural heritage of those who are already Lithuanian *citizens*. The key difference was that at the time of independence it was relatively easy to become a Lithuanian citizen. Subsequently, several new citizenship laws have been introduced, mainly aimed at new arrivals acquiring Lithuanian citizenship, which are decidedly less liberal and inclusive. The most recent prescribed a qualifying period of ten years' permanent residence in Lithuania and knowledge of the language and constitution.[46]

---

[43] The United Nations Committee on the Elimination of Racial Discrimination has commented that the decision to adopt the 'zero option' approach on citizenship has 'led to the construction of a more stable society': United Nations, Concluding Observations of the Committee on the Elimination of Racial Discrimination, CERD/C/60/CO, 8 March 2002.

[44] In 1994, the government suspended the operation of a local council in a predominantly Polish region, accusing it of deliberately blocking reform. This caused considerable tensions which were alleviated by subsequent elections.

[45] Law on Ethnic Minorities, 23 November 1989.

[46] Law on Citizenship, 17 September 2002, No. IX-1079. This law amended the previous law to ensure those ethnic Lithuanians or those of previous Lithuanian citizenship who left Lithuania after the 1941 German invasion and Russian annexation were able to reclaim their original Lithuanian citizenship, regardless of whether they had acquired a new citizenship in the interim. Originally, such persons did not have the right, once they had acquired citizenship of another country, to retain Lithuanian citizenship. Chapter III, Articles 17 and 18.

It was only when the time came for Lithuania to comply with the European *acquis* on EU citizens' right to vote and stand as candidates in local elections, that Article 119 of the Lithuanian Constitution relating to local government was amended to make this possible, and a legal framework enacted which applied to both EU citizens and third country nationals. The constitutional amendment in June 2002 allowed the introduction of further legislation[47] which extends beyond the basic requirements of EU law as it entitles *all* third country nationals the right to vote and stand as a candidate in municipal elections. This will be applied for the first time in local elections in December 2007.

The situation in Lithuania is not, however, without its problems for EU citizens and third country nationals. Whilst all persons are constitutionally guaranteed freedom of expression, thought, conscience and religion (Articles 25–27), only Lithuanian citizens are allowed to form political parties and associations (Article 35). This restriction is elaborated further in the law relating to political parties.[48] While this conditionality does not prevent a non-Lithuanian citizen from standing as a candidate for a municipal council (or in the case of EU citizens the European Parliament) and being elected, in practice parties have hitherto had a monopoly over the nomination of candidates for election (Zukauskiene, 2005: 30). Thus this restriction seems likely to be a problem in the future, although this has been denied by officials.[49] The conditionality may therefore be seen as an indirect hindrance to the inclusion of non-Lithuanian citizens into the political society of Lithuanian (and European) politics and may produce knock-on effects relating to the ability to raise funds to finance electoral campaigns without the financial support of a political party. This is a restriction based not on ethnicity, but on citizenship. Despite accession to the EU, the law in Lithuania regarding political parties remains unchanged, notwithstanding mounting pressure within the EU to grant the right to join and found political parties to EU citizens (if not to third country nationals).[50] An amendment to the existing law was tabled in the Lithuanian Parliament in January 2005[51] which envisaged the right of

---

[47] Law on Elections to Municipal Councils, 19 September 2002.
[48] Law on Political Parties, 23 March 2004.
[49] Interview with Zenonas Vaigauskas, Chairman of the Central Electoral Committee, 28 April 2004.
[50] See the Opinion of the Network of Experts on Fundamental Rights, above n. 30.
[51] Draft Law on the amendment of the Law on Political Parties, Draft Law No. XP-220, 21 January 2005.

all permanent residents to join political parties, but this was revoked shortly after its introduction. In Lithuania, there are a number of political parties established within national minorities such as the Election Action of the Lithuanian Poles (established in 1994), the Union of Lithuanian Russians (established in 1995) and the Alliance of Lithuanian Citizens (established in 1996). Indeed, representatives of both the Polish and the Russian communities have been prominent in national politics, in particular at the elections to the *Seimas* (the national Parliament) in 2000 and 2004. However, again these are confined to citizens.

IV Slovenia and the case of 'the erased'

Slovenia is another of the states of Central and Eastern Europe amongst the group which acceded to the EU in May 2004 which has already enacted local electoral rights for all non-nationals. Article 43(3) of the Slovenian Constitution provides that: 'The law may provide in which cases and under what conditions aliens have the right to vote.' Amendments to the Law on Local Elections in 2002 made provision for third country nationals, as well as EU citizens, to vote and stand for election in local elections, with the proviso that only a Slovene national is eligible to hold the office of elected head of the executive body of a local government (mayor). Since the EU directive on local elections, which is said by officials in the Ministry of the Interior to constitute the inspiration for the legislation,[52] entails provisions for such opt-outs, the Slovene legislature adopted the position that municipal executive functions (mayor) are part of the national competences which are transferred to the local level, that they can have national security functions, and that they can thus be reserved to nationals. The legislation was applied for the first time in 2002, even in advance of EU accession, although in practice there have been no reported cases of non-nationals standing for election (Andreev, 2005: 23). This 'mainly symbolic gesture' is nonetheless said to show 'the willingness of the country's political elite to follow the most advanced European practice in this field' (Andreev, 2003: 17).

There is little more, therefore, that can be said directly about the electoral rights themselves. They should, however, be placed in a wider context of minority protection and citizenship issues, which relate to Slovenia's status as a new state under international law as a consequence

---

[52] Interview with Ministry official, December 2003.

of its secession from the SFRY in 1991 and its creation of new governing norms of the polity, including a law on national citizenship.

As regards minority rights protection, it should be noted that Slovenia has adopted a number of measures which reflect its commitment to the protection of minority rights, based on Articles 64 and 65 of the Constitution which guarantee the status and special rights of the autochthonous Italian and Hungarian national communities and the Roma community in Slovenia. The former groups enjoy special representation at the national and local levels, through their recognition as self-governing communities, and the latter have special representation at the local level (Petričušić, 2004). This protection, especially for the former groups, is a little anomalous, as Hungarians only represent 0.4 per cent of the population, and Italians as little as 0.16 per cent. However, they are long-standing historic minorities, and their status can be addressed without the need for controversial engagement with the effects of the break-up of the former SFRY, but rather by reference to the historic continuities from the Austro-Hungarian empire, of which Slovenia was once part. In contrast, no special measures have been taken – other than conceivably the provisions on electoral rights for non-nationals – to protect the status of other ethnic groups from the other former SFRY territories within Slovenia, whether they have national citizenship or not. These groups are rather larger than the autochthonous groups: Croats make up 2.7 per cent of the population, Serbs 2.4 per cent and Bosnians 1.3 per cent.[53]

The initial definition of national citizenship in Slovenia was based in substantial measure on the only reference point which it had as a new state, namely, the 'republican' citizenship which existed within the SFRY (Zorn, 2005; Andreev, 2005). It did not have a legacy citizenship, such as that which existed from a prior period of statehood, which could be used as it was, in the cases of Estonia and Latvia, to define the initial scope of national citizenship, by reference to descent from an historic nation. In addition to those with 'republican' citizenship of Slovenia as a republic within the SFRY, who were presumed to be ethnically Slovenian, it was also possible, for a period of six months after the promulgation of the 1991 Citizenship Act, for others who had been permanent residents of Slovenia, who were actually residing in Slovenia on the day of the independence plebiscite (23 December 1990), to apply to become

---

[53] European Centre on Racism and Intolerance (ECRI), 'Second Report on Slovenia', December 2002, at 16.

Slovenian citizens. Such applications did not require proof of linguistic competence, nor did they set other tests of affiliation. The figures cited by Jelka Zorn (2005: 136) show that 171,000 people (some 8.5 per cent of the population) obtained Slovenian national citizenship by applying during the six-month period up until 26 December 1991, but that about 0.9 per cent of Slovenia's population overall (18,305 people) did not succeed in obtaining Slovenian citizenship either because they did not apply, or because their application was rejected. This group were treated thereafter as foreigners, and their status regulated according to the Aliens Act; this treatment was also given to the war refugees who arrived in Slovenia from this time onwards, who were escaping the conflicts in Croatia, Bosnia and Serbia. However, most controversially for the group of existing residents who became foreigners in their state of residence, in February 1992 they were erased from the Register of Permanent Residents when the Aliens Act began to apply to them, and they were moved to the inactive or dead register, of persons presumed to have died or have emigrated. Consequently, this group came to be known as 'the erased'.

What happened to 'the erased' has been a matter of great controversy within Slovenia since the issue started to come to public attention in the late 1990s, and it reflects both an underlying ethnic definition of citizenship which belied the original approach which appeared to be closer to the 'zero option' of Lithuania than to the ethnic approaches of Latvia or Estonia, and also a worrying element of anti-democratic action, as the measures which were taken with regard to this non-citizen group were undertaken predominantly in secret and without parliamentary scrutiny (Zorn, 2005; Dedić et al., 2000). Furthermore, notwithstanding a constitutional court judgment in 1999,[54] which found that the principles of the rule of law, trust in law and equality were violated by the acts of the state in respect of the erased, no comprehensive changes to the situation of the erased were made. A further 1999 Act on the Regulation of the Status of Citizens of other Successor States of the former SFRY in Slovenia was declared unconstitutional in 2003, not least because it failed to deal with the situation of those who had been deported as a consequence of losing their residence status, and because it did not recognise the underlying illegality of the erasure. The issue has been taken up by bodies such as the Slovenian Helsinki monitor, the Slovenian Human Rights Ombudsman and latterly Amnesty International; negative international

---

[54] U-I-284/94, 4 February 1999, Official Gazette RS, No. 14/99.

attention has included criticisms in the ECRI 2002 report on Slovenia;[55] and from 2003 onwards there was substantial public attention given to the issue. This was partly because the 2003 constitutional court judgment, which sought to draw a line under the issue, in fact touched upon some issues which were highly sensitive for both the Slovenian state and, as it turned out, the wider Slovenian public. The judgment included a list of five points for action:

- The state should make a formal apology and recognise its wrongdoing.
- The state should provide a transparent account of what had actually happened and should identify the lines of political and legal responsibility in that respect.
- There should be unconditional retrospective restoration of status.
- General reparations should be granted to all those affected by way of symbolic compensation.
- In addition, where individuals could show specific loss, they should be able to claim additional damages.

The difficulty was that these fundamentally liberal and rule-of-law oriented precepts encountered a negative response amongst both the majority of politicians and within public opinion. There was a deep resistance to the possibility of paying compensation to individuals who might be former officers of the hated Yugoslav federal army, and perhaps persons who opposed Slovenian independence. Many of the group of erased were also Roma, and it has been suggested that the erasure manoeuvre was intended to prevent them becoming Slovenian citizens (Weissbrod and Collins, 2006: 264). A further 'technical law', which had been put forward by the government to deal with the circumstances of a limited group of the erased, was put to a non-binding referendum at the initiative of a group of nationalist politicians in April 2004. Although most politicians and NGOs urged citizens to boycott the vote, the majority view (95 per cent) of those who did vote (on a turnout of 30 per cent) was that the law, and thus in effect the judgment of the constitutional court, should be rejected, and in effect the erasure was reinforced. The Amnesty International annual report in May 2006 highlighted that, by the end of 2005, approximately 6,000 of the erased still did not have a permanent residence permit or, in the alternative,

---

[55] ECRI Report, above n. 53, at 19–22.

Slovenian citizenship.[56] The case of the erased could not provide a sharper contrast to the case of electoral rights for non-nationals, characterised, as we noted above, as an instance of the Slovenian political elite seeking to position itself at the forefront of European best practice in matters of citizenship and political inclusion. Once again, therefore, as with the cases discussed in Chapter 8, we can see that what at first sight is a policy of inclusion can sometimes be a mask for other policies of exclusion.

V Conclusions

This chapter has concentrated on two sets of cases where new states in Central and Eastern Europe, which acceded to the EU in 2004, have grappled with the intersections between the definition of national citizenship in the post-1989 world, the creation of new minority groups whose treatment has led to scrutiny by international organisations of national state action, and the evolving norms of inclusion which are characterised not only by Article 19 EC but also by the more general, if not yet conclusive, trend towards the extension of local electoral rights to third country nationals. The cases of the Russians (and others) in the Baltic states and the citizens of other republics of the SFRY in Slovenia have posed challenges both to the internal definition of these new polities and the norms which underpin their emerging senses of national identity, and to their search for international acceptability, especially in the form of accession to the European Union.

It is apparent that variety is as evident in relation to these states as it is in relation to the narratives of inclusion and exclusion in the states of the 'old' EU, charted in Chapters 8 and 9. Even within the Baltic area, there is considerable variety. One possible provisional conclusion to be drawn from the very different experiences of Estonia, Latvia and Lithuania is that each of the states has experienced the effects of 'Europeanisation' – the 'return' to Europe comprising the search for, and achievement of, international acceptance through membership of bodies such as NATO and the EU – very much through the prism of its own political identity.

---

[56] See the Amnesty International Annual Report 2006, http://web.amnesty.org/ report2006/svn-summary-eng/; see also Amnesty International Press Release, 'Restore the Rights of the Erased', AI Index, EUR 68/001/2005, 4 March 2005; Amnesty International's Briefing to the UN Committee on Economic, Social and Cultural Rights on Slovenia, 35th Session, November 2005, http://www.amnesty-eu.org/static/ documents/2005/CESCR_briefing_Slovenia_final.pdf.

Moreover, each state has approached the question of Europeanisation by reference to the different domestic constellations of political interests, such as the perceived role of, and threat posed by, minorities, both those who have, and those who have not, acquired national citizenship, as well as the specific interests of domestic political elites, including political parties. These variables account for the differing trajectories of the three states, despite their shared heritages and geopolitical situations.

The 'return to Europe' for Slovenia, formerly part of the Austro-Hungarian empire and historically a borderland state in both geographical and geopolitical terms, has been mediated through its status as much the most stable state to have emerged from the ashes of the SFRY in the 1990s, a state which has been lauded for both its orderly democratic transition and its achievement of economic success. Yet, when the case of the erased came to public attention in the late 1990s, it highlighted deep-seated divisions within society in relation to the SFRY heritage (and indeed older divisions within the South Slav area) which Slovenian success in relation to EU membership and other markers of transition had not wholly effaced. On the one hand, Slovenian legislators were capable of moving Slovenia ostensibly to the front rank of European good practice, extending electoral rights in local elections to third country nationals. At the same time, the state organs have remained complicit in what has been widely condemned, internationally, as a major breach of human rights norms, by effectively denying the personhood of a large group of permanent residents (Zorn, 2005).

PART IV

Conclusions

Conclusions: citizenship and electoral rights in the multi-level 'euro-polity'

During the lengthy period of gestation and preparation of this book, there has been considerable activity at both the national and the EU levels in relation to the use of the criterion of national citizenship as setting the boundaries of the suffrage. Some of the national legislative developments are highlighted briefly below, but in relation to the EU itself, the emphasis has been on the practical application of the Article 19 electoral rights at the national level. Since 1994, there have been no further changes or reforms to the legislative scheme governing the Article 19 electoral rights other than those strictly necessitated by enlargement. However, the body of practice and experience with the operation of these rights has expanded considerably. Three sets of European Parliamentary elections have now taken place under the Article 19 regime, and by 2002 every Member State (then fifteen) had held at least one set of local elections under the equal treatment rules for EU citizens, allowing the Commission to report satisfactory national compliance, at least in principle.[1] As we saw in Chapter 5, however, satisfactory formal compliance does not indicate in itself that the electoral rights for resident EU citizens have become fully part of the political cultures of the Member States.

2004 saw the first phase of eastward enlargement completed, extending the territorial reach of Article 19 from fifteen to twenty-five states, which was then extended to twenty-seven in January 2007 when Bulgaria and Romania joined the Union. Many of these states have also applied the Article 19 rules to local elections since enlargement, although there is no hard evidence as yet of their impact. At the same time enlargement introduced an ambiguous relationship between the legal status of 'EU citizen' and the rights of the citizens of the new

---

[1] 'Report from the Commission to the European Parliament and the Council on the Application of Directive 94/80/EC on the Right to Vote and Stand as a Candidate in Municipal Elections', COM(2002) 260, 30 May 2002.

Member States to take advantage of labour mobility under Article 39 EC. This is because of the reluctance of the majority of the 'old' Member States immediately to open their labour markets to workers from the so-called EU8 states, and later the A2 states of Bulgaria and Romania. This has introduced a paradox into the heart of EU citizenship which will last at least as long as the end of the transitional period (2011), and which challenges the idea of a single legal status linking all nationals of the Member States.

Meanwhile, the *Gibraltar* and *Aruba* cases[2] have provided the first opportunity for the Court of Justice to clarify the nature of the 'right to vote' for the European Parliament. While these cases do not directly discuss the equal treatment rights in Article 19, they nonetheless add some substance to our evolving understanding of European citizenship, in particular its political dimension. Although it did so only indirectly, the Court has given expression in the *Gibraltar* and *Aruba* cases to the notion that there can be a direct, democratic connection between the EU institutions and 'their' citizens. Thus these cases have offered perhaps the first shoots of growth in the development of an autonomous euro-political figure linked both horizontally and vertically to political institutions at various levels, national and European, according to the isopolity/sympolity distinction which was borrowed from Paul Magnette in Chapters 1 and 2 of this book (Magnette, 2005).

In *Gibraltar*, the Court confirmed that, if the right to vote for the European Parliament is indeed a right attaching to European citizenship (which it did not say explicitly, but which it implied was the case), then it is not an *exclusive* right but one which the Member States may also, provided they act otherwise in compliance with EU law, confer upon nationals of third countries. This would be the case, in particular, if a Member State such as the UK, which has certain constitutional traditions in relation to the boundaries of the suffrage, chooses to apply those traditions in relation to European Parliament elections. However, this case seems to have limited implications for what the EU and its institutions could themselves do in relation to developing the potentially fuzzy outer boundaries of EU citizenship rights, because it seems to confirm that it is the Member States which are at liberty to confer these rights upon third country nationals as well as EU citizens.

---

[2] Case C-145/04 *Spain* v. *United Kingdom (Gibraltar)*, 12 September 2006; Case C-300/04 *Eman and Sevinger* v. *Het College van Burgemeester en Wethouders van Den Haag (Aruba)*, 12 September 2006.

But Member States are not under a duty to confer any such rights. At best, the possibility of the rights being extended may free up the space for political campaigns at the national level to be mounted which seek the extension of the electoral rights given to resident EU citizens in European Parliament elections also to third country nationals.

Aruba is potentially the more far-reaching of the two cases, because it opens the way for the Court of Justice to scrutinise more closely the inner workings of EU citizenship *within* the Member States, albeit so far in relation only to the operation of a specific EU institution, namely, the European Parliament and its elections. It confirmed the general applicability of principles upheld in the ECHR regarding the nature of direct universal suffrage as the basis for elections to democratic representative institutions. It confirmed, again implicitly, that nationals of the Member States have the right in principle to vote in European Parliament elections, although this is not an unconditional or absolute right. Member States may make certain choices, for example in relation to the place of residence of their nationals. But Member States are not completely free to assign the right to vote to different groups of nationals as they wish. EU citizens enjoy the protection of the general principle of equal treatment, which is part of the general principles of EU law, as well as, presumably, the various rights in relation to democratic participation and universal suffrage conferred by the ECHR. They enjoy that protection *within* the Member States, as *EU citizens*. Previously, in all circumstances where the Court of Justice has conferred the protections offered by EU law in a wholly internal situation (for example, where a Member State has been in breach of an EU law or directive), it has done so not because the complainants were EU citizens, but because they were *subjects of law*. This would be the situation where a case is brought before a national court claiming breach by a Member State of directly effective rights conferred by a Treaty provision or a directive in a field such as equal pay, or health and safety. In respect of the enjoyment of such rights, there is no citizenship qualification.

The implications of the *Aruba* case for European citizenship in general may prove to be just as important as the judicial developments in relation to Articles 17 and 18 EC charted in Chapter 2, which have seen the Court of Justice gradually dissolving the need for a market link to be established before the mobile EU citizen can take advantage of his or her right to non-discrimination. Increasingly, it would seem that Advocate

General Jacobs' words in *Konstantinides*[3] are proving to be prescient forerunners of the current situation, and they can now even be edited down to remove any reference to economic activity and to refer to the Union and to citizenship of the Union instead of the nationality of the Member States. Thus we can say that:

> a [Union citizen] who goes to another Member State ... [is] ... entitled to assume that, wherever he goes ... in the European [Union], he will be treated in accordance with a common code of fundamental values, in particular those laid down in the European Convention on Human Rights. In other words, he is entitled to say 'civis europeus sum' and to invoke that status in order to oppose any violation of his fundamental rights.

Perhaps, if this claim is becoming true, the EU will also in due course see the affirmation of another bold normative claim, this time made by the European Commission in the 1970s, namely, that the 'complete assimilation with nationals as regards political rights is desirable in the long term from the point of view of a European Union'.[4] Some comments on this question will be developed below.

Turning now to electoral rights developments at the national level, it is worthy of comment that half of the ten Member States which acceded in 2004 have since 1992 introduced electoral rights for third country nationals (Estonia, Hungary, Lithuania, Slovakia and Slovenia), in most cases in circumstances broadly linked to the processes of state-building and transition after the break-up of multinational states and empires, which were themselves necessary precursors to accession to the EU. In contrast to the development of electoral rights for third country nationals in most of the old Member States, however, some of these changes have had more to do with resident minorities than they have with processes of and consequences of migration and mobility. Slovenia is, perhaps, an example of a new Member State wanting, with its electoral rights legislation, to put itself in the first rank of 'European' good practice.

Within the Member States whose membership pre-dates 2004, numerous important developments have occurred. In these cases, the developments have been connected above all to the issue of immigration and the integration of immigrants, and to the ongoing debate about whether the allocation of political rights should be a reward to

---

[3] Case C-168/91 *Konstantinides* v. *Stadt Altensteig* [1993] ECR I-1191 at 1211.
[4] Bull. EC Supp. 7/75, point 3.1.

non-nationals for integration already achieved, or an incentive on the pathway towards greater integration. Belgium (after lengthy debate) and Luxembourg (although not the right to stand) have each instituted electoral rights for all third country nationals satisfying certain residence conditions, and held local elections in which they have been applied. Ireland has seen its long-standing provisions brought into the political spotlight at the 2004 local elections, with a number of non-national candidates being elected for the first time at the town council level, and with much greater political salience being given to the right to vote. Austria, France, Germany, Italy and Spain have all seen active political contestation over electoral rights, especially between 'national' and 'subnational' units of government. However, in none of the latter five cases has there so far been concrete legislative developments (beyond the very limited rights which exist in Spain for Norwegian citizens).

These new developments are important additions to the regimes of comprehensive and rather well-established electoral local rights for third country nationals which already existed in Denmark, Finland, the Netherlands and Sweden, and the partial, reciprocity-based, electoral rights in Portugal. These states have seen no policy or legislative change although in some cases, such as Denmark and the Netherlands, an increasingly problematic national politics concerned with immigration, integration and ethnic minority and religious issues has spilled over into hostility regarding the political participation rights of immigrants and their descendants (whether those with or without national citizenship) from some quarters. In both states, radical-right parties are receiving a substantial share of the vote in elections, as indeed they are in Belgium and Austria. One exception to the generally positive trend in relation to third country national electoral rights is Greece, where there is a much weaker institutional strategy for the integration of immigrants than in most other Member States (Kasimis and Kassimi, 2004; Apostolatou, n.d.). Meanwhile, in the UK, where there exists the EU's most peculiar patchwork of voting and standing rights for non-nationals, the debate about the political participation of non-nationals has, in contrast to many of the cases mentioned above, been noticeably absent in recent years. There has been debate about immigration and integration issues, but it has concentrated on the questions associated with radical Islam and the terrorist attacks of 7 July 2005, with the future of what is postulated as the UK's multicultural model being brought into question. In addition, substantial political and media attention has been directed towards the question of intra-EU mobility from the states of Central and Eastern Europe since enlargement in 2004. The absence of a wider debate on the boundaries of an already fuzzy suffrage in the UK is somewhat ironic, in view of the general salience of issues of immigration and belonging in the UK at the present time.

Indeed, the UK case reminds us that debate about citizenship can often reveal simultaneously what appear to be conflicting impulses. For example, what should we make of the almost simultaneous appearance of initiatives which reassert the *national* content of the citizenship concept, for example in the form of ever stricter integration tests for immigrants and non-nationals (both at the point of first entry into the host state and later at the point of national citizenship acquisition), and other developments which stress the blurred and fuzzy edges of belonging, such as new electoral rights for *non-nationals* conferred in states such as Belgium and Luxembourg? Is this a case of political incoherence, or of the Janus-faced nature of the citizenship figure, which can simultaneously both exclude and include the outsider?

Furthermore, the national and EU levels have not proceeded on two separate and diverging tracks. On the contrary, there are frequently synergies or elements of overlap between developments which occur at the two levels. Obvious points of contact were seen in Chapters 6 and 7, which explored the nature of the (citizens') right to vote for the European Parliament, the case for extending electoral rights in national elections to EU citizens, and the case for pushing out the boundaries of the personal scope of EU local electoral rights by bringing in third country nationals. It is perhaps in deference to these evident and evolving relationships between EU citizenship and national citizenship, which go beyond the text of the existing EC Treaty which calls the former merely *complementary* to the latter (Article 17(1) EC), that a notion of 'dual citizenship' is sometimes mooted as the best way to describe the relationship between EU citizenship and national citizenship. For example, in an October 2002 Praesidium draft of the introductory articles of what eventually became the Constitutional Treaty, signed by the Member States in October 2004, the *dual* rather than *complementary* nature of EU citizenship and national citizenship was cited.[5] However, by the time this text had been more fully fleshed out ready for discussion in the plenary of the Convention on the Future of Europe in February 2003, the section on citizenship had already

---

[5] CONV 369/02 of 28 October 2002, Article 5.

reverted to a version which essentially repeated the text of provisions of the EC Treaty.[6]

In some respects, in addressing issues of immigration, nationality and citizenship, this book has joined a crowded field. There has been a good deal of scholarly attention of a philosophical or theoretical nature to the question of electoral rights for non-nationals over recent years, in some cases linking the issue to that of electoral rights for expatriates as well, and the more general question of the transnational political activities of immigrants and non-nationals (Bauböck, 2005; Carens, 2005; Dobson, 2006; López-Guerra, 2005; Rubio-Marín, 2000). Other work has asked more analytical questions about the behaviour of states and why they might choose (or refuse) to adjust the boundaries of the suffrage (Beckmann, 2006; Earnest, 2006), and some work has collected substantial empirical evidence in the field about the huge variety of different national practices (Waldrauch, 2005). Furthermore, in an area where it is equally important to track changes in the boundaries of national citizenship itself (i.e. processes of acquisition and loss), there has been important new work in this field, including on questions of dual nationality (Bauböck *et al.*, 2006a and 2006b; Howard, 2005; Hansen and Weil, 2002). This work on the legal boundaries of citizenship has been matched by a continuing trend within much social sciences and humanities scholarship to use 'the citizen' and citizenship as a prism of analysis for many aspects of the human condition. To that end, Chapter 2 sought to review the main lines of thinking which challenge the (nationally) bounded nature of citizenship, whether by focusing on questions about the citizenship of aliens (Bosniak, 2006) or by questioning whether citizenship can take on (or has taken on) either transnational or postnational characteristics (Fox, 2005; Tambini, 2001).

However, what has been lacking thus far in the literature has been a focus on the issues which are raised by the EU's involvement in the issue of electoral rights for non-nationals, and the complex interactions which are developing within the EU's multi-level constitutional framework between the national and the EU levels. There has been important new work looking at Union citizenship generally, particularly from the perspective of the case law of the Court of Justice which has been rather activist over recent years (Dougan, 2006; Kostakopoulou, 2005; Mather, 2005; Reich 2001 and 2005) or from the perspective of enlargement (Adinolfi, 2005; Carrera, 2005a; Kochenov, 2006). Commentators appear confident that, at least as regards the relationships pertaining to the

---

[6] CONV 528/03, 16 February 2003 (Articles 1–16), Article 7.

citizens of the 'old' Member States, the EU has gone beyond the stage of 'market citizenship'. They appear less confident about what has replaced market citizenship. In contrast, since the first inception of EU citizenship and the Article 19 electoral rights in the mid-1990s, at which point the innovation of equal treatment in relation to electoral rights did receive a good deal of legal scholarly attention (Lardy, 1996; O'Leary, 1996; Oliver, 1996), there have been very few attempts to provide a comprehensive interpretation of what the theory and practice of EU electoral rights might mean, especially when it is placed against the backdrop of national developments as well as the constitutional development of the Union itself.

The ambitions of this book in that respect have been limited, even if it has ranged across a rather broad range of legal and political material. In the tradition of constitutional ethnography (Scheppele, 2004), I have looked at the fixing and the shifting of the boundaries of the suffrage in the EU and its Member States, not in order to explain variations between national systems, but in order to excavate the key themes in relation to institutional change, in a manner which emphasises the interactions between the different levels and units of government in the 'euro-polity'. I take the 'euro-polity' to be the complex sum of the twenty-seven national polities of the Member States, plus the EU itself as a legal, constitutional and political order, each overlapping and intersecting with the others. Throughout the book, I have sought to emphasise the different ways in which citizens are citizens of multiple units of government, at different times, in different places, and under different conditions. The concepts of postnational and transnational citizenship are useful in this respect, but what is most important is to focus on the specifics of institutional change rather than what are essentially normative or ideological terms. But the patterns and themes revealed by the investigation do bring into play many conflicting ideas which are constantly debated between political and legal actors when they look at the polities which make up the EU. More specifically, the book seeks to demonstrate that debates about the boundaries of the suffrage can in turn generate arguments about the limits of legitimate political order within these multiple overlapping polities.

It is hard to summarise the findings of this book, and the project upon which it reports, in a short conclusion. All seven empirical chapters have shown that 'progress' towards electoral inclusion is by no means unilinear, whether in the context of the EU or at the national level, and whether in relation to EU citizens or third country nationals. Moreover, it should never be assumed that constitutional or legislative changes to extend the boundaries of the suffrage to categories of persons who lack national citizenship will be irreversible. The case of the United States, which once had rather extensive alien suffrage rules, is illustrative of this possibility (Varsanyi, 2005). In Chapter 3, I argued that, in order to understand better the ideas and practices which shape the boundaries of the suffrage, it was important to look at the incremental institutional changes which take place around the notion of polity membership, as well as the related debates and contestations which frame these changes. But the granting of political rights hardly conforms to a single model. Although political rights can be made contingent upon both immigration status and nationality in some cases, in other cases they are accorded on a more universal basis to non-nationals so long as they have settled residence. It is clear that, whatever the national diversity of such laws, the complex textures and practices of immigration and nationality laws, and related fields such as legal protection for ethnic and other minorities, are probably the most important elements structuring the contestation of political rights for non-nationals, whether these are granted or denied by national law. Moreover, despite some evidence of convergence in relation to the practice of giving local electoral rights to non-nationals, both within and beyond the EU, there is no substantial evidence of convergence across national systems in relation to other issues of citizenship status, such as citizenship acquisition. Furthermore, there may be significant differences between mobility as it occurs in the EU context, other forms of international labour migration, and the wide range of other types of voluntary and forced migration which appear increasingly common in a globalised world. Other factors shown to be most relevant to the inclusion/exclusion dynamic at the national level have included issues related to the organisation of local elections and local democracy, the role of political parties and other voluntary associations, and the interface with other political participation rights which might accrue to migrants and minorities in a transnational and a domestic context.

Rather than simply repeat the complex conclusions drawn out of the many issues discussed and analysed in the seven empirical chapters, the rest of this concluding chapter will seek to bring out some of the themes which cut across the chapters, and which link together cases of electoral inclusion or exclusion that one might not initially have expected to find linked together. At the end of the chapter I shall then turn to the question posed in Chapter 3 about the judgment of the types of changes which have been charted throughout this book: at what point and in what manner would it be correct to say that citizenship has been transformed within the contemporary euro-polity?

A number of chapters have addressed the uneasy climate surrounding questions of immigration and integration at the present time. While migration issues are not the only ones which impact upon the evolution of citizenship at the present time (whether that relates to issues of first entry into the state, integration and assimilation of non-nationals, or acquisition of host-country nationality, as well as emigration which remains an important question for the new post-2004 Member States of the European Union), they remain rather dominant across the EU, in national and official EU discourse. All of the Member States, without exception, are facing demographic issues relating to an ageing workforce, and, while immigration is often postulated by scholars and some political actors as one possible response to demographic issues, it is evident that where immigration issues are handled badly there can quickly be slippage, especially in media coverage, into xenophobia and racism. There is an insistence in many 'old' Member States on treating the issues relating to labour mobility involving the 'new' Member States as questions of immigration, to be dealt with in the same way as other forms of international migration with a focus on repressive rather than facilitative mechanisms, rather than as what it is: mobility structured and regulated by EU law within an area of political and economic integration. In that domain too, in the haste to generate sensationalist headlines which justify repressive measures even against other EU citizens (such as a proposal to create new criminal offences involving on-the-spot fines to be imposed on Romanian and Bulgarian workers found working in the UK), political actors often forget to draw a distinction between stocks and flows of migration. If there is evidence that 600,000 new Member State citizens have been in the UK at one time, then that is wrongly treated by many commentators as the basis for the proposition that there are still that number of persons present. It is easy to play upon popular fears of the unknown, and of strangers, with such headlines.

In relation to questions of political participation, it is clear that the right to vote in local elections is treated, for EU citizens under EU law, not as a reward for integration, but as a mechanism which is central to protecting the equal treatment rights which they enjoy. Yet there is no generalised willingness amongst political forces in the Member States at the national level to apply the same logic to third country nationals. For such groups of non-nationals, the argument is commonly made that denying electoral rights of all kinds will in fact encourage the third country nationals to assimilate (rather than simply making them feel excluded), and will thus give them the requisite incentives to acquire national citizenship through naturalisation. Yet migrants from third countries are surely in the same position with regard to the host country political institutions as are those who exercise free movement rights under EU law, and there seems little logic in treating them quite so differently, whether in law or in political discourse. Moreover, while little account is taken in political discourse of whether EU citizens resident in other Member States participate politically or not (most of them do not), third country nationals seem 'damned if they do, and damned if they do not'. That is to say, the failure to exercise whatever political voice they may have, or to assimilate, integrate and naturalise in order to gain a formal political voice, leads to many third country national communities in the Member States being condemned for creating closed societies, which pay little account to the host political environment, if it is not for the purpose of attacking its very integrity, whether by advocating Sharia law or failing to prevent members of the community turning to political violence and acts of terrorism. Equally, where groups can and do engage politically, this too can be found problematic unless the ideas which are advocated are immediately acceptable to the host state; individuals who seek to participate politically often face unwarranted hostility and discrimination.

But migration, as such, has not been the only theme which has emerged strongly in this book. The cases in Central and Eastern Europe examined in Chapter 10 expose the close interactions between processes of democratisation and consolidation in what are now Member States of the EU and the setting of the boundaries of the suffrage. It is interesting to reflect whether there may be a connection to be drawn between the challenge of setting the boundaries of the suffrage for new political institutions in those states, and the challenges of setting the boundaries of the suffrage for a relatively new political institution in the EU context, namely, the European Parliament. What parallels may be drawn between the two processes of (still unfinished) democratisation?

Furthermore, it is interesting to see how the question of the political participation of non-nationals can bring out contestation within polities, not only between competing political forces and parties of the left and the right, or of a more cosmopolitan or communitarian inclination, but also between governmental institutions at different levels of the state, or located in different parts of the state. In some cases, a political climate in favour of greater electoral inclusion in a particular part of one Member State, which has been unable to prevail at the national level, seeks an outlet through local initiatives, including autonomous attempts (thus far always thwarted) to confer limited electoral rights upon disenfranchised groups of non-nationals. If the political and economic case can be made that certain migration issues are best dealt with at the subnational level, allowing tailored responses to be developed to situation-specific economic needs or cultural awareness (e.g. to co-ethnics from another neighbouring state), then it might make sense that the power of the state to define the suffrage at the national level should be disaggregated and decentralised in like manner.

Before moving to consider the issue of the transformation of citizenship, we should pause for a moment to consider where developments might occur in the future at the EU or the national level. It certainly seems probable that, in the years to come, some further Member States will enact electoral rights for some or all third country nationals, overcoming as necessary the types of constitutional and political obstacles which were discussed in Chapter 9. Of course, other Member States may choose not to adopt electoral rights for non-nationals, or may choose to reverse their existing measures. The possibility of such changes occurring seems to depend upon the constellations of political forces holding power in the states where the issue is under consideration, but is also bound to continue to be affected by the diffuse effects of EU law, including experiences at the local level with the Article 19(1) electoral rights to vote in municipal elections. One of the paradoxes of political developments regarding electoral rights is that the argument can most easily be made in favour of extending the boundaries of the suffrage on the basis that the suffrage in question does not matter. Thus a national government which is largely indifferent to the question of local government could be the one most susceptible to an argument in favour of extension. The point is borne out by the case of Luxembourg and the two EU electoral rights directives, as its insistence on maintaining derogations in its favour, in the form of insisting on longer qualifying residence periods by Community voters, is justified precisely on the basis that it hosts a larger proportion of EU citizens within its territory.

But can we expect to see any further developments in the electoral domain at the EU level? Given the generally 'forward' logic of European integration, it seems safe to assume that, unless the European Union as it presently exists unravels completely (which is not completely inconceivable given recent developments and the continuing challenge of enlargement), the current tranche of rights under Article 19 will not be reversed. The possibility of further developments was canvassed in Chapter 6 with regard to national electoral rights for EU citizens, and in Chapter 7 with regard to local electoral rights for third country nationals. As to the latter, it is worth recalling that it took nearly thirty years from the inception of the original ideas and proposals, in the European Parliament and amongst some commentators, for local electoral rights for EU citizens to become a reality in the Treaty of Maastricht. The same logic of a gradual shift from soft law to hard law may apply to the case of third country nationals, as the EU gradually, but perhaps inexorably, moves onto the terrain of regulating the status of third country nationals within the Member States, as one dimension of the task of developing an area of freedom, security and justice. However, just as there was a 'tipping point' in relation to the debate on electoral rights for EU citizens in the 1980s, which saw the Commission shift its position from being rather neutral about local electoral rights for nationals of the Member States to being firmly in favour, so a similar tipping point would have to occur for third country nationals to attract the necessary constellation of political forces in favour of change.

As to the former question of EU citizens' rights, it is not improbable that the Commission may present a proposal under Article 22 EC, based on the reports which it has compiled over the years which show some pressure for EU citizens' rights to be developed further, not least because this would be part of a longer-term strategy on the part of the Commission to place this issue on the agenda. In practice, such a proposal is not likely to be accepted with the requisite unanimity amongst the Member States in the Council of Ministers in the near future. These types of truncated Treaty amendment procedures, which avoid the need for a full-blown intergovernmental conference, have very rarely been used throughout the history of European integration, except where they have applied to institutional matters, rather than to substantive competences. In truth, revisions of the scope of the competences conferred upon the Union under the Treaties, whether concerning citizenship or any other topic, have always occurred via the full intergovernmental conference process where, even if there have been relatively narrow agendas (for example, the Single European Act or the Treaty of Nice), the Member States have had at least some scope to trade their interests off against those of their partners in order to reach a compromise acceptable to all parties. Such an intergovernmental conference seems likely to occur in the wake of the failure of the Constitutional Treaty, for the purposes of limited institutional change, but the Member States are most likely to avoid sensitive issues of national sovereignty which could arouse hostility to ratification at the national level, or increase the likelihood that a referendum on ratification has to be called. Electoral rights, and the question of citizenship generally, would fall into this type of 'red line' category. Furthermore, limited electoral rights have been enacted for EU citizens even though the Member States have never removed from the Treaties the residual national sovereignty controls they insist on maintaining in relation to the free movement of EU citizens, relating to expulsion on public security, public policy and public health grounds (e.g. Article 39(3) EC) and relating to employment or the provision of services in the public sector (Articles 39(4) and 45 EC). Even EU citizens enjoying the right of permanent residence can still be expelled from the host state, if only on 'serious grounds of public policy and public security'.[7] To that extent, as in the sphere of political rights, permanent residence as defined in Directive 2004/38/EC does not amount to a form of *ersatz* citizenship, but is – at best – a 'citizenship-of-residence-lite', with distinct limitations.

However, it would be foolish to predict that the EU will never see the development of greater electoral rights for EU citizens. Perhaps there will be a new initiative in the future which carries both the rhetorical force and engenders the same practical support as the market-making and political union initiatives of the late 1980s and early 1990s. In the shorter term, however, any developments would be most likely to stem from the national level, whether in the form of unilateral action, such as that taken in 1984 by Ireland to enfranchise UK citizens and to create a gateway to enfranchise EU citizens, or in the form of the type of laboratory for developing mutual trust and understanding through an international agreement outwith the scope of the Union, suggested in Chapter 6. Such initiatives can contribute to the further development of Union citizenship, albeit indirectly (Shaw, 2007).

In Chapter 4, I suggested that observing the evolution of the EU electoral rights showed how this case could be treated as a microcosm of the EU as a whole. That is, the variables at play and the forces which came into conflict with each other, over a period of years, are much the same as those which have shaped the successes and failures of the European integration process more generally over fifty years or more. As

---

[7] Directive 2004/38/EC on citizens' free movement rights, OJ 2004 L158/77, Article 28(3).

regards the issue of citizenship, we remain far from any certain answers about what either citizenship of the Union now is, what value-added it gives, or what it might become in the future. Clearly, the evolution of citizenship depends upon the trajectory of the EU more generally, and the situation in the mid-2000s, especially with regard to the so-called 'Future of Europe' process which saw the negotiation of the now-stalled Constitutional Treaty, calls for caution in this respect. Furthermore, speaking of citizenship more generally, we cannot always be confident of the resilience of either the concept, or of all of the practices which underpin it. At some points, citizenship appears vibrant, an effective framework for giving expression to all manner of claims. At other points, it appears in crisis, as participation in elections declines in more or less all states and at all levels of government.

But what we can say with certainty is this. Despite the differences between the two types of 'citizenship' and the uncertainties as to meaning, citizenship of the Union and national citizenship now co-exist in the complex multi-level euro-polity. Each contributes, in different ways, to the process of polity-building. Citizenship in both the national and the EU cases is rhetorically and symbolically connected to the project of polity-building (Shaw, 2007). Each is also changing, sometimes in subtle ways, and sometimes more dramatically. Some of those changes result from points of contact, overlap or friction between the national and the EU levels. Some occur autonomously (or apparently autonomously). Citizenship as a whole is a political and legal figure in a process of transformation, a transformation which is reflected in a rich scholarly literature which can sometimes be criticised for attempting to see all social, political and legal phenomena through the prism of citizenship, when at times other tools such as equality or justice may be more useful as frames of analysis. However, in the field of electoral rights for nonnationals, which has been the central focus of this book, there can be little doubt that the practices and institutions of citizenship, if not necessarily all of the symbolic aspects of citizenship such as identity and belonging, have been decisively re-shaped by the progress of European integration.

BIBLIOGRAPHY

Adinolfi, A. (2005) 'Free Movement and Access to Work of Citizens of the New Member States: The Transitional Measures', 42 *Common Market Law Review* 469–98.

Aleinikoff, T. and Klusmeyer, D. (2001a) 'Plural Nationality: Facing the Future in a Migratory World', in Aleinikoff and Klusmeyer, 2001b, 63–88.

(eds.) (2001b) *Citizenship Today: Global Perspectives and Practices*, Washington, DC: Carnegie Endowment for International Peace.

Ambrosio, T. (2002) 'Vanquishing the Ghost of Trianon: Preventing Hungarian Irredentism through Western Integration', 3 *Seton Hall Journal of Diplomacy and International Relations* 39–52.

Anderson, M., den Boer, M. and Miller, G. (1994) 'European Citizenship and Cooperation in Justice and Home Affairs', in A. Duff, J. Pinder and R. Pryce (eds.), *Maastricht and Beyond: Building the European Union*, London: Routledge, 104–22.

Andreev, S. (2003) 'Making Slovenian Citizens: The Problem of the Former Yugoslav Citizens and Asylum Seekers Living in Slovenia', 4 *Southeast European Politics* 1–24.

(2005) 'Active Civic Participation of Immigrants in Slovenia', Country Report prepared for the European research project POLITIS, Oldenburg, 2005, www.uni-oldenburg.de/politis-europe/.

Anil, M. (2005) 'No More Foreigners? The Remaking of German Naturalization and Citizenship Law, 1990–2000', 29 *Dialectical Anthropology* 453–70.

Apostolatou, K. (n.d.) 'Immigrant and Immigration Policy-Making: A Review of the Literature of the Greek Case', IMISCOE Working Paper: Country Report, www.imiscoe.org.

Arena, M., Nascimbene, B. and Zincone, G. (2006) 'Italy', in Bauböck *et al.*, 2006b, 328–66.

Arendt, H. (1973) *The Origins of Totalitarianism*, San Diego: Harcourt-Brace-Jovanovich.

Aron, R. (1974) 'Is Multinational Citizenship Possible?', 41 *Social Research* 638–56.

Bańkowski, Z. and Christodoulidis, E. (1999) 'Citizenship Bound and Citizenship Unbound', in K. Hutchings and R. Dannreuther (eds.), *Cosmopolitan Citizenship*, Basingstoke: Macmillan, 83–104.

Bańkowski, Z. and Scott, A. (eds.) (2000) *The European Union and Its Order: The Legal Theory of European Integration*, Oxford: Blackwell.

Barbieri, W. (1998) *Ethics of Citizenship: Immigration and Group Rights in Germany*, Durham/London: Duke University Press.

Bast, J. (2006) 'The Legal Position of Migrants – German Report', report presented to the XVIIth International Congress on Comparative Law, Utrecht, 16–22 July 2006.

Bauböck, R. (1994a) 'Changing the Boundaries of Citizenship: The Inclusion of Immigrants in Democratic Polities', in R. Bauböck (ed.), *From Aliens to Citizens: Redefining the Status of Immigrants in Europe*, Avebury/European Centre Vienna, Aldershot, etc., 1994, 199–232.

(1994b) *Transnational Citizenship: Membership and Rights in International Migration*, Aldershot: Edward Elgar.

(2003) 'Reinventing Urban Citizenship', 7 *Citizenship Studies* 139–60.

(2005) 'Expansive Citizenship – Voting beyond Territory and Membership', *PS Online* 763–7.

Bauböck, R. and Çinar, D. (2001) 'Nationality Law and Naturalisation in Austria', in Hansen and Weil, 2001, 255–72.

Bauböck, R., Ersbøll, E., Groenendijk, K. and Waldrauch, H. (eds.) (2006a) *Acquisition and Loss of Nationality: Policies and Trends in 15 European States*, vol. 1, *Comparative Analyses*, Amsterdam: Amsterdam University Press.

(eds.) (2006b) *Acquisition and Loss of Nationality: Policies and Trends in 15 European States*, vol. II, *Country Analyses*, Amsterdam: Amsterdam University Press.

(2006c) 'Introduction', in Bauböck *et al.*, 2006a, 15–34.

Barry, K. (2006) 'Home and Away: The Construction of Citizenship in an Emigration Context', 81 *New York University Law Review* 11–59.

Béaud, O. (1992) 'Le droit de vote des étrangers: l'apport de la jurisprudence constitutionnelle allemande à une théorie du droit de suffrage', *Revue française de droit administratif* 409–24.

Becker, F. (2003) 'The Decision of the German Constitutional Court on the Immigration Act', 4 *German Law Journal* 91–106.

Beckmann, L. (2006) 'Citizenship and Voting Rights: Should Resident Aliens Vote?', 10 *Citizenship Studies* 153–65.

Bell, M. (2007) 'Civic Citizenship and Migrant Integration', 13 *European Public Law*, 311–33.

Bellamy, R. (2001) 'The "Right to Have Rights": Citizenship Practice and the Political Constitution of the EU', in Bellamy and Warleigh, 2001, 41–70.

Bellamy, R., Castiglione, D. and Shaw, J. (eds.) (2006) *Making European Citizens*, Basingstoke: Palgrave.

Bellamy, R. and Warleigh, A. (eds.) (2001) *Citizenship and Governance in the European Union*, London: Continuum.

Bencini, C. and Cerretelli, S. (2005) *Racism in Italy*, ENAR Shadow Report, 2005.

Benhabib, S. (2004) *The Rights of Others*, Cambridge: Cambridge University Press.

Berg, E. and Ehin, P. (2006) 'What Kind of Border Regime Is in the Making?', 41 *Cooperation and Conflict* 53–71.

Bergh, J. and Bjørklund, T. (2003) 'The Political Representation of Immigrants in Oslo and Copenhagen: A Study of Electoral Systems and Voting Behavior', in G. Brochmann (ed.), *The Multicultural Challenge: Comparative Social Research 22*, Oxford: Elsevier Science, 2003, 102–22.

van den Berghe, G. (1979) 'Direct Elections in Accordance with a Uniform Procedure', 4 *European Law Review* 331–40.

Besch, S. (2004) 'Les candidates portugais aux élections locales luxembourgeoises', *Cahiers de l'Urmis*, No. 9, February, 77–87.

Bidegaray, C. and Strudel, S. (2002) 'De la Citoyenneté et autres Cocquecigrues: Remarques sur la participation des citoyens de l'Union Européenne aux élections municipales françaises de mars 2001', *Annuaire Français de Relations Internationales*, Brussels: Bruylant, 424–31.

Blais, A., Massicotte, L. and Yoshinaka, A. (2001) 'Deciding Who Has the Right to Vote: A Comparative Analysis of Election Laws', 20 *Electoral Studies* 41–62.

Böhning, W. (1972) *The Migration of Workers in the United Kingdom and the European Community*, New York, Toronto and London: Oxford University Press for the Institute of Race Relations, London.

   (1973) 'The Scope of the EEC System of Free Movement for Workers: A Rejoinder', 10 *Common Market Law Review* 81–4.

Bosniak, L. (1994) 'Membership, Equality and the Difference That Alienage Makes', 69 *New York University Law Review* 1047–149.

   (2000a) 'Universal Citizenship and the Problem of Alienage', 94 *Northwestern University Law Review* 963–84.

   (2000b) 'Citizenship Denationalized', 7 *Indiana Journal of Global Legal Studies* 447–509.

   (2002) 'Constitutional Citizenship through the Prism of Alienage', 53 *Ohio State Law Review* 1285–324.

   (2003) 'Citizenship', in P. Cane and M. Tushnet (eds.), *The Oxford Handbook of Legal Studies*, Oxford: Oxford University Press, 183–201.

   (2006) *The Citizen and the Alien*, Princeton, NJ: Princeton University Press.

Bostock, D. (2002) 'COREPER Revisited', 40 *Journal of Common Market Studies* 215–34.

Boswell, C. (2000) 'European Values and the Asylum Crisis', 76 *International Affairs* 537–57.

(2001) *Spreading the Costs of Asylum: A Critical Analysis of Dispersal Policies in the UK and Germany*, Anglo-German Foundation Report 1314, London and Berlin, June 2001.

(2007) 'Theorizing Migration Policy: Is There a Third Way?', 41 *International Migration Review* 75–100.

British Council Brussels, Foreign Policy Centre and Migration Policy Group (2005) *European Civic Citizenship and Inclusion Index*, British Council: Brussels.

Brubaker, R. (1992) *Citizenship and Nationhood in France and Germany*, Cambridge, MA: Harvard University Press.

(1996) *Nationalism Reframed: Nationhood and the National Question in the New Europe*, Cambridge: Cambridge University Press.

Burkholz, B. (1995) 'Teilnahme von Unionsbürgern an kommunalen Bürgerentscheiden?', *Die Öffentliche Verwaltung* 816–19.

Carens, J. (2000) *Culture, Citizenship and Community*, Oxford: Oxford University Press.

(2002) 'Citizenship and Civil Society: What Rights for Residents?', in Hansen and Weil, 2002, 100–18.

(2005) 'The Integration of Immigrants', 2 *Journal of Moral Philosophy* 29–46.

Carrera, S. (2005a) 'What Does Free Movement Mean in Theory and Practice in an Enlarged EU?', 11 *European Law Journal* 699–721.

(2005b) '"Integration" as a Process of Inclusion for Migrants? The Case of Long-Term Residents in the EU', CEPS Working Document, No. 219, March 2005.

(ed.) (2006a) *The Nexus between Immigration, Integration and Citizenship in the EU*, Challenge Liberty and Security, Collective Conference Volume, April 2006.

(2006b) 'A Comparison of Integration Programmes in the EU: Trends and Weaknesses', CHALLENGE Papers, No. 1, March 2006.

Castles, S. (2005) 'Hierarchical Citizenship in a World of Unequal Nation-States', 38 *PS Online* 689–92.

Chan, K. (2004) 'Central and Eastern Europe in the 2004 European Parliament Elections: A Not So European Event', SEI Working Paper No. 81, EPERN Working Paper No. 16, November 2004, http://www.sussex.ac.uk/sei/documents/wp81.pdf.

Chinn, J. and Truex, L. (1996) 'The Question of Citizenship in the Baltics', 7 *Journal of Democracy* 133–47.

Çinar, D. and Waldrauch, H. (2006) 'Austria', in Bauböck *et al.*, 2006b, 19–61.

Cole, D. (2006) 'The Idea of Humanity: Human Rights and Immigrants' Rights', 37 *Columbia Human Rights Review* 627–58.

Connolly, A. (2003) 'The Theory and Practice of Alien Suffrage in the European Union', unpublished PhD dissertation, University of Manchester.

Connolly, A., Day. S. and Shaw, J. (2006) 'Alien Suffrage in the European Union: Contested and Incomplete?', in Bellamy, Castiglione and Shaw, 2006, 31–55.

Connolly, W. (1993) *The Terms of Political Discourse*, 3rd edn, Princeton, NJ: Princeton University Press.

Dauvergne, C. (2004) 'Sovereignty, Migration and the Rule of Law in Global Times', 67 *Modern Law Review* 588–615.

Davies, N. (1997) *Europe: A History*, London: Pimlico.

Davy, U. (2005) 'Integration of Immigrants in Germany: A Slowly Evolving Concept', 7 *European Journal of Migration and Law* 123–44.

Day, S. and Shaw, J. (2002) 'EU Electoral Rights and the Political Participation of Migrants in Host Polities', 8 *International Journal of Population Geography* 183–99.

(2003) 'The Boundaries of Suffrage and External Conditionality: Estonia as an Applicant Member State of the EU', 9 *European Public Law* 211–36.

(2006) 'Transnational Political Parties', in Bellamy, Castiglione and Shaw, 2006, 99–117.

Dedić, J., Jalušič, V. and Zorn, J. (2000) *The Erased: Organized Innocence and the Politics of Exclusion*, Ljubljana: Mirovni inštitut.

DeVoretz, D. (2004) 'Immigrant Issues and Cities: Lessons from Malmö and Toronto', Willy Brandt Series of Working Papers in International Migration and Ethnic Relations, 2/04.

DG Justice, Freedom and Security (2004) *Handbook on Integration for Policy-Makers and Practitioners*, Brussels: European Communities.

Dietz, G. (2004) 'Frontier Hybridisation or Culture Clash? Transnational Migrant Communities and Sub-National Identity Politics in Andalusia, Spain', 30 *Journal of Ethnic and Migration Studies* 1087–112.

Dill, G. (1999) 'Kommunales Wahlrecht für EU-Bürger. Studien und Materialien im internationalen Vergleich', Interne Studien No. 143/1999, Sankt Augustin: Konrad Adenauer Stiftung.

Dobson, L. (2006) 'Aliens, Citizens and Social Contracts', mimeo, June 2006.

Dougan, M. (2005) 'Fees, Grants, Loans and Dole Cheques: Who Covers the Cost of Migrant Education within the EU?', 42 *Common Market Law Review* 943–86.

(2006), 'The Constitutional Dimension to the Case Law on Union Citizenship', 31 *European Law Review* 613–41.

Douglas-Scott, S. (1998) 'In Search of Union Citizenship', 18 *Yearbook of European Law* 29–66.

Duff, A. (2005) 'Introduction: Crime and Citizenship', 22 *Journal of Applied Philosophy* 211–16.

Earnest, D. (2003) 'Voting Rights for Resident Aliens: A Comparison of 25 Democracies', paper prepared for the Northeast Political Science Association and International Studies Association-Northeast 2003 Annual Meeting, 7 November 2003.

(2004) '*Voting Rights for Resident Aliens: Nationalism, Postnationalism and Sovereignty in an Era of Mass Migration*', PhD dissertation,

Columbian College of Arts and Sciences, George Washington University, Washington, DC.

(2006) 'Neither Citizen Nor Stranger: Why States Enfranchise Resident Aliens', 28 *World Politics* 242–75.

Easton, A. (2006) 'Electing the Electorate: The Problem of Prisoner Disenfranchisement', 69 *Modern Law Review* 443–52.

Ellis, E. (2003) 'Social Advantages: A New Lease of Life?', 40 *Common Market Law Review* 639–59.

Evans, A. (1984) 'European Citizenship: A Novel Concept in EEC Law', 32 *American Journal of Comparative Law* 679–715.

Everson, M. (1995) 'The Legacy of the Market Citizen', in Shaw and More, 1995, 73–90.

Evia, G. (2003) 'Consent by All the Governed: Reenfranchising Noncitizens as Partners in America's Democracy', 77 *Southern California Law Review* 151–86.

Faist, T. (2005) 'From Nationhood to Societal Integration, or: "We Are All 'Republican' Now" – The Change, Prospects and Limits of Citizenship in Germany', paper delivered to a conference on 'Dual Citizenship: Democracy, Rights and Identity in a Globalizing World', University of Toronto, March 2005.

Fanning, B. (2002) *Racism and Social Change in Ireland*, Manchester: Manchester University Press.

Farrell, D. and Scully, R. (2005) 'Electing the European Parliament: How Uniform Are "Uniform" Electoral Systems?', 43 *Journal of Common Market Studies* 969–84.

Føllesdal, A. (1999) 'Third Country Nationals as European Citizens: The Case Defended', in D. Smith and S. Wright (eds.), *Whose Europe? The Turn Towards Democracy*, Oxford: Blackwell, 104–24.

Ford, R. (2001) 'City-States and Citizenship', in Aleinikoff and Klusmeyer, 2001, 209–33.

Forde, C. (2005) 'Participatory Democracy or Pseudo-Participation? Local Government Reform in Ireland', 31 *Local Government Studies* 137–48.

Fowler, B. (2004a) 'Nation, State, Europe and National Revival in Hungarian Party Politics: The Case of the Millennial Commemorations', 56 *Europe-Asia Studies* 57–83.

(2004b) 'Fuzzing Citizenship, Nationalising Political Space: A Framework for Interpreting the Hungarian "Status Law" as a New Form of Kin-State Policy in Central and Eastern Europe', in Kántor *et al.*, 2004, 177–238.

Fox, G. and Roth, B. (2001) 'Democracy and International Law', 27 *Review of International Studies* 327–52.

Fox, J. (2005) 'Unpacking "Transnational Citizenship"', 8 *Annual Review of Political Science* 171–201.

Fraser, N. (2005) 'Reframing Justice in a Globalising World', *New Left Review* No. 36, 69–88.

Fries, S. and Shaw, J. (1998) 'Citizenship of the Union: First Steps in the Court of Justice', 4 *European Public Law* 533–59.

Gallie, W. B. (1955–6) 'Essentially Contested Concepts', 6 *Proceedings of the Aristotelian Society* 157–91.

Gardner, J. P. (ed.) (1997) *Citizenship: The White Paper*, London: Institute for Citizenship Studies/The British Institute of International and Comparative Law.

(ed.) (1997) *Citizenship: The White Paper*, London: 1997, Hallmark 3: Right to Vote, 42–51.

Gärtner, R. (2002) 'The FPÖ, Racism and Foreigners in the Haider Era', in R. Polak and A. Pelinka (eds.), *The Haider Phenomenon in Austria*, New Brunswick, NJ: Transaction Publishers, 17–32.

Geddes, A. (2005) 'Europe's Border Relationships and International Migration Relations', 43 *Journal of Common Market Studies* 787–806.

Gelazis, N. (2004) 'The European Union and the Statelessness Problem in the Baltic States', 6 *European Journal of Migration and Law* 225–42.

Golynker, O. (2005) 'Jobseekers' Rights in the European Union: Challenges of Changing the Paradigm of Social Solidarity', 30 *European Law Review* 111–22.

Goodin, R. (2003) *Reflective Democracy*, Oxford: Oxford University Press.

Green, S. (2000) 'Beyond Ethnoculturalism? German Citizenship in the New Millennium', 9 *German Politics* 105–24.

(2001) 'Citizenship Policy in Germany: The Case of Ethnicity over Residence', in Hansen and Weil, 2001, 24–51.

(2004) *The Politics of Exclusion: Institutions and Immigration Policy in Contemporary Germany*, Manchester: Manchester University Press.

Groenendijk, K. (2006) 'The Status of Quasi-Citizenship in EU Member States: Why Some States Have "Almost-Citizens"', in Bauböck *et al.*, 2006a, 411–29.

Groenendijk, K., Guild, E. and Barzilay, R. (2000) 'The Legal Status of Third Country Nationals Who Are Long-Term Residents in a Member State of the European Union', Council of Europe Community Relations Series, Strasbourg, August 2000.

de Groot, R. (2004) 'Towards a European Nationality Law', 8 *Electronic Journal of Comparative Law*, No. 3, http://www.ejcl.org.

Guild, E. and Carrera, S. (2005) 'No Constitutional Treaty? Implications for the Area of Freedom, Security and Justice', CEPS Working Document, No. 231, October 2005.

Habermas, J. (1994) 'Citizenship and National Identity', in van Steenbergen, 1994, 20–35.

Hailbronner, K. (2006a) 'Nationality in Public International Law and European Law', in Bauböck *et al.*, 2006a, 35–104.

(2006b) 'Germany', in Bauböck *et al.*, 2006b, 213–51.

Halfacree, K. (2003) 'Book Review', 10 *European and Regional Urban Studies* 187.

Hammar, T. (1990) *Democracy and the Nation State*, Aldershot: Avebury.

Handoll, J. (2006) 'Ireland', in Bauböck *et al.*, 2006b, 289–328.

Hansen, R. (2006), 'The Danish Cartoon Controversy: A Defense of Liberal Freedom', 19 *EUSA Review*, No. 2, Spring, 1 and 3–6.

Hansen, R. and Weil, P. (eds.) (2001) *Towards a European Nationality: Citizenship, Immigration and Nationality Law in the EU*, London: Palgrave.

(eds.) (2002) *Dual Nationality, Social Rights and Federal Citizenship in the US and Europe: The Reinvention of Citizenship*, New York and Oxford: Berghahn Books.

Harper Ho, V. (2000) 'Non-Citizen Voting Rights: The History, the Law and Current Prospects', 19 *Law and Inequality* 271–322.

Harrington, J. (2005) 'Citizenship and the Biopolitics of Post-Nationalist Ireland', 32 *Journal of Law and Society* 424–49.

Hayduk, R. (2004) 'Democracy for All: Restoring Immigrant Voting Rights in the US', 26 *New Political Science* 499–523.

(2006) *Democracy for All*, New York: Routledge.

Hedrich, I. (2001) *Le droit de vote et d'éligibilité des ressortissants communautaires aux élections municipales en France*, PhD dissertation, University of Grenoble.

Heisler, M. (2005) 'Introduction – Changing Citizenship Theory and Practice: Comparative Perspectives in a Democratic Framework', 38 *PS Online* 667–70.

Held, D. (1991) 'Between State and Civil Society: Citizenship', in G. Andrews (ed.), *Citizenship*, London: Lawrence and Wishart.

Heleniak, T. (2006) 'Latvia Looks West, But Legacy of Soviets Remains', Migration Information Source, February 2006, www.migrationinformation.net.

Helton A. *et al.* (2000) 'Protecting the World's Exiles: The Human Rights of Non-Citizens', A Dialogue, 22 *Human Rights Quarterly* 282–97.

Hervey, T. (1995) 'Migrant Workers and Their Families in the European Union: The Pervasive Market Ideology of Community Law', in Shaw and More, 1995, 91–110.

Hilson, C. (2004) 'What's in a Right? The Relationship between Community, Fundamental and Citizenship Rights in EU law', 29 *European Law Review* 636–51.

(2006) 'EU Citizenship and the Principle of Affectedness', in Bellamy *et al.*, 2006, 56–74.

Hirschl, R. (2005) 'The Question of Case Selection in Comparative Constitutional Law', 53 *American Journal of Comparative Law* 125–55.

Ho, N. (2004) 'A Rocky Road: The Political Fate of Gibraltar', *Harvard International Review*, Winter, http://hir.harvard.edu/articles/1177/.

Honig, B. (2001) *Democracy and the Foreigner*, Cambridge and Princeton, NJ: Princeton University Press.

Howard, M. (2005) 'Variation in Dual Citizenship Policies in the Countries of the EU', 39 *International Migration Review* 697–720.

Hughes, J. (2005) '"Exit" in Deeply Divided Societies: Regimes of Discrimination in Estonia and Latvia and the Potential for Russophone Migration', 43 *Journal of Common Market Studies* 739–62.

Hunger, U. (2001) 'Party Competition and Inclusion of Immigrants in Germany', 1 *German Policy Studies* 302–30.

Iglicka, K. (2005) 'EU Membership Highlights Poland's Migration Challenges', Migration Information Source, Country Profile, April 2005, http://www.migrationinformation.org.

ILPA (Immigration Law Practitioners' Association) and Migration Policy Group (eds.) (2000) *The Amsterdam Proposals: The ILPA/MPG Proposed Directives on Immigration and Asylum*, London and Brussels, www.migpolgroup.com.

Iordachi, C. (2004a) 'Dual Citizenship and Policies toward Kin-Minorities in East-Central Europe: A Comparison between Hungary, Romania, and the Republic of Moldova', in Kántor *et al.*, 2004, 239–69.

(2004b) '"Entangled Histories": Re-thinking the History of Central and Southeastern Europe from a Relational Perspective', *Regio: A Review of Studies on Minorities, Politics and Society* 113–47.

Ireland, P. (2000) 'Reaping What They Sow: Institutions and Immigrant Political Participation in Western Europe', in Koopmans and Statham, 2000b, 233–52.

Isin, E. (ed.) (2000) *Democracy, Citizenship and the Global City*, London: Routledge.

Jachtenfuchs, M., Diez, T. and Jung, S. (1998) 'Which Europe? Conflicting Models of a Legitimate European Political Order', 4 *European Journal of Political Research* 409–45.

Jacobs, D. (1998) 'Discourse, Politics and Policy: The Dutch Parliamentary Debate about Voting Rights for Foreign Residents', 32 *International Migration Review* 350–73.

(1999) 'The Debate over Enfranchisement of Foreign Residents in Belgium', 25 *Journal of Ethnic and Migration Studies* 649–64.

(2000a) 'Multinational and Polyethnic Politics Entwined: Minority Representation in the Region of Brussels-Capital', 26 *Journal of Ethnic and Migration Studies* 289–304.

(2000b) 'Giving Foreigners the Vote: Ethnocentrism in Dutch and Belgian Political Debates', in J. ter Wal and M. Verkuyten (eds.), *Comparative Perspectives on Racism*, Ashgate: Aldershot, 117–38.

Jacobs, D., Martiniello, M. and Rea, A. (2002) 'Changing Patterns of Political Participation of Immigrants in the Brussels Capital Region: The October

2000 Elections', 3 *Journal of International Migration and Integration* 201–21.

Jandl, M. and Kraler, A. (2003) *Austria: A Country of Immigration?*, Country Report, Migration Information Source for the Migration Policy Institute, March 2003, www.migrationinformation.org.

Janmaat, J. (2006) 'Popular Conceptions of Nationhood in Old and New European Member States: Partial Support for the Ethnic-Civic Framework', 29 *Ethnic and Racial Studies* 50–78.

Jenny, M. (2002) 'Politische Partizipation von MigrantInnen in Wien. Erwartungen der Betroffenen an ein AusländerInnen-Wahlrecht', unpublished report, SORA, Vienna.

Joppke, C. (1999) *Immigration and the Nation States: The United States, Germany, and Great Britain*, Oxford: Oxford University Press.

(2003) 'Citizenship between De- and Re-Ethnicization', 44 *Archives européennes de sociologie* 429–58.

Kadelbach, S. (2003) 'Union Citizenship', in 'European Integration: The New Germany Scholarship', Jean Monnet Working Paper 9/03.

Kalvaitis, R. (1998) 'Citizenship and National Identity in the Baltic States', 16 *Boston University International Law Journal* 231–71.

Kántor, Z., Majtényi, B., Ieda, O., Vizi, B. and Halász, I. (eds.) (2004) *The Hungarian Status Law Syndrome: A Nation Building and/or Minority Protection*, Sapporo: Slavic Research Center, Hokkaido University.

Kasimis, C. and Kassimi, C. (2004) *Greece: A History of Migration*, Migration Information Source, Country Profile, June 2004, http://www.migrationinformation.org.

Kastoryano, R. (2005) 'Citizenship, Nationhood, and Non-Territoriality: Transnational Participation in Europe', 38 *PS Online* 693–6.

Katz, R. (1997) *Democracy and Elections*, Oxford: Oxford University Press.

Kavanagh, A. (2004) 'The 2004 Local Elections in the Republic of Ireland', 19 *Irish Political Studies* 64–84.

Keane, J. (2005) 'European Citizenship? Contested Histories, Current Trends, Future Perspectives', CSD, June 2005, http://www.johnkeane.net/essays/essay_eurocitizens.htm.

Kempen, O. (1989) 'Kommunalwahlrecht der Ausländer – Schutzwall für die nationale Provinz oder Baustein für ein soziales Europa?', 40 *Gewerkschaftliche Monatshefte* 414–21.

Kionka, R. (1993) 'Estonia: A Difficult Transition', *RFE/RL Research Report*, Vol. 2, No. 1, 1 January 1993, 89–91.

Kirsch, G. (1995) 'The New Pluralism: Regionalism, Ethnicity, and Language in Western Europe', in K. Knop, S. Ostry, R. Simeon and K. Swinton (eds.), *Rethinking Federalism: Citizens, Markets and Governments in a Changing World*, Vancouver: UBC Press, 59–74.

Klopp, B. (2002) 'The Political Incorporation of EU Foreigners Before and After Maastricht: The New Local Politics in Germany', 28 *Journal of Ethnic and Migration Studies* 239–57.

Kochenov, D. (2003) 'The European Citizenship Concept and Enlargement of the Union', 3 *Romanian Journal of Political Science* 71, http://www.ciaonet.org/olj/rjps/rjps_v3n2/rjps_v3n2_kod01.pdf.

(2004) 'Pre-Accession, Naturalisation and "Due Regard to Community Law"', 4 *Romanian Journal of Political Science* 71.

(2006) 'European Integration and the Gift of Second Class Citizenship: The Absence of the Tools within the European Legal System to Combat Temporary Discrimination of European Citizens on the Basis of Nationality Institutionalized by the Acts of Accession', 13 *Murdoch University Electronic Journal of Law*, No. 1, 209–24.

Koenig-Archibugi, M. (2003) 'National and European Citizenship: The Italian Case in Historical Perspective', 7 *Citizenship Studies* 85–109.

Kofman, E. (2005) 'Citizenship, Migration and the Reassertion of National Identity', 9 *Citizenship Studies* 439.

Kohn, H. (1944) *The Idea of Nationalism: A Study in Its Origins and Background*, New York: Macmillan.

Kokott, J. (2005) 'EU Citizenship – Citoyens sans Frontières?', Durham European Law Institute, European Law Lecture 2005.

Kokott, J. and Rudolf, B. (1996) Case note on *Piermont* v. *France*, European Court of Human Rights, 27 April 1995, 90 *American Journal of International Law* 456–60.

König, K. and Perchinig, B. (2003) 'Austria', in J. Niessen, Y. Schibel and R. Magoni (eds.), *EU and US Approaches to the Management of Migration*, Migration Policy Group, May 2003.

Koopmans, R. and Statham, P. (2000a) 'Migration and Ethnic Relations as a Field of Political Contention: An Opportunity Structure Approach', in Koopmans and Statham, 2000b, 13–56.

(eds.) (2000b) *Challenging Immigration and Ethnic Relations Politics*, Oxford: Oxford University Press.

Koopmans, R., Statham, P., Guigni, M. and Passy, F. (2005) *Contested Citizenship. Immigration and Cultural Diversity in Europe*, Minneapolis and London: University of Minnesota Press.

Kostakopoulou, D. (2000) 'The European Citizenship Menu: Modes and Options', 7 *Journal of European Public Policy* 477–92.

(2001a) 'Invisible Citizens? Long-Term Resident Third-Country Nationals in the EU and Their Struggle for Recognition', in Bellamy and Warleigh, 2001, 180–206.

(2001b) *Citizenship, Identity and Immigration in the European Union: Between Past and Future*, Manchester: Manchester University Press.

(2002) '"Integrating" Non-EU Migrants in the European Union: Ambivalent Legacies and Mutating Paradigms', 8 *Columbia Journal of European Law* 181–201.

(2003) 'Why Naturalisation?', 4 *Perspectives on European Politics and Society* 85–115.

(2005) 'Ideas, Norms and European Citizenship: Explaining Institutional Change', 68 *Modern Law Review* 233–67.

(2006) 'Thick, Thin and Thinner Patriotisms: Is This All There Is?', 26 *Oxford Journal of Legal Studies* 73–106.

Krahler, A. and Sohler, S. (2005) *Active Civic Participation of Immigrants in Austria*, Country Report prepared for the European research project POLITIS, Oldenburg, 2005, www.uni-oldenburg.de/politis-europe/.

Krieger, H. and Fernandez, E. (2006) 'Too Much or Too Little Long-Distance Mobility in Europe? EU Policies to Promote and Restrict Mobility', European Foundation for the Improvement of Living and Working Conditions, Presented at Foundation Seminars on Worker Mobility, Latvia and Lithuania, 7 and 9 June 2006.

Krūma, K. (2004) 'EU Citizenship: Unresolved Issues', RGSL Working Papers No. 22, Riga.

Kymlicka, W. (1999) 'Citizenship in an Era of Globalization: Commentary on Held', in I. Shapiro and C. Hacker-Cordón (eds.), *Democracy's Edges*, Cambridge: Cambridge University Press, 112–26.

Kymlicka, W. and Norman, W. (1994) 'Return of the Citizen: A Survey of Recent Work on Citizenship Theory', 104 *Ethics* 352–81.

Lardy, H. (1996) 'The Political Rights of Union Citizenship', 2 *European Public Law* 611–33.

(1997) 'Citizenship and the Right to Vote', 17 *Oxford Journal of Legal Studies* 75–100.

(2001) 'Democracy by Default: The Representation of the People Act 2000', 2 *Modern Law Review* 63–81.

Laursen, F. and Vanhoonacker, S. (eds.) (1992) *The Intergovernmental Conference on Political Union – Institutional Reforms, New Policies and International Identity of the European Community*, Maastricht: EIPA/Martinus Nijhoff.

Layton-Henry, Z. (1990) 'Citizenship or Denizenship for Migrant Workers?', in Z. Layton-Henry (ed.). *The Political Rights of Migrant Workers in Western Europe*, London: Sage.

(1991) 'Citizenship and Migrant Workers in Western Europe', in U. Vogel and M. Moran (eds.), *The Frontiers of Citizenship*, London: Macmillan, 112–30.

Lefebvre, E. (2003) 'Republicanism and Universalism: Factors of Inclusion or Exclusion in the French Concept of Citizenship' , 7 *Citizenship Studies* 15–36.

Legomsky, S. (1995) 'Why Citizenship?', 35 *Virginia Journal of International Law* 279–300.

Lewis, J. (1998) 'Is the "Hard Bargaining" Image of the Council Misleading? The Committee of Permanent Representatives and the Local Elections Directive', 36 *Journal of Common Market Studies* 479–504.

López-Guerra, C. (2005) 'Should Expatriates Vote?', 13 *Journal of Political Philosophy* 216–34.

Luther, K. R. (2003) 'The Self-Destruction of a Right-Wing Populist Party? The Austrian Parliamentary Election of 2002', 26 *West European Politics* 136–52.

Lyons, C. (1997) 'A Voyage around Article 8: An Historical and Comparative Evaluation of the Fate of European Union', 17 *Yearbook of European Law* 135–64.

Mac Éinrí, P. (2005) 'Ireland', in J. Niessen, Y. Schibel and C. Thompson (eds.), *Current Immigration Debates in Europe: A Publication of the European Migration Dialogue*, Migration Policy Group, September 2005.

McCrone, D. (2001) *Understanding Scotland: The Sociology of a Nation*, 2nd edn, London: Routledge, 2001.

Magnette, P. (2005) *Citizenship: The History of an Idea*, London: ECPR.

Marias E. (ed.) (1994) *European Citizenship*, Maastricht: EIPA.

Marshall, T. H. (1950) *Citizenship and Social Class*, Cambridge: Cambridge University Press.

Martiniello, M. (2005) 'Political Participation, Mobilisation and Representation of Immigrants and Their Offspring in Europe', Willy Brandt Series of Working Papers in International Migration and Ethnic Relations, 1/05.

Martiniello, M. and Statham, P. (1999) 'Introduction', 25 *Journal of Ethnic and Migration Studies* 565–73.

Mather, J. (2005) 'The Court of Justice and the Union Citizen', 11 *European Law Journal* 722–43.

Maveety, N. and Grosskopf, A. '"Constrained" Constitutional Courts as Conduits for Democratic Consolidation', 38 *Law and Society Review* 463–88.

Mayer, H. (2002) 'Einführung eines Ausländerwahlrechtes zu den Bezirksvertretungen in Wien', *Österreichische Gemeinde-Zeitung*, No. 8/2002, no page given.

Meehan, E. (1993) *Citizenship and the European Community*, London: Sage.

van der Mei, A. (2005) 'Union Citizenship and the "De-Nationalisation" of the Territorial Welfare State', 7 *European Journal of Migration and Law* 203–11.

Méndez Lago, M. (2005) 'The Participation of Non-National EU Citizens in Spanish Local Elections', paper prepared for the ESF/LESC-SCSS Exploratory Workshop on 'Citizens, Non-Citizens and Voting Rights in Europe', Edinburgh, 2–5 June 2005.

Menocal, M. (1990) *The Arabic Role in Medieval Literary History: A Forgotten Heritage*, Pittsburgh: University of Pennsylvania Press.

Merlingen, M., Mudde, C. and Sedelmeier, U. (2001) 'The Right and the Righteous? European Norms, Domestic Politics, and the Sanctions Against Austria', 39 *Journal of Common Market Studies* 59–77.

Meyer-Teschendorf, K. and Hofmann, H. 'Teilnahme von Unionsbürgern nicht nur an Kommunalwahlen, sondern auch an kommunalen Plebisziten?', *Zeitschrift für Rechtspolitik* 290–3.

Miller, D. (1995) *On Nationality*, Oxford: Oxford University Press.

Mouffe, C. (1992) 'Preface: Democratic Politics Today', in C. Mouffe (ed.), *Dimensions of Radical Democracy*, London: Verso.

Mullaly, S. (2005) 'Citizenship and Family Life in Ireland: Asking the Question: "Who Belongs?"', 25 *Legal Studies* 578–600.

Munz, R. (2006) 'Europe: Population and Migration in 2005', Migration Information Source, 1 June 2006, www.migrationinformation.org.

Neuman, G. (1992) '"We Are the People": Alien Suffrage in German and American Perspective', 13 *Michigan Journal of International Law* 259–335.

Nic Shuibhne, N. (2003) 'Article 13 EC and Non-Discrimination on Grounds of Nationality: Missing or in Action?', in C. Costello and E. Barry (eds.), *Equality in Diversity: The New Equality Directives*, Dublin: Equality Authority, 269–93.

Niessen, J. (2000) 'The Amsterdam Treaty and NGO Responses', 2 *European Journal of Migration and Law* 203–14.

Nowak, M. and Lubich, A. (2005) 'Report on the Situation on Fundamental Rights in Austria in 2004', EU Network of Experts on Fundamental Rights (CFR-CDR).

Nowak, M., Pritz, C., Weyss, B. and Lubich, A. (2006) 'Report on the Situation on Fundamental Rights in Austria in 2005', EU Network of Experts on Fundamental Rights (CFR-CDR).

O'Connell, R. (2005) 'Legal Responses to Racism: Innovation and Retrenchment in Ireland', 6 *International Journal of Discrimination and the Law* 199–222.

O'Keeffe, D. (1994) 'Union Citizenship', in D. O'Keeffe and P. Twomey (eds.), *Legal Issues of the Maastricht Treaty*, Chichester: Wiley, 87–107.

(1996) 'Reflections on European Citizenship', *Current Legal Problems* 347–74.

O'Leary, S. (1995) 'The Relationship between Community Citizenship and the Protection of Fundamental Rights in Community Law', 32 *Common Market Law Review* 519–54.

(1996) *The Evolving Concept of Community Citizenship*, The Hague: Kluwer Law International.

Odmalm, P. (2005) *Migration Policies and Political Participation*, Basingstoke, Palgrave.

d'Oliveira, H. U. J. (1994) 'European Citizenship: Its Meaning, Its Potential', in R. Dehousse (ed.), *Europe after Maastricht: An Ever Closer Union?*, Munich: Law Books in Europe, 126–48.

Oliver, P. (1996) 'Electoral Rights under Article 8B of the Treaty of Rome', 33 *Common Market Law Review* 473–98.

Ong, A. (1999) *Flexible Citizenship: The Cultural Logics of Transnationality*, Durham, NC: Duke University Press.

(2005) '(Re)Articulations of Citizenship', 38 *PS Online* 697–9.

Oosterom-Staples, H. (2004) Case note on *Collins*, 42 *Common Market Law Review* 205–23.

Painter, J. (2003) 'European Citizenship and the Regions', Queen's Papers on Europeanisation, 7/2003.

Palermo, F. and Woelk, J. (2003) 'No Representation without Recognition: The Right to Political Participation of (National) Minorities', 25 *Journal of European Integration* 225.

Peers, S. (2000) *EU Justice and Home Affairs Law*, Harlow: Longman.

Penninx, R. (2005) 'Dutch Integration Policies after the Van Gogh Murder', Contribution to the Expert Panel on Social Integration of Immigrants, Ottawa, 24 January 2005.

Penninx, R., Kraal, K., Martiniello, M. and Vertovec, S. (eds.) (2004) *Citizenship in European Cities: Immigrants, Local Politics and Integration Policies*, Aldershot: Ashgate.

Penninx, R. and Martiniello, M. (2004) 'Integration Processes and Policies: State of the Art and Lessons', in Penninx *et al.*, 2004, 139–63.

Perchinig, B. (2004) 'Kein Wahlrecht ohne rotten Pass', Juridikum. Zeitschrift im Rechtsstaat 2004/04, 178–81.

(2005) 'Blocked by Constitution: How the Constitutional Court Stopped Municipal Voting Rights for Third Country Nationals in Vienna', paper prepared for the ESF/LESC-SCSS Exploratory Workshop on 'Citizens, Non-Citizens and Voting Rights in Europe', Edinburgh, 2–5 June 2005.

Pescatore, P. (1987) 'Some Critical Remarks on the Single European Act', 24 *Common Market Law Review* 9–18.

Péteri, G. (2000) 'Between Empire and Nation-State: Comments on the Pathology of State Formation in Eastern Europe during the "Short Twentieth Century"', 9 *Contemporary European History* 367–84.

Petričušić, A. (2004) 'Slovenian Legislative System for Minority Protection', *NoveSSL Revista de Sociolingüística*, Autumn.

Pettai, V. (1997) 'Political Stability through Disenfranchisement', *Transition*, Vol. 3, No. 6, 4 April 1997, 21–3.

Pettit, P. (2005) 'Two-Dimensional Democracy, National and International', IILJ Working Paper 2005/8, www.iilj.org.

Pickus, N. (ed.) (1997) 'Becoming American. America Becoming', Final Report, Duke University Workshop on Citizenship and Immigration, http://kenan. ethics.duke.edu/PDF/BecomingAmerican–AmericaBecoming.pdf.

Pinder, J. (2000) 'Steps Towards a Federal European Parliament', 35 *International Spectator* 13–20.

Plender, R. (1976) 'An Incipient Form of European Citizenship', in F. Jacobs (ed.), *European Law and the Individual*, Dordrecht: North Holland, 39–52.

(1990) 'Competence, European Community Law and Nationals of Non-Member States', 39 *International and Comparative Law Quarterly* 599–618.

Pogany, I. (2004) *The Roma Café: Human Rights and the Plight of the Roma People*, London: Pluto.

Preuss, U. (1995) 'Problems of a Concept of European Citizenship', 1 *European Law Journal* 267–81.

(2003) 'Citizenship and the German Nation', 7 *Citizenship Studies* 37–56.

Preuss, U., Everson, M., Koenig-Archibugi, M. and LeFebvre, E., 'Traditions of Citizenship in the European Union', 7 *Citizenship Studies* 3–14.

Rambour, M. (2004) 'Elections et citoyenneté européennes: une mise en perspective post-nationale', paper presented at a Conference on 'La construction européenne au prisme des elections au Parlement européen de juin 2004', Strasbourg, 18–19 November 2004.

Raskin, J. (1993) 'Legal Aliens, Local Citizens: The Historical, Constitutional and Theoretical Meanings of Alien Suffrage', 141 *University of Pennsylvania Law Review* 1391–470.

Rath, J. (1990) 'Voting Rights', in Z. Layton-Henry (ed.), *The Political Rights of Migrant Workers in Western Europe*, London: Sage, 127–57.

Raun, T. (1997) 'Democratization and Political Development in Estonia 1987–1996', in K. Dawisha and B. Parrott (eds.), *The Consolidation of Democracy in East-Central Europe*, Cambridge: Cambridge University Press, 334–74.

Rawls, J. (1993) *Political Liberalism*, New York: Columbia University Press.

Reich, N. (2001) 'Union Citizenship – Metaphor or Source of Rights?', 7 *European Law Journal* 4–23.

(2005) 'The Constitutional Relevance of Citizenship and Free Movement in an Enlarged Union', 11 *European Law Journal* 675–98.

Ress, G. (1981) 'Free Movement of Persons, Services and Capital', in Commission of the European Communities (ed.), *Thirty Years of Community Law*, Luxembourg: OOPEC.

Rostek, K. and Davies, G. (2006) 'The Impact of Union Citizenship on National Citizenship Policies', *European Integration online Papers (EioP)*, Vol. 10, No. 5.

Rubio-Marín, R. (1998) 'National Limits to Democratic Citizenship', 11 *Ratio Juris* 51–66.

(2000) *Immigration as a Democratic Challenge*, Cambridge: Cambridge University Press.

(2006) 'Transnational Politics and the Democratic Nation-State: Normative Challenges of Expatriate Voting and Nationality Retention of Emigrants', 81 *New York University Law Review* 117–47.

Ruhs, M. (2004) 'Ireland: A Crash Course in Immigration Policy', Country Profile, Migration Information Source, October 2004, www.migrationinformation.org.

Ryan, B. (2004) 'The Celtic Cubs: The Controversy over Birthright Citizenship in Ireland', 6 *European Journal of Migration and Law* 173–93.

Salt, J. (2005) *Current Trends in International Migration in Europe*, Report for the Council of Europe, CDMG (2002) 2, January 2005.

Sasse, G. and Thielemann, E. (2005) 'A Research Agenda for the Study of Migrants and Minorities in Europe', 43 *Journal of Common Market Studies* 655–71.

Sassen, S. (1998) 'The *De Facto* Transnationalizing of Immigration Policy', in C. Joppke (ed.), *Challenges to the Nation-State: Immigration in Western Europe and the United States*, Oxford: Oxford University Press, 49–85.

Scheppele, K. (2004) 'Constitutional Ethnography: An Introduction', 38 *Law and Society Review* 389–406.

Schmid-Drüner, M. (2006) 'Germany's New Immigration Law: A Paradigm Shift?', 8 *European Journal of Migration and Law* 191–214.

Schmitt, H. (2005) 'The European Parliament Elections of 2004: Still Second Order?', 28 *West European Politics* 650–79.

Schmitter, P. and Trechsel, A. (eds.) (2005) *The Future of Democracy in Europe: Trends, Analyses and Reforms*, Council of Europe Green Paper.

Schuck, P. (2000) 'Citizenship in Federal Systems', 48 *American Journal of Comparative Law* 195–226.

  (2004) 'Only Citizens Should Hold Voting Rights, http://www.law.yale.edu/outside/html/Public_Affairs/491/yls_article.htm, 2 August 2004.

Schuster, L. and Solomos, H. (2002) 'Rights and Wrongs across European Borders: Migrants, Minorities and Citizenship', 6 *Citizenship Studies* 37–54.

Schwellnus, G. and Wiener, A. (2004) 'Contested Norms in the Process of EU Enlargement: Non-Discrimination and Minority Rights', Constitutionalism Web-Papers, ConWEB, No. 2/2004.

Seglow, J. (2005) 'The Ethics of Immigration', 3 *Political Studies Review* 317–34.

Shah, P. and Menski, W. (eds.) (2006) *Migration, Diasporas and Legal Systems in Europe*, London: Routledge-Cavendish.

Sharpe, M. (2005) 'Globalization and Migration: Post-Colonial Dutch Antillean and Aruban Immigrant Political Incorporation in the Netherlands', 29 *Dialectical Anthropology* 291–314.

Shaw, J. (1998a) 'Citizenship of the Union: Towards Post-National Membership?', in Academy of European Law (ed.), *Collected Courses of the Academy of European Law*, Vol. VI, Book 1, The Hague: Kluwer Law International, 237–347.

  (1998b) 'The Interpretation of European Union Citizenship', 61 *Modern Law Review* 293–317.

  (2000) 'The Problem of Membership in European Union Citizenship', in Bańkowski and Scott, 2000, 65–89.

  (2003) 'Sovereignty at the Boundaries of the Polity', in N. Walker (ed.), *Sovereignty in Transformation*, Oxford: Hart Publishing, 461–500.

  (2005) 'Europe's Constitutional Future', *Public Law* 132–151.

(2007) 'EU Citizenship and Political Rights in an Evolving European Union', 71 *Fordham Law Review* 101–30.

Shaw, J. and More, G. (eds.) (1995) *New Legal Dynamics of European Union*, Oxford: Oxford University Press.

Shaw, J. and Wiener, A. (2000) 'The Paradox of the "European Polity"', in M. Green Cowles and M. Smith (eds.), *State of the Union*, vol. 5, *Risks, Reforms, Resistance or Revival*, Oxford: Oxford University Press, 64–88.

Sheehy, A. (1993) 'The Estonian Law on Aliens', *RFE/RL* Vol. 2, No. 38, 24 September 1993.

Sieveking, K., Barwig, K., Lörcher, K. and Schumacher, C. (eds.) (1999) *Das Kommunalwahlrecht für Ausländer*, Baden-Baden: Nomos Verlagsgesellschaft.

Smith, G. (1996) 'The Ethnic Democracy Thesis and the Citizenship Question in Estonia and Latvia', 24 *Nationalities Papers* 199–216.

Smith, M. and Shaw, J. (2006) 'Changing Polities and Electoral Rights: Lithuania's Accession to the EU', in Shah and Menski, 2006, 145–63.

Smith, R. (1997) *Civic Ideals: Conflicting Visions of Citizenship in US History*, New Haven: Yale University Press.

(2001) 'Citizenship and the Politics of People-Building', 5 *Citizenship Studies* 73–96.

(2003) *Stories of Peoplehood: The Politics and Morals of Political Membership*, Cambridge: Cambridge University Press.

Smyth, C. (2005) 'The Right to Vote and Participate in Local Elections: Citizens' Right or Human Right?', paper prepared for the ESF/LESC-SCSS Exploratory Workshop on 'Citizens, Non-Citizens and Voting Rights in Europe', Edinburgh, 2–5 June 2005.

Smyth, C. and O'Connell, D. (2006) 'The Irish Citizenship Referendum of 2004: A Solution in Search of a Problem?', in Shah and Menski, 2006, 127–43.

Soysal, Y. (1994) *Limits of Citizenship: Migrants and Postnational Membership in Europe*, Chicago and London: University of Chicago Press.

(2004) 'Postnational Citizenship: Reconfiguring the Familiar Terrain', Campbell Public Affairs Institute Conference, on 'Transforming Citizenship? Transnational Membership, Participation and Governance', 30 April 2004.

Spiro, P. (1997) 'Dual Nationality and the Meaning of Citizenship', 46 *Emory Law Journal* 1411–85.

(2005) 'Dual Citizenship – A Postnational View', paper presented to the conference on dual citizenship at the Munk Centre for International Studies, University of Toronto, March 2005.

(2006) 'Protecting Political Diaspora', 81 *New York University Law Review* 207–33.

van Steenbergen, B. (ed.) (1994) *The Condition of Citizenship*, London, etc.: Sage.

Strudel, S. (2002) 'Les citoyens européens aux urnes: les usages ambigus de l'article 8B du traité de Maastricht', 9 *Revue Internationale de Politique Comparée* 47–63.

(2003) 'Polyrythmie européenne: le droit de suffrage municipal des étrangers au sein de l'Union, une règle électorale entre détournements et retardements', 53 *Revue Française de Science Politique* 3–34.

(2004) 'La participation des Portugais aux élections européennes et municipales en France', *Cahiers de l'Urmis*, No. 9, February, 69–76.

Szczepaniková, A., Čanek, M. and Grill, J. (eds.), *Migration Processes in Central and Eastern Europe: Unpacking the Diversity*, Prague: Multicultural Center, 2006, www.migrationonline.cz.

Taggart, P. (2006) 'Questions of Europe: The Domestic Politics of the 2005 French and Dutch Referendums and Their Challenge for the Study of European Integration', 44 *JCMS Annual Review* 7–25.

Tambini, D. (2001) 'Post-National Citizenship', 24 *Ethnic and Racial Studies* 195–217.

Taube, C. (2003) 'Latvia: Political Participation of Linguistic Minorities', 3 *International Journal of Constitutional Law (I.CON)* 511–40.

Tienda, M. (2002) 'Demography and the Social Contract', 39 *Demography* 597–616.

Togeby, L. (1999) 'Migrants at the Polls: An Analysis of Immigrant and Refugee Participation in Danish Local Elections', 25 *Journal of Ethnic and Migration Studies* 665–84.

Toggenburg, G. N. (2006) 'A Remaining Share or a New Part? The Union's Role vis-à-vis Minorities After the Enlargement Decade', EUI Working Paper, Law No. 2006/15.

Tóth, J. (2003) 'Connections of Kin-Minorities to the Kin-State in the Extended Schengen Zone', 5 *European Journal of Migration and Law* 201–27.

Tully, J. (2000) 'The Challenge of Reimagining Citizenship and Belonging in Multicultural and Multinational Societies', in C. McKinnon and I. Hampsher-Monk (eds.), *The Demands of Citizenship*, London: Continuum, 212–34.

Uçarer, E. (2001) 'From the Sidelines to Center Stage: Sidekick No More? The European Commission in Justice and Home Affairs', *European Integration Online Papers (EioP)*, Vol. 5, No. 5.

Uitermark, J., Rossi, U. and van Houtum, H. (2005) 'Reinventing Multiculturalism: Urban Citizenship and the Negotiation of Ethnic Diversity in Amsterdam', 29 *International Journal of Urban and Regional Research* 622–40.

Urth, H. (2005) 'Building a Momentum for the Integration of Third-Country Nationals in the European Union', 7 *European Journal of Migration and Law* 163–80.

Vagts, A. (1946) 'The Foreigner as Soldier in the Second World War, I', 8 *Journal of Politics* 174–200.

Varsanyi, M. (2005) 'The Rise and Fall (and Rise?) of Non-Citizen Voting: Immigration and the Shifting Scales of Citizenship and Suffrage in the United States', 9 *Space and Polity* 113–34.

Vink, M. (2005) *Limits of European Citizenship: European Integration and Domestic Immigration Policies*, Basingstoke: Palgrave.

Waldrauch, H. (2005) 'Electoral Rights for Foreign Nationals: A Comparative Overview', paper prepared for the ESF/LESC-SCSS Exploratory Workshop on 'Citizens, Non-Citizens and Voting Rights in Europe', Edinburgh, 2–5 June 2005.

Wallace, C. (2002) 'Opening and Closing Borders: Migration and Mobility in East-Central Europe', 28 *Journal of Ethnic and Migration Studies* 603–25.

Walzer, M. (1993) *Spheres of Justice: A Defense of Pluralism and Equality*, New York: Basic Books.

Weatherill, S. (2005) *Cases and Materials on EU Law*, 7th edn, Oxford: Oxford University Press.

Weiler, J. (1998) 'European Citizenship, Identity and Differentity', in M. La Torre (ed.), *European Citizenship an Institutional Challenge*, The Hague: Kluwer Law International, 1–24.

Weissbrod, D. and Collins, C. (2006) 'The Human Rights of Stateless Persons', 28 *Human Rights Quarterly* 245–76.

Wheeler, S. (1997) 'Corporations as Citizens?', in Gardner, 1997, 224–44.

Wiener, A. (1994) 'Citizenship Policy in a Non-State: Implications for Theory', paper delivered to the 2nd ECSA World Conference on Federalism, Subsidiarity and Democracy in the European Union, Brussels, May 1994.

(1998) *'European' Citizenship Practice: Building Institutions of a Non-State*, Boulder, CO: Westview Press.

(1999) 'From *Special* to *Specialized* Rights: The Politics of Citizenship and Identity in the European Union', in M. Hanagan and C. Tilly (eds.), *Extending Citizenship, Reconfiguring States*, Lanham, etc.: Rowman and Littlefield, 194–227.

(2003) 'Citizenship', in M. Cini (ed.), *European Union Politics*, Oxford: Oxford University Press, 397–414.

(2006) 'Constructivism and Sociological Institutionalism', in M. Cini and A. Bourne (eds.), *Palgrave Advances in European Union Studies*, Basingstoke: Palgrave, 53–5.

Wilkinson, B. 'Towards European Citizenship? Nationality, Discrimination and Free Movement of Workers in the European Union', 1 *European Public Law* 417–37.

Williams, A. M. (2001) 'New Forms of International Migration: In Search of Which Europe?', in H. Wallace (ed.), *Interlocking Dimensions of European Integration*, Basingstoke: Palgrave, 103–21.

de Witte, B. (2000) 'Old-Fashioned Flexibility: International Agreements between Member States of the European Union', in G. de Búrca and J. Scott (eds.), *Constitutional Change in the EU*, Oxford: Hart Publishing, 31–58.

Wüst, A. (2004) 'Naturalised Citizens as Voters: Behaviour and Impact', 13 *German Politics* 341.

Zincone, G. (2006) 'The Making of Policies: Immigration and Immigrants in Italy', 32 *Journal of Ethnic and Migration Studies* 347–75.

Zolberg, A. (2000) 'The Dawn of Cosmopolitan Denizenship', 7 *Indiana Journal of Global Legal Studies* 511–18.

Zorn, J. (2005) 'Ethnic Citizenship in the Slovenian State', 9 *Citizenship Studies* 135–52.

Zukauskiene, R. (2005) *Active Civic Participation of Immigrants in Lithuania*, Country Report prepared for the European research project POLITIS, Oldenburg, 2005, www.uni-oldenburg.de/politis-europe/.

Zuleeg, M. (2001) 'Kommunalwahlrecht für Unionsbürger', in *Demokratie und Selbstverwaltung in Europa, Festschrift für Dian Schefold*, Baden-Baden: Nomos Verlagsgesellschaft, 117–127, available at http://www.uni-frankfurt.de/fb01/zuleeg/kommwahleu.rtf.

Zürn, M. and Leibfried, S. (2005) 'Reconfiguring the National Constellation', in S. Leibfried and M. Zürn (eds.), *Transformations of the State?*, Cambridge: Cambridge University Press, 1–36.

INDEX